India Betrayed

The Role of Nehru

India Betrayed

The Role of Nehru

Brig. (Retd.) B.N. Sharma

1997

MANAS PUBLICATIONS

NEW DELHI 110 002

MANAS PUBLICATIONS
(Publishers, Distributors & Exporters)
4819/XI, Varun House, Mathur Lane,
24, Ansari Road, Darya Ganj,
New Delhi-110002 (INDIA)
Ph.: 3260783, 3265523, 2523865
Fax : 011 - 3272766 & 2927854
E-Mail : manas.vkgarg@axcess.net.in

Rs 795/-

ISBN 81-7049-082-0

First Published 1997

Typeset at
Innovative Processors
New Delhi 110 002

Printed in India at
Print Perfect, Delhi
and Published by Mrs. Suman Lata for
Manas Publications, 4819/XI, Varun House,
Mathur Lane, 24, Ansari Road, Darya Ganj,
New Delhi-110002 (INDIA)

To

To my daughter Gunjan and son Aseem
without whose inspiration and constant encouragement
this book would not have seen the light of day

My Acknowledgement is due to Shri Dinesh Chandra without whose active assistance in the form of suggestions and typing assistance this work would not have become possible

Preface

We are a great nation, but hungry for heroes and idols whom we remove with the same rapidity as we instal them. This is more true of our leaders after Independence. Those before Independence had shown more staying power. Take the toll of icons that we have made and destroyed since Independence. Gandhi is now merely a name to the new generation, and a convenient brand name for wily politicians to sell their wares. Patel, Subhas, Azad and then Jaya Prakash Narain—all with the exception of Jaya Prakash—were awarded Bharat Ratna and then forgotten; Patel, partly in his own lifetime, due to reasons which will be stated later. Subhas was resurrected partly; Azad revived and forgotten at convenience; Jaya Prakash Narain buried forever with the demise of the Janata Party. But one name endures and that defies logic. That is Nehru. Partly because he and his dynasty are inextricably interlinked with what happened to us as a nation after Independence. With brief interludes of a year and a half of Shastri, three years of Janata Party and a short span of Janata Dal and later Samajwadi Janata Party, the country has been ruled by Congress for almost 43 years, of which Nehru family accounts for 39 years. Thus, Nehru's legacy and family name cannot be wished away from the history of this country.

Again with all our virtues, which are considerable we tend to lose objectivity. We had been more discerning in our ancient years, a legacy which we now seen bent upon to destroy. The Nehru legacy is, to my mind, a reflection of the immaturity of our intelligentsia, the ignorance of our masses and a deliberate effort at disinformation. A good man may have many failings, Nehru had his. He gave many things to this country but there is much more that he could, but did not do. To my mind, his historical balance sheet will be taken as red. Enormous material exists today including his own writings that shed light on Nehru, the man and the leader. Most of this is irrational idolatory. Unfortunately, most of the biographers of Nehru did not possess the philosophical detachment, so essential for any effort of this kind. They started as admirers and ended up as idolators.

Is it not a misfortune for a country that for almost two decades, which partly included pre-Independence years, the writ of one man ran in the country? The conscientious objectors were spurned, many potential leaders sent to oblivion and today's generation is faced with problems which should never have arisen.

As a young boy, I was a great admirer of Nehru, the man and the leader. Then, somewhere along my growth something snapped. It was a trauma for me. Nehru, the icon, showed feet of clay. Disillusionment soon set in. My thirst for truth made me unhappy and then later many things happened to turn my childhood suspicion into verified evidence. Nehru was not the man he was made out to be. The Congress Party, press and public went crazy over him. I had my reservations. The pre- and post-Independence hoi polloi, simple and contented souls, were happy with Nehru, but came nowhere near the truth regarding the real man. I for one, decided to know and live with the truth and risk the unhappiness.

I could have written about Nehru much earlier, even as early as 1963 after the Chinese debacle. I could have done it even during Indira Gandhi's regime, but the code of military conduct, forestalled any such attempt on my part. Further, any such attempt would have been instant history. Now that the past is distant and the dust has settled, the perspective is clearer and the harvest of Nehru's actions has become more visible. Now I am an ordinary citizen of Bharat, the highest classification for any individual, unencumbered by office, unrestrained by political hypocrisy and unburdened with vulgar wealth, whose acquisition, retention and increase breeds vested interest and robs a man of his innate sincerity. I can, thus, bare my thoughts.

India Betrayed, thus, is not a biography of Nehru nor an attempt to malign him by focussing on the negative aspects of his personality; rather this is an effort to restore objectivity to our assessment of the man. Since much praise has already been showered on Nehru and all the facts of his life meticulously documented, what has emerged is a larger than life-size picture of the man, entirely to his advantage. I shall confine myself to those issues which had a negative impact on this country and showed the other side of the man. Later history will judge the man better. But I write while the memory serves. Another aim of this endeavour is to inform so that this nation does not repeat the mistakes of the past.

We as a nation should be more discerning and it is for our intelligentsia, if such a class at all exists, to present unvarnished facts and a balanced viewpoint before the public. My chief attempt is to present the unrevealed Janus-like face of the man, who to a large extent, shaped the destiny of this subcontinent called Bharat. Placed as he was at the steering wheel of history, after we had won our 'freedom by midnight', he had the power and the authority, unparalleled in a democratic polity, to chalk out a path for this country that could lead to progress and glory. Instead, he dithered and fumbled and took us where we stand today. To now correct the course, and reach our rightful destiny, it is incumbent on all of us to know what went wrong and why? It is difficult to imagine how a nation as well endowed as India in human and natural resources, with a headstart on many other countries similarly enslaved, crawled to its present state of development. We are so far behind from where we should have been. Even today, we are still freeing ourselves from the intellectual bondage and ideological baggage of the past, so aptly called by Nani Palkhiwala as the "Lost Decades". Admittedly, no one man can be held responsible for the lack of performance of a nation. But if that man happens to be the undisputed leader of the country, the man who received adulation beyond measure from all, the heart throb of the youth, and in whom the poor teeming millions of this country had put unquestioning love and trust, not for the brief space of a few years but almost two decades, should we then not hold that man responsible for what happened to that nation? Hence, this book. It is not a pleasant story to tell but the truth must be told.

B.N. Sharma

Contents

Part III

Part IV

Part I

1 *The Beholder's Eye*

Our perception of things external depends upon our mental make up, personal predilections and conscious and unconscious response of our inner self to the objects perceived. Sir Aurthur Eddington, a renowned British mathematician and philosopher, has held that our knowledge of the external world is governed by the limitations of our mind, just as the size of a fisherman's catch depends upon the shape and size of the net holes. It will not hold any fish smaller. Thus, a certain amount of subjectivity conditioned by our mental frame is inherent in any study. However, as enunciated by another great philosopher of our times, Bertrand Russel, weight of evidence, reasoned analysis and a correct choice of axioms can lead to a very reliable approximation to truth. "What is truth"? asked Pontius Pilate during the trial of Jesus of Nazareth. The answer is still elusive.

In my study of Nehru, I began with my own personal impressions, visual glimpses and what was generally talked about and appeared on him in the print media. This stage lasted till the age of adolescence, when I entered University. I was considered intelligent by the standards of 1930s and 40s when academic achievements, being the visible criteria of human excellence, were the rule. Till the end of my intermediate examination from U.P. Board of Education, a period devoted solely to studying for examinations, I did remarkably well passing out in the top bracket well above the first division with a number of distinctions to my credit. With no exposure to the free thought and discussions and confined to curricular studies, I fell in line with the public perception of Nehru, the glamour boy of the freedom struggle, the heart throb of the millions, the 'emperor of India's youthful heart', beloved of the masses, especially women; and above all, the uncrowned prince and the inheritor of Mahatma Gandhi's legacy. These were the identification marks of Nehru, the man and the leader. Two things happened during this period, both around 1937, during the hectic campaigning for the Provincial Assembly elections, which Congress had decided to contest.

One was his visit to Shri Gandhi Ashram, Meerut. I lived there as a young boy where my father and uncle were working, the latter in the capacity of General Secretary of the Ashram. The institution was a volunteer organisation under Gandhiji's constructive programme to give employment to the weavers and spinners producing khadi. One of the main planks of Gandhi's movement was charkha and khadi, which later became the symbols and watchwords for our struggle for freedom and a badge of honour for all freedom fighters. With its wide influence and coverage over rural and urban areas and its vast array of dedicated workers devoted to the cause of freedom, it was an asset that could be effectively put to use for the election campaign. It was winter. Nehru came to us dressed in an overcoat and a khadi dhoti, sometime late in the evening, his throat hoarse after a series of speeches. Soon on arrival, he engaged in an animated conversation with a group of khadi workers. All of a sudden, he left the group and I saw him move quietly behind a tree, to light a cigarette. He drew a few quick puffs and extinguished the butt with the sole of his dusty shoes and rejoined the group. To me, schooled in the monastic discipline of the Ashram a man's deeds spoke better than his words. Smoking was a taboo with Gandhiji and his followers. We at Gandhi Ashram were his true disciples. This act of Nehru, smoking on the sly, aroused my indignation and I, a young boy of nine, considered him as a hypocrite and an apostate, to Gandhiji's cause. I had often read about Nehru's foreign visits to 'European countries' while he was a member of the All India Congress Committee. He dropped his khadi dress on the shores of India and with consummate ease slipped into his Western clothes. To me this was heresy, and the mask of the hero fell away.

The next thing happened very soon after. Nehru was to deliver an election speech at the Town Hall in Meerut. The stage was decked up as a newly wedded bride to welcome the groom, the handsome Nehru, then called Panditji. The chief organiser was a local richman and an ardent supporter of the Congress. There were special lights in *papier-mache* of all kinds, petromax lamps and other electric bulbs of all colours and plenty of flowers. The beautiful shamiana was highly decorated. The place was overflowing with people eager to obtain a glimpse of their beloved leader. Nehru arrived late as usual, a practice later picked up by his tribe with much less justification. He gave one look to the shamiana and the decorated lights, and blew off his top. The organisers with folded hands asked his forgiveness for being extra lavish in the decoration. 'It was our love and enthusiasm that overstepped the bounds of simplicity,' exclaimed the organisers. But Nehru was not the one to listen. For a poor and slave country, this was a lavish display indeed. Nehru was livid with anger and refused to calm down. Even J.B. Kripalani who was present there tried to pacify him, but once aroused Nehru was hard to pacify. He harangued, he shouted and threatened to go back. Then as a last resort and in order to atone for his sin, the man bowed with folded hands before Nehru and pleaded with him not to leave and start his speech. This gesture appeared to be a sign of servility and it enraged Nehru the more. Then in full public view of thousands of men crowding the place, Nehru kicked the man, already prostrate at his feet. Everyone was shocked and dismayed. Kripalani felt it too. Enough was enough. He held Nehru by the hand, scolded him and physically pulled him away and stopped him from further creating a scene. After a pause, the meeting started.

To my young mind a few things left a permanent imprint. That Nehru was arrogant, that he exulted in public display of anger on those who appeared meek and submissive. And Jesus had declared in his Sermon from the Mount, 'Blessed are the meek for they shall inherit the earth'. That he was highly impulsive and was playing to the gallery. That the fate of the country cannot be safe in the hands of a person who so totally lacked self-control. His subsequent speech, when compared to Kripalani was a rambling though forceful denunciation of the Raj. Kripalani's was a well reasoned scholarly discourse. Calm and collected Kripalani gave solid arguments, made points with irrefutable logic and won the hearts of the educated people while Nehru only appealed to the eyes and ears of the uneducated and these outnumbered the former.

I carried these impressions to the Allahabad University where I did my graduation in Science. During the next two years, i.e., 1946-48, momentous events were taking place in our country. I opened out myself to a variety of disciplines, least of these being my course curriculum. I read and imbibed Bertrand Russell, almost everything written by him, A.H. Whitehead, his co-author of the 'Principia Mathematica'; C.E.M. Joad's political thoughts, George Bernard Shaw, D.H. Lawrence, Havelock Ellis; all English and continental novelists from Victor Hugo to Dostoevesky, Ibsen to Zola, Goethe and Schiller, Gustav Flaubert to Anatole France; scientists like Sir James Jeans on astronomy; Max Plank, Fermi and Dirac on quantum mechanics, not to mention Einstein's relativity, tensors and matrices, much beyond the scope of our class studies. I read almost all philosophers from Berkeley and Hume downwards and everything available on Western Philosophy, Science and Political Thought from Harold

Laski to H.G. Wells, Shaw's Fabian Socialism, Karl Marx, Hegel and Hume. In fact, reading became my grand obsession, almost a physical necessity.

It was during this period of intense mental activity, reasoning and formulation of views with almost no experience of the outside world that I heard another speech of Nehru in August 1946. Accustomed to precision in thought and speech, I was disappointed in him again. He was charming, made you feel exalted, but left no permanent thought or worthwhile ideas. Much later in life, I was to come across a similar experience mentioned by J.R.D. Tata of his meeting with Nehru. One year afterward, I missed Nehru's "Tryst with Destiny" speech on Independence eve, mainly due to lack of radio facility, though, I heard his speech on the death of Mahatma Gandhi. It was almost a soliloquy, a lament that moved all of us at the University. We fasted for two days and the messes were closed. Then we got busy with studies for the final examination and Nehru and Gandhi were forgotten. But my thirst for knowledge and truth continued even then. The evening before my Chemistry practical examination, I was studying Bertrand Russell's `Sceptical Essays' and Shaw's `Man and Superman'. I heard Nehru again at the Red Fort on 15th August, 1948. It was an exhilarating experience. However, earlier during October-November 1947, I heard Nehru's broadcast on Pakistan's attack on Kashmir. It was more of a dirge than a clarion call to the nation to rise and fight. Unlike Churchill's `we shall fight from the beaches' speech, it was a somnolent waking up to the glare of daylight, an indecisive Hamlet, soliloquing, `To be or not to be'. The pain in his voice was audible but there was no challenge to steel the nerves. I heard him often thereafter during the 1952 general elections. He was a crowd puller par excellence, his husky voice and charming demeanour disarmed his worst critics and swayed the masses—mostly uneducated.

Then finally, I was at the receiving side of his rambling

speech at the National Defence Academy, Dehradun, during the passing out parade in December 1953. Instead of being crisp, clear and brief to Army cadets who would be officers tomorrow, he presented a rather muddled picture of our nation's first Prime Minister. The speech was long and winding dealing with politics, something alien to the culture of a Military Institution, least of all to budding soldiers who are taught to shun politics. It was long on platitudes and short on substance.

Finishing my Master's degree in Physics from Delhi University, I joined as a lecturer in Physics in Meerut College in 1950, and before I could have appeared for the Civil Services Examination, I was charmed into Defence forces by the then Commander-in-Chief General K.M. Carriappa. It is here that I felt the hurting edge of Nehru's defence policies, his shabby treatment of General Thimayya engineered by V.K. Krishna Menon, the Kashmir imbroglio and the Chinese disaster. More about it later.

Comparisons are odious, but there is a need to consider some of his peers, chief among them being Patel as a reference point on the political matrix of our nation, to assess Nehru's actions and thoughts. One could include Jaya Prakash Narain and J.B. Kripalani too but that will not be fair either to them or to Nehru, since they hardly exercised any power in the governance of this country. I do not include Gandhi in this list as that would be an insult to the Mahatma. Nehru had the habit of addressing the public almost as a necessity. Whether it was an opening ceremony, a University function, a science congress or a medical conference, Nehru had no reservations in accepting the invitation to act as a chief guest. Patel and Kripalani were less visible and talked less. Nehru set the lead for a politician to act as a decorative piece to any function, which the Congressmen and the subsequent leaders have followed to this day. Whether they know even the rudiments of the subject is a different matter altogether. There are script writers, dime a dozen among the bureaucracy who are only too willing, to do the job.

In his desire to be constantly visible and heard, Nehru neglected more pressing affairs of the State. His homework on matters of vital national importance was patchy. Nehru often said that he felt invigorated by these exposures. But the debit side of his forays into the public is not so re-assuring. His last convocation address which I heard in Delhi University was not a picture of erudition or a stimulation to the budding scholars to contribute to the nation's priorities but a melange of inanities, platitudes and generalisations.

I have tried hard to assess the real substance of the so-called sacrifice made by Nehru in joining the freedom struggle. Motilal Nehru had a roaring legal practice and had lived in a style, that was envy of many of the lesser Maharajas. Patel had a lucrative practice both at Ahmedabad and Bombay. Nehru admitted to the Harrow Public School, with the influence of his father, never rose in his studies above mediocrity and predictably had a poor legal practice later on. He never distinguished himself either in pursuit of education and knowledge or a single minded devotion to a cause. Nehru was born to greatness and a great part of the credit goes to his father. Patel and Kripalani worked for it. We Indians have a weakness for the white skin and venerate the "Gaurang Prabhu". Nehru was the inevitable beneficiary of this Indian psyche. A canard often heard and propagated in early Thirties was that his family was so rich that they had their clothes sent to Paris for a wash. He sacrificed this all and jumped into the freedom struggle. Nehru could indulge into this luxury only on his father's expense account. It was he who made the sacrifice, changed his lifestyle, and put on khadi dhoti and kurta. Undoubtedly, Nehru initially joined the freedom struggle on his own volition, much against the wishes of his father, but his subsequent rise in the Congress as we shall see owed not a little to the efforts of his father, whose contribution to Nehru's eminence has been largely ignored by historians and political analysts.

In habits an Englishman, 'the last Viceroy of India', Nehru fully epitomised the Western Oriental Gentleman (WOG) and there was little indigenous or Indian in his make up, worth mention. His private affairs and dealings with women is not the subject of this book. However, it is necessary to stress one point. There is an old saying, "Caesar's wife should be above reproach". What about Caesar himself? People in public life owe a responsibility to the people, more so in India where the poor, uneducated and deprived masses still worship all the values of this ancient land. They who put him on a pedestal and reposed unquestioning trust in him, have a right to know that their idol was true to their trust. In contrast, Gandhiji's life and that of Patel were an open book with nothing to hide. Nehru's daughter later used to cover her head with the sari in public meetings to impress the village voters, the sons of the soil. Nehru did the same. It was a put on. There is a lot of evidence to suggest that Nehru's life away from the gaze of public scrutiny was not entirely and truly Indian. Patel and Gandhi were the opposite end of this brand of leadership. To them private life was equally important.

These were the personal glimpses and impressions which have been analysed with the highest objectivity and precision possible to a lay observer, and an average citizen of this country. The rest is documented evidence which the ensuing chapters unfold.

In law there are two types of evidence, direct and indirect. The direct is always considered more valuable of the two, and if this happens to be documented it becomes the more reliable and thereby more admissible. A great thinker has said that 'a man is what he thinks'. Thus Nehru's writings are the best mirror to his personality. Though there has always been considerable hiatus between his speech and action, thought and practice, it is still the best possible measure available to us to assess the man. To find out what Aristotle says, you must read

Aristotle and not someone who writes about him. You are likely to get a tutored version of Nehru's thoughts if you read other's interpretation of his thoughts. In other words you are like a tourist who travels with a guide book in his hand and who sedulously observes Mr. 'A's idea on say London, while having only half an eye on the city itself. Much has been written on Nehru by others but I have quoted extensively Nehru himself on his views. However, regarding facts of history and events I have tried to obtain more than one account of the events to ensure objectivity.

2 Making of the Man

Begotten of an extrovert father who liked good things of life, Nehru was a born aristocrat. He retained this elitist trait even in his later life. When fifteen years old, he was taken to Harrow by his father Moti Lal Nehru to receive the finest education that money could buy. In 1907, Nehru moved to Trinity College, Cambridge, and from there to the Inner Temple in London to become a barrister like his father. Fashioned in the liberal Western mould, he was inspired by Garibaldi, the Italian, and the Irish national movement. While his father, who enjoyed wealth found much to admire and emulate in the British way of life and the British Raj, his mother Swarup Rani had her roots firmly embedded in Hindu religion and culture. Shaped by these countervailing forces, Nehru's personality acquired a superficial Indianness and a love for English mores without developing a deep insight into the core of either culture or philosophy. However, it served him well to mediate between the two world poles and champion the cause of the third to which he belonged. But this did not afford him the wherewithal of a great leader like Gandhi or Lincoln rooted and nourished in his native soil. No great leaders of men have emerged who do not resonate to the fundamental identity of their own country.

Born at the Anand Bhawan, Nehru pursued a lavish lifestyle after he became the Prime Minister of India. After 1952 general elections, Congress workers from lower and middle class families came to occupy positions of power and occupied ministerial posts. Against Gandhi's admonitions, they followed the British model not only in governance but in lifestyle too. There was a scramble for the best bungalows. My uncle, jailed many times from 1921 onwards, was invited to Lucknow by Pandit Govind Ballabh Pant to join the State Government as a Cabinet Minister. I doubt if at that time there was a system to appoint Deputies or Ministers of State. Except him, everyone accepted the pay scales offered by the Congress Government. He drew only Rs. 500/- as salary which he donated to his parent organisation, Shri Gandhi Ashram, and lived on what Shri Gandhi Ashram gave him as his old salary of General Secretary. He travelled in third class as before. What did we see in Delhi? Nehru on the advice of Lord Mountbatten occupied the official residence of the Commander-in-Chief opposite the Teen Murti Memorial, while the Governor-General and later the President of the Republic moved into the Viceregal Lodge on the Raisina Hill. The move was symbolic. It was the typical civil lines approach of the erstwhile British rulers. Nehru's lead was eagerly followed by the rest of the pack and all Central leaders rushed to the best available bungalows. Even in countries like USA and UK, the size of the Ministerial residence would appear as a measly hutment of the low born compared to the sprawling residential estates of the ministers of this country known for its simple living and high thinking. Simple and unostentatious lifestyle was given a go by. Many a time, Sardar Patel, the Home Minister, raised a point in the Parliament to limit Ministerial remunerations, perks and privileges but was outvoted by a majority who had tasted blood. It was in this vein that some uncharitable observers once described Nehru as the last Viceroy of India rather than the first Prime Minister of a poor country. He was fair, fashioned in the British style and filled the role. But it was not so funny seeing the erstwhile jail birds, the freedom fighters of yesteryears, wallowing in luxuries of the colonial lifestyle of governance.

Nehru set the pace and others followed. Nehru was personally honest, but corruption flourished under his nose. He was too busy with his dams and steel mills to see the rot setting in under his benevolent gaze. The nation later had to pay a heavy price for this lapse. The government overspending is, today, the main cause of our mounting fiscal deficit and the crushing debt burden. After the Mundhra deal and Jeep Scandal and the oil scandal of K.D. Malaviya, the band of Congressmen set all-time record in corruption. Probity in public life became an exception rather than the rule.

Nehru never believed in Gandhi's Gram Swaraj or his constructive programme of khadi and cottage and village industries. This will be discussed later. What is of relevance to us here is his attitude to khadi. He accepted with reservations khadi as the uniform of the freedom fighter, the symbol of swadeshi and the march to Swaraj. While in India he scrupulously avoided any breach of this code. But, no sooner did he leave the Indian shores, than he was transformed into a Westernised diplomat wearing the apparels of an Englishman, to boot, with his tie and bowler hat. As an impressionable young boy living through the drama of our freedom struggle in which many of my kith and kin were involved and true to Gandhi's creed, I myself wore khadi in Gandhi Ashram. To me this chameleon type change in Nehru appeared not only incomprehensible but macabre. Gandhiji's heir designate flouting the cherished symbol of freedom struggle at the first available opportunity. In fact, in some of the photographs, appearing in newspapers of those days in the Thirties and Forties, it was difficult to identify Nehru, the bald headed man in English suit, whose head was seldom seen without the cover of the Gandhi cap. Used to his attractive Indian attire of dhoti kurta, khadi or woollen jacket and Peshawari chappals, this was a new face of Nehru revealed to me. The argument often advanced by his defenders that 'When in Rome do as the Romans do' did not quite convince. I saw the leaders of other countries dressed in their national dress when they visited foreign countries away from their native lands. Why couldn't Nehru do the same. Till today, I have not found the answer to my query. Gandhiji attended the Round Table Conference in a loin cloth and a warm shawl. Many other national leaders wore national dress but not Nehru. Later in life, I saw even foreign heads of states from Africa and Middle East countries, visiting abroad in their own traditional attire, and took pride in doing so. Did Nehru then have a complex about wearing dhoti kurta when going abroad? One does not know. It certainly shows lack of moral strength, confidence in one's own country, and pride in its culture.

I have discussed earlier the incident of Nehru's arrogance, when he kicked in public a respectable citizen of Meerut who had organised a reception function for him during the run up to the Provincial Assembly elections. Contrast this with what Fred Doughlas, a black journalist, wrote of Lincoln, "Lincoln was the first great man, I talked with freely in the United States, who in no single instance reminded me of the difference between himself and me of the difference in colour." George Washington having successfully fought the nation's war of independence had no further ambitions of holding any office. Unable to read clearly the farewell address that he had prepared for his troops, who followed him faithfully through the vicissitudes of the struggle, he apologised and took out his glasses saying "Gentlemen, I have grown old in the service of my country and my eyesight is fading," and he continued his address. This man who had paid from his pocket the salary of the troops since the arrears had not been passed by the Congress, later, walked through the ranks saying goodbye to his comrades. An observer records that the soldiers who had steeled themselves against all hardships and miseries of war and had learnt to suppress emotions were so moved that there was not a single dry eye that day. Later, George Washington quietly went to his home estate at Mount Vernon in Virginia. What a different scene was witnessed in India during the `Freedom At Midnight.' Bapu, the feeble old man, the tallest of them all who won us our freedom, was walking barefoot in the streets of Noakhali, East Bengal, saving human lives, while the surrogates were making speeches at Delhi. Later, some of this genre were fighting for the loaves of office which soon developed into the Congress culture.

Being heir to Gandhi, though, outvoted by the majority of the All India Congress Working Committee members, who preferred Patel, but had to bow to the Mahatma's wishes, Nehru wore the mantle of the crowned King with no compunctions. Later, unobtrusively, he groomed his daughter for this role and in his own lifetime, helped by his fawning supporters, allowed her to become Congress President and later a Minister in the Government. From there to the throne was but a short step, hastened by the sudden demise of Lal Bahadur Shastri. During his lifetime, Nehru nominated no heir but had no qualms in grooming his daughter for the role. Everytime, someone mentioned that the weak health of Indira might not allow her to shoulder so heavy a burden as the All India Congress Committee President, Nehru roundly snubbed him, asking with irritation, what was wrong with her health? She was all right. From Moti Lal to Jawaharlal to Indira to Rajiv, it has been a dynastic rule all along. Some lady of high station once came to Abraham Lincoln about the claims of her son in the Army of Potomac saying that the scions of the family in the past had rendered great service to the country. Lincoln politely replied to the lady that there was, in fact, more reason for this illustrious family, who had done more than their share of national service to let others now have a chance. One only wishes that Mahatma Gandhi could have told the same to Moti Lal Nehru when the latter was pleading for his son to succeed him as the President of the Indian National Congress in

1929. Can such a thing be ever imagined in our country? During Nehru's lifetime, there was any number of Pandits, Saprus, Kauls, Katjus, Dhars and of course Nehrus and other kins and next to next of kins of the first family who served the nation in different capacities. One Nehru who was not even a qualified bureaucrat was made an Indian Foreign Service (IFS) Officer and put in the foreign service, an elitist service then by any standards. Why do we blame the family rule now? The son and nephew syndrome in politics is nothing new, only the public memory is proverbially short. This is what Neville Maxwell says in his book 'India's China War'.

"An official (non-Kashmiri, non-Brahmin) who worked closely with Nehru for a time wrote that enemies of the Prime Minister used to say that his search for talent and gift for talent spotting was limited to those around him and particularly to Kashmiris, and amongst them, those who were in one way or another connected with the Nehru family; certainly the record does substantiate the suspicion that Nehru was drawn to Kashmiris, and he never found in close family ties reasons not to appoint people to high office. But it can be said that often such appointees had—or appeared to have—high qualities, and probably Nehru's favouritism was unconscious."

Once when questioned on these preferences, Nehru replied without hesitation that he should have the freedom to choose his team and the choice obviously fell on the men, he knew well. But, how many men can the Prime Minister know well? And is knowing well some person, a passport to merit and competence? While it could be true for personal appointments, can such a rule be applied to important positions where national interests are involved. And pray what was the job of the Department of Personnel or its equivalent organisation, if such a thing existed in Nehru's time? Is it not to find the right man for the right job? The trouble with personal appointments is that they tend to be yes men, and time servers; they bring to their master only that which he likes to see or hear, thus removing all objectivity from their advice. Krishna Menon, K.M. Pannicker and G. Parthasarthy, whom Nehru knew well, all did this very successfully and in full measure. It is a common failing with people in power who nurse an enormous self-esteem. Cullen Hightower once said, "Those who agree with us may not be right, but we admire their astuteness". These hand-picked men of Nehru did no service to his China Policy.

The apotheosis of Nehru has always been based on his outer charm rather than inner substance; the superficial sweep of his concern over many issues, than abiding commitment to any. Before coming to events connected with Nehru's thought process, it would be pertinent to examine his own stated ideas, mostly expressed in 'The Discovery of India'. Consistency in thought and hardheadedness in decisions were not Nehru's strong points. Superficiality of thought and confused thinking led him wandering into the realm of philosophy and metaphysics. By his own confession, he came rather late to history and still had strong convictions on historical issues sometimes to the disregard of accumulated evidence of millennia. These have been given in a separate chapter in this book. He was not a student of either metaphysics or philosophy but modesty in expression of opinions was not his strong point. He will theorise and stride with hobnailed boots where angels fear to tread, particularly on the delicate issues of metaphysics and philosophy and then draw self-deluding or self-justifying conclusions utterly unrelated to the issues raised by himself. The following paragraphs from his book, 'The Discovery of India' would be of interest:

"Metaphysics and philosophy, or a metaphysical philosophy, have a greater appeal to the mind. They require hard thinking and the application of logic and reasoning, though all this is necessarily based on some premises, which are presumed to be self-evident, and yet which may or may not be true. All thinking persons, to a greater or less degree, dabble in metaphysics and philosophy, for not to do so is to ignore many of the aspects of this universe of ours. Some may feel more attracted to them than others, and the emphasis on them may vary in different ages. In the ancient world, both in Asia and Europe, all the emphasis was laid on the supremacy of the inward life over things external, and this inevitably led to metaphysics and philosophy. The modern man is wrapped up much more in these things external, and yet even he, in moments of crisis and mental trouble often turns to philosophy and metaphysical speculations.

"Some vague or more precise philosophy of life we all have, though most of us accept unthinkingly the general attitude which is characteristic of our generation and environment. Most of us accept also certain metaphysical conceptions as part of the faith in which we have grown up. I have not been attracted towards metaphysics; in fact, I have had a certain distaste for vague speculation, and yet I have sometimes found a certain intellectual fascination in trying to follow the rigid lines of metaphysical and philosophic thought of the ancients or the moderns. But I have never felt at ease there and have escaped from their spell with a feeling of relief.

"Essentially, I am interested in this world, in this life, not in some other world or a future life. Whether there is such a thing as a soul, or whether there is a survival after death or not, I do not know; and, important as these questions are, they do not trouble me in the least. The environment in which I have grown up takes the soul (or rather the *atma*) and a future life, the *Karma* theory of cause and effect, and reincarnation for granted. I have been affected by this and so, in a sense, I am favourably disposed towards these assumptions. There might be a soul which survives the physical death of the body, and a theory of cause and effect governing life's actions seems reasonable, though it leads to obvious difficulties when one thinks of the ultimate cause. Presuming a soul, there appears to be some logic also in the theory of reincarnation.

"But I do not believe in any of these or other theories and assumptions as a matter of religious faith. They are just intellectual speculations in an unknown region about which we know next to nothing. They do not affect my life, and whether they were proved right or wrong subsequently, they would make little difference to me.

"Spiritualism with its seances and its so-called manifestations of spirits and the like has always seemed to me a rather absurd and impertinent way of investigating psychic phenomena and the mysteries of the afterlife. Usually it is something worse, and is an exploitation of the emotions of some over-credulous people who seek relief or escape from mental trouble. I do not deny the possibility of some of these psychic phenomena having a basis of truth, but the approach appears to me to be all wrong and the conclusions drawn from scraps and odd bits of evidence to be unjustified.

"Often, as I look at this world, I have a sense of mysteries, of unknown depths. The urge to understand it, in so far as I can, comes to me: to be in tune with it and to experience it in its fullness. But the way to that understanding seems to me essentially the way of science, the way of objective approach, though I realise that there can be no such thing as true objectiveness. If the subjective element is unavoidable and inevitable, it should be conditioned as far as possible by the scientific method.

"What the mysterious is I do not know. I do not call it God because God has come to mean much that I do not believe in. I find myself incapable of thinking of a deity or of any unknown supreme power in anthropomorphic terms, and the fact that many people think so is continually a source of surprise to me. Any idea of a personal God seems very odd to me. Intellectually, I can appreciate to some extent the conception of monism, and I have been attracted towards the *Advaita* (non-dualist) philosophy of the Vedanta, though I do not presume to understand it in all its depth and intricacy, and I realise that merely an intellectual appreciation of such matters does not carry one far. At the same time the Vedanta, as well as other similar approaches, rather frighten me with their vague, formless incursions into infinity. The diversity and fullness of nature stir me and produce a harmony of the spirit, and I can imagine myself feeling at home in the old Indian or Greek pagan and pantheistic atmosphere, but minus the conception of God or gods that was attached to it.

"Some kind of ethical approach to life has a strong appeal for me, though it would be difficult for me to justify it logically."

In sum, Nehru, the half-baked political theorist was bad enough; Nehru, the sermoniser on metaphysics, the essence of the soul, spiritualism and the law of *Karma*, was a bit too much. And yet our Westernised leftist elite avidly took over where Nehru left and completed the process of the total alienation of intellectuals from the cultural past of this land and the spirit of Geeta and Upanishads. If only some one could tell Nehru the famous words of William Cowper:

> *Knowledge is proud that he has learned so much;*
> *Wisdom is humble that he knows no more.*

For an ascetic meditating in wilderness, or even an armchair philosopher and a drawing room social conversationalist such indecision and semantics are pardonable. But in a man who is going to chart out the paradigms of our national ethos and shall in due course hold forth on almost any subject under the sun in his addresses at colleges, institutions, academia, Parliament and other national fora such waywardness of thought is unpardonble. It can produce a generation of confused thinkers and that is what we see today. The so-called elite, escapist, leftist intelligentsia.

There was a Byronic streak in Nehru minus his poetry. Byron went out as a volunteer to fight alongside the

Greeks in their struggle for freedom against the Turks. Nehru almost volunteered to fight with the International Volunteer Brigade against General Franco's Fascist forces in Spain in 1938 as a soldier of International Socialism. It was only on Gandhi's persuasion that he decided to give up this quixotic venture. Nehru's mercurial temperament often led to the pursuit of a highly idealistic approach, with total disregard to the more mundane realities of the Indian polity.

Here is the case of Simon Commission. During the tenure of the British Tory Government the Commission consisting of seven members visited India with a view to investigate the possibility of granting Dominion Status. Nehru described them: "The seven uninvited gentlemen from England". While Gandhiji, more realistic than Nehru, was not keen to outright reject the idea, saying "we need not worry if freedom is spelt dominion status or independence". But he was informed that `Jawaharlal was outraged at the suggested compromise on total independence' and had explained: "It passes my comprehension how a national organisation can have as its goal dominion status"! It is further recorded—`But the Mahatma knew how to control his idealistic protege when necessary'. "The difference between you and me appear to be so vast that there seems to be no meeting ground between us. I cannot conceal from you my grief that I should lose a comrade so valiant, so faithful and so honest..."

Again the records: 'Jawaharlal quickly climbed down'. "No one has moved me and inspired me more than you. And am I not your child in politics—though perhaps a truant and errant child?".

'Gandhi: "Well, it is now your duty to devote your whole energy to national unity and to boycott the Simon Commission".

'Here in this city of Lucknow, Nehru warned," we cannot rest, for rest is a betrayal of the millions who never eat"', Nehru's rhetoric!

We shall now turn to the leadership qualities of Nehru, generally accepted without demure. In his own lifetime, he has been described as the undisputed leader of the Indian masses. Effective and inspiring leadership is not necessarily based on charisma, a factor often quoted in favour of the Nehru dynasty, though, this may help. There are countless examples in history of great leaders with hardly any pleasant exterior or even mannerism for sale. In fact, charismatic leaders have often proved a disaster. The people get so hypnotised by their charm, physical or vocal, that they lose all power of rational judgement and often follow him to disaster. There is one recent example, Adolph Hitler. Philip of Macedonia, father of Alexander the Great, once remarked that "he is afraid of no other person than Demosthenes, a great orator, because if he heard him long enough, he would be roused to wage a war against himself". With the exception of Alexander, no great leader of men had what we Indians so fondly describe as `charisma'. Aristotle, Plato, Kant, Hume, and recently Bertrand Russel in philosophy; the one eyed Hannibal, Caesar the bald and middle aged; Scipio Africanus, Genghis Khan, Napoleon the little Corporal, the one eyed Nelson and the long nosed Duke of Wellington, Garibaldi and Mao Tse Tung in war; in political leadership, Pericles, Bismark, George Washington in peace and war; Voltaire, Rousseau and the Robespierre during the French Revolution; Abraham Lincoln, the greatest of all American Presidents, Disraeli, Gladstone and Lenin, were not attractive to men or women. And nearer home Mahatma Gandhi. But they all had one thing in common, a moral authority over people born out of selfless service to a cause, transparent honesty of purpose and the capacity to inspire trust and confidence. Patel, described by many as the rough hewn Roman patrician, inspired trust and confidence, while Nehru the Greek hero only blind worship. Hitler led Germany to disaster, Nehru did not lead India to any great heights.

Durga Das, the author of the book 'India From Curzon To Nehru', in one of his addresses to a distinguished audience on the subject of Sardar Patel, put this very succinctly, "Gandhi and Vallabbhai Patel carved out destiny for themselves, Jawaharlal was the child of destiny; Lal Bahadur Shastri was thrown up by destiny; Indira Gandhi is the instrument of destiny". In the same address he says again," I will take you back to the psyche. We worship or revere or salute an uncommon man. Gandhi became an uncommon man when he wore the garb of a saint and became a Mahatma in word and deed. Nehru was sold to the people by Gandhi as a Prince who had put on the garb of a Sadhu".

Where would have Nehru been without being anointed by Mahatma and born to Moti Lal Nehru? McNamara, one of the ablest bureaucrat of the United States, was candid enough to admit his part of the mistake in the continuation of the Vietnam war. He believed strongly that leaders are there to lead and not pander to public paranoia or attempt to win elections on wrong emotive issues. This is what he said, "The press, the public and Congress throughout the time I was there all supported the war. Damn it, the leaders of this country are not elected to respond to polls and the press and to follow solely the views of the Congress. The leaders are elected to lead and we are led wrong". McNamara had the candour of Mahatma Gandhi in accepting his mistake. This is the common error of populist stances. Inspite of the public being keyed up not to accept any deviation from the fight for freedom, Gandhiji had the moral courage to stop freedom struggle and go on a fast for the removal of untouchability and the cause of Harijans. His aim was to lead in a true sense rather than look to the next elections. He showed the same courage and capacity to lead when he called off the Satyagrah after the violence at Chauri Chaura. Nehru need not have bothered about public approval or winning elections. He held such undisputed sway over the masses. He could force his will for causes that he espoused only if he had chosen to do so. Instead he only played to the gallery. He did not lead. He failed to lead India since he did not know what was good for the country, and fumbled with his priorities. His daughter by her own admission was a politician and the pursuit of political power became her sole aim. Her populist slogans like Garibi Hatao, Bank Nationalisation and Abolition of Privy Purses, were all examples in political gimmickry. Nehru was not Gandhi. He did not learn from his master how to stand for the right and national good, even though, there was no risk to his position or leadership.

Nehru did not lead in building character. No nation can attempt anything of value nor achieve much without this basic asset. Whatever little progress our people have made is not due to anything that Nehru or the later Indian State has done for them but inspite of it. It is their innate sense of identity with our age-old culture, much deprecated by Nehru and ridiculed by our leftist elitist press that they have not lost faith in the future of this country. Taking the best from Science and Technology that the West has to offer it is our own Indianness that has put up people here and abroad above most people of the world. How is it that the same talent, stifled by the system created after Independence, goes to seed in this country, while it flowers in the Western countries under more creative conditions. Is then all well with the State created by Nehru and perpetuated by his less worthy successors? The signs were clear in his own lifetime, but instead of rooting out the evil, he allowed it to grow and not all his planning and big constructions, could put the nation firmly on its feet. His great speech of 'Tryst with Destiny' proved only a pious hope. Nehru, as was true of P.B. Shelley, was "The ineffectual angel beating his luminous wings in the void in vain".

What did Mahatma do for a cause he held even more important than freedom and political change in the Indian Government? The cause of Hinduism, the soul of India.

He decided to go on fast not for the fight for freedom but on a religious issue. He condemned the caste Hindus for the detestable manner in which they treated the Harijans who though forming a large part of undivided Hindu society were treated as untouchables. He thought it morally indefensible that these wretched be segregated politically too. Though Nehru and other Congressmen did not see the issue in that perspective, to Gandhi it was a matter on which he was prepared to stake his life. To others, it was a mere distraction from the main effect towards freedom. But to Gandhiji it was a matter of life and death. All appeals of Nehru and his friends were lost on the Mahatma who called for religious reforms as a prerequisite for freedom. The demand for separate electorate was a devious attack on Hindu solidarity and an affront to Gandhiji's idea of regenerating Hindu society, which should embrace the Harijans. While Ambedkar was ready with alacrity to pick up the cause of separate electorates for the untouchables to break them away from the Hindus, the Mahatma stood solidly against this effort. His going on fast shook the nation. The Britishers thought that Gandhiji dead was more dangerous than the one alive. Hindu leaders visited Gandhiji, and Ambedkar who did not take kindly to Gandhiji's fast was put under tremendous pressure. Four days later Ambedkar buckled under on the issue of separate electorates for the Harijans. However, he forced a caveat that the Harijans were to be given reserved seats from the quota of Hindus. In the bargain, they got twice the number of seats they were entitled to under the law. But for the Hindus and Gandhiji, it was a battle worth the fight, and Hinduism survived.

Nehru's insensitiveness to serious issues of lasting nature which make a nation is not generally known, though, the results of these important omissions are for everyone to see. Unlike Gandhi, Nehru never really grasped the importance of developing human potential. He was too much concerned with the spectacular and the superficial but not with the substance of which nations are made.

Nehru decried totalitarianism and dictatorship but by nature, he was as irrational and dictatorial as any despot. That he was an elected dictator in a democratic India is a phenomenon that has baffled many observers of the Indian scene. One factor is, our people's desire to seek a redeamer and worship him regardless of his failings. We as a nation are slow to react and not sharp enough to correctly size up a man or see through the magic words of a mountebank. Be that as it may, here is an interesting sidelight on Nehru's continued preeminence in politics. An article appeared in November 1937 in a Calcutta journal that stated of Nehru thus:

"He has all the makings of a dictator in him—vast popularity, a strong will, energy, pride... and with all his love of the crowd, an intolerance of others and a certain contempt for the weak and inefficient." The writer went on, "In normal times he would just be an efficient and successful executive, but in this revolutionary epoch Caesarism is always at the door, and is it not possible that Jawaharlal might fancy himself a Caeser? Therein lies the danger for Jawaharlal and India". The man who penned this piece of inverted snobbery, apparently candid, but misleading in content, was no other than Nehru himself.

It was a foregone conclusion among the Congressmen at the beginning of 1951 that Congress now completely under the spell of Nehru was bound to turn into an autocracy. In a way, they were right about Nehru being a Caeser but it was to be an autocracy of his weakness. Nehru's pride and arrogance was in full view. Though much resented, this had to be tolerated because all power flowed through Nehru's popularity through which the acolytes drew their position and sustenance. Nehru's self-imposed democratic veneer ultimately became a source of status quoism. Though not a Caesar in so many words all power was centered in one man and all decisions flowed from one fount. Unfortunately, a less than efficient executor and an ineffective administrator, Nehru never learnt the art of delegation. The link between Nehru and Congress was a marriage of weaknesses. Congress needed Nehru and it was only Nehru who could have led a party as supine as the Congress. For the survival of Congress, Nehru was a necessity since he alone could keep it in power through his hold over the Indian masses.

It will become clear by subsequent events, described later, that Nehru just could not accept being No. 2 in any organisation. His entry by back door as he himself was to confess later to the Presidentship of All India Congress Committee through the influence of his father is well known and is discussed in detail in the chapter "Nehru before Independence". He never had any doubts whatsoever that after the freedom struggle, he would become the first Prime Minister of India. The anointed one would have accepted nothing less.

There was a search for the head of the Indian State as Mountbatten was due to leave in the summer of 1948. True to his promise of working in Nehru's team as a loyal soldier, Patel discussed the subject of Mountbatten's successor with Nehru in March 1948 and Rajaji appeared to be a consensus candidate. While Mountbatten was away in England for the marriage of his nephew, Prince Philip to Princess Elizabeth, the heiress to the throne, Rajaji sounded Nehru if he himself could accept the position vacated by Mountbatten and allow Patel to become the Prime Minister. Rajaji stressed his view further saying that this "would be of great international value besides being an efficient arrangement for internal affairs". C.R.'s choice of Patel thus became obvious, and Nehru thereupon with renewed vigour persuaded Rajaji to accept the post of Governor General, leaving Madras for Delhi. Nehru need not have feared Patel's ambition for Prime Ministerial chair. With his characteristic candour Patel wrote to Rajaji that, "After

Bapu's death it is all the more essential that the remnant of his circle should pull its weight together". That settled the issue conclusively and Rajaji accepted the suggestion. Thus Nehru, never prepared to be No. 2, got his choice with the active support of Sardar Patel, the man whom he feared as the most powerful contender for the throne. A month after Mountbatten's departure, in true royal style, Nehru moved in the grand mansion of the British Commander-in-Chief on Teenmurti Road. It appears that this shift from his earlier residence, opposite Sardar's at No. 1, Aurangzeb Road, was advised by Mountbatten while Patel was away and recuperating from his sickness. This almost put a stop to the informal meetings that he used to have with the Sardar from his earlier abode.

Nehru on his part had an almost unquestioning reliance on his own charm and pulling power on the crowds, to foist on the unsuspecting and gullible masses decisions which were not only not well reasoned but also against national interest. In contrast to this attitude, witness a candid confession by no less a person than Nelson Mandela, who spent 25 years in jail, almost three times as much as Nehru's total period of incarceration. When asked in a Television interview during his visit to India in 1994, the world hero and Noble Prize winner said, "I have always been warning my people to put issues above personalities. Mandela will come and go but issues will stay. My people must think of the issues I stand for and not focus on Mandela, the man". The true disciple of Gandhi was born in South Africa but not in Anand Bhawan. A man spoilt by mass adulation was the one Gandhiji appointed as the heir to his legacy.

Nehru knew that his position was unassailable and he could indulge in dramatics. His frequent threats to resign later became a joke with the intelligentsia. Michael Edwardes said, "Warnings had been there for all to hear in many of his speeches. He was feeling `flat and stale' he said, but he had said that before. In 1951, before the Tandon clash, he had talked about retirement.

In 1954, he had also said that `he was tired'. But Congressmen had judged him as they did themselves. Their motives for hanging on to power were certainly different but no less compelling. Some gestures were made. In 1953, he had been relieved of the Congress presidency, but in his place was elected a handpicked successor. In 1957, Nehru had also expressed a desire to give up office. Everyone then took it for what it was, a fit or pique at not being able to get his own choice as the second President of India."

An idealistic dreamer, Nehru often lacked what the French called "Le Sens Practique". His lack of practical wisdom and ignorance of the nitty-gritty of running an organisation honed to fight the freedom struggle has been brought to light by an interesting incident before the Quit India Movement and after the failure of the Cripps Mission. Again Michael Edwardes, "He wrote to President Roosevelt that Indians would do their utmost not to submit to Japanese aggression. They could not support the British war effort but they would organize their own. Nehru's solution was guerrilla warfare against the invader. Gandhi dismissed it in his newspaper *Harijan:* `I am sorry that he [Nehru] has developed a fancy for guerrilla warfare. But I have no doubt that, it will be a nine days' wonder'. As usual, Gandhi was right".

It has been said elsewhere that Nehru had a personal charm that could move the masses. He had the veneer of a demagogue, though never clear and precise in his exhortations or reasoning. He had a rambling speech with a pleasant, husky, melancholy timbre to his voice, but the effect on the masses was transient. It never left a permanent mark. All great men and movers of a nation, possess much more than effective speech. They have the ability to stir the masses to rise above themselves, for causes higher than themselves even involving the highest sacrifice. This power comes from character and something greater than the sum total of their known achievements. To quote Orisson Swett Marden:

"I have read", Emerson says, "that they who listened

to Lord Chatham felt that there was something finer in the man than anything which he said". It has been complained of Carlyle that when he has told all his facts about Mirabeau they do not justify his estimate of the latter's genius. The Gracchi, Agis, Cleomenes, and others of Plutarch's heroes do not in the record of facts equal their own fame. Sir Philip Sidney and Sir Walter Raleigh are men of great figure and of few deeds. We cannot find the smallest part of the personal weight of Washington in the narrative or his exploits. The authority of the name of Schiller is too great for his books. This inequality of the reputation to the works or the anecdotes is not accounted for by saying that the reverberation is longer than the thunderclap; but something resided in these men which begot an expectation that outran all their performance. The largest part of their power was latent. This is that which we call character—a reserve force which acts directly by presence, and without means. What others effect by talent or eloquence, the man of character accomplishes by some magnetism. Half his strength he puts not forth. His victories are by demonstration of superiority, and not by crossing bayonets. He conquers, because his arrival alters the face of affairs.

There are men and women in every country who conquer before they speak. They exert an influence out of all proportion to their ability, and people wonder what is the secret of their power over men."

Lincoln was awkward and ungainly. But in just four years of his Presidency and death in the fifth, he achieved much more than any other world leader; far more than Nehru in his whole lifetime including seventeen years of unchallenged rule. Lincoln reunited a nation divided against itself, abolished slavery and gave America its soul. Like Gandhi, he had character. Again Swett Marden:

"Lincoln, although President of a great people, was the laughing stock of the aristocratic and fashionable circles of Europe. The illustrated papers of all Christiandom caricatured the awkwardness and want of dignity of this backwoods graduate. Politicians were shocked at the simplicity of his state papers, and wished to make them more conventional; but Lincoln only replied, 'The people will understand them'. Even in Washington he was ridiculed as the ape, stupid blockhead, and 'satyr'. On reading these terrible denunciations and criticisms, he once said, 'Well Abraham Lincoln, are you a man or are you a dog'? After the repulse at Fredericksburg he said, 'If there is a man out of hell that suffers more than I do, I pity him'. But the great heart of the common people beat in unison with his. The poor operatives in European cotton mills sometimes nearly starved for lack of cotton, but they never petitioned their government to break Lincoln's blockade. Working people the world over believed in and sympathised with him.

"No man ever lived of whom it could have been more truly said that, 'The elements so mixed in him that Nature might stand up. And say to all the world, 'This is a man'!

"Lincoln always yearned for a rounded wholeness of character; and his fellow lawyers called him 'perversely honest.' Nothing could induce him to take the wrong side of a case, or to continue on that side after learning that it was unjust or hopeless. After giving considerable time to a case in which he had received from a lady a retainer of two hundred dollars, he returned the money, saying: 'Madam, you have not a peg to hang your case on'. 'But you have earned that money', said the lady. 'No, no', replied Lincoln, 'that would not be right. I can't take pay for doing my duty'.

"There should be something in a man's life greater than his occupation or his achievements, grander than acquisition of wealth; higher than genius; more enduring than fame. Men and nations put their trust in education, culture, and the refining influence of civilized life, but these alone can never elevate or save a people. Art, luxury, and degradation have been boon companions all down the centuries.

"If there is any one power in the world that will make itself felt, it is character. There may be little culture, slender abilities, no property, no position in 'society'; yet, if there be a character of sterling excellence, it will demand influence and secure respect.

"A right act strikes a chord that extends through the whole universe, touches all moral intelligence, visits every world, vibrates along its whole extent, and conveys its vibrations to the very bosom of God".

Gandhi's choice of Nehru as his successor and Prime Minister may be baffling to a superficial observer of the Indian political scene. But for all his personal idealism, Gandhi had a strong streak of commonsense and a cool headed realism. He wanted Nehru the idealistic and impulsive to be reigned in by Patel, the cool headed realist. He wanted them both to work as team. While he could rely on Patel to support Nehru from No. 2 position, he did not trust Nehru to play a second fiddle to Patel as the Prime Minister. Nehru was too ambitious and proud. The crowd puller and darling of masses was to rouse the nation and Patel, the realist, to chart out, plan and execute the task of nation building. He hoped the combination would last for some time till India came into it's own and became a nation of substance. But he did not reckon with Nehru's arrogance. Even before Gandhiji's death, Nehru complained against the Sardar. He wanted to cut loose from Patel's influence and play a dictatorial role. Examples are legion. Gandhiji always advised restraint and never even once imagined Nehru governing the country without Patel's guidance, help and support.

A very objective assessment of the initial stage of the functioning of Indian Government after Independence brings out vividly Nehru's inadequacy and the pre-eminence of Sardar Patel on the political scene.

However, snatching away the Prime Ministership from Nehru was farthest from Patel's thoughts. He knew he was old and enfeebled due to sickness, and he did not have Nehru's popular support. His only aim was to influence the nation's policies to the good, to restrain Nehru when needed, but not to remove him. During his lifetime Patel acted as a sobering influence on Nehru as also a check on the radicals and extremists. On 15th December, 1950, when the Sardar died in Bombay this last restraint on Nehru was removed. The funeral was to be held at Bombay. As recorded, Nehru acted double facedly even at this solemn hour of the Sardar's death. While he indulged in public praise for the great man, he resorted to pettiness in private. He tried to restrain Dr. Rajendra Prasad from attending the ceremony on the specious plea that as Head of the State, by attending the funeral of a Minister will be setting a bad precedent. The real reason, however, was his fear that Dr. Prasad might praise the Sardar in glowing terms. Prasad, however, saw through Nehru's ruse for what it was, a petty effort to tarnish the Sardar's reputation. As it turned out, the President and the Prime Minister travelled by the same plane to Bombay, and Nehru learnt a lesson. Later, he was forced to offer encomiums to the deceased Deputy Prime Minister in Parliament in the following words:

'We shall remember him as a friend, and a colleague and comrade above all, and I, who have sat here on this bench side by side with him, feel rather forlorn and a certain emptiness will steal upon me when I look to his empty seat'.

But Nehru to ensure that the seat forever remained empty, never appointed a Deputy Prime Minister after Patel's death.

The Congress leaders, inexperienced in the art of governance persisted in their behaviour as a volunteer force for freedom with hardly any semblance of a party in power. The prominent leaders of the freedom struggle continued to dominate the government and the most conspicuous among these was Sardar Patel who dealt with Home Affairs and the Department of States and not Nehru, the Prime Minister. Though outside the Government, Gandhi wielded considerable influence and continued to act as a referee between Nehru and Patel, due almost entirely to his great moral authority. It was because of Bapu's support for Nehru and efforts at mediation that the real break between Nehru and Patel never came. The challenge from Patel and the organisational wing was aimed not at Nehru's position as Prime Minister but at his policy prescriptions. The division of responsibility between the two was not very well defined, though indicated vaguely during the interim government. In his dealings with External Affairs, Kashmir and Commonwealth, Nehru the Prime Minister was seldom questioned. His views on Kashmir, even though radical, were accepted by the communalists, though, for the wrong reasons. However, in the domestic field, it was Patel's writ that prevailed, though he always informed Nehru on major issues and obtained his concurrence. In addition to Information and Broadcasting, Patel also retained a complete hold on the Congress organisation. Because of the significance of these portfolios, and his hold on the domestic scene, Patel has been truly described as the architect of the Indian state. He and V.P. Menon, working together as a team, changed the shape of the country. Thus one after another, all the 565 Princely States were merged in the Indian Union. These principalities amounting to twelve administrative units brought about 10 lakh square miles and nine crore people into the Union, almost as much as was lost due to the partition. The princes were offered generous terms and the process of assimilation went on smoothly. Nehru had no role to play in this great national undertaking. It was Patel who created the steel framework of bureaucracy, on which Nehru was to rely so much later on. Nehru had earlier decried both the Armed Forces and the Civil Services. But later, though he changed his views about the bureaucracy, his attitude to the military remained unchanged and was one of the principal causes of the poor showing of the Indian Army during the Chinese conflict in 1962. Patel had a better understanding of the needs of the modern state than Nehru. He presided over the transformation of the services and the Army from their colonial role to an instrument of the independent state of Bharat. Nehru, however, headed the pack of Congressmen, in heaping calumny on the Civil Services and Armed Forces branding them "as traitors" and had advocated drastic changes. It was Patel's restraining hand which allowed a smooth transformation of these dedicated Indians into the best Civil Services and Armed Forces of the time.

Nehru meant well, but he missed the essence of Plato's distinction, "between 'willing what is right' and 'knowing what is right to will.'" It is not possible to evaluate all Nehru's thoughts and writings at this stage. This would be done later by discussing his thoughts on history and his approach to Indian identity. What can be attempted at this stage is only to focus on those thoughts that translated into his policy prescriptions, almost without a whimper of protest or criticism by a supine national press, and specialists who should have known better; thoughts that shaped the policy and economic development of our country. These must be analysed ruthlessly for their validity, involving as they do the destiny of a nation being shaped by a benevolent dictatorial man.

Nehru had a facile pen and his prose could be lucid. His "Tryst with Destiny" speech ranks among some of the best pieces of public speeches. Yet to a discerning mind, most of his speeches lack coherence or direction. His exhortations and denunciations notwithstanding, the central thread was weak. Above all, unlike great leaders and makers of history whose words mirrored their deeds, his public utterances lacked candour. To illustrate this point, I shall juxtapose Nehru's best speech mentioned above against one of the shortest speeches known to history lasting barely two minutes delivered by Abe Lincoln at Gettysburg, which ranks amongst the two best pieces of English prose. First the "Tryst with Destiny".

"Long years ago we made a tryst with destiny, and now the time comes when we shall redeem our pledge, not wholly or in full measure, but very substantially. At the stroke of the midnight hour, when the world sleeps, India will awake to life and freedom. A moment comes, which comes but rarely in history, when we step out from the old to the new, when an age ends, and when the soul of a nation, long suppressed, finds utterance. It is fitting that at this solemn moment we take the pledge of dedication to the service of India and her people and to the still larger cause of humanity.

"The appointed day has come—the day appointed by destiny—and India stands forth again after long slumber and struggle, awake, vital, free and independent. The past clings on to us still in some measure and we have to do much before we redeem the pledges we have so often taken. Yet the turning point is past, history begins anew for us, the history which we shall live and act, and the others will write about.

"It is a fateful moment for us in India, for all Asia and for the world. A new star rises, the star of freedom in the East, a new hope comes into being, a vision long cherished materializes. May the star never set and that hope never be betrayed.

"We rejoice in that freedom, even though clouds surround us and many of our people are sorrow-stricken and difficult problems encompass us. But freedom brings responsibilities and burdens and we have to face them in the spirit of a free and disciplined people.

"On this day, our first thoughts go to the architect of this freedom, the Father of our Nation who, embodying the old spirit of India, held aloft the torch of freedom and lighted up the darkness that surrounds us. We have often been unworthy followers of his, and we have strayed from his message, but not only we, but the succeeding generations, will remember this message and bear the imprint in their hearts of this great son of India, significant in his faith and strength and courage and humility. We shall never allow that torch of freedom to be blown out however high the wind or stormy the tempest.

"Our next thoughts must be of the unknown volunteers and the soldiers of freedom who without praise or reward, have served India even unto death.

"We think also of our brothers and sisters, who have been cut off from us by political boundaries and who unhappily cannot share at present the freedom that has come. They are of us and will remain of us, whatever may happen, and we shall be sharers in their good and ill fortune alike.

"The future beckons to us. Whither do we go and what shall be our endeavour? To bring freedom and opportunity to the common man, to the peasants and the workers of India. To fight and end poverty and ignorance and disease. To build up a prosperous, democratic and progressive nation, and to create social, economic and political institutions, which will ensure justice and fullness of life to every man and woman.

"We have hard work ahead. There is no resting for anyone of us, till we redeem our pledge in full, till we make all the people of India, what the destiny intended them to be. We are citizens of a great country, on the verge of bold advance, and we have to live up to that high standard. All of us, to whatever religion we may belong, are equally the children of India, with equal rights, privileges and obligations. We cannot encourage the communalism or narrow-mindedness, for no nation can be great whose people are narrow in thought or in action.

"To the nations and the peoples of the world, we send greetings and pledge ourselves to co-operate with them in furthering peace, freedom and democracy.

"And to India, our much loved motherland, ancient, eternal and ever new, we pay our reverent homage and we bind ourselves afresh to her service. Jai Hind".

Now compare this with Lincoln's address.

The Gettysburg Address

"Four score and seven years ago our fathers brought forth on this continent, a new nation, conceived in liberty, and dedicated to the proposition that all men are created equal.

"Now we are engaged in a great civil war, testing whether that nation, or any nation so conceived and so dedicated, can long endure. We are met on a great battlefield of that war. We have come to dedicate a portion of that field, as a final resting place for those who here gave their lives that nation might live. It is altogether fitting and proper that we should do this.

"But in a larger sense, we cannot dedicate, we cannot consecrate, we cannot hallow, this ground. The brave men, living and dead, who struggled here, have consecrated it, far above our poor power to add or detract. The world will little note, nor long remember what we say here, but it can never forget what they did here. It is for us, the living, rather to be dedicated here to the unfinished work which they who fought here have thus far so nobly advanced.

"It is rather for us to be here dedicated to the great task remaining before us, that from these honored dead we take increased devotion to that cause for which they gave the last full measure of devotion; that we here highly resolve that these dead shall not have died in vain; that this nation, under God, shall have a new birth of freedom, and that this government of the people, by the people, and for the people shall not perish from the earth".

While Nehru's speech is a work of art and sophistry, Lincoln's is a mirror of simplicity and candour but unmistakable in its intent. Each brings out a different man. The first suave, sophisticated, seeking effect; the other a rough hewn human full of candour and endowed with almost Biblical simplicity. Nehru's "The history, which we shall live and act and others will write about," is a rather presumptuous statement taking for granted the success of his efforts, most of which in fact failed.

In any case, it lacks modesty. If this speech is his covenant with the people of India or his testament, then it only deals with generalities while missing the most important single point, i.e., "to build up national character through education" so that democracy can have a meaning. Without education of masses, democracy is mere slogan mongering, a clap trap about social justice and radical rhetoric by which many a tinpot dictator have fooled people. Today's talk of social justice by dividing the communities on caste lines, the "forwards" and "backwards" has a strange feeling of deja vu. The speech is rambling, lacks direction and is certainly not abounding in modesty.

Assured of his superior standing and greatness bestowed on him by the Mahatma, Nehru often treated his equals and colleagues with less than due regard to their wisdom and experience. Later, when his equals and challengers to his superiority disappeared from the national scene, he became even more irreverent. He began to pontificate and deliver long homilies. In his writings, even in official communications he tended to over-emphasise and became repetitive, while, as stated above, the content lacked coherence and brevity. Nehru was never known to be a "Man of few words". We all have heard of Byron's essay on a Biblical episode set in an examination paper where he stood first in the class in the briefest of answers, ''The water saw its master and blushed''. In another examination for which he was ill-prepared, he was honest enough to write, ''Forgive me my master, I do not know my subject well enough to be brief". Patel's correspondence published by Durga Das is replete with concise and clear letters, making no pretensions to ideal prose, but unmistakable in direction. They left the recipient in no doubt whatsoever about what was stated and what action was required. This is the hallmark of a man of action and builder of a nation's destiny.

In a man as attractive to women as Nehru, there were bound to be many women in his life. His relationship with them is not our concern. The Indian press too has been very generous to Nehru in sweeping all these affairs under the carpet unlike the British London tabloids. Many of Nehru's indiscretions on this count have been overlooked and scrupulously suppressed. To reword Oscar Wilde's famous remarks on the discovery of America which runs thus, "America has been discovered many times before Columbus but it was always hushed up". It can be said with some justification that Nehru was discovered many times but it was always hushed up. A mention has already been made regarding the need for transparency in the private lives of people in public life. Caeser's wife must be above reproach. In the assessment of Nehru, 'the man' while we can ignore some women in his life, we cannot brush aside those who, though, not attached to him in any way, did influence and shape his political actions. His closeness to Lady Mountbatten is well known. This definitely gave his decisions a pro-Mountbatten and pro-British tilt. Much to the disagreement of many nationalist leaders, chief among them being Jaya Prakash Narayan, Nehru opted to stay on in the British Commonwealth, an achievement that redounds to the credit of Lord Mountbatten who had promised to the diehard imperialist, Winston Churchill, that with Nehru's support, he would still be able to keep India as a dominion in the British Commonwealth, 'The Jewel in the Crown.' Nehru's almost total reliance on Lord Mountbatten in Kashmir affairs, inspite of the rocklike opposition of Sardar Patel was the single decisive factor that led Nehru to take this issue to the United Nations with disastrous results.

The retention of Lord Mountbatten as the first Governor-General of free India in preference to Shri Rajagopalachari was another example of this distinct pro British bias. The request by Nehru and Patel to Lord Mountbatten to continue as a caretaker head of Government during the partition has been well documented in the famous book *Freedom At Midnight* by Larry Collins and Dominique

Lapierre. It did not exactly cover our leaders with glory. This episode was labelled as a deliberate piece of disinformation and was later roundly criticised by our leaders. Both Nehru and Patel made unquestionable efforts to deal with the problem of partition of India and it does not convince the people of India. Part of the answer lies in Mountbatten's own sense of paranoia and his lack of compunction in distorting the truth as also a very human desire to project himself as a great master in handling critical situations. No doubt he averred that the task was beyond them. But even if there was a particle of truth in this confession of their weakness, it can be stated without doubt that Patel was not a party to this unusual request. By Lord Mountbatten's own accounts, Patel was a strong man. He records, "Patel essentially a realist and very sensible and not Nehru was to be made State Minister, a department created to bring the 565 princely states into the Indian Dominion". Again, Lord Wavell's first impression of Sardar Patel written on January 19, 1946, reads, "I saw Sardar Vallabhbhai Patel for the first time in the morning. Not an attractive personality and uncompromising but more of a man than most of the Indian politicians, I have met". Later he wrote to King George VI, "Sardar Vallabhbhai Patel is the recognised tough in the Congress Working Committee and by far the most forceful among them. He is probably the only one of those capable of standing upto Gandhi". If it could not be Patel, the needle of suspicion points only to Nehru who even otherwise had a great admiration for and dependence on Lord Mountbatten. It is also doubtful that the doughty Home Minister could easily let go his charge. His record of maintaining peace in Delhi has been thoroughly documented in Patel's correspondence published by Durga Das and his biography written by Raj Mohan Gandhi. He did restore normalcy in Delhi under extremely difficult conditions and frequent meddling by Nehru. Thus, this total subservience and abdication of responsibility to

Lord Mountbatten to handle the partition crisis, if true, can only be attributed to Nehru. All this does not speak of a capable administrator and a ruler of men. Coming back to women, at a different level frequent meddling by Mridula Sarabhai in Congress affairs and her habit of carrying tales vitiated some of his decisions and caused unnecessary differences with the Sardar. As a result, he was less than fair to some of his Congress colleagues and definitely hurt Patel grievously many times. Mani Ben, Patel's daughter, made no secret about the evil influence of Mridula Sarabhai on Nehru, whom she considered the prime source of many frustrations to the Sardar resulting in a sharp deterioration of his health leading to an early death in December, 1950.

Nehru's weakness for some of his Muslim friends such as Maulana Azad and Rafi Ahmed Kidwai endeared to him no doubt by their proximity, but also his blinkered perception of the so-called 'nationalist and secular Muslims', a rare breed indeed, even during the freedom struggle, is brought out by the blind support to Maulana inspite of his deviousness. Here is an example of the duplicity practised by Maulana Azad as described by D.P. Mishra in his book, 'India's March to Freedom' Vol. I (Vikas Publishing House).

"Maulana Abul Kalam Azad also has expressed his own views through his autobiography. Despite his assertion that 'it was impossible for me to tolerate this abject surrender on the part of the Congress', the fact remains that he had supported the plan both in the working committee and in the AICC. He said in the AICC that partition was a tragedy for India and the only thing that could be said in its favour was that we had done our best to avoid division but we had failed'. This only means that he too accepted partition under compulsion. However, the Maulana has also indulged in a fling against Patel, who, he says, 'did not like my speech' and 'spent almost the whole of his speech in trying to refute what I had said'. The fact is that all through the negotiations the Maulana had praised the Cabinet Mission plan with its provisions for coercing provinces to join sections and permitting them to secede from the Indian Union if they so desired after ten years. In the light of the Muslim League's resolution accepting the plan and Jinnah's assertion that the plan was being accepted only as a stepping stone to Pakistan, Patel had reached the conclusion that if that plan had been accepted by the Congress 'the whole of India would have gone the Pakistan way'. Govind Ballabh Pant, the mover of the resolution in the AICC, had criticized the Cabinet Mission plan and the Maulana had refuted Pant's arguments in his speech. But for Pant's criticism by the Maulana there would have been no occasion for Patel to challenge the Maulana's views. As a matter of fact Patel was the only Congress leader who, instead of playing to the gallery, manfully defended the action of the working committee as being right under the circumstances."

Lack of Nehru's realism and ineffectual statecraft is echoed by no less a person than Mountbatten himself to whom Nehru was drawn so naturally with the fervor of a devout worshipper. "I am glad", "Mountbatten wrote to Attlee, "that Nehru has not been put in charge of the new States Department, which would have wrecked everything. Patel who is essentially a realist and very sensible, is going to take it over...."

Very few of us are aware that to some extent the credit of alienating Jinnah from the Congress fold in early 1935 and later goes to Nehru. The British, no doubt, continued in their power game of divide and rule. But Nehru undoubtedly forced Jinnah to adopt a more strident posture than he was willing to take.

After his return to India in 1935, Jinnah united the Indian Muslims for the ensuing elections under the new Constitution. Once a protagonist of Hindu-Muslim unity and not still rooting for the partition, he even now only demanded a partnership for a separate Muslim personality in the Indian polity. He was not so sure that the Muslims whom Hindus considered as converted Hindus would rejoin the Indian mainstream. It was the Congress which forced him to acquire an extremist posture of a communal leader, mainly a Nehru effort. Though not far off the mark from his ideological stand Nehru echoed the sentiment that it was Congress that through its exertions had overcome the virus of communalism. At this stage, Jinnah also conformed to this picture of an Indian nationalist and was prepared to join the Congress again in the fight for freedom. A look at the correspondence between Nehru and Jinnah of this time, however, gives a glimpse of Nehru's manner of negotiation which uncompromising in its character was later to lead to the Indo-China border dispute. Nehru the idealist was always prepared to "talk but not negotiate". He refused to understand the motives and compulsions of the other man's stand, but felt extremely righteous in a self-deluding manner about the sanctity of his own stand. There is a saying that when people say they are thinking, they are merely rearranging their prejudices. In Nehru's case it could truly be said that when he negotiated he only rearranged and restated his preset positions. In other words, Nehru could never be wrong. Nehru apparently gave the semblance of accommodation but his intolerance of the other man's viewpoint always prevented him from seeing the sincerity of the other party. It was this unfortunate trait that led to the 1947 partition and the Chinese punitive expedition against India in 1962. Jinnah's failure to negotiate with Nehru and what he considered the pro-Hindu stance of Congress provincial government forced him into converting the Muslim League into the sole mouthpiece of the majority of the Muslims.

Again, inspite of Mahatma's restraints Nehru's impulsiveness and hurt pride made him answer and counter-charge on almost each of Jinnah's vitriolic utterances against Congress. Silence would have been gold and cut Jinnah to size but there was no stopping of Nehru. He thus gave Jinnah the centre stage during pre-partition days, undoubtedly, assisted by the British whose game plan he was so ably executing.

As has been brought out Nehru exulted in mass adulation. It acted as a tonic and gave him tremendous energy. He loved addressing masses. All charismatic leaders do that, but it is a double-edged weapon and can easily turn the head of the man. Nehru confessed as much in an article comparing himself with Caeser. The following is an account from "The Discovery of India" regarding his whirlwind election campaign in 1937 and his honeymoon with the masses:

"Someone took the trouble to estimate that during these months some ten million persons actually attended the meetings I addressed, while some additional millions were brought into some kind of touch with me during my journeys by road. The biggest gatherings would consist of about one hundred thousand persons, while audiences of twenty thousand were fairly common. Occasionally in passing through a small town I would be surprised to notice that it was almost deserted and the shops were closed. The explanation came to me when I saw that almost the entire population of the town, men, women, and even children, had gathered at the meeting place, on the other side of the town, and were waiting patiently for my arrival.

"How I managed to carry on in this way without physical collapse, I cannot understand now, for it was a prodigious feat of physical endurance. Gradually, I suppose, my system adapted itself to this vagrant life. I would sleep heavily in the automobile for half an hour between two meetings and find it hard to wake up. Yet I had to get up and the sight of a great cheering crowd would finally wake me. I reduced my meals to a minimum and often dropped a meal, especially in the evening, feeling the better for it. But what kept me up and filled me with vitality was the vast enthusiasm and affection that surrounded me and met me everywhere I went." Public adulation often leads to populist postures and drives away reason. It can lead to impatience with dissent, hauteur and a tendency towards impulsiveness, all known characteristics of Nehru. As long as a counter poise and sobering influence in Sardar Patel lived to restrain him, Nehru performed effectively and in a democratic manner. After Patel's passing away, it was a one man Government which could do no wrong.

The title of the Thomas Hardy's book "Far From The Madding Crowd' aptly states the age old truth that crowds are not only mad but can also madden. Many a great statesman has fallen victim to this lure of mass approval and crowd adulation. Bertrand Russel in his admirable autobiography so succinctly observes that crowds are seldom infallible. They can be mean and wicked and always irrational. Think of the glee of the cheering crowds in the Roman amphitheatre when a helpless plebeian is devoured by lion or a gladiator pierced to death by his looming victor. Having been in the Army and faced with mob frenzy in helping civil administration restore order, I am only too conscious of the craziness that can overcome even rational individuals once they form part of a mob. How quickly the crowd's temper can change. I still remember this extract from Orisson Swett Marden's book "Pushing To The Front" which I read as a young boy.

"On the 2nd September, 1792, the populace broke into the prisons of Paris, crowded almost to a suffocation with aristocrats and priests. These fell like grain before the scythe of the reaper. But in the midst of that wild revel of blood, `a sans culotte' recognised the Abbe Sicard, who had spent his life teaching the deaf and dumb."

"The cunning fingers finely twined
The subtle thread that knitteth mind;
There that strange bridge of signs was built where roll
The sunless waves that sever soul from soul;
And by the arch, no bigger than a hand,
Trust travelled over to the silent land".

"Behold the bosom through which you must pass to reach that of this good citizen", said Mounot, who knew the Abbe only by sight and reputation; "you do not know him. He is the Abbe Sicard, one of the most benevolent of men, the most useful to his country, the father of the deaf and dumb". And the murderers around not only desisted from attacking, but embraced the Abbe, and wished to carry him home in their arms. Even in that blood stained throng the power of a noble character was supreme."

My emphasis is not on character but the sudden change in the mood of a blood thirsty crowd. Nehru's hold over the fawning masses gave him tremendous power to build and innovate. Did he use this power for the glory of the nation? Did he give them character? He gave us big dams, steel mills and large white elephants in the form of public sector undertakings. Did he ever think of investing in national character or set a personal example like Gandhiji? If he had, we would not have been in a sorry mess in which we find ourselves today. This one single contribution of Nehru, investment in education and character could have made this nation. The rest would have followed as surely as day follows night. If only Nehru had read and assimilated the following quote, again from the above book:

'Louis XIV asked Colbert how it was that ruling so great and populous a country as France, he had been unable to conquer so small a country as Holland.' 'Because' said the Minister, 'The greatness of a country does not depend upon the extent of its territory, but on the character of its people.' If only Nehru had imbibed this basic truth, he need not have bothered about the future of our country.

In an interesting book 'The Patriots', I read during my stay in America, I was impressed to find that the first thing the early immigrants into North-Eastern parts of America, New England, as it was then called, did was to establish two things, a church and a school for each parish. The foundations of the Harvard School were laid then. That showed the importance they attached to education over other material needs. The result is history. It is also interesting to note that the majority of the first immigrants were not men of high education or moral standards. They were the social outcasts, persecuted religious groups, poor and indigent, criminals and fugitives from justice the flotsams and dregs of society. But the few people, the patriots who pioneered the formation of modern America were men of vision. They educated the lowly and the meek and the criminals and the outcasts and showed what education can do to a nation. They consummated the successful revolt of the American colonies against the exploitative regime of the mother country and won their independence. They chose as their first President, George Washington, the man who was 'first in war, first in peace, and the first in the hearts of his countrymen'. We had Nehru as the first prime minister. After Washington, the country produced a galaxy of distinguished Presidents the most respected among them being Abraham Lincoln, the emancipator. Mahatma Gandhi made men out of clay. Nehru was a banyan tree under which nothing grows. Who did we have after Nehru? Only power seekers. How many of us know that the last desire of another outstanding American President, Thomas Jafferson, on whom superlatives could be showered in almost every field of human achievement, chose for the final epitaph on his grave, the following words: "Here lies Thomas Jefferson, the founder of Virginia University". That is the value American leaders attached to education. In contrast the records of our leaders right from Nehru downwards is dismal.

With a cultural heritage as rich as ours, and a generation successor to this highest level of civilization known to history, it should not have been difficult for our leaders to convince the masses of the value of education and raise them into better human beings. That they failed to do so is a measure of their lack of character and vision. The fountain head of this order of leadership can only be Nehru.

In our country with all his love and romance with the masses, Nehru's planning priorities did not put education as number one on his agenda. His successors faithfully perpetuated this tradition and today we have the largest illiterate population of the world. To be fair to Nehru, he did talk of science and a scientific outlook and helped establish many such institutions but he missed the wood for the trees. He neglected the roots, the early education which forms character. His trickle down theory of development, which was based on the assumption that prosperity and wealth generated above by giant undertakings will, somehow, reach the masses below, presumed that the instruments of such transfer would have character and sincerity of purpose. They lacked both. Public wealth filled the pockets of the ruling elites, power brokers and vested interests even in his own time. Later, in a rare show of candour his grandson and the Prime Minister, Rajiv Gandhi, did confess that out of every one rupee spent for the benefit of the weaker sections of the society, only 15 paise reached the intended beneficiary. Thanks to the first sin of the Nehru's planning order, we have today a country headed by the most venal trinity of politicians, bureaucrats and businessmen combine, aped and sustained by a torso of criminalised upper and middle class, the 'noveau rich' and fly by night operators, lording it over with a crushing and intolerable burden on the paralytic lower limbs of society, the vast world of the wretched of the earth, the 'Daridra Narayan' whom Gandhiji wished to serve. The number of memorials and monuments, institutions and anniversaries that commemorate Nehru and his familial legacy are legion. Gandhi is remembered but once and then consigned to oblivion.

3 Nehru's Historical Thought

Nehru's reading of India's historical past is heavily coloured through the Western glasses that he wore. Here is his own confession which he so candidly made in his magnum opus, 'The Discovery of India'.

"India was in my blood and there was much in her that instinctively thrilled me. And yet I approached her almost as an alien critic, full of dislike for the present as well as for many of the relics of the past that I saw. To some extent I was eager and anxious to change her outlook and appearance and give her the garb of modernity. And yet doubts arose within me. Did I know India—I who presumed to scrap most of her past heritage. There was a great deal that had to be scrapped, that must be scrapped; but surely India could not have been what she undoubtedly was, and could not have continued a cultured existence for thousands of years, if she had not possessed something very vital and enduring, something that was worthwhile. What was this something?"

Here is a school boy approaching the Indian culture and history with almost a juvenile naivete. Contrast this with another scholar, Dr. K.M. Munshi, who says in his foreword to the voluminous and authentic work, "The History and Culture of the Indian People", published by Bhartiya Vidya Bhawan, Bombay.

"I know the difficulties which beset the path of any enterprise which seeks to write such a history. In the past Indians laid little store by history. Our available sources of information are inadequate, and in so far as they are foreign, are almost invariably tainted with a bias towards India's conquerors. Research is meagre and disconnected.

"*Itihasa,* or legends of the gods, and *Purana,* legends of origin, had different spheres in the ancient literary tradition of India. But later, both came to mean the same thing, traditional history. The *Kali Yuga,* the current Iron Age, was considered too degenerate a period to deserve recording. The past was only cherished as the pattern for the present and the future. Works by ancient Indian authors which throw light on history are few. Religious and literacy sources like the *Puranas* and *Kavyas* have not yet fully yielded up their chronological or historical wealth. Epigraphic records, though valuable, leave many periods unrelated.

"Foreign travellers from other countries of Asia and from Europe, like Megasthenes of Greece, Hiuen Tsang of China, Al-Masudi of Arabia, Manucci of Venice, and Bernier from France, have left valuable glimpses of India, but they are the results of superficial observation, though their value in reconstructing the past is immense. Chroniclers in the courts of the Turk, Afghan or the Mughal rulers wrote "histories" which, in spite of the wealth of historical material, are partially legendary and partially laudatory. The attempts of British scholars, with the exception of Todd, wherever they have taken these "histories" as reliable source-books, have hindered rather than helped the study of Indian history. Sir H. M. Elliot, the foremost of such scholars, for instance, has translated extracts from Persian and Arabic "histories" with a political objective, *viz.* to make, to use his own words, 'the native subjects of British India more sensible of the immense advantages accruing to them under the mildness and equity of the present rule.....' So high an authority as Dr. Maulana Nadvi, in his presidential address at the "Early Medieval India" section of the seventh session of the Indian History Congress, expressed the verdict of modern scholars, that both the selection and translation of these extracts have not been honest. But unfortunately, Elliot's volumes became the source-book for most of our modern histories of Medieval India. As a result, they do not present a true picture of India's past, nor do they explain how Indians resisted the Turk, Afghan and Mughal incursions, how they reacted to the vicissitudes through which in consequence they passed, and how a Renaissance sprang up out of the impact of Indian with Persian and Turkish cultures.

"The treatment of the British period in most of our histories is equally defective. It generally reads like an unofficial report of the British conquest and of the benefits derived by India from it. It does not give us the real India; nor does it present a picture of what we saw, felt and suffered, of how we reacted to foreign influences, or of the values and organizations we created out of the impact with the West.

"The history of India, as dealt with in most of the works of this kind, naturally, therefore, lacks historical perspective. Unfortunately for us, during the last two hundred years we had not only to study such histories but unconsciously to mould our whole outlook on life upon them. Few people realise that the teaching of such histories in our schools and universities has substantially added to the difficulties which India has had to face during the last hundred years, and never more than during recent years.

"Generation after generation, during their school or college career, were told about the successive foreign invasions of the country, but little about how we resisted them and less about our victories. They were taught to decry the Hindu social system; but they were not told how this system came into existence as a synthesis of political, social, economic and cultural forces; how it developed in the people the tenacity to survive catastrophic changes for millennia; how it protected life and culture in times of difficulty by its conservative strength and in favourable times developed an elasticity which made ordered progress possible; and how its vitality enabled, the national culture to adjust its central ideas to new conditions."

Nehru's refusal to see Hinduism as the core of Indian culture even doing the period before the Muslim Invasion is a unique example in confused thinking and also shows a definite bias against associating Indian cultural thought with Hindu thought as the inheritor of the Dravidian, the Aryan and the Vedic civilizational mores. Sample this extract from 'The Discovery of India'.

"We might say that the first great cultural synthesis and fusion took place between the incoming Aryans and the Dravidians, who were probably the representatives of the Indus Valley civilization. Out of this synthesis and fusion grew the Indian races and the basic Indian culture, which had distinctive elements of both. In the ages that followed there came many other races: Iranians, Greeks, Parthians, Bactrians, Scythians, Huns, Turks (before Islam), early Christians, Jews, Zoroastrians; they came, made a difference, and were absorbed. India was, according to Dodwell, 'infinitely absorbent like the ocean.' It is odd to think of India, with her caste system and exclusiveness, having this astonishing inclusive capacity to absorb foreign races and cultures. Perhaps it was due to this that she retained her vitality and rejuvenated herself from time to time. The Moslems, when they came, were also powerfully affected by her. 'The foreigners (Muslim Turks)', says Vincent Smith, 'like their forerunners the Sakas and the Yueh-chi, universally yielded to the wonderful assimilative power of Hinduism, and rapidly became Hinduised'"

What is Hinduism?

"In this quotation Vincent Smith has used the words 'Hinduism' and 'Hinduised'. I do not think it is correct to use them in this way unless they are used in the widest sense of Indian culture. They are apt to mislead today when they are associated with a much narrower, and specifically religious, concept. The word 'Hindu' does not occur at all in our ancient literature. The first reference to it in an Indian book is, I am told, in a *Tantrik* work of the eighth century *A.D.,* where 'Hindu' means a people and not the followers of a particular religion. But it is clear that the word is a very old one, as it occurs in the Avesta and in old Persian. It was used then and for a thousand years or more later by the peoples of western and central Asia for India, or rather for the people living on the other side of the Indus river. The word is clearly derived from Sindhu, the old, as well as the present, Indian name for the Indus. From this Sindhu came the words Hindu and Hindustan, as well as Indus and India."

Any lingering doubts regarding the eligibility of Hinduism as a sole inheritor of the ancient Dravidian culture prevailing in the Indus Valley civilization, now further back-dated by at least by 2000 years as lately discovered, with its subsequent Aryan and Vedic underpinnings should be removed by a simple question. If not Hinduism, which is a way of life, what other culture or religion is the inheritor of this legacy? Is it Islam? Is it Christianity? The answer obviously is in the negative. Even after the Muslim Invasion the vast countryside and masses away from the seat of governance remained essentially Hindu. Hinduism overpowered and assimilated the new religion without losing the essential ingredients of its own. The Hindu converts into Islam from rural areas still retained their identity, language, ways of life and occupation. Even in smaller cities this was so. Urdu remained the language of Durbars, land settlement and records and courts of Law; a system that was followed by the British for convenience. But the rest of the vast masses remained attached to their local dialect and tradition, a fact accepted by Nehru. Yet he flinches in giving the Indian culture its legitimate status of a Hindu culture or civilisation. Even for the sake of semantics, Hindu is synonymous with Indian being its true derivative word.

His subsequent random and incoherent, sometimes self-contradictory views on Hinduism are revealed from the following extracts from the same book.

"The expression *Vedic dharma* was also used in ancient times to signify more particularly and exclusively all those philosophies, moral teachings, ritual and practices, which were supposed to derive from the Vedas. Thus all those who acknowledged the general authority of the Vedas could be said to belong to the *Vedic dharma*.

"*Sanatana dharma,* meaning the ancient religion, could be applied to any of the ancient Indian faiths (including Buddhism and Jainism), but the expression has been more or less monopolized today by some orthodox sections among the Hindus who claim to follow the ancient faith.

"Buddhism and Jainism were certainly not Hinduism or even the *Vedic dharma*. Yet they arose in India and were integral parts of Indian life, culture and philosophy. A Buddhist or Jain in India is a hundred per cent product of Indian thought and culture, yet neither is he a Hindu by faith. It is, therefore, entirely misleading to refer to Indian culture as Hindu culture. In later ages this culture was greatly influenced by the impact of Islam, and yet it remained basically and distinctively Indian. Today it is experiencing in a hundred ways the powerful effect of the industrial civilisation, which rose in the west, and it is difficult to say with any precision what the outcome will be.

"Hinduism, as a faith, is vague, amorphous, many-sided, all things to all men. It is hardly possible to define it, or indeed to say definitely whether it is a religion or not, in the usual sense of the word. In its present form, and even in the past, it embraces many beliefs and practices, from the highest to the lowest, often opposed to or contradicting each other. Its essential spirit seems to be to live and let live. Mahatma Gandhi has attempted to define it: 'If I were asked to define the Hindu creed, I should simply say: Search after truth through nonviolent means. A man may not believe in God and still call himself a Hindu. Hinduism is a relentless pursuit after truth... Hinduism is the religion of truth. Truth is God. Denial of God we have known. Denial of truth we have not known.' Truth and nonviolence, so says Gandhi; but many eminent and undoubted Hindus say that nonviolence, as Gandhi understands it is no essential part of the Hindu creed. We thus have truth left by itself as the distinguishing mark of Hinduism. That, of course, is no definition at all."

"It is, therefore, incorrect and undesirable to use 'Hindu' or 'Hinduism' for Indian culture, even with reference to the distant past, although the various aspects of thought, as embodied in ancient writings, were the dominant expression of that culture. Much more is it incorrect to use those terms, in that sense, today. So long as the old faith and philosophy were chiefly a way of life and an outlook on the world, they were largely synonymous with Indian culture; but when a more rigid religion developed, with all manner of ritual and ceremonial, it became something more and at the same time something much less than that composite culture. A Christian or a Moslem could, and often did, adapt himself to the Indian way of life and culture, and yet remained in faith an orthodox Christian or Muslim. He had Indianized himself and become an Indian without changing his religion.

"The correct word for 'Indian', as applied to country or culture or the historical continuity of our varying traditions, is 'Hindi', from 'Hind', a shortened form of Hindustan. Hind is still commonly used for India. In the countries of Western Asia, in Iran and Turkey, in Iraq, Afghanistan, Egypt, and elsewhere, India has always been referred to, and is still called, Hind; and everything Indian is called 'Hindi'. 'Hindi' has nothing to do with religion, and a Moslem or Christian Indian is as much a Hindi as a person who follows Hinduism as a religion. Americans who call all Indians Hindus are not far wrong; they would be perfectly correct if they used the word

'Hindi'. Unfortunately, the word 'Hindi' has become associated in India with a particular script—the *devanagri* script of Sanskrit—and so it has become difficult to use it in its larger and more natural significance. Perhaps when present-day controversies subside we may revert to its original and more satisfying use. Today, the word 'Hindustani' is used for Indian; it is, of course, derived from Hindustan. But this is too much of a mouthful and it has no such historical and cultural associations as 'Hindi' has. It would certainly appear odd to refer to ancient periods of Indian culture as 'Hindustani."

He makes a tentative statement and then has second thoughts leaving the reader puzzled as to his own line of reasoning. The same inconsistency informs many subsequent thoughts and actions of Nehru which spelt disaster for the country. Contrast this with the clarity of vision displayed by Dr. K.M. Munshi in his foreword to the earlier mentioned book.

"The multiplicity of our languages and communities is widely advertised, but little emphasis is laid on certain facts which make India what she is. Throughout the last two millennia, there was linguistic unity. Some sort of a *lingua franca* was used by a very large part of the country; and Sanskrit, for a thousand years the language of royal courts and at all times the language of culture, was predominant, influencing life, language, and literature in most provinces. For over three thousand years, social and family life had been moulded or influenced by the *Dharma-Sastra* texts, containing a comprehensive code of personal law, which, though adapted from time to time to suit every age and province, provided a continuous unifying social force. Aryan, or rather Hindu culture (for there was considerable Dravidian influence) drew its inspiration in every successive generation from Sanskrit works on religion, philosophy, ritual, law and science, and particularly the two epics, the *Mahabharata* and *Ramayana*, and the *Bhagavata*, underwent recensions from time to time, and became the one irresistible creative force which has shaped the collective spirit of the people. Age after age the best of Indians, from the mythical Vasishtha to the modern Gandhiji, found self-fulfilment in living up to an ideal of conduct in accordance with a code of life which may be traced back as far as the *Upanishads.*"

Historiological scrutiny down the millennia has been crying out loud and clear about the inalienable uniqueness of the character and identity of our cultural heritage and the immanence of this ethos in the lives of people of India. Any effort to prove otherwise is futile. But it does not prevent the so-called modern historians from trying. This deep down feeling was voiced by no less a person than the learned philosopher and poet of this land, Dr. Mohammad Iqbal, a converted Kashmiri Pandit in his famous verse, 'Sare Jahan se Achcha'.

"Yunan, Misro, Roman sub mit gaye jahan se, baqi magar hai abbhi namo nishan hamara. Kuchh baat hai ki hastee mitatee nahin hamaree, Sadiyon raha hai dushman daure jahan hamara".

Translated, it means; Greece, Egypt and Rome have disappeared from the surface of the earth. But the evidence of our being still endures. There is something in us that our existence is not easy to be wiped out. And that despite the fact that the world order had been inimical to us for centuries together.

Iqbal did not talk of the Moslem conquest, or the British India which came much later. He was talking of India and its cultural identity as early as the Greek, the Egyptian and the great Roman civilizations beginning from 1000 B.C. into the Anno Domini era. It was that basic and core culture that remained immanent, the rest were subsequent additions and outcroppings.

Nehru's original distortion propounded in the 'Discovery of India' in robbing the Indian culture of its soul of Hinduism, and almost making it appear as a composite culture of diverse religious faiths, mainly Islam and Christianity had far reaching influence on our modern historians. Spurred by the 'King's religion' it became the 'in thing' to decry the Hindu core of our culture. The pack of leftist and socialist historians 'nursed on Nehru's half baked thoughts' 'lost no time' in rewriting history according to the maxims of Marx and Lenin Now that Marx, Lenin and Socialism have been consigned to the dustbin of history, these authors are still clinging precariously to their philosophy and the discerning are having the last laugh. It is a fashion with these converts to describe ours as a composite culture. Let us look at the evidence.

The earliest culture in the Indian subcontinent thus far known as the Indus Valley Civilization dating back to 3000 B.C. has, with latest archaeological finds and research, been pushed back to 5000 BC. Starting from that date in proto history it reached its zenith in 3000 BC testified by the excavation at Mohanjodaro and Harappa. From that date till today, through the transfer of power in 1947, is a period of seven millennia. Of this vast time frame, the Muslim domination from 1300 to 1707 AD, a period of four centuries is very small indeed. During the period beyond 1707 to 1818 AD. the Marathas reigned supreme, while the British paramount lasted only 139 years, less than one and a half century. Thus the alien influence which was superimposed on our culture, call it by whatever name you like, lasted only five and a half century out of a total period of seven millennia of indigenous thought. By what law of evidence, even if we equate culture with the mores of the ruling class, can a seven millennia old civilization and culture be transformed into a composite culture by a cosmetic change of just five and a half centuries. Such contrived arguments influence only those who are either ignorant or have a vested interest in perpetrating the biggest historical fraud on the Indian people. Nehru, possibly inadvertently, like Adam perpetrated the 'original sin', subsequent leftist and western oriented historians compounded it and the gullible masses believed it. Thus followed 'all our woes and loss of Eden, till one greater man restore us and regain the blissful seat' (to quote Milton from the opening lines of 'Paradise Lost'). This was first done by Swami Dayanand and later Vivekanand, but how many Indians study Vivekanand? Where is the national cultural renaissance? We have to wait for another day Christ in the like of Vivekanand.

Look at the irrefutable logic of Dr. R.C. Majumdar, in his preface to the book, 'The History and Culture of Indian People' at page 23:

"It has been hitherto customary to divide Indian history into the Hindu, Muslim, and British periods, and assign equal space to each. The *Cambridge History of India* has set its seal of approval upon this plan, which has also been adopted by the Indian History Congress for its projected history of India. But it can hardly be regarded as equitable. Looking at the matter from a broad standpoint, it would be difficult to maintain that the 4,000 years of pre-Muslim India, of the history and culture of which we possess a definite knowledge, though in brief outline, should rank in importance as equal with that of the Muslim period of about 400 or 500 years, or the British period of less than 200 years. It is true that we possess more historical material for the later ages, but if we are to judge by that standard alone, the British period should have twice or thrice the number of volumes assigned to the Muslim period. After all, the contribution of different ages to the evolution of national history and culture should be the main criterion of their relative importance, though the space devoted to each should also be largely determined by the amount of historical material available. There is, no doubt, a dearth of material for the political history of ancient India, but this is to a large extent made up for by the corresponding abundance for the cultural side. Taking everything into consideration we have modified the historically accepted plan, and have allotted nearly half of the entire work to the Hindu period."

Historically the signs of the Moslems and British, the so-called medieval and modern period are more recent, and hence visible. But that is true of all new phenomena in nature. Their impact, however on the psyche of a nation, depends on their innate worth and acceptability. Here also with the exception of the Vedic period and later attempts, few excerpts from recorded texts exist and we have not much on record and little to go on. But the monuments of these three periods, ancient, medieval and modern, are an interesting study. In sheer number and quality of architecture, the temples and forts of ancient and later Hindu Kings even during the medieval and Moslem period far surpass those built by the Moslem rulers themselves. The British monuments of course are a miniscule lot and the fact that they are new and visible cannot erase the past which forever exists. Just as a man cannot wish away the existence of his ancestors, the few British monuments and the recorded history cannot wipe away the existence of our long past. Nehru's greatest disservice to the nation was his attempt, while thoroughly romanticising the past, to denigrate the core Hindu cultural past of our glorious national heritage. From this stemmed our slavish imitation of the West, adoption of irrational economic models, hero worship of Marx and Lenin, the gods that failed, and putting the planning process on its head by investing in the visible monuments, dams and steel mills at the cost of investment in the invisible sector of our national ethos, Indian values, national character, and human resource, the foundation of any nation's greatness.

Pandit Sampurnanand, a great Sanskrit scholar and a profound student of Hindu history and culture, did not subscribe to Nehru's constant refrain branding the Hindu values and culture as obscurantist. To Nehru a scrutiny by the methods of modern science were the only true guide to evaluate the worth of our past. Sampurnanand made a strong case saying, "To write off our millennia old heritage of knowledge in the name of science is another form of blind belief; because the conclusions of true science can only be drawn after a proper enquiry through proven methods. Our tradition and heritage has been one of search and enquiry. That we should re-examine our past and reject what is found irrational and unacceptable is understandable. But under the pretext of the new system of development, is it wise to declare our whole tradition and past as worthless?"

The biggest damage to the study of ancient Indian History has been caused by the British authors whose sole aim was to negate the antiquity and nobility of our heritage and make the future generation feel uncomfortable with their past. In this attempt they were eminently successful. The dubious theory of Aryan migration is one such myth and an attempt at disinformation. Lack of existing material evidence is not always enough to discard a belief. There are innumerable incidents and events in our Shastras, Puranas and epics which have been described in graphic details. The fact that there is no artifect, stone pellet, pottery or numismatic evidence of these happenings, is no reason to question their authenticity. All that it means is that enough and sincere efforts have not been made to unearth this storehouse of evidence. There are many references in *Ramayana* and *Mahabharata* to existing names of cities, forts, ponds and even temples connected with various events. But still our pick and shovel, calliper carrying historian is unconvinced of their authenticity. The Israelis are the only people amongst the nations of the world who are most attached to the soil of their ancient land, Ertz Israel, based on their ancient Kingdom that comprised Israel in the north and Judea in the South and the neighbouring lands. After acquiring their homeland Israelis have spared no efforts to rediscover their past and their roots. Thanks to the efforts of their dedicated archaeologists which include many great soldiers, they have been able to discover and identify all the ruins of place names mentioned in the Old Testament. Just as the relics of ancient Troy and even the earlier Cretan civilization around the islands in the Aegean Sea have been found, so have signs of the submerged Dwarika; but our leftist historians, true to the Nehru model of history, refuse to accept the evidence. Unfortunately, very little genuine effort has been made by our archaeologists too to dig up more evidence of our forgotten era.

The other blind spot, not confined to Nehru, was the so-called immigration of Aryans. If we accept the hypothesis that the Aryans did indeed come from outside and drove the indigenous Dravidians to the south, then many weighty questions need to be answered. Firstly, if we do not know the exact place of their origin, how can we be so sure of their arrival? So many outsiders came to this country; the Persians, the Scithians and the Bactrians, the Huns, the Turks, and the Mongols, the Arabs, the Moghuls, and the French, the Portuguese, the Dutch and the British. They all had a home of their own and their identity is related to their place of origin; and that is where there still exists a storehouse of historical evidence of these peoples. There is no place on earth where such a legacy that the Aryans might have left in their original homeland, before they came over to India, can be identified. The second question is, why did the Aryans move out of their old habitat and left no trace behind? The Aryans in India wrote the Vedas and had the ability for profound thoughts as expounded in Vedanta, the Upanishads and such other erudite works and founts of human knowledge, as religion, cosmology, science, medicine, mathematics and astronomy. How is it that people with such enormous capability left no such literature or any trace of their activity in their original homeland? There is no place outside India where such literature or anything even remotely similar exists. In this country, nothing happens without invoking the Vedic rites; even the so-called Dravidians also invoke the Vedic rites and rituals in the performance of their religious activities. How is it that no living race elsewhere in the world has such a heritage? The third point is that without knowing their place of origin, how can we say with any degree of certainty that the Aryans came from that place, if at all they did? If someone said that the present inhabitants of Britain are not the original occupiers of the land and that those who were, have been driven away by the later immigrants into Ireland and now the Irish are waging a struggle to reclaim their lost land, would anyone believe it? On the other hand, historians of all hues, starting from Nehru and followed by the Leftist School are emphasising on an imaginary distant homeland and telling us that we have no roots and no origin in this soil. We are the product of a race that came from nowhere, the back of beyond, which nobody knows. In other words, India or Bharat is not our native land. We are only intruders into this country while our roots lie elsewhere. We are not entitled to call this land our own. By their logic, we have as much claim on this land as a temporary tenant, almost at par with the Persians, the Turks, the Afghans, the Moghuls, the French, the Portuguese or the English. This country is a caravanserai or a guest house for footloose travellers. Anyone can come and stay here as he wishes, since it does not belong to any one race or people in particular. There is hardly any country in the world which can claim such a dubious distinction. This is beyond doubt a well hatched game plan of the British historians, lapped up by our elite westernised leftist historians, with no core race or culture claiming it as its own. Even an educated poet like Firaq fell victim to this vicious mindset. He wrote, *'Sar zameene hind par Aquauame Alam ke Firaq, Karvan baste gaye, Hindustan Banata Gaya.* In simple English this means:

'As the caravans of the different world races arrived and settled down in this land of Hind, Hindustan continued to be formed.'

It is the same verse that our state sponsored TV continued to din into our ears day after day. Was it an anodyne to the supposedly bruised feelings of the minorities in the aftermath of the demolition of the Babri structure?

Even America, the so-called melting pot of multiple cultures, civilizations and ethnic groups, still has a core of its basic identity as an Anglo-Saxon outpost of the English speaking people of Christian denomination. The great historian Churchill fervently believed in it with his heart and soul. Tacitly accepted, but seldom articulated, is this basic concept of the Anglo-Saxon core with an addendum of multiple races in the unstated order of precedence, i.e., the British, Irish, Scottish, Dutch, Germanic, Italian, Hispanic and the East European white races, followed by the Asians and the African Americans. We who have an almost seven millennia old civilization are still grappling with the question of proving that we have a core cultural identity, thanks to Nehru and his school of historiography.

That we are a conglomerate of multiple races and nationalities. That we are not a nation yet, say the modern westernised historian echoing the words of Jawaharlal Nehru that 'India is a nation in making'. It is due to this mindset that we are even now made to feel that we are not even a nation. The question to ponder is, why has the issue of Aryans being indigenous or immigrants to this landmass that is Bharat, is being raised by the historians. The same question can be raised about any race and aimed to make them feel alien to their land. A well calculated, mischievous effort is on to make us feel that we are not even a nation and in any case do not really belong to Bharat. No one really asked Nehru or these historians to whom Bharat then belongs? Is it the immigrants or invaders like the Greeks, the Huns, the Shakas, the Ghaznis, the Ghoris, the Slaves, the Lodhis, the Khilzis, the Tughlaks, the Moghuls, the Turks or the Britishers, who came and ruled? Most only laid claim to their kingdoms. But the English did not even claim this country to be their own or that they were the sons of the soil. They did not need to be told that they did not belong here. It is nothing, if not an irony, that our own land-born are teaching us this alienation of our own people from this landmass in the state prescribed books of history. Going by the text of the Shastras and Brahmipath, which Nehru never read, the boundaries of our old land were much more distant. This landmass of Bharat-agni included Bharatvarsh or Aryavarta and the land around was called 'Varunpradesh'. Our epics speak of much larger areas beyond the present geographical confines, but historians, as mentioned earlier, do not take written text as evidence. And this, when two of our epics *Ramayana* and *Mahabharta* were written by Sant Valmiki and Ved Vyas who actually lived these times and were witness to the epochal events taking place there. Still our historians class them as mere legends and myths and not hard history. River Saryu, Ayodhya, Chitrakoot, Panchavati, Setu Bandh Rameshwaram, the coral island bridge, ruins of Hastinapur, Kurukshetra, Draupadis' Bawri and Brahmkund at Kurukshetra, the Old fort of Pandavas, Purana Quila, Indraprastha, Bhimgoda and innumerable relics speak out aloud. But that according to our state textbooks is not history. Nehru, the historian, said so. This is his contribution to the antiquity and rich heritage of our history. To ensure that this lesson is not lost on us the state sponsored TV kept on screening this serial 'Bharat Ek Khoj' to the gullible, in order to put history on its head. Nehru's reading of Indian history was thoroughly flawed by the influence of Western writers and his own predilections of looking at it from his Cambridge perch. Coming late to history as he himself confesses in his book 'Discovery of India', he with little evidence to support, holds forth the thesis of a splintered India during the age of Mahabharata. To him there was no civilizational or cultural unity in the land and whatever little there existed, was confined to the north of Vindhyas, a natural barrier at which the tide of Aryan invasion was stemmed. Here is an extract from his same book:

"In the *Mahabharata* a very definite attempt has been made to emphasize the fundamental unity of India, or Bharatvarsha as it was called, from Bharat, the legendary founder of the race. An earlier name was Aryavarta, the land of the Aryas, but this was confined to northern India up to the Vindhya mountains in Central India. The Aryans had probably not spread beyond that mountain range at that period. The *Ramayana* story is one of Aryan expansion to the south. The great civil war, which occurred later, described in the *Mahabharata*, is vaguely supposed to have taken place about the fourteenth century B.C. That war was for the overlordship of India (or possibly of northern India), and it marks the beginning of the conception of India as a whole, of Bharatvarsha. In this conception a large part of modern Afghanistan, then called Gandhara (from which the name of the present city of Kandhar), which was considered an integral part of the country was included. Indeed the queen of the principal ruler was named Gandhari, the lady from Gandhara. Dilli or Delhi, not the modern city but ancient cities situated near the modern site, named Hastinapur and Indraprastha, becomes the metropolis of India.

Sister Nivedita (Margaret Noble), writing about the *Mahabharata*, has pointed out: "The foreign reader...is at once struck by two features: in the first place its unity in complexity; and, in the second, its constant efforts to impress on its hearers the idea of a single centralized India, with a heroic tradition of her own as formative and uniting impulse".

Here are further rumblings of a confused mind who has not studied the subject in depth and is too quick to hand out opinions, and even judgements. This one on idol worship:

"It is an interesting thought that image worship came to India from Greece. The Vedic religion was opposed to all forms of idol and image worship. There were not even any temples for the gods. There probably were some traces of image worship in the older faiths in India, though this was certainly not widely prevalent."

Here is another pearl of wisdom on Chanakya's *Arthashastra*, questioning the validity of some statements made therein, 'It is interesting to note that Chanakya in his *Arthashatra*, in discussing weapons of warfare, mentions machines which can destroy a hundred persons at one time and also some kind of explosives. He also refers to trench warfare. What all this meant it is not possible to say now. Probably the reference is to some traditional stories of magical exploits. There is no ground for thinking that gunpowder is meant'.

Clearly it shows that Nehru had not studied military history nor the development of military art, and weapons of war. I was lucky to work on a thesis on Chanakya or Kautilaya's Art of War propounded in his *Arthashastra*. Kautilaya's *Arathshastra* is a comprehensive treatise on statecraft, an authority on the rules of governance, war policy, coordination of diplomacy and the higher direction of war. It deals with strategy and comes down to the details of minor tactics. It discusses war timings and better campaigning seasons, employment of spies, battle formations, use of earthworks and so on. Though gunpowder was discovered in China much after Vishnu Gupta was born, there did exist the use of some fire producing material such as lac, the material out of which Lakshagraha was made at Varna Varta to burn alive the Pandavas, as mentioned in *Mahabharta*. Then there is the mention of *agnivana* too. During the times of Kautilaya, fortification was a practised art. If only Nehru had cared to read Suntzu's Art of War, a valuable book dated 5th Century B.C. he would not have made the remarks that he did, accusing Chanakya, the hard headed realist, of indulging in fancies.

Nehru's romance with the ancient Indian history is highly theoretical, and such as it was, is wide off the mark on the important facts of its antiquity. Its predominantly Sanskrit or Hindu underpinnings, as distinct from solely Vedic or Aryan as he assumes; its potent indigenous content as compared to an imported one and the existence of a unified civilizational and cultural thread from well before almost 3000 BC till his time, is totally ignored. Here are extracts from the most authentic book, 'The History and Culture of the Indian People" mentioned earlier which has a foreword by Dr. K.M. Munshi and a preface by Dr. R.C. Muzumdar.

"Until as recently as 1922, early Indian history had little actual remains to offer besides the meagre Paleolithic and Neolithic finds, described above (CH. VII), and the Piprahwa relic was the oldest object of which the date (*c.* fifth century B.C.) could be approximately determined. The antiquity of Indian history and culture as gleaned from Vedic literature is also not supposed to go beyond the second millennium before Christ. But the archaeological discoveries at Harappa, Mohenjo-daro and other localities (see map No.2) in the Indus valley have pushed back this limit, at a single stretch, to 3000 B.C., if not to a still remoter period, and India can now lay claim to the honour of being a pioneer of civilization along with Sumer, Akkad, Babylon, Egypt, and Assyria.

The fascinating story of the excavations at various places in the Indus valley has been told above (Ch. III) and we shall now try to reconstruct a picture of the culture and civilization that flourished in this region from the remains found principally at Harappa and Mohenjo-daro."

"Now working backwards from the earlier date, the age of Manu Vaivasvata, who flourished, according to the genealogies prepared on the basis of traditional accounts, 95 generations before the Bharata War, can be put as (95 × 18 + 1400=) 3110 B.C., taking one generation to average 18 years (as we have to deal with very long genealogies extending over 90 generations, we would be erring on the side of caution if we assumed 18 years as the average reign). This date, viz. 3110 B.C., curiously enough, approaches 3102 B.C. which has been taken as the beginning of the hypothetical Kali age for astronomical calculations. There is no doubt that the date 3102 B.C.

signifies some important and epoch-making event in the traditional history of India. If it denotes the period of the beginning of the rule by Manu Vaivasvata, that means that it stands for the date of the Great Flood recorded in the *Satapatha Brahmana* and other accounts, in which Manu was the saviour of humanity. The devastating Flood undoubtedly was the most important landmark in the history of the ancient world, and common Flood legends suggest that the same event has been described in India, Hebrew, and Babylonian accounts. The Flood in Mesopotamia is generally held to have occurred about 3100 B.C. The Flood in India probably also occurred at the same time, and the date 3102 B.C., supposed to be the beginning of the Kali era, may therefore, commemorate this event.

"The year 3102 B.C. thus represents the age of Manu, the first traditional king in India. Yayati, who is fifth in descent from Manu and figures also in the *Rigveda,* thus flourished (18 x 5 =) 90 years after Manu or in (3100 ~ 90 =) 3010 B.C. Mandhatri, coming after twenty generations, has to be placed in (3100 ~ 20 x 18=) 2740 B.C. The period of Arjuna Kartavirya, Visvamitra, Jamadagni, Parasurama, and Harischandra can be put between (3100 ~ 20 x 18 =) 2542 B.C., and (3100 ~ 33 x 18 =) 2506 B.C. or roughly between 2550 and 2500 B.C. Sagara of Ayodhya and Dushyanta and Bharat of Hastinapura flourished between (3100 ~ 41 x 18 =) 2362 B.C. and 3100 ~ 44 x 18 =) 2308 B.C or roughly between 2350 and 2300 B.C. Rama flourished 65 generations after Manu, i.e. in (3100 ~ 65 x 18 =) 1930 B.C. or roughly in 1950 B.C. and the famous Dasarajna which occurred about three or four generations after Rama, in *c.* 1900 B.C. These dates will, of course, have to be lowered by 400 years if the Bharata War is placed in *c.* 1000 B.C.)"

And now the latest discoveries of artifacts similar to those at Mohenjo-daro at a number of other places, such as the tribal area of Santhal Pargana, Chhota Nagpur, Gujarat and southern Maharashtra conclusively prove that the high watermark of civilisation reached around 3000 B.C. was not localised in the Indus valley alone, but included within its reach almost the entire land of Bharat and much before the so-called advent of the Aryans. A civilisation that spreads itself over an entire subcontinent cannot be born, nourished and expanded in a short period of time. May be, more such finds will establish our historical antiquity even beyond 5000 B.C. and nearer to 7000 to 10,000 B.C., the Biblical times, while Noah has a parallel in Manu, the first human of Bharat.

The indigenous content so well established during the racial movements and the proto-history period before Aryans and even Mohenjo-daro, is described further.

"Some of the fundamental bases of Indian civilisation on the material side would thus appear to be the gifts of the Austric-speaking Pro-Australoid people: the cultivation of rice, the raising of some important vegetables, the manufacture of sugar from cane, and the use of the betel vine in life and in ritual; the habit of counting on the basis of twenty (Bengali kudi, Hindi *kodi)*, and probably also the use of turmeric and vermilion in religious rituals and social life (e.g. in marriage), combined with some notions of future life (survival of the soul after death, and the germs of the idea of transmigration) and some mythological and religious as well as romantic notions and stories appear to have come from the same source. Weaving of cotton cloth was also an Austric or Pro-Australoid invention; and probably the Pro-Australoids were the first people to domesticate and train the elephant."

"Certain magical-religious rituals, e.g., the removal of the evil eye by the rite known in Northern India as *nichhawar* or *baran*, which have a strong place in Hindu society, would seem to be of Austric origin. The idea of taboo would seem to be another trait derived from the mentality of the Pro-Australoids (or Austric speakers) in prehistoric times, when *Arya* and *Nishada*—the Aryan and the dark-skinned Austric dwellers in the forests—

first met in the Punjab: Sylvan Levi has drawn our attention to the fact that the *Atharvaveda* world *tabuva* was connected with the Polynesian word *tapu* or *tabu* by Weber in 1876 and by Barth later on; and it is likely that the word passed on with the Pro-Australoid immigrants into Austronesia, the distant Polynesian islands, while in India it was borrowed in the *Atharvaveda*. Cosmic and creational myths and ideas as they had originated among the pre-Aryan Austric-speaking peoples of India were adopted into the cosmopolitan or composite Aryan-non-Aryan or Hindu religion and legend, while these made their steady way into the oceanic regions of the Pacific through the islands of Indonesia with the expanding Pro-Australoids. Certain remarkable agreements between the cosmogony of the Polynesians and that of the *Nasadiya* hymn of the *Rigveda* (X 129) have to be taken note of in this connection. The enumeration of the days by the phases of the moon—the *tithis*—which was early adopted by the Hindu people probably simultaneously with its formation and has still been retained in the sacred or religious (ritualistic) calendar of the Hindus, is again an Austric custom which survived in Polynesia; even the old Austric names for two of the phases of the moon, which are still found in the Polynesian group of Austronesian were adopted in India by Sanskrit (*raka* = "full moon", and *kuhu* = "new moon"). It has also been suggested that Sanskrit name of at least one constellation is of Austric origin, *viz. matrika* = "the Pleiades", the present day Polynesian form of which is *matariki*.

"The culture-world of India has thus among its material and other ideological bases some fundamental things derived from the Austric speakers, assuming that they were also, in their pure state, Pro-Australoid in race, which became fully characterized on the soil of India. That would be only natural, as this racial element forms one of the most important in the present-day Indian people, as anthropologists tell us, the masses or the lower classes throughout the greater part of the India being largely of this stock. The bedrock of Indian civilisation is agriculture, and that in all likelihood in connection with the cultivation of rice, goes back to the Austric Pro-Australoids of India. The germs of the idea of transmigration, which has been so potent a force in Indian thought, religion and life, would probably go back to this source; also some of the fundamental cults and rituals.

"In the domain of myth and legend, a number of Austric notions and tales appear to have survived in the myths of the Puranas and of the popular Hinduism. The legends of the creation of the world from an egg or eggs, of the *avataras* or incarnations of Vishnu, e.g.; that of the tortoise incarnation, of the princess smelling of fish (*matsya-gandha*), of the Nagas as serpent spirits of the water and the underworld, and many more, which do not form part of the Aryan or Indo-European inheritance in Hinduism, and do not seem to have come from the Dravidian world either, can reasonably be expected to have been derived from the Austric or Pro-Australoid world.

"All these have been more or less distorted or transformed in the Sanskrit Puranas, in the traditions surviving among the Austric-speaking tribes of the present day, or in popular Hindu folklore of today. The use of the rude block of stone as symbol of the divinity is also Austric— it may also have been Dravidian in addition. Some fairy or folk tales would also go back to the same source. Zoomorphic deities, appear also to be survivals from Austric or Pro-Australoid totemism which also was reinforced by the Dravidian cults possessing a similar character (e.g. the Nagas or snake deities, the tortoise, the *makara* or crocodile, the monkey god, Ganesa with his elephant's head, etc.)."

Where does Nehru's thesis of idol worship, mentioned earlier, stand in view of this evidence.

The final nail in the coffin of the belief that all that was best in our past was brought in by the white skinned Aryans is provided by the following extracts from the same source.

"India was first proposed some four generations ago, it was believed that the white-skinned, blue-eyed, and golden-haired Aryans, like their kinsmen of Northern Europe, entered India from the plateau of Central Asia, which was then a land of romantic mystery, came to this land of the black-skinned non-Aryans, made an easy and matter-of-course conquest of them, and imposed upon an inferior race or races their superior religion, culture, and language. It was believed that all the better elements in Hindu religion and culture—its deeper philosophy, its finer literature, its more reasonable organization, everything in fact which was great and good and noble in it—came from the Aryans as a superior white race; and whatever was dark and lowly and superstitious in Hindu religion and civilization represented only an expression of the suppressed non-Aryan mentality. This view is now being gradually abandoned. It has been generally admitted, particularly after a study of both the bases of Dravidian and Aryan cultures through language and through institutions, that the Dravidians contributed a great many elements of paramount importance in the evolution of Hindu civilization, which is after all (like all other great civilizations) a composite creation, and that in certain matters the Dravidian and Austric contributions are deeper and more extensive than that of the Aryans. The pre-Aryans of Mohenjo-daro and Harappa were certainly in possession of a higher material culture than what the seminomadic Aryans could show.

"The assumption that the Mohenjo-daro and Harappa people spoke a primitive Dravidian speech accords best with the subsequent trend of Indian history and civilization. From various aspects, a Mediterranean origin of the Dravidian people, its religion and civilization, appears to find good support. Reference may be made in this connection to the city culture of Harappa and the ancient cities of Sind described in the next chapter. On the positive side, the cult of Siva and the institution of yoga appear to have been characteristic of the religious life of the people of Sind and South Punjab. The Aryans knew of Sky Father—*Dyaush Pita*—and of an Earth Mother—*Prithivi Mata*—but these divinities were vague nature deities, who merely typified the falling of the rain from the sky to help earth to produce corn and fruits. The Kols (e.g. the Santals) had similarly a Sun god (*Sin Bonga)* and a Moon goddess (*Ninda Chando)* who were the great Father and Mother deities in the Kol pantheon. But the Dravidians had a conception of the forces of Life and of the Universe in the forms of a Great Mother Goddess and her male counterpart a Father God, and this conception, which was more profound, more mystic, more all-embracing and more deeply philosophical as well as more poetic than the simple Aryan idea of a material Sky Father and an equally material Earth Mother, the Dravidians appear to have brought to India from their original homeland in the islands of the Aegean and the tracts of mainland along the Aegean Sea—Greece and Asia Minor. Ma or Kubele (Cybele) and Atthis, or Hepit and Teshup, the great Asianic Mother Goddess and Father God, the former having as her symbol or vehicle the lion, the latter the bull, form undoubtedly one of the bases on which the Siva-Uma cult of Hindu India grew up."

"The extent to which the Aryan religion has been modified by Austric and Dravidian contacts is sufficient indication of the profound influences exerted by the latter in the evolution of the Hindu religion. There has been a widespread racial mixture, as anthropology has indicated. In culture, speaking in the Indian way, one may say that over twelve annas in the rupee is of non-Aryan origin. The bases of Indian economy—food (rice or wheat or millet with pulses or lentils as relish, milk products like *ghee* and curds, vegetables, occasionally a little goat or mutton, and fish and oil of various sorts where milk is not common, as opposed to the Aryan meal of barley cakes and meat and butter), dress (unsewn cotton cloth worn in three pieces as *dhoti* or *sari* i.e. loincloth, *dupatta* or shawl, and head-cloth or turban, in place of the woollen garments of the Aryans), and dwelling, are pre-Aryan; our way of thinking is un-Aryan—the syntax of the later Indo-Aryan dialects agrees more with that of the Dravidian languages than with that of Vedic and of the extra-Indian Indo-European languages; our counting and computation is largely on the basis of *eight,* which is Dravidian (Mark Collins has explained *ompattu* the Tamil word for "nine" as being really the Aryan una "one less" plus Tamil *pattu* "ten," and the Telugu *tommidi* as really meaning "broken ten" thus suggesting that *eight* was the common number in computation), combined to some extent with counting by *tens,* which is Aryan, and to a slight extent on the basis of *twenty* as the highest number, which is Austric (as Jean Przyluski has shown). Many of our social institutions and conventions (e.g., certain usages regarding prohibited degrees in marriage, and customs like a wife being on familiar terms with her husband's younger brother but regarding his elder brother as her father) and a good many of our wedding and other customs (e.g. the practice known as *stri-achara* with its attendant paraphernalia of the various produce of the earth arranged in a winnowing fan, the use of turmeric and vermilion in the wedding ritual, the employment of the coconut and betel-leaf in many of our ceremonies) are of non-Aryan origin. We have a fairly extensive element from the Austric and the Dravidian languages in our Indo-Aryan speech: the number—at least a hundred for Austric, and some four hundred and fifty for Dravidian as given by Kittel in his *Kannada Dictionary*—seems to be on the way to increase the more our knowledge of this matter is deepening and widening. In their phonetics, Indo-Aryan, Austric and Dravidian have converged more or less to a common Indian sound-system. Despite a number of noteworthy differences due to original diversity of race and speech and to climatic and economic conditions, the bases of Indian pre-Aryan (Austric and Dravidian) life and culture, modified by the language and ideology of the Aryans, and later by the ideology of Islam, still remain, and they form a specifically Indian background for a civilization and an outlook that may be described as pan-Indian.

"The discovery of Mycenaean artifacts in Greece has proved the truth of what the great explorer of AEgean culture, Sir Arthur Evans, had suspected, that a good deal of the heroic legends of Greece as well as of the legends of their gods and goddesses was of pre-Hellenic, i.e. pre-Indo-Europena, AEgean or Mediterranean origin, and these were simply Hellenizd by being rendered into the Indo-Europena language of the Greeks as soon as this language became established on its new territory. The stories of the *Iliad* and the *Odyssey* and of Oedipus and other heroes were according to this view of AEgean origin, and this has been corroborated, in spirit at least, for some other connected legends. A similar thing appears to have taken place in India. Myths and legends of gods and heroes current among the Austrics and Dravidians, long ante-dating the period of Aryan advent in India (*c.* 1500 B.C.), appear to have survived the Aryan impact and to have been rendered into the Aryan language in late and garbled, or "improved", versions accommodating themselves to the Aryan God and Hero-worlds; and it is these myths and legends of gods, kings, and sages which we largely find in the Puranas. The Rama legend looks like a blend of three distinct stories without any historicity put together at different times (the Ayodhya intrigue and the banishment of Rama, the abduction of Sita and her recovery by Rama, and the episode of the monkey princes), and seems to have grown up in Eastern India with an Austric background; but later it was re-edited as a national poem within the gorgeous framework of the composite and highly complex Hindu civilization of 2,000 years ago. The Mahabharata story, on the other hand, which developed in the Midland (present-day western United Provinces and eastern Punjab), would appear to embody a good deal of the legends, traditions, and history of the Aryans as well as of the mixed Aryan-non Aryan peoples and was created consciously as the national poem of a new Hindu nation of mixed origin welded into one people under Brahmana guidance. Viewed in this light, the pre-Vedic antiquity of a number of heroic tales and legends and dynastic "histories" as being really pre-Aryan, possibly Dravidian, can be properly understood, as cases of rendering in the Aryans' language of pre-Aryan material."

Note the mention of a new Hindu nation of mixed origin welded into one people under the Brahminical guidance.

How correct is Nehru rejecting the Hindu civilizational origin of our history with almost a disdain.

An oft-repeated charge against Hinduism, levelled by Nehru in his book, "Discovery of India", and later picked up with unseemly alacrity by the leftist school of historians, is regarding the evils of the so-called caste system. Ignorance of history and lack of authentic knowledge was the sole reason for this uninformed criticism and its continuation by the so-called intellectuals to this date. Let us survey the facts as brought out in records.

"The elaborate institution known as the Caste System among the Hindus in India may almost be said to be without a parallel in the world, although there is hardly a country where classes or orders of society or grades of social distinction of some kind or other are not met with. A common origin, name, tutelary deity, occupation, and ceremonies generally distinguish one homogeneous caste-group from another, but to-day caste is rigidly fixed by birth, and exclusive *commensality* and *connubium* between the members of a caste-group to the exclusion of all others are its fundamental and outstanding characteristics. Further, the conception of impurity communicable to a higher caste by contact with a lower one underlies this fissiparous tendency, and has resulted in the untouchability of the so-called Ṣudra, who by popular error is almost identified with the *panchama,* or one outside the framework of the *Chaturvarnya.* Again, in place of the four original *varnas* or class-groups, there are today thousands of caste divisions and sub-divisions, and the number is still growing. This unique development of an ordinary social phenomenon naturally invests its history with a special importance.

"The extent to which caste had been developed in the age of the *Rigveda Samhita* has formed a subject of keen controversy among scholars. The uncertainty regarding the exact interpretation of the basic words and phrases in the *Rigveda,* and the relative chronology of the various relevant passages scattered throughout that Veda, make it difficult to arrive at any conclusion that is likely to meet with general acceptance. We shall, therefore, state first of all in detail the most widely accented version—in a sense, almost the recognized version—of the development of caste in the *Rigveda,* contenting ourselves with only a brief statement of divergent views. Much confusion will be avoided, if we keep in view the fact, generally agreed to that the development of caste has been a progressive one, and that we should not expect in the *Rigveda Samhita* the picture of the Caste System which is presented even in the *Yajurveda Samhitas.*

"There are various speculations in later Braminical literature regarding the origin of castes. The most common is that which represents the Brahmanas, Kshatriyas, Vaisyas, and Sudras to have been created respectively from the head, breast or arms, the thighs, and the feet of the Creator. An echo of this is found in a hymn of the RV (X. 90), the famous Purusha-sukta, which describes the mythical legend of the sacrifice of a primeval giant called Purusha, the ideal "Man" or World-Spirit. The relevant passage has been translated thus:

"When (the gods) divided Pursha, into how many parts did they cut him up? What was his mouth? What arms (had he)? What (two objects) are said (to have been) his thighs and feet? The Brahmana was his mouth; the Rajanya was made his arms; the being (called) the Vaisya, he was his thighs; the Sudra sprang from his feet".

"This passage refers to the first three Castes not as sprung from, but as identical with, the mouth, arms, and the thighs of the Creator. But in spite of this difference many regard this hymn of the *RV* as the earlier exposition of the later Brahmanical view, and regard the essential features of the Caste System as existing even in the earliest Aryan society in India.

"This theory has been challenged by many scholars whose views may be briefly stated as follows:

"The evidence of the Purusha-sukta, an admittedly late hymn, is not valid for the bulk of the *Rigveda,* which was produced by the as yet un-Brahmanized tribes of Vedic Indians living in the Indus region and the Punjab. The Caste System was developed only later, when a section of these Vedic tribes migrated farther east. Their term Varna (*lit.,* Aryan colour) is used in the *Rigveda* of all the three highest castes of later times, being contrasted only with Dasa (the dasya-varna or "aboriginal colour"). The terms "Rajanya," "Vaisya" an "Sudra" occur only in the Purusha-sukta, the term "Brahmana", also, being rare in the *Rigveda*. The term "Kshatriya", of which "Rajanya" is an earlier variant, occurs but seldom in the *Rigveda*. The term "Brahman" denotes "a priest by profession" only in some passages, while in others it denotes any person who was distinguished by genius or virtue, or one who, for some reason, was deemed specially receptive of the divine inspiration.

"The transition from the casteless, though classified, society of the bulk of the *Rigveda* to the elaborate Caste System of the *Yajurveda* is to be traced to the complication of life resulting from the further migration of the Vedic Aryans from the Punjab to the east. The necessity of carrying on a ceaseless fight with, and the conquest of, the aborigines called for an organisation of the conquering people by the merger or fusion of petty tribes into centralised kingdoms. Thus emerged the powerful monarch, while the lesser tribal princes, deprived of their royal rank, sank to the position of nobles. The monarchy, moreover, needed now a standing armed force, prepared to meet all eventualities, such as resisting the sudden incursions of native or other Aryan tribes and quelling revolts on the part of the subdued aborigines. This standing army was naturally recruited from the ranks of the nobility of tribal princes and the chief armed retainers of the king. This is the genesis of the warrior class. At the same time, the "people" of the Aryan masses, secure in the protection afforded by the warrior class, ceased to take interest in military matters and settled down to a peaceful life devoted to agriculture, pastoral pursuits, trade and industry. They constituted the third class, the *Vis,* later called "Vaisyas".

"Side by side also grew a distinct community of priests. In the earlier period, not only the householder but even the petty prince could offer sacrifice to the gods for himself and his people, the ritual being very simple. But when the size of the kingdom grew and military and administrative affairs kept the hands not only of the king but also of the warrior class full, while, at the same time, the ritual tended to become more complicated and elaborate, the need was keenly felt of a hierarachic order composed of the more intellectual elements among the non-fighters who could dedicate themselves, undisturbed by the distractions of war or peace, to the faithful and exact performance of the highly developed ritual, and to the preservation (by word of mouth) of the traditional formulae and sacred hymnology of the Aryans, a heritage in part at least from almost prehistoric times.

"As regards the fourth class, the Sudra is mentioned for the first and only time in the "Purusha-sukta". But *dasya* and *dasa* are known to the *Rigveda,* both as aborigines independent of Aryan control and as conquered slaves.

The latter may reasonably be supposed to represent the Sudras of the later texts. But not all the defeated aborigines could be absorbed as slaves in the royal household or in the houses of individual owners. There must have been whole villages of the aborigines, though under Aryan control. The term "Sudra" was evidently applied to the inhabitants of these villages as well as to wild hill tribes which lived by hunting and fishing and acknowledged the overlordship of their Aryan neighbours. In course of time it included even *dasya-varna* (or dark-skinned) people who remained beyond the pale of the Aryan state and who were virtually excluded from the religious and ritual cult of the Aryans. The development of the Caste System in a rigid form, with strictly hereditary and mutual exclusive castegroups, did not take place till the time when the Vedic Aryans had settled down in the Middle Country and were already Brahminised enough to look upon the inhabitants of the North-West—-the home of the *Rigveda*—as uncivilized Vratyas because they did not follow the strict Caste System.

"The view summed up above may be regarded as the one now generally accepted by scholars. According to this recognized version, in the earliest society represented by the bulk of the *Rigveda,* there were probably different classes and professions, but none, not even the priestly and the warrior classes, were hereditary; the warriors were drawn from the people at large, and any person with the requisite qualifications could officiate as a priest."

Such rigidities, distortions and evils that creep with time in all old religions is a well known phenomenon. Christianity and Islam are no exceptions though they may not be very old. However, as would be clear, the caste was never sacrosanct and interconvertibility from one caste to another was commonplace as is evident from the following extract:

"On the whole, it is difficult not to agree with the views, propounded long ago by Muir, that the Brahmanas (far less the Kashtriyas or Vaisyas) did not constitute an exclusive caste or race, and that the prerogatives of composing hymns and officiating at the services of gods were not regarded, in the age of the *Rigveda,* as entirely confined to men of priestly families. The same thing was equally, or perhaps more, true of the minor professions, as the hymn, quoted above, refers to the father, mother and the son following three different vocations in life, viz. those of a poet, a grinder of corn, and a physician. The heredity of occupation was, therefore, not yet a recognized principle, far less an established fact. The utmost that can be said is that there were recognized professions like priesthood, or distinctions of nobility, and these had in many cases a tendency to become hereditary, but, as in other countries or societies, their ranks might have been recruited from all sections of the community. Of the other essential features of the Caste System *viz.,* prohibition of interdining and intermarriage, no such restriction is even remotely hinted at in the hymns of the *Rigveda.*"

Now, we come to the most controversial issue. The nature of the early Muslim conquests, and the process and means used by these invaders for the expansion of their kingdoms and the process of their assimilation into their new found homeland. Nehru described this process as benign. His understanding of the flowering of Arab culture and its benevolent influence on our age-old civilisation is not what most scholars believe. Even before the Arab conquest, India had been having regular informal visits and trade between western India and Arabia and East Africa. Both sides gained from this intercourse. To say that Arab advent into India had a reforming influence on our value systems is to fly in the face of truth. He further made a case that it was Indian conceit which prevented them from learning from Arabs as much as the latter did from the former.

Nothing could be further from the truth. All chroniclers accompanying a conqueror and living on his largesse and benevolence cannot but be expected to describe events and facts in a light most favourable to him. Al-Beruni, the chronicler accompanying Mahmud of Ghazni, the most rapacious of invaders known to history, looked at the Hindu people through the eyes of Islam. The official historian of a proseletysing religious monarch finds Indians arrogant and proud. Nehru endorses his judgement. To justify Mahmud's conquest and avarice, a justification had to be found in the so-called 'Jehad' against the non-believers or 'Kafirs', especially if such a venture could bring untold riches from conquered kingdoms and desecrated temples to make Ghazni, the richest Muslim Kingdom of the Middle East. Nehru had no such compulsions. The whole genesis of the Indian psyche down the ages is based on tolerance, humility and natural acceptance of outsiders. Hindus were frequently invaded and subdued but never really conquered. They did not learn the brutality of the invaders. Nehru's description of Al-Beruni's observations and later of Mahmud's raids is not only flattering to the ruthless conqueror but an insult to the civilisation that he intended to conquer and failed. Quoting Al-Beruni in "Discovery of India," he observed:

"Of the Indians, Alberuni says that they are 'haughty, foolishly vain, self-contained and stolid', and that they believe 'that there is no country like theirs, no nation like theirs, no kings like theirs, no science like theirs'. Probably a correct enough description of the temper of the people."

"Mahmud's raids are a big event in Indian history, though politically India as a whole was not greatly affected by them and the heart of India remained untouched. They demonstrated the weakness and decay of north India, and Alberuni's accounts throw further light on the political disintegration of the north and west.

"These repeated incursions from the north-west brought many new elements into India's closed thought and economy. Above all they brought Islam, for the first time, to the accompaniment of ruthless military conquest. So far, for over 300 years, Islam had come peacefully as a religion and taken its place among the many religions of India without trouble or conflict."

In fact, Mahmud's invasions only brought death and destruction in their wake. It was only the local genius of the people of the conquered land that flowered after peaceful conditions prevailed. Leaving the Muslim conquest for a later stage, let us first attend to the two points made i. e. the haughty veneer of the Indian people and their insularity. This has been contradicted on many accounts by many historians, not the least, H.G. Wells who writes in his book, "The Outline of History":

"The commercial and intellectual importance of Alexandria continued for many centuries. Anticipating the account we shall presently give of the rise of the Roman power, we may tell here that under the Empire, Alexandria became the greatest trade centre in the world. The Roman Alexandrian merchants had numerous settlement in South India. At Cranganore on the Malabar coast there was a temple dedicated to Augustus, and the settlement was defended by two Roman cohorts. Embassies were sent from the Emperor to various South Indian potentates. Moreover, Clement, Chrysostom and other early Christian writers speak about the Indians in Alexandria and their cults."

But Nehru is too mesmerised by the flowering of Arab culture and Islam. It is well known that most people in Harun-al-Rashid court were outsiders who brought their knowledge to Baghdad. This is borne out by historical records and Nehru himself acknowledges this in the following extract from "The Discovery of India."

"Having rapidly conquered large parts of Asia, Africa and a bit of Europe, the Arabs turned their minds to conquests in other fields. The empire was being consolidated, many new countries had come within their ken and they were eager to find out about this world and its ways. The intellectual curiosity, the adventures in rationalist speculation, the spirit of scientific inquiry among the Arabs of the eighth and ninth centuries are very striking.

"Normally, in the early days of a religion based on fixed concepts and beliefs, faith is dominant and variations are not approved or encouraged. That faith had carried the Arabs far and that triumphant success itself must have deepened that faith. And yet we find them going beyond the limits of dogma and creed, dabbling with agnosticism, and turning their zeal and energy towards adventures of the mind. Arab travellers, among the greatest of their kind, go to far countries to find out what other peoples were doing and thinking, to study and understand their philosophies and sciences and ways of life, and then to develop their own thought."

How much of all this confluence of multicultural and multiethnic talent and learning was truly Arab?

And then sample the following, where carried away by his admiration of the Arab ferment, its conquests and invigorating influence, Nehru does concede that the Arab mind was in close and effective contact with India and Sanskrit and later, he not only contradicted what he has said earlier but further obfuscates the issue:

"But when we write Arab here, we must write it with a certain reservation. The Arabic culture of Islam has something of the same relation to the original Arab as the Hellenic culture after the days of Alexander had to the original European Greek. It was no longer racially pure. It had incorporated with it a group of pre-existing cultures, the Persian of the Arabian dynasty, and the Coptic of Hellenized Egypt. Persia and Egypt learnt to talk Arabic with great promptitude, but they remained in quality Persia and Egypt.

"The early conquests of the Arabs had brought the Arabic culture into close contact with the Greek literary tradition—not, it is true, in the original Greek but through the Syrian translations of the Greek writers. The Nestorian Christians, the Christians to the east of orthodoxy, seem to have been much more intelligent and active-minded than the court theologians of Byzantium, and at a much higher level of general education than the Latin speaking Christians of the west. They had been tolerated during the latter days of the Sassanids, and they were tolerated by Islam until the ascendancy of the Turks in the eleventh century. They were the intellectual backbone of the Persian world. They had preserved much of the Hellenic medical science, and had even added to it. In the Omayyad times most of the physicians in the Caliph's dominions were Nestorians, and no doubt many learned Nestorians professed Islam without any serious compunction or any great change in their work and thoughts. They had preserved much of Aristotle both in Greek and in Syrian translations. They had a considerable mathematical literature. Their equipment makes the contemporary resources of Saint Benedict or Cassiodorus seem very pitiful. To these Nestorian teachers came the fresh Arab mind out of the desert, keen and curious, and learnt much and improved upon its teaching. It learnt much and acquired much. Persia had been for many centuries a country of intense and subtle theological and speculative activity. These activities now clothed themselves in Arabic phrases and became a process of heresy and schism in the Moslem Church. The Shitte schism was essentially Persian.

"But the Persians with the Hellenic learning were the only teachers available for the Arabs. Throughout all the rich cities of the East the kindred Jews were scattered with their own distinctive literature and tradition, and the Arab and the Jewish mind reacted upon one another to a common benefit. The Arab was informed and the Jew sharpened to a keener edge. The Jews have never been pedants in the matter of their language; we have already noted that a thousand years before Islam they spoke Greek in Hellenized Alxandria, and now all over this new Moslem world they were speaking and writing Arabic. Some of the greatest of Jewish literature was written in Arabic, the religious writings of Maimonides, for example. Indeed, it is difficult to say, in the case of this Arabic culture, where the Jew ends and the Arab begins, so important and essential were its Jewish factors.

"Moreover, there was a third source of inspiration, more particularly, in mathematical science, to which at present it is difficult to do justice—India. There can be little doubt that effective contact with Sanskrit literature and with Indo-Persian physical science. The Afghans differed also from the more highly cultured and sophisticated Arabs and Persians. They were hard and fierce like their mountain fastneses, rigid in their faith, warriors not inclined towards intellectual pursuits or adventures of the mind. They behaved to begin with as conquerors over a rebellious people and were cruel and harsh.

"But soon they toned down. India became their home and Delhi was their capital, not distant Ghazni as in Mahmud's time. Afghanistan, where they came from, was just an outlying part of their kingdom. The process of Indianisation was rapid, and many of them married women of the country. One of their great rulers, Alauddin Khilji, himself married a Hindu lady, and so did his son. Some of the subsequent rulers were racially Turks, such as Qutbud-Din Aibak, the Sultana Razia, and Iltutmish; but the nobility and army continued to be mainly Afghan. Delhi flourished as an imperial capital."

As an example of perversity of perception and deliberate suppression of truth, nothing can beat the following extracts from 'The Discovery of India'.

"It is thus wrong and misleading to talk of a Moslem invasion of India or of the Moslem period in India, just as it would be wrong to refer to the coming of the British to India as a Christian invasion, or to call the British period in India a Christian period. Islam did not invade India; it had come to India some centuries earlier. There was a Turkish invasion (Mahmud's and an Afghan invasion, and then a Turco-Mongol or Mughal invasion, and of these the two latter were important. The Afghans might well be considered a border Indian group, hardly strangers to India, and the period of their political dominance should be called the Indo-Afghan period. The Mughals were outsiders and strangers to India and yet they fitted into the Indian structure with remarkable speed and began the Indo-Mughal period.

"Through choice or circumstances or both, the Afghan rulers and those who had come with them, merged into India. Their dynasties became completely Indianized with their roots in India, looking upon India as their homeland, and the rest of the world as foreign. In spite of political conflict, they were generally considered as such and many even of the Rajput princes accepted them as their over-lords. But there were other Rajput chiefs who refused to submit and there were fierce conflicts. Feroze Shah, one of the well-known Sultans of Delhi, had a Hindu mother; so had Ghyasud-Din Tughlak. Such marriages between the Afghans, Turkish, and the Hindu nobility were not frequent, but they did take place. In the south the Moslem ruler of Gulbarga married a Hindu princess of Vijayanagar with great pomp and ceremony."

When Nehru talks of a happy mingling of Hindus and Moslems resulting into a composite culture, he conveniently forgets that not only during the period of the Delhi Sultanates, but even during the Moghal rule the religious life of Moslems was agitated not infrequently by periodic outbursts of puritanism, directed mostly against any tendency that smacked of Hinduising Islam. The two nation theory later propounded by Jinnah was nothing new. It had its roots even in the early period of our history.

If only Nehru had bothered to read what Will Durrant, one of the greatest scholars of history, had to say in his book "The Story of Civilisation, Part-I: Our Oriental Heritage" about Moslem conquest of India, he would have harboured serious doubts about the benign nature of the Moslem conquest. Sample the following from this book.

"The Mohammedan conquest of India is probably the

bloodiest story in history. It is a discouraging tale, for its evident moral is that civilisation is a precarious thing, whose delicate complex of order and liberty, culture and peace may at any time be overthrown by barbarians invading from without or multiplying within. The Hindus had allowed their strength to be wasted in internal division and war; they had adopted religions like Buddhism and Jainism, which unnerved them for the tasks of life; they had failed to organise their forces for the protection of their frontiers and their capitals, their wealth and their freedom, from the hordes of Scythians, Huns, Afghans and Turks hovering about India's boundaries and waiting for national weakness to let them in. For four hundred years (600-1000 A.D.) India invited conquest; and at last it came".

"In the year 997 a Turkish chieftain by the name of Mahmud became sultan of the little state of Ghazni, in eastern Afghanistan. Mahmud knew that his throne was young and poor, and saw that India, across the border, was old and rich; the conclusion was obvious. Pretending a holy zeal for destroying Hindu idolatry, he swept across the frontier with a force inspired by a pious aspiration for booty. He met the unprepared Hindus at Bhimnagar, slaughtered them, pillaged their cities, destroyed their temples, and carried away the accumulated treasures of centuries. Returning to Ghazni he astonished the ambassadors of foreign powers by displaying "jewels and unbored pearls and rubies shining like sparks, or like wine congealed with ice, and emeralds like fresh sprigs of myrtle, and diamonds in size and weight like pomegranates". Each winter Mahmud descended into India, filled his treasure chest with spoils, and amused his men with full freedom of pillage and kill; each spring he returned to his capital richer than before. At Mathura (on the Jumna) he took from the temple its statues of gold encrusted with precious stones, and emptied its coffers of a vast quantity of gold, silver and jewelry; he expressed his admiration for the architecture of the great shrine, judged that its duplication would cost one hundred million *dinars* and the labor of two hundred years, and then ordered it to be soaked with naphtha and burnt to the ground". Six years later he sacked another opulent city of northern India, Somnath, killed all its fifty thousand inhabitants, and dragged its wealth to Ghazni. In the end he became, perhaps, the richest king that history has ever known. Sometimes he spared the population of the ravaged cities, and took them home to be sold as slaves; but so great was the number of such captives that after some years no one could be found to offer more than a few shillings for a slave. Before every important engagement Mahmud knelt in prayer, and asked the blessing of God upon his arms. He reigned for a third of century; and when he died, full of years and honors, Moslem historians ranked him as the greatest monarch of his time, and one of the greatest sovereigns of any age."

"Seeing the canonization that success had brought to this magnificent thief, other Moslem rulers profited by his example, though none succeeded in bettering his destruction. In 1186 the Ghuri, a Turkish tribe of Afghanistan, invaded India, captured the city of Delhi, destroyed its temples, confiscated its wealth, and settled down in its palaces to establish the Sultanate of Delhi—an alien despotism fastened upon northern India for three centuries, and checked only by assassination and revolt. The first of these bloody sultans, Kutb-Din Aibak, was a normal specimen of his kind—fanatical, ferocious and merciless".

To quote Moslem historians,"His gifts were bestowed by hundreds of thousands, and his slaughters likewise were by hundreds of thousands". In one victory of this warrior (who had been purchased as a slave), "fifty thousand men came under the collar of slavery, and the plain became black as pitch with Hindu blood". Another sultan, Balban, punished rebels and brigands by casting them under the feet of elephants, or removing their skins, stuffing these with straw, and hanging them from the gates of Delhi. When some Mongol inhabitants who had settled in Delhi, and had been converted to Islam, attempted rising, Sultan Alau-d-din (the conqueror of Chitor) had all the males—from fifteen to thirty thousand of them—slaughtered in one day. Sultan Muhammad bin Tughlak acquired the throne by murdering his father, became a great scholar and an elegant writer, dabbled in mathematics, physics and Greek philosophy, surpassed his predecessors in bloodshed and brutality, fed the flesh of a rebel nephew to the rebel's wife and children, ruined the country with reckless inflation, and laid it waste with pillage and murder till the inhabitants fled to the jungle. He killed so many Hindus that, in the words of a Moslem historian, "there was constantly in front of his royal pavilion and his Civil Court a mound of dead bodies and a heap of corpses, while the sweepers and executioners were wearied out by their work of dragging" the victims "and putting them to death in crowds". In order to found a new capital at Daulatabad he drove every inhabitant from Delhi and left it a desert; and hearing that a blind man had stayed behind in Delhi, he ordered him to be dragged from the old to the new capital, so that only a leg remained of the wretch when his last journey was finished". The Sultan complained that the people did not love him, or recognize his undeviating justice. He ruled India for a quarter of a century, and died in bed. His successor, Firoz Shah, invaded Bengal, offered a reward for every Hindu head, paid for 180,000 of them, raided Hindu villages for slaves, and died at the ripe age of eighty." And for these great 'Services' to India one of the important roads in the national metropolis is named after him even today. Sultan Ahmad Shah feasted for three days whenever the number of defenseless Hindus slain in his territories in one day reached twenty thousand.

"All of them were armed with a religion militaristic in operation, but far superior in its stoical monotheism to any of the popular cults of India; they concealed its attractiveness by making the public exercise of the Hindu religions illegal, and thereby driving them more deeply into the Hindu soul. Some of these thirsty despots had culture as well as ability; they patronized the arts, and engaged artists and artisans—usually of Hindu origin—to build for them magnificent mosques and tombs; some of them were scholars, and delighted to converse with historians, poets and scientists. One of the greatest scholars of Asia, Alberuni, accompanied Mahmud of Ghazni to India, and wrote a scientific survey of India comparable to Pliny's *Natural History* and Humboldt's *Cosmos*. The Moslem historians were almost as numerous as the generals, and yielded nothing to them in the enjoyment of bloodshed and war. The Sultans drew from the people every rupee of tribute that could be exacted by the ancient art of taxation, as well as by straight-forward robbery; but they stayed in India, spent their spoils in India, and thereby turned them back into India's economic life. Nevertheless, their terrorism and exploitation advanced that weakening of Hindu physique and morale which had been begun by an exhausting climate, an inadequate diet, political disunity, and pessimistic religions.

"The usual policy of the Sultans was clearly sketched by Alau-d-din, who required his advisers to draw up "rules and regulations for grinding down the Hindus and for depriving them of that wealth and property which foster disaffection and rebellion". Half of the gross produce of soil was collected by the government; native rulers had taken one-sixth. "No Hindu", says a Moslem historian, "could hold up his head, and in their houses no sign of gold or silver ... or of any superfluity was to be seen.... Blows, confinement in the stocks, imprisonment and chains, were all employed to enforce payment". When one of his own advisers protested against this policy, Alau-d-din answered: "Oh, Doctor, thou lart a learned man, but thou hast no experience; I am an unlettered man, but I have a great deal. Be assured, then, that the Hindus will never become submissive and obedient till they are reduced to poverty. I have therefore given orders that just sufficient shall be left to them from year to year of corn, milk and curds, but that they shall not be allowed to accumulate hoards and property".

Inspired by the words in Quran "Oh Prophet, make war upon infidels and unbelievers and treat them with severity" the learned Mullahs sanctified the invasion of India. "Thereupon Taimur crossed the Indus (1398), massacred or enslaved such of the inhabitants as could not flee from him, defeated the forces of Sultan Mahmud Tughlak, occupied Delhi, slew a hundred thousand prisoners in cold blood, plundered the city of all the wealth that the Afghan dynasty had gathered there, and carried off to Samarkand with a multitude of women and slaves, leaving anarchy, famine and pestilence in his wake". Later, the Sultans of Delhi, much praised by Nehru, reoccupied their throne and recovered their losses by selective taxation of the Hindus of India.

It is mentioned in one of the Children's Encyclopedia that the credit for raising the largest pyramid of human skulls in history goes to Timur, who heaped one hundred thousand Hindu skulls outside Delhi after the famous massacre. And the same Will Durant records Gandhi's actions centuries later, as if to compare the extreme form of human cruelty indulged in by the Moslem invaders into India with the nobility and benevolence of one of its greatest sons who was a Hindu. "Shortly after the worst of all riots between Moslems and Hindus, when the Moplah Mohammedans butchered hundreds of unarmed Hindus and offered their prepuces as a covenant to Allah, these same Moslems were stricken with famine; Gandhi collected funds for them from all over India, and, with no regard for the best precedents, forwarded every anna, without deduction for "overhead" to the starving enemy". It was Gandhi, the quintessential Hindu, the epitome of purity of means in our national political struggle who acted thus. And finally, the cruelty of the conquest of the Vijayanagar Kingdom in the battle of Talikota fought by the confederation of three Muslim kingdoms of Decan against the Hindu king.

"The superior numbers of the attackers prevailed; Rama Raja was captured and beheaded in the sight of his followers, and these, losing courage, fled. Nearly a hundred thousand of them were slain in the retreat, until all the streams were colored with their blood. The conquering troops plundered the wealthy capital, and found the booty so abundant "that every private man in the allied army became rich in gold, jewels, effects, tents, arms, horses and slaves". For five months the plunder continued: the victors slaughtered the helpless inhabitants in indiscriminate butchery, emptied the stores and shops, smashed the temples and palaces, and labored at great pains to destroy all the statuary and painting in the city; then they went through the streets with flaming torches, and set fire to all that would burn. When at last they retired, Vijayanagar was as completely ruined as if an earthquake had visited it and had left not a stone upon a stone. It was a destruction ferocious and absolute, typifying that terrible Moslem conquest of India which had begun a thousand years before, and was now complete."

The early Moslem conquerors used force to vanquish the Hindu princes in order to establish their Kingdom. Having done that they used coercion and sword to convert them into Islam. But the sheer magnitude of the task of conversion was daunting enough to force them to abandon it. There were more heads than the sword could sever. In sheer desperation they gave up. India was simply too vast and populous. Akbar realised this truth very early in his life. His father Humayun had received assistance and shelter from the Rajput princes to regain his lost Kingdom from Sher Shah Suri, the Pathan warrior. He never forgot the might of the Rajput sword and it was during one of these flights from the enemy in a shelter provided by a Rajput prince at the fort of Amarkot in the pristine desert wilderness too difficult for the pursuer, that his pregnant queen, Hamida Begum, gave birth to Akbar in 1542. Akbar owed his safe arrival in this world to Rajput chivalry and clemency. He never forgot the might of the Rajputs and was forced, not out of philanthropy, but real politic to the conclusion that no empire could survive if the swords of Rajput princes would unite against it. His policy, therefore, rested solely on obtaining Rajput support while keeping them divided, and it paid handsome dividends. It would be too presumptuous to say that he loved the Rajputs; but he made good use of them to build and extend his empire. Rewards were offered and the Rajput loyalty obtained. But, inspite of all the services and sacrifices, the Hindu princes were mainly used for military campaigns in far off places like Kabul, Kandhar to the North-West and against rulers in South and East. His own trusted Muslim generals were kept nearer at the royal court. Even amongst the Muslim nobles and notables, those who had a Turko-Moghul descent were given the overlordship of all states and principalities, as well as the command positions in the royal armies. But those Muslims who were Indian born were kept scrupulously out of the royal favours and privileged ranks. So much Akbar's love of this land which he intended to rule. The Rajput princes were ofcourse the sons of a lesser God and treated as such. To prove their loyalties, these princes were made to undertake extremely hazardous campaigns and to fight even their own kith and kin. That was the price for a few loaves of royal favour. Nehru called Akbar, a great King almost in the same class as Ashoka. There could be no greater travesty of truth. Akbar was certainly clever but greatness is made of different stuff. He married Rajput princesses to cement friendships and forged alliances in order to expand his rule. There was not a single known example of a Moghul princess marrying a Rajput prince. It was always a one way street. To some degree, the trend continues till today. Col. James Todd had this to say in his book, 'Annals and Antiquities of Rajputana' in the chapter 'Annals of Mewar', regarding the Rajput pride against offering its allegiance to Akbar. In the letter written by Prithi Raj, a Bikaner prince in Akbar's Court, he exhorts Rana Pratap thus:

"The hopes of the Hindu rest on the Hindu; yet the Rana forsakes them. But for Pratap, all would be placed on the same level by Akber; for our chiefs have lost their valour and our females their honour. Akbar is the broker in the market of our race: all has he purchased but the son of Oodoh; he is beyond his price. What true Rajpoot would part with honour for nine days (*Noroza)*; yet how many have bartered it away? Will Cheetore come to this market, when all have disposed of the chief article of the Khetri? Though Putto has squandered away wealth, yet this treasure has he preserved. Despair has driven many to this mart, to witness their dishonour: from such infamy the descendant of Hamir alone has been preserved. The world asks, whence the concealed aid of Pratap comes? None but the soul of manliness and his sword: with it, well has he maintained the Khetri's pride. This broker in the market of men will one day be overreached; he cannot live for ever: then will our race come to Partap, for the seed of the Rajpoot to sow in our desolate lands. To him all look for its preservation, that its purity may again become resplendent.

"This effusion of the Rahtore was equal to ten thousand men; it nerved the drooping mind of Pratap, and roused him into action: for it was a noble incentive to find every eye of his race fixed upon him."

Todd sheds further light on the character of 'Akbar The Great' by describing his Noroza festival.

"The allusion of the princely poet in the phrase, 'bartering their honour on the 'Noroza', 'requires some explanation. The *Noroza,* or 'New Year's Day', when the sun enters Aries, is one of great festivity among the Mahomedan princes of the East; but of that alluded to by Pirthi Raj we can form an adequate idea from the historian Abul Fuzil.

"It is not New Year's Day, but a festival especially instituted by Akbar, and to which he gave the epithet *Khooshroz,* 'day of pleasure', held on the ninth day (no roza), following the chief festival of each month. The court assembled, and was attended by all ranks. The queen also had her court, when the wives of the nobles and of the Rajpoot vassal princes were congregated. But the Khooshroz was chiefly marked by a fair held within the precincts of the court, attended only by females. The merchants' wives exposed the manufactures of every clime, and the ladies of the court were the purchasers'. "His majesty is also there in disguise, by which means he learns the value of merchandise, and hears what is said of the state of the empire and the character of the officers of government". The ingenuous Abul Fuzil thus softens down the unhallowed purpose of this day; but posterity cannot admit that the great Akbar was to obtain these results amidst the *Pushto* jargon of the dames of Islam, or the mixed *Bhaka* of the fair of Rajasthan. These 'ninth day fairs' are the markets in which Rajpoot honour was bartered, and to which the brave Pirthi Raj makes allusion.

"It is scarcely to be credited that a statesman like Akbar should have hazarded his popularity or his power, by the introduction of a custom alike appertaining to the Celtic races of Europe as to these the Goths of Asia and that he should seek to degrade those whom the chances of war had made his vassals, by conduct so nefarious and repugnant to the keenly cherished feeling of the Rajpoot. Yet there is not a shadow of doubt that many of the noblest of the race were dishonoured on the 'Noroza' and the chivalrous Pirthi Raj was only preserved from being of the number by the high courage and virtue of his wife, a princess of Mewar, and daughter of the founder of the Suktawuts. On one of these celebrations of the Khooshroz, the monarch of the Moguls was struck with the beauty of the daughter of Mewar, and he singled her out from amidst the united fair of Hind as the object of his passion. It is not improbable that an ungenerous feeling united with that already impure, to despoil the Seesodias of their honour, through a princess of their house under the protection of the sovereign. On retiring from the fair, she found herself entangled amidst the labyrinth of apartments by which egress was purposely ordained, when Akbar stood before her: but instead of acquiescence she drew a poniard from her corset, and held it to his breast, dictating, and making him repeat, the oath of renunciation of the infamy to all her race. The anecdote is accompanied in the original with many dramatic circumstances. The guardian goddess of Mewar, the terrific 'Mata', appears on her tiger in the subterranean passage of this palace of pollution, to strengthen her mind by a solemn denunciation, and her hand with a weapon to protect her honour. Rae Singh, the elder brother of the princely bard, had not been so fortunate; his wife wanted either courage or virtue to withstand the regal tempter, and she returned to their dwelling in the desert despoiled of her chastity, but loaded with jewels; or as Pirthi Raj expresses it: "She returned to her abode, tramping to the tinkling sound of the ornaments of gold and gems on her person; but where, my brother, is the moustache on thy lip?"

Akbar is often described as a magnanimous king and an epitome of chivalry. These were the Rajput virtues, never displayed by Muslim conquerors. Akbar's attack on Chittor from October to February 1567 amply demonstrated that in moments of victory he could be as cruel as his forebears. The seige of the Fort, heroically defended by a small garrison of brave Rajputs under the command of Jaimal, had already lasted five long months. Ultimately, before the dawn on the 23rd February Jaimal died, while supervising the repairs to the breach in the fortress wall caused by the heavy Mughal artillery, shot in the forehead by Akbar himself. The mantle of command now fell on his young nephew Phatta who gallantly fought a losing battle and died. When no one was left to command, the brave Rajput women committed their last rite of 'Jauhar' by jumping into the fire leaving the men-folk to continue the fight. Early in the morn of 23rd February, Akbar made a triumphal entry into the fortress and ordered a general massacre "which ceased only for lack of victims". Like a gesture of tokenism he got the statue of two elephants installed at the gate in the memory of the brave duo. This was nothing more than a gimmick to consolidate his Rajput support and winning their goodwill.

In all his descriptions of historical events relating to the invasions of Moslems and subsequent events, Nehru's judgement against all these researched records shows a less than honest effort to read history correctly and interpret our own native culture and tradition.

Nehru's views on the British conquest of India are recorded in chapter Seven of the book 'The Discovery of India' titled "The Last Phase-1". Nehru quotes from some British writer and admits that there is always a definite bias in the record of events as seen by the victor or his scribe. This time he could be more objective. "Our writing of India's history is perhaps resented more than anything else we have done—so writes an Englishman well acquainted with India and her history. It is difficult to say what Indians have resented most in the record of British rule in India; the list is long and varied. But it is true that British accounts of India's history, more especially of what is called the British period, are bitterly resented. History is almost always written by the victors and conquerors and gives their viewpoint; or, at any rate, the victors' version is given prominence and holds the field. Very probably all the early records we have of the Aryans in India, their epics and traditions, glorify the Aryans and are unfair to the people of the country whom they subdued. No individual can wholly rid himself of his racial outlook and cultural limitations, and when there is conflict between races and countries even an attempt at impartiality is considered a betrayal of one's own people. War, which is an extreme example of this conflict, results in a deliberate throwing overboard of all fairness and impartiality so far as the enemy nation is concerned; the mind coarsens and becomes closed to almost all avenues of approach except one. The overpowering need of the moment is to justify one's own actions and condemn and blacken those of the enemy. Truth hides somewhere at the bottom of the deepest well and falsehood, naked and unshaded reigns almost supreme."

Nehru would treat the British conquest differently from that of the Moslem. He had earlier endorsed the views of the chronicler, Al-Beruni, who accompanied Mahmud of Ghazni during his bloody conquests, on the character of Hindus in contemporary India. Cleverly hidden in this romantic foray into India's past, is the running thread of an anti-Hindu bias in one form or the other. This shows Nehru's true face. Sample another piece from the same book:

"All over the widespread domains of the Mughal Empire there was a mixture of religion and nationalism. That nationalism was certainly not of the modern secular type, nor did it, as a rule, embrace the whole of India in its scope. It was coloured by feudalism, by local sentiment and sectarian feeling. The Rajputs, more feudal than the rest, thought of their clan loyalties; the Sikhs, a comparatively small group in the Punjab, were absorbed in their own self-defence and could hardly look beyond the Punjab. Yet the religion itself had a strong national background and all its traditions were connected with India. 'The Indians', writes Professor Macdonell, 'are the only division of the Indo-European family which has created a great national religion—Brahmanism—and a great world religion—Buddhism; while all the rest far from displaying originality in this sphere have long since adopted a foreign faith'. That combination of religion and nationalism gained strength and cohesiveness from both elements, and yet its ultimate weakness and insufficiency were also derived from that mixture. For it could only be an exclusive and partial nationalism, not including the main elements in India that lay outside that religious sphere. Hindu nationalism was natural growth from the soil of India, but understandably it comes in the way of the larger nationalism which arises above differences of religion or creed.

"It is true that during this period of disruption when a Moghul empire was breaking up and many adventurers, Indian and foreign, were trying to carve out principalities for themselves, nationalism in its present sense, was hardly in evidence at all. Each individual adventurer sought to augment his own power, each group fended for itself. Such history as we have only tells us of these adventurers, attaching more importance to them than the more significant happenings below the surface of events. Yet there are glimpses to show that it was not all adventurism, though many adventurers held the field."

Nehru describes the resurgence of nationalist feelings in India after Aurangzeb as attempts at personal aggrandisements leading to a confused kaleidoscope of local chieftains fighting each other or the Rajputs, the eternal feudals and the Marathas the marauders. These to him were petty fights for limited personal gains and not an effort inspired by a pan-Indian upsurge to shake off the Muslim yoke, and the final signs of a nationalist awakening. Any student of history would know that Shivaji, inspired in his boyhood by the lays of the ancient Hindu gods and goddesses, was a Hindu to the core. And he fought to overthrow the Moslem rule. Any local treaties and compromises with Muslim chiefs were merely tactical ploys to gain temporary advantage for the achievement of this ultimate goal, a Hindu Kingdom and Hindu Nationalism, which had in it, a place for all minorities, including the Dutch, the Christians, the Portuguese, the English and the Muslims. No wonder, Hindu renaissance and nationalism always started from the soil of Maharashtra. Even Warren Hastings' observations quoted by Nehru and given below confirm the seeds of this nationalistic fervour planted in the Maratha mind from where it was trying to spread and embrace the whole country in its sweep. This is what he said, "The Marathas, especially, had a wider conception and as they grew in power this conception also grew". He again wrote in 1784, "The Marathas possess, alongwith all the people of Hindostan and Deccan, a principle of national attachment, which is strongly impressed on the minds of all individuals of the nation, and would probably unite their chiefs into one common cause, if any great danger were to threaten the general state. Probably, this national sentiment of their was largely confined to the Marathi-speaking areas. Nevertheless, the Marathas were catholic in their political and military systems as well as in the habits, and there was a certain internal democracy among them. All this gave strength to them. Shivaji, though, he fought Aurangzeb, freely employed Moslems". What Nehru, the Indian could not see, Warren Hastings, the foreigner, could see with amazing objectivity and clarity. Removal of Moslem overlordship was one of the essential pillars of this resurgence, which aimed, through Hindu renaissance, to re-establish the Hindu pride. This included, with few exceptions, even the Rajput princes as Col. Todd mentions in his book, 'The Annals and Antiquities of Rajputana'.

Nehru's study of history sometimes displays a philosophical connotation, often superficial in its content and confused in its direction. See the following passage.

"Yet the past is ever with us and all that we are and that we have comes from the past. We are its products and we live immersed in it. Not to understand it and feel it as something living within us is not to understand the present. To combine it with the present and extend to make of all this the pulsating and vibrating material for thought and action—that is life.

"Any vital action springs from the depths of the being. All the long past of the individual and even of the race has prepared the background for that psychological moment of action. All the racial memories, influences of heredity and environment and training, subconscious urges, thoughts and dreams and actions from infancy and childhood onwards, in their curious and tremendous mix-up, inevitably drive to that new action, which again becomes yet another factor influencing the future. Influencing the future, partly determining it, possibly even largely determining it, and yet, surely, it is not all determinism."

Past is the father of the present, which in turn determines the future. But there this relationship ends. A son may excel the father and still owe a lot to him. This is common knowledge. The first paragraph is generally incontrovertible. The second one is confused. He repeats the earlier thoughts but then in the last sentence doubts himself, 'partly determining it possibly even largely determining it' and then negating it in the last words. There is no razor edge clarity or logical thinking. Contrast this with Bertrand Russel's thoughts, who derives a soothing pleasure from the past since it is unchangeable and cannot be destroyed. He stops there. He knows as all of us do that the past affects the present, but refrains from stating the obvious or even trying to quantify it. A rationalist and a philosopher, Bertrand Russell suffers from no confusions. Nehru, the self confessed rationalist, fumbles and makes ambiguous statements. This trait, in his thinking, is forever present in his later life, even while answering important questions in the Parliament.

In Nehru's thinking action determines thoughts. Sample this from 'Discovery of India'.

"This urge to action. . . . apart from being itself a kind of action, becomes part of the action to come. It is not something entirely abstract, in the void unrelated to action and life. The past becomes something that leads up to the present, the moment of action, the future something that flows from it; and all three are inextricably intertwined and interrelated.

"Even my seemingly actionless life in prison is tacked on somehow, by some process of thought and feeling, to coming or imagined action, and so it gains, for me a certain content without which it would be a vacuum in which existence would become intolerable. When actual action has been denied me I have sought some such approach to the past and to history. Because my own personal experiences have often touched historic events and sometimes I have even had something to do with the influencing of such events in my own sphere, it has not been difficult for me to envisage history as a living process with which I could identify myself to some extent."

Any meaningful action follows a rational thought. Thought precedes action. That is the wisdom of the sages. It is only an impulsive man whose action precedes thought. The whole wisdom of the Vedas and Upanishads places thought before and above action. A calm, cool, well meditated thought controls the body and its actions. A restless mind driven by urges of the body can only lead to hasty and unwise deeds. There are many examples from Nehru's later life to prove how far such a thought process ruled his actions.

Nehru's thoughts on national issues such as foreign relations, economic planning and socialism were amptly adumbrated in page after page of his book, *The Discovery of India,* his magnum opus that he wrote from his cloistered existence while incarcerated alongwith other national leaders at Ahmednagar jail. His knowledge of Islam and possibly a pro-Moslem bias was the inevitable outcome of his proximity to Maulana Abul Kalam Azad, and his earlier associations with other Muslims leaders such as Rafi Ahmed Kidwai, Hafiz Mohammad Ibrahim and Asaf Ali. He had read widely but not wisely, extensively but superficially. The canvas of his vision was large but lacked depth of vision. Inspite of its wide sweep it merely brushed the obvious and failed to read the meaning of shapes and forms. He failed to see the Indianness of our culture viewing it, as he did, through borrowed glasses. He mistook the cosmetics of Moslem influence as a positive ingredient of what he called the composite Indian culture. Yet the soul of India had remained unchanged millenia after millenia. But it was too much to expect a politician in a hurry to go deep into the past and read the buried message of our civilisational existence.

Nehru's later life concept of secularism became our national creed; but the foundation of his perception was flawed from the very beginning. Even before independence, he had often expressed, such views in his 'Discovery of India'. Nehru was not quite clear by what he meant by a secular thought. For all practical purposes, the essence of Nehru's scheme of the secular thought was the subsuming of the Hindu content of her cultural identity, which he considered obsolete, backward looking, regressive and full of distortions. It demanded a thorough assimilation of two alien influences, the Islam and Christianity which to him appeared both catholic and egalitarian. This was a travesty of facts. Islam and Christianity with all their virtues were not content with enriching themselves and stay where they were. Their essential creed was to proselytise; by persuation, inducement and if necessary by force. While the former mainly relied on the use of force, the latter used both. But force was an essential element in both. But Hinduism never left its domain to conquer and convert. Christianity moved out from Jerusalem westwards and conquered the whole of the Mediterranean rim and later Europe and the Western hemisphere. Islam first moved out from Mecca to Medina and later westwards to Spain by the power of the sword and finally right upto the East Indies. But Hinduism remained within India and the tiny Nepal which was once a part of Aryavarta. It had the tolerance to absorb all that was good outside and the magnanimity to accept dissent within. Such a religion according to Nehru was obscurantist and inward looking, much of which according to him was to be scrapped. Today's leaders blindly follow this concept of Nehru and his historical thought. Even the mention of the Hindu identity of ancient India was anethema to Nehru, who would only think in terms of a composite culture.

What is Hinduism or Hindutva? Hindu and Hinduism is not a body or a form of religious worship and thought; it is the heartbeat and the music note of our Vedic worldview and a philosophic understanding of life; the eternal fragrance of the soil of this ancient Bharat; it is our identification mark; the creative urge of our sages and saints; the expression of our rich cultural heritage and the definition of our Vedic consciousness. Hindu or Hinduism is nothing if not the amalgam and congealing of the essence of proto-historical and ancient Indian thought, embracing all forms of individual worship which could include believers, monotheism, polytheism and even atheism, idols of gods and their worship, even concepts of astrology and cosmogeny and most importantly the universality of human values. It is a belief in 'Vasudhaiv Kutumbukam', Fatherhood of God and Brotherhood of man. It teaches respect for all religions and thoughts. Can such a system ever militate against or be inimical to any religion, or aggressive in its objectives?

4 Nehru Before Independence

Jawaharlal Nehru's legal practice did not show much promise. He had yet to make up his mind on joining the Indian National Congress and was almost entirely dependent on his father for his living. His father, Moti Lal Nehru, was well established in the Indian National Congress, having wound up his Swaraj Party. He, however, still carried with him his western ways, except for the fact that he wore khadi. A great leader, his sacrifice in giving up a lucrative legal practice for the freedom movement need not detain us here. What is significant is that like his elite education, preordained by birth, Nehru's entry into Congress could be equally smooth, should he so desire. His father once jokingly remarked that on his meagre professional earnings, Jawahar could not even sustain himself and his wife. The remark stung Nehru to the quick. We need not dwell on his process of entering the Congress, which is well documented by his biographers. However, the story of J. L. Nehru being catapulted to centre stage in Indian politics and his ascent to the much coveted position of the president of the Indian National Congress, makes interesting reading.

The main issue in the election of Congress President in 1929 was a successor to Moti Lal Nehru. This was a crucial election, which would launch Congress into a movement for complete Independence. As Bose was to write later--"the general feeling in the Congress circles was that the honour should go to Sardar Vallabhbhai Patel". However, a large section of the Congress insisted that Gandhiji himself should take over the presidency and lead the struggle against England. Rajagopalachari supported this view and Patel also felt the same way. He mentioned in September that "Everyone is anxious to make Gandhiji as President". Ten provincial Congress Committees had put up Gandhiji's name and he was elected unanimously. But the Mahatma refused to oblige. The next step was to pick up the next candidate. Five provincial committees of the Congress recommended Patel only three suggested Nehru. However, as a last ditch effort the AICC in its meeting in Lucknow implored Gandhiji to reconsider his decision but the Mahatma was adamant. From the young crowd two luminaries--Narendra Dev and Balkrishna Sharma from U.P. sounded the Sardar regarding his views, just to ensure the election of Nehru on the odd chance that Patel too may quit. This dubious approach somehow irritated Patel and later, on Gandhiji's instructions, he quit the field. The events are very aptly described by Rajmohan Gandhi in his book `Patel—A Life'.

"Vallabhbhai's prompt compliance was expected in a man of his record but, as the "hounds" remark indicates, it left unpleasant memories. There were several reasons. To begin with, Congress's 1929-30 President was going to be more than that: he would inaugurate the struggle to which Congress was pledged, declare complete independence as India's goal and possibly, project himself as Gandhi's successor. Secondly, Jawaharlal was a much younger man, and yielding to a younger man was not part of the Patidar code. Letting Vithalbhai have that passage to the U.K. in 1905 may have been in excess of the code but it was not contrary to it. Yielding to Jawaharlal was. Thirdly, Vallabhbhai did not believe that Jawaharlal's views were all sound or that he would make a better president. Fourthly, Vallabhbhai was aware that, given the age difference, any precedence now established would be hard to reverse later.

"Fifthly, and this may have been the most hurtful reflection of all, he had been found wanting by the one for whose sake he had given up home and hearth and whose opinion mattered more to him than anything else. The "hounds" preferring Jawarharlal was one thing, Gandhi doing it another, Finally, Vallabhbhai would have felt unhappy about the very thing that delighted Motilal and sent Jawaharlal's mother, Swaruprani, to "a sort of ecstasy"—the succession from father to son". Presiding at the Lahore Congress at the end of the year, Jawaharlal would affirm that he was "a republican and no believer in kings and princes", yet the succession was described by admirers of Motilal and Jawarharlal in terms of 'a king passing on the scepter of the throne to his logical successor". Though less touchy than Jawaharlal about Dominion status, Vallabhbhai had an inner republicanism that could not have rejoiced at Congress's throne passing directly from a father to his son".

The unanswered question for posterity is why did Gandhi settle for Nehru in preference to the Sardar? One obvious reason was the persistent efforts mounted by Moti Lal Nehru from 1927 onwards, even to the extent of imploring Gandhiji, to see his son succeeding him while he was still alive, as a president of the Congress. In 1927, Gandhiji had installed Dr. M.A. Ansari; but in 1928, Moti Lal again reminded him of Jawaharlal's rights and repeated his request in 1929 again. The second reason as Kripalani put it "were personal rather than political". According to him Nehru and Gandhi were emotionally attached to each other in spite of their denials. He further thought that "Gandhiji . . . like the good shepherd, left the many going straight and ran after the one going astray". This view gained credence by Gandhiji's own statement in 1929 that "Sardar Patel would be with him in any case". However, the Mahatma did his best to dispel this "emotional bond" theory and emphasised the "vast" and "radical" differences existing between him and Nehru which left "no meeting ground between us". While Gandhiji took Patel for granted and certainly had soft feelings towards the latter, it was the attitude of an elder brother to the younger. But with Nehru it was a father to son relationship, as Kishorlal Mashruwala remarked later:

"I would describe the Gandhi-Patel relationship as that of brothers, Gandhi being the senior brother, and Gandhi-Nehru as that of father and son".

While Gandhiji regarded Nehru as a son notwithstanding with all the ideological differences, Nehru confirmed the same in his statement in early 1928, saying, "Am I not your child in politics, though perhaps a truant and errant child?" The younger brother Patel, dependable and loyal, could be taken for granted; the truant son could not, should he see the possibility of being disinherited. The Sardar could only aspire to become a Regent but Nehru, the son, was to be the coveted heir as was prophetically proved later.

The younger brother could wield influence only during the time of the king, the son may acquiesce till the latter's death and launch out on his own once he climbs the throne. To quote again Rajmohan Gandhi:

"Gandhi's choice, as he looked to the future, was confined to Patel and Jawaharlal. True, there was Subhas. There was Rajaji whom, indeed, Gandhi had described in 1927 as 'the only possible successor". There was Rajendra Prasad. There was Abul Kalam Azad. All four had serious disqualifications, however, Subhas's commitment to democracy seemed uncertain. C.R. could not communicate with the Hindi heartland. Prasad was too mild and Azad too aloof. Gandhi's choice in the autumn of 1929 was thus restricted to Vallabhbhai who alone had caused the Raj to bend, and Jawaharlal, whom the youth loved. If Patel swallowed the pill with only a fleeting grimace, Jawaharlal, doubtless aware of what his biographer Gopal describes as "the general feeling that he was still unseasoned for the presidency", felt an acute embarrassment that he would later recall:

"I have seldom felt quite so annoyed and humiliated—it was not that I was not sensible of the honour--But I did not come to it by the main entrance or even a side entrance. I appeared suddenly by a trap door and bewildered the audience into acceptance". According to Michael Edwardes in his book `Nehru--A Political Biography:

"Nehru was not altogether pleased by Gandhi's steam-roller methods of getting what he wanted. That he could not be elected on merit and without the rather obvious interference of the Mahatma wounded his sense of pride. In his autobiography, Nehru claimed that he almost felt 'like handing back the honour'. But he did not. Gandhi knew him better than he did himself. A soothing letter from Gandhiji and three days of reflection calmed me.'"

Gandhiji, having refused the crown now settled for Nehru who according to him represented the youth of the country. He also hoped that Nehru would bring the radicals to the Congress fold and that responsibility "will mellow and sober youth". To those who did not like Gandhiji being substituted by Nehru, he reassured that it will be just like having him in the chair.

Nehru used to royal privilege shows a sign of annoyance purely for public consumption, but nonetheless quietly accepts the crown. He had no moral compunction in easing out a senior colleague who had, for a longer period, put in much more political ground-work in the field and was recommended by a majority of the members of the Pradesh Congress Committees. This trait we shall see develop further in his later political career and the same has been successfully passed down to his next two generations. This was the beginning of the process of the dynastic rule whereby the Nehru family line contrived for itself the centre stage in the Indian politics. Moti Lal Nehru canvassed for his son while the latter quietly accepted the reserved space on the stage for the First Family in the Indian political pantheon. Nehru often violently differed with Gandhi but always stopped short of a total breach with an eye on future dividends that would accrue out of the emotional bonds he had forged with the Mahatma, the king maker. Nehru could be naive on many counts but never on those of personal glory. This trait is typical of what a later date astrologer found in Nehru's horoscope, called Gura Chandal Yoga. This is a combination of the planets which confers on the man the instinct and an insatiable desire to eliminate with finesse all personal opposition and threat to his position. Such a person would have no qualms in destroying his enemies regardless of the means and possible consequences to the country in a single handed pursuit of personal glory.

Nehru never really intended to abandon the centre stage nor relinquish power, inspite of his principles and public posturing. This side to his personality became even clearer in his second run to presidentship of the Indian National Congress. Treading on many toes, disappointing many colleagues, blessed by Gandhiji, the royal prince strode to his lawful throne, a second time. His belief in socialism notwithstanding, he had no moral qualms in sacrificing his principles to retain power.

Patel later expressed himself thus, 'I was and still am doubtful about Jawaharlal's fitting in with the parliamentary programme and policy, even though, I readily agreed that on personal and general grounds we could not pitch on a better choice for the Congress President's place this year". This was Patel's magnanimity of heart. And later Gandhi wrote to Nehru, "Something should be done by you to see that Vallabhbhai's decisions as regards parliamentary policy are not challenged but given full cooperation from the Working Committee and by the Congress President". Why should such an advice be necessary to Nehru, described by his admirers later as a great democrat, if he was not in the habit of meddling into other peoples business? Here is another example of Nehru's character trait of expediency. While talking straight faced on high idealism and his principles, expediency prevailed when it came to the crunch of staying in power. The run up to presidency in 1937 is a replay of the 1936 act with differences of dates and issues. But the running thread is Nehru's love of power, public posturing of principles and then giving in rather than resign, when faced with the opposition from all sides. This served a double purpose. The image of a disciplined soldier, who shall fall in line with the objectives of the organisation inspite of sharp personal differences even on fundamental issues, was being carefully cultivated and remained Nehru's trade mark. Side by side, he tested the waters for his ideas and acquiesced, when outmanoeuvered, to remain in power, waiting for the time when he would have no rivals. Expediency paid. An interesting sidelight is thrown on the hiatus between Nehru's postures and performance in relationship with Bose.

Subhas Chandra Bose was a known radical and found himself ill at ease with the moderate approach adopted by Mahatma Gandhi in achieving independence. In 1928, he had collaborated with Nehru in challenging the Congress establishment on the question of dominion Status versus Independence. Subhas, as we know, stood for complete Independence and not any half-way measures. But Nehru's response to overtures from Bose was rather ambivalent; fickle as ever, he had not yet made up his mind. Bose, however, did not approve of Nehru's vacillation and castigated him for leaving the Indian Independence League by making common cause with the dominion school headed by Gandhiji. Subhas Bose while greatly admiring Gandhiji confided to a German friend in 1932 that the Mahatma was going rather slow on the Civil Disobedience Movement; that he allowed distractive issues, such as the cause of untouchability, to interfere with the main struggle for Independence. Bose certainly did not like Gandhiji's calling off the Civil Disobedience Movement when it was at its tide and going on a fast for the cause of the Harijan uplift and removal of untouchability. He also did not take kindly to Gandhi-Irvin Pact and

Gandhiji's attendance at the Round Table Conference. According to Bose, Gandhiji lacked political finesse and coherence; his ways of dealing with the British verged on a tendency to compromise. All this was frustrating to the rebel and the radical in Bose. He also deplored the religious and moral overtones of Gandhiji's Satyagraha. In his own words:

"Gandhiji is too good and too moderate in his views and his actions. We want a more radical and more militant policy. Nehru's ideas are more in our favour, but in his action he gives full support to Gandhiji. His hand pulls one way and his heart in another direction. His heart is with Gandhi".

Eight years later again in 1936, Bose and Nehru would again be allies in weaning the Congress away from its conservative moorings. Bose urged Nehru to seize the opportunity which the Lucknow Congress, over which Nehru was due to preside, offered them to achieve this goal. But Nehru was never cast in the role of a true radical in spite of all his posturings. Again Nehru disappointed Bose and ditched him, preferring the role of the radical mediator between the two wings of the Congress—the radicals and the conservatives. This was in tune with Nehru's character as shall be seen later.

Nehru's indulgence towards Communists caused further irritation between him and Patel. The issue was that of the attitude of the Congress Ministry on the acts of lawlessness indulged in by the Communists. Nehru charged K.M. Munshi who was the law minister in the cabinet of Bombay Province of becoming a police officer. Munshi in his first few weeks in office had imposed restrictions on the activities of some twenty communist activists. Patel asked Munshi to stick to his own views and go by his judgement without being influenced by Nehru's fuming. Gandhiji gave the same advice. Another incident which caused Nehru to flare up, was the Bombay Ministry decision to offer police protection to workers who disobeyed the strike call given by the Communists. The flash point was reached when a socialist, S.S. Batliwala in Bombay was arrested at Vellore for inciting violence. Nehru felt that the provincial Ministry should consult the working committee before ordering such actions. However, C.R. stood against this proposal with Patel's backing, and Gandhiji and the working committee killed the proposal. Again Nehru was not in favour of the Congress policy of non-intervention in the princely States, contrary to the stand of Patel and Gandhiji, who with more common sense felt that any intervention in the States' policy would force these princes closer to the British Raj.

The policy was that the struggle against the princely rulers should be carried out by their own subjects and Congress should not put its foot into it. Once more Nehru was out-voted and sane counsel prevailed.

These constant rebuffs to Nehru's radicalism and impetuousness made Nehru feel "out of place and a mis-fit" in Congress and he said as much to Gandhiji. But the break never came. On most of these issues, Nehru and Patel stood on the opposite sides of the pole but Nehru was not a fool to declare an open break with Patel who had a very strong organisational support. He could only go to Gandhiji complaining against Patel, like a child informing the father of the mis-treatment meted out to him. While Nehru was vocal and hasty, Patel kept his silence and cool.

The Congress Session at Lucknow in March-April, 1936, brought out the by now familiar Nehru trait to fit in rather than break. Both on the issue of socialism and acceptance of office as mentioned earlier, he gave in. He not only refused to join the Congress Socialist Party but put his support behind the Lucknow decision for acceptance of office. In spite of the occasional "acrimonious" verbal duel Patel and Nehru did agree on many points and Nehru was to remark later that, "our points of agreement were more numerous than our points of disagreement". That attainment of freedom should over-ride all other considerations and that Gandhiji was indispensable to Congress were the two points on which Nehru and Patel had no differences. Nehru's expediency is again evident from the composition of his working committee which contained ten old timers headed by Patel, C.R., Prasad, while Kripalani was allowed to function as General Secretary. This was as much as Gandhiji could have wished for. Three odd socialists, Narendra Dev, Jaya Prakash and Achyut Patwardhan were there not because of Nehru but Gandhiji.

Nehru, the ever radical, preached and emphasised socialism but always fell with the working committee "against his better judgement". But Patel did not take kindly to this double speak. Forthright, as ever, he objected to Nehru indulging in his socialistic rhetoric, the creed "which the Congress has not accepted". Other working committee members, including C.R. and Prasad, agreed with Patel and these members sent their resignations through Prasad to protest against Nehru's behaviour. This extreme step was caused by Nehru's irresponsible remarks against certain members of the working committee who did not subscribe to his socialistic tirade. Thus Nehru's socialistic rhetoric not only caused avoidable acrimony within his team, but also showed him for what he was, a socialist in speech but opportunist in action. Constantly taunted by his socialist friends and admirers, like Rafi Ahmad Kidwai on the one hand and restrained by the old heads on the other, Nehru created confusion for himself. Now Gandhiji had to step in and persuaded these members to withdraw their resignations. In the process, he reprimanded Nehru for creating a crisis, when none existed, thereby forcing the AICC members into divided loyalties between his radical friends and himself. Gandhiji said, "if they are guilty of intolerance, you have more than your share of it. The country should not be made to suffer for your mutual intolerance", and the crisis passed with everyone agreeing to the Congress manifesto for the provincial elections of 1937.

On his release from jail in September, Nehru proceeded to Europe to see his ailing wife. Gandhiji had already made up his mind to nominate Nehru to take over the presidency of the Congress, while Vallabhbhai felt strongly in favour of Rajaji and through Prasad informed Gandhiji accordingly. The logic was simple. Jawaharlal had already been the President. But somehow, C.R. shied away from the responsibility of the onerous position. Now Gandhiji had no compunction in inviting Nehru to wear the mantle. In spite of the gross injustice done to C.R., Patel, however did not make it a prestige issue and bowed to Gandhiji's wish. In fact, he had publicly praised Nehru in the summer of 1935, "No one has rendered as much service to the peasants as Pandit Jawaharlalji and his sick wife have. For your sake he has sacrificed a life of comfort and readily shared your troubles. Your poverty infuriates him. How can we move a step forward without his help".

Again in 1937, the election for the Congress President was due and the new incumbent would assume responsibilities in December, 1936 at Faizpur in Maharashtra. Nehru again, true to form, expressed his willingness to stand for the presidency, though he modified his stand by conceding that he would extend complete cooperation even if someone else was elected. Patel did not take kindly to Nehru's presumption to sit on the throne endlessly. He expressed his views to Mahadev that the "decked-up groom-prince is ready to marry at one stroke as many girls as he can find". Again Patel tried to persuade C.R. thinking that if he showed interest Nehru would have to withdraw. He mentioned as much to Gandhiji who in turn wrote to C.R. "The Sardar is desperately anxious for you to wear the thorny crown. I shall be pleased if you will, but I have no heart to press it on you. If you (can) be persuaded into shouldering the burden, you should unhesitatingly say yes and end the agony of the Sardar".

The ever vacillating C.R. again demurred Patel's

next choice felt on Govind Ballabh Pant of U.P. and he mentioned it to Mahadev, "How about Pantji? Bapu had mentioned his name at one point. You can raise it with him. As far as I am concerned, I would break loose and quit if he (Jawaharlal) continues. Jivat (Kripalani) too is very cut up".

Patel too was a choice of many Congressmen who did not belong to the radical platform. In the meantime Nehru had made it clear that should he be the next President, Congressmen will have to put up with his socialistic ways. In the words of Kripalani this is what happened--"Jawaharlal approached Gandhiji and told him that he felt that one term of 8 months was not sufficient for him to vitalise the Congress. He would like a second term of office—Gandhiji remained thoughtful for sometime. Then he said, 'I shall see what can be done'. I was present when the conversation between Gandhiji and Jawaharlal took place'.

"In pursuance of Jawaharlal's talks with Gandhiji regarding a second term, Gandhiji asked Sardar to withdraw, which he did".

Nehru stuck to his socialistic pretensions and somehow, by his own contrived logic, felt that Congress was not against socialism. However, one thing led to another and Patel announced his withdrawal from the contest. But there were stipulations in his offer to withdraw. These were based on a draft that Gandhiji had sent to him on 24th November 1936—"If you do not like the draft, write out another, and if you think it your duty to enter into competition, do so. You may change the draft where you think it necessary. Whatever you do must be done with confidence, because we shall have to cross many deserts". Patel did not consider it necessary to rival Nehru and hanker for vote nor was he holding a threat to leave. However, the statement that he made showed that he always kept organisational interests above those of his own person. He issued a statement:

"After consultations with friends, I have come to the

conclusion that I must withdraw from the contest . . . . At this critical juncture, a unanimous election is most desirable.

"My withdrawal should not be taken to mean that I endorse all the views Jawaharlalji stands for. Indeed Congressmen know that on some vital matters my views are in conflict with those held by Jawaharlalji. For instance, I do not believe in the inevitability of class war.

"(Also) I can visualise the occasion when the acceptance of office may be desirable to achieve the common purpose. There may then be a sharp division of opinion between Jawarharlalji and myself.

"We know Jawaharlalji to be too loyal to the Congress to disregard the decision of the majority".

"The Congress President has no dictatorial powers. He is the chairman of a well-knit oganisation . . .The Congress does not part with its ample powers by electing any individual no matter who he is".

Nehru, however, with an eagle's eye on the main chance gladly accepted Patel's terms as enunciated above and further observed that "it would be absurd for me to treat this presidential election as a vote for socialism or against office-acceptance".

Namboodiripad's assessment of the Congress strategy was very near the truth. "Nehru to attract the masses and secure their votes, and Patel to control the ministries after winning the elections— such was the division of labour inside the Congress"; and so Gandhiji could say at Faizpur session, "I have cast all my cares on the broad shoulders of Jawaharlal and the Sardar". The outcome of the Assembly Polls in 1937 was a foregone conclusion and Congress won an absolute majority in eleven provinces. Having won the election, Jawaharlal had his own reservations on accepting the ministerial berths and strongly advocated his stand. But Patel, the realist, in spite of his opposition to 1935 Act realised that the Congress should not miss this opportunity to seize power. Nehru, the President, and the Congress were bent upon wrecking this Act. Patel knew that Nehru would fume if he was thwarted. So he let others do the job and Rajaji made a strong case for accepting ministerial office alongwith many Congress provincial committees and all the elected legislative members. Nehru persisted in his opposition to accept office but was outvoted by a large majority. Now Gandhiji stepped in and used his authority in favour of acceptance, stipulating that British Raj had given an assurance that the governors would not over-ride the Ministers by invoking their special powers.

Beatrice Webb, the British socialist, on meeting Nehru in 1938, had observed that she was "struck more by his charm than by his force". She could see through Nehru and took note of "Nehru's aristocratic refinement and culture dedicated to the salvation of the underdog", but qualified her assessment in the following words:

"But I doubt whether he has the hard stuff of a revolutionary".

With Patel it was the reverse. It was the force of his character, not his charm by which he was remembered. In the ultimate reckoning, Gandhiji preferred charm to force and thereby hangs a tale and the beginning of our misfortunes. The factors which weighed in the mind of Gandhiji, against Patel and for Nehru as his heir, and subsequently our Prime Minister, was Nehru's acceptability amongst the youth, the Left and the Muslims in the country. Another was the fact of age—Patel was 14 years older to Jawaharlal and not in sound health. In addition, there were two other reasons equally important. In Gandhiji's mind Patel could act as a stabilizing influence on Nehru who would only be the first among equals and not the sole authority. In a letter that Gandhiji wrote to Patel in 1939, he confirmed this view that Patel was to be the sheet-anchor, robust and critical, to Nehru and expressed himself thus, "Kishorlal was telling me yesterday that you had said, 'Bapu has placed us in Jawaharlal's charge, so we must go on doing as he says'. I hope this was only a joke. I have not handed you over to anyone -- it will not do if all of you do not exercise your independent judgment".

Gandhiji was also convinced that Nehru was not the one to accept No. 2 position while Patel as the disciplined disciple could. He was also sure that Patel's services and dedication will not be influenced by the position that he would hold. This is what Gandhiji wrote to Nariman in 1937 regarding Patel:

"The Sardar has no parliamentary ambition. He has no ambition for leadership. Nature has endowed him with certain qualities and he uses them. You won't find him going to the press and complaining if he loses hold on the populace".

He was not so sure of Nehru. Against the back drop of these events it is almost impossible not to compare Jawaharlal Nehru with Sardar Patel. The two worked together for the national cause as a team as ordered and umpired by Gandhiji. One had the shine, the other substance. One was a puller of crowds, the other an organiser par excellence and the orchestrator of the Congress machinery. After the Assembly elections were won and Provincial Governments formed, differences arose between the two regarding the running of the Governments. Patel was the man who had a better hold on the Congress Committee and thereby could counsel and control the actions of Provincial Governments much better, though Nehru was the All India Congress President. But Nehru struck with his socialistic rhetoric and a sympathy for the communists caused considerable embarrassments to these governments.

Very early, almost immediately, after Mountbatten's arrival in India, Nehru made an entry on the stage of international politics. It mattered to him the least that there were far more urgent and important matters in the national politics to be attended to, a curious fact that can only be termed as 'escapism', from the local to the international. This early trait amply adumbrated subsequent exertions of Nehru to trumpet his prominence in the international field in order to make up for his deficiencies on the home front. On 23rd March, 1947, a formidable structure was erected within the Purana Quila where the first Asian Relations Conference took place with considerable euphoria. Though the inspiration may have been some other sources too, the organization had a definite Nehru imprint. The idea of holding such a conference had been germinating in Nehru's mind for sometime now where-in he intended to invite a large number of Asian delegates after seeing such a show under the UN auspices at San Francisco. To this august assembly, his sister Vijay Lakshmi had been nominated as the Indian delegate and the idea never left him since then, and was repeatedly mentioned in his utterances in the winter of 1945. In December, 1945, Nehru gave an interview expressing his desire to hold such a conference and the same was published in the *Hindu*, national daily from Madras and the *Manchester Guardian*. Nehru had undoubtedly been working for this conference and had approached many Asian leaders in this regard in March, 1946.

The planning was subsequently taken up by the Indian Council of World Affairs, an ad hoc body, formed to meet this specific requirement. It is surprising that during the blood letting and carnage during the riots in India and Pakistan and amidst the negotiations for the nation's independence, Nehru could take time off for his international hobby. In a veiled attempt to disguise official backing to this Council, it was rumoured that the event would be merely a scholarly discourse on Asian culture. Nehru was also keen to hold the conference in Delhi, a more visible venue, in January 1947 and employed a British officer from the External Affairs Division of the Foreign Affairs Ministry to attend all meetings of the organising committee of this Council. Further help was sought from the British diplomatic mission in Delhi to help with the invitations, but this was politely declined; a fitting rebuff to Nehru's untimely concern. Because of the inadequacy of this unofficial council, hardly three years old, with little resources or expertise, Nehru had to do most of the home work himself. To many international observers, it appeared almost perverse that the leader of an emerging independent India was more concerned with an international extravaganza than the more serious problems confronting the nation passing through a bloody period of riots, social turmoil and uncertainties. Thus, Nehru's efforts towards the Asian conference were in almost total and callous disregard of urgent national interests; an act of glamour display and a self-serving exposure. And what was the sum total of the achievement of this conference? Nehru justified such labours in a speech delivered in early 1946 claiming that the aim of such a conference would be promotion of good neighbourly relations and development of ideas among the Asian countries. He, however, did not mention a word about cooperation and the anti-colonial struggle that was the need of the hour.

Nehru's preoccupation with international affairs at the cost of more pressing issues at home is an unending thread that runs through his entire political life. Even one of his close friends and admirers, Maulana Azad mentioned:

"I may also mention that Jawaharlal has always been more moved by international considerations than most Indians. He looked at all questions from an international rather than a national point of view. I also shared his concern for the international issues but to me the question of India's independence was paramount."

He was equally unduly influenced by foreign leaders of non-British origin, possibly with the exception of Mountbatten. This is what Azad observed on Nehru's return from China.

"He had returned from China recently and been greatly influenced by Generalissimo and Madame Chiang Kai-shek. It was clear to him that India's help was essential if China was to resist Japan successfully. During the meeting of the Working Committee Jawaharlal came to me one evening. Our discussions convinced me that he was in favour of accepting the Cripps offer even though there was no change in the British stand."

Maulana Abul Kalam Azad's (MAK Azad) observations during the crucial period of negotiations on the Cabinet Mission Plan in the summer of 1946, when he, being Congress President, had been carrying these out, throws another light on Nehru's personality. In his book "India Wins Freedom" published 30 years after his death, he refers to Nehru's opposition to his suggestion of a coalition with the Unionist Party in Punjab to form the provincial government. He says:

"Jawaharlal is however very vain and cannot stand that anybody else would receive greater support or admiration than he; Jawaharlal has also a weakness for theoretical considerations and they took advantage of this to turn him against me. They spoke to him and said that the alliance of Congress with the Unionist Party was in principle wrong. They argued that the Muslim League was a mass organization and the Congress should have formed a coalition with the Muslim League and not with the Unionist Party in the Punjab. This was the line which the communists had adopted openly. Jawaharlal was partially influenced by their views and may have thought that I was sacrificing leftist principles in forming a coalition with the Unionist Party.

"Those who wanted to create a division between Jawaharlal and me also kept on telling him that the praises howered on me was a reflection on other Congress leaders including him. If his own paper, *The National Herald,* should speak so highly of me, the result would be that soon I would achieve an unrivaled position in the Congress Organization.

"I do not know how far these persuasions had any effect on Jawaharlal's mind but during the meeting of the Congress Working Committee at Bombay, I found that he began to oppose my line of action on almost every item. Jawaharlal took the line that the policy I had adopted in the Punjab was not correct. He even said that I had brought down the prestige of the Congress. I was both surprised and sorry to hear this. What I had done in the Punjab was to put Congress into the Government in spite of the fact that the Governor had been working for installing a Muslim League Ministry."

Azad had been the Congress President continuously since 1939 onwards till 1946 and thus there was a need for a change and the search for a successor. In his own words:

"I thought carefully over the matter and finally came to the conclusion that since I had been President for seven years from 1939 to 1946 I must now retire. I therefore decided that I should not permit my name to be proposed.

"The next point which I had to decide was about the choice of my successor. I was anxious that the next President should be one who agreed with my point of view and would carry out the same policy as I had pursued. After weighing the pros and cons, I came to the conclusion that the election of Sardar Patel would not be desirable in the existing circumstances. Taking all facts into consideration, it seemed to me that Jawaharlal should be the new President. Accordingly, on 26 April, 1946, I issued a statement proposing his name for the presidentship and appealing to Congressmen that they elect Jawaharlal unanimously".

But he soon repents his decision:

"I acted according to my best judgement but the way things have shaped since then has made me realize that this was perhaps the greatest blunder of my political life. I have regretted no action of mine so much as the decision to withdraw from the presidentship of the Congress at this critical juncture. It was a mistake which I can describe in Gandhiji's words as one of Himalayan dimension". And he goes on:

"My second mistake was that when I decided not to

stand myself I did not support Sardar Patel. We differed on many issues but I am convinced that if he had succeeded me as Congress President he would have seen that the Cabinet Mission Plan was successfully implemented. He would have never committed the mistake of Jawaharlal which gave Mr. Jinnah the opportunity of sabotaging the plan. I can never forgive myself when I think that If I had not committed these mistakes, perhaps the history of the last ten years would have been different".

He also gives Gandhiji's preference in the matter again.

"One factor which gave greater strength to my decision was Gandhiji's view. He agreed with me that I should not continue as president but he was not wholly pleased that I had proposed that Jawaharlal should succeed me. Perhaps he was somewhat inclined towards Sardar Patel, but once I had proposed Jawaharlal's name, he gave no public indication of his views".

It is necessary here to clarify that the substance of the Cabinet Mission Plan was to transfer power to undivided India composed of several zones each including province with mixed population of Hindus, Muslims and other minorities. These were to be united on a federal basis with the Central Government which would execute control of matters such as defence, currency and foreign affairs. However, provinces were free to join in or opt out of the grouping from the one zone to another zone.

And here is Azad's final judgement on Nehru when the latter against the sane advice given by him and Gandhiji decided to visit the North West Frontier Provinces (NWFP) in October 1946, in rather uncertain and inopportune circumstances.

"In the latter half of October, Jawaharlal took a step which was unnecessary and which I had then opposed. His nature is however such that he often acts on impulse. He is generally open to persuasion but sometimes he makes up his mind without taking all facts into consideration.

Once he has done so, he tends to go ahead regardless of what the consequences may be".

We have seen D.P. Mishra's version of Maulana Azad's handling of the delicate issue of the Cabinet Mission Plan. Here are Azad's own words:

"The Muslim League Council had accepted the Cabinet Mission Plan. So had the Congress Working Committee. It however needed the approval of the AICC. We thought this would be a formal matter as the AICC had always ratified the decisions of the Working Committee. Accordingly, a meeting of the AICC was called at Bombay on 7 July, 1946. Once this decision was taken there was no need for me to stay on in Delhi."

"My speech had a decisive influence on the audience. When the vote was taken, the resolution was passed with an overwhelming majority. Thus the seal of approval was put on the Working Committee's resolution accepting the Cabinet Mission Plan". After a few days I received telegrams of congratulation from Lord Pethick-Lawrence and Sir Stafford Cripps. They were happy that Congress had accepted my resolution and congratulated me on my able presentation of the Cabinet Mission Plan. But he goes on to say:

"Now happened one of those unfortunate events which change the course of history. On 10 July, Jawaharlal held a press conference in Bombey in which he made an astonishing statement. Some press representatives asked him whether, with the passing of the Resolution by the AICC, the Congress had accepted the plan in toto, including the composition of the Interim Government. Jawaharlal in reply stated that Congress would enter the Constituent Assembly 'completely unfettered by agreements and free to meet all situations as they arise'.

"Press representatives further asked if this meant that the Cabinet Mission Plan could be modified".

Thus Azad himself, one of Nehru's closest friends and confidantes was disappointed in him. As is well known this volte face by Nehru gave Jinnah the opportunity he was looking for to repudiate the Cabinet Mission Plan.

"The Muslim League had accepted the Cabinet Mission Plan only under duress. Naturally, Mr. Jinnah was not very happy about it. In his speech to the League Council, he had clearly stated that he recommended acceptance only because nothing better could be obtained. His political adversaries started to criticize him by saying that he had failed to deliver the goods. They accused him that he had given up the idea of an independent Islamic State. They also taunted him that if the League was willing to accept the Cabinet Mission Plan—which denied the right of the Muslims to form a separate State—why had Mr. Jinnah made so much fuss about an independent Islamic State?"

This according to Azad led to Jinnah's tactical victory.

"Mr. Jinnah was thus not at all happy about the outcome of the negotiations with the Cabinet Mission. Jawaharlal's statement came to him as a bombshell. He immediately issued a statement that this declaration by the Congress President demanded a review of the whole situation. He accordingly asked Liaqat Ali Khan to call a meeting of the League Council and issued a statement to the following effect. The Muslim League Council had accepted the Cabinet Mission Plan in Delhi as it was assured that the Congress also had accepted the scheme and the plan would be the basis of the future constitution of India. Now that the Congress President had declared that the Congress could change the scheme through its majority in the Constituent Assembly, this would mean that the minorities would be placed at the mercy of the majority. His view was that Jawaharlal's declaration meant that the Congress had rejected the Cabinet Mission plan and as such the Viceroy should call upon the Muslim League, which had accepted the plan, to form the Government".

As will be brought out later these events show a lack

of perception and Nehru's total inability to negotiate effectively.

Mention has been made of the policy of avoiding a collision course with the princely states. While Nehru, the ever impetuous was keen to go, Patel advised caution. His policy towards the British Raj was the same. "We have not accepted office in order to carry out a few reforms. We accepted office with a view to moving on towards a far greater thing—Complete Independence. If by accepting office our ability to move towards that goal is increased, well and good. But if we find that our final goal is jeopardized, we must immediately give up office".

In the final analysis, Patel, the pragmatist, did a better job with the states. He displayed that he could assimilate all these states in the Indian Union. Nehru tackled only one, that is Kashmir, and failed. On both these issues Patel's stand was clear and pragmatic compared to Nehru's idealistic, radical and confrontationist. Within a year, however, the Assemblies fell as the war clouds gathered and the Second World War broke out in September, 1939.

As has been stated earlier, Nehru had invested wisely and well in forging an emotional bond with the Mahatma from whom he differed almost in all respects. This carefully cultivated image of a disciplined soldier and his magic over the crowds ultimately paid off. Gandhi anointed Jawaharlal his successor. Gandhiji had said, "Pandit Jawaharlal and I have had differences from the moment we became co-workers, yet I have said for some years and say it now that not Rajaji, not Sardar Vallabhbhai, but Jawaharlal will be my successor. You cannot divide water by repeatedly striking it with a stick. It is just as difficult to divide us—when I am gone, he will speak my language."

This was a momentous decision of the Mahatma. In all his thoughts and deeds there is but nothing that one can blame him for except possibly for the minor tactical mistake of withdrawal from the State Assemblies. This had left a vacuum for the Muslim League to fill during the War, thereby forcing the British to favour Jinnah over the Congress. But now his decision to anoint Nehru was of the greatest importance. It was a blunder that affected the destiny of this county, not necessarily for good. As we shall see, from this original act flowed all our miseries.

Nations and governments need statesmen and men of substance, not of charm and woolly idealism. Mahatma Gandhi, apparently struck by the outer face of Nehru, settled for a man who was confused in thoughts, a romantic idealist, impulsive to a degree, and not farseeing against one having substance, farsight and solid organisational skills. He preferred Hamlet, the Prince of Denmark, to Prince Bismark of Prussia. J.R.D. Tata compared the simple good sense and logic of Patel with Nehru's thinking thus, "While I usually came back from talks with Jawaharlal fired with emotional zeal but often confused and unconvinced, meetings with Vallabhbhai were a joy from which I returned with renewed confidence in the future of our country". Events moved fast since then, with Quit India Movement, release of leaders and the arrival of Cabinet Mission in 1946.

We have assessed Nehru's thoughts penned by him, during his incarceration at Ahmednagar jail, in his book, "The Discovery of India". While Nehru was thus engaged in studying the past, Patel seldom wrote but thought of the future, the struggle for independence and the shape of his India after independence. We notice in one (Nehru) the urge to act first and think later, hoping the act to stimulate thought. The other (Patel) thinks first and then acts decisively, taking his actions to their logical end and not leaving them unfinished or halfway. There would be many examples in future to illustrate this difference.

But now back to the main events. Nehru nursed the ambition for being the first Prime Minister of Independent

India, and his success against all odds depended entirely on the blessings of one man whom the nation could not defy.

It was at this time that Nehru succeeded Azad as the Congress President while the Interim Government was being formed, and this meant a Prime Ministerial throne. There were many aspirants for this post—Azad who wanted re-election not exactly to Nehru's liking and of course there was always Sardar Patel, a clear aspirant on merit. The last date for nomination was April 29 but Gandhiji had already indicated his preference for Nehru, in spite of some kite-flying in the press regarding Azad's re-election. He chided Azad for such indiscretion in his note of April 20, 1946.

"Please go through the enclosed cutting—I have not spoken to anyone of my opinion. When one or two Working Committee members asked me, I said that it would not be right for the same president to continue . . . If you are of the same opinion, it may be proper for you to issue a statement about the cutting and say that you have no intention to become president again . . . In today's circumstances I would if asked prefer Jawaharlal. I have many reasons for this. Why go into them?".

Equally strong as Gandhiji's reasons to favour Nehru, Congress Party had its own for settling for Patel, who according to them was "a great executive, organizer and leader" and who had his feet firmly on the ground. They had also not forgotten the Sardar's tremendous contribution during the `Quit India' movement which was far above that of Jawaharlal. In 1946, shortly after the release of the Working Committee members from jail, with Patel's role still fresh in public thought, twelve of the fifteen provincial committees nominated Patel. Gandhiji's less than convincing reasons for Nehru were publicly announced by him later, where he said, "Jawaharlal cannot be replaced today, whilst the charge is being taken from Englishmen. He, a Harrow boy, a Cambridge graduate and barrister is wanted to carry all the negotiations with the Englishmen." Nehru's constituency among the Muslims was another reason. But the most important reason was that "Jawaharlal will not take second place". He also knew that Nehru was known in International circles and would make India play a role in International affairs. Deep down in his consciousness the wise old man knew that Jawaharlal's elevation would not ipso facto lead to Patel's walking away. He knew, "they will be like two oxen yoked to the Government cart. One will need the other and both will pull together". Nehru had almost missed his chance but for Gandhiji. Till April 29, the deadline for receiving nominations, not a single provincial Congress committee had sent his name. As Kripalani was to record later, "in deference to Gandhiji's wishes he sent a paper round proposing the name of Jawaharlal". After this there was nothing more to be said and all members of the Working Committee signed this. Kripalani withdrew his own nomination and offered Patel a piece of paper to sign his own withdrawal. Kripalani's draft read that Patel was withdrawing from the contest "so that Nehru could be elected unopposed". Before signing the paper, Vallabhbhai showed it to Gandhiji. In spite of his openly espousing Jawaharlal's cause, Gandhiji gave Jawaharlal a choice to step down in favour of the Sardar. He said, "No provincial Congress committee has put forward your name, only the Working Committee has". But it was not in Nehru's nature to renounce power and the throne. He maintained a "complete silence". In the meantime, Gandhiji got information from some other sources that "Jawaharlal will not take second place". Thus Gandhiji was left with no choice but to ask Patel to sign the paper that Kripalani had given him. Patel promptly complied. For him it was a repeat performance of stepping down in favour of Nehru because the latter could not forego his lust for power. It had happened in 1929, 1939 and was to be repeated now. Later, many Congressmen alongwith Prasad complained that, "Gandhiji had once again sacrificed his trusted lieutenant for the sake of the glamorous Nehru". Patel neither complained nor disobeyed Gandhiji. He knew fully well that being already 71, he could never get an opportunity again to head the Government. While he did not mention it, it is almost certain that Patel must have been deeply hurt, but he showed no outward sign of his deep anguish. While Patel could withstand the temptation of unlimited power and privilege, Nehru could not. The voice of reason within him followed Gandhiji's thought process that Nehru would either take first position or leave the cabinet. He should not do the same. It was also obvious that once rejected, Nehru even could join the opposition and Patel did not wish to create a crisis that could lead to the division of India.

What would one call a man who not even once in his lifetime renounced this lust for power. He just could not efface himself for a single moment, though, he knew that he was young and would almost certainly get a chance soon enough. Knowing the state of Patel's health, he would have been sure of a long innings after his death. But Nehru the pampered prince could not say no to power. In his characteristic fashion, he would stick to power till struck by the Chinese Thunderbolt in 1962 and later weakened by a stroke at Bhubaneshwar. Even then, he stuck to power, keeping the reigns of Government in his shaking hands till death took him away on 27th May, 1964. Unlike Gandhi, he did not even name his successor. After me the deluge? In the meantime, Patel's candid assessment of Nehru conveyed to D.P. Mishra, a leader of Madhya Pradesh, is not a disparaging remark of a colleague who lost out on merit but that of a great patriot who knew his comrade's weakness but allowed himself to act as the second man to him. He did not esteem Nehru less but loved his country more. One who considered service to the nation above the lure of power. His remarks on Nehru:

"Though Nehru has been elected (President) for the fourth time, he often acts with childlike innocence.. but we must not allow our anger to get the better of ourselves... His press conference was an act of emotional insanity. But in spite of all his innocent indiscretions, he has unparalleled enthusiasm and a burning passion for freedom which make him restless and drive him to a pitch of impatience where he forgets himself. Opposition sometimes drives him mad, as he is impatient. You may, however, rest assured that as long as one of us is inside the group that governs the policy of the Congress, the straight and steady march of the ship will not be interrupted."

Nehru started with a faux pas at the very beginning of his Presidency by making it clear to the AICC that, "we are not bound by a single thing except that we have decided to go into the Constituent Assembly" knowing fully well that the Working Committee had put its seal on the May 16 proposal. He reiterated three days later that Congress would be "completely unfettered by agreements." And that "the Central Government was likely to be much stronger than what the Cabinet Mission envisaged." He further amplified:

"The big probability is... (that) there will be no grouping. Obviously Section A (the Hindu majority provinces) will decide against grouping. In betting language, there is a four-to-one chance of the N.W.F.P. deciding against grouping. Then Group B collapses. (As for Section Cl, I can say with every assurance and conviction that there is going to be finally no grouping there, because Assam will not tolerate it under any circumstances whatever."

Jinnah took strong exception to Nehru's remarks as a complete repudiation of May 16 agreement, and requested the British Government to "remove the impression that the Congress has accepted the long-term scheme." When the British Government refused, Jinnah reacted by getting the Muslim League to revoke its earlier acceptance of May 16 proposal and prepare for "direct action to achieve

Pakistan." Vallabhbhai was stunned at Jawaharlal's indiscretion which literally forced the League to resort to this drastic action.

And for the way the hereditary ruler treated Patel who made his accession to the throne possible, there were many instances. His constant complaining to Bapu against Patel was not new. Even before Independence, cracks had already developed in the Nehru-Patel relationship. The situation was not improved by Nehru's unexpected statement at the Meerut Session of the Congress in November, 1946 that the Congress Ministers would soon resign. This was not the policy of the Congress nor Patel's desire; and the latter intended to make a public statement to set the records straight. This he did in Bombay, while addressing a huge crowd, and made it absolutely clear that "Congress has no intention of quitting office". Earlier at Meerut, Patel had told the votaries of Pakistan that, "Whatever you do, do it by the method of peace and love. You may succeed. But the sword will be met by the sword." The statement was lustily cheered by the crowd, since the event was so near to the Noakhali and Bihar killings of Hindus. Nehru, as usual, reacted sharply to Patel's remarks and went with his complaint to Mahatma who was then walking in the streets of Noakhali. In all probability, Gandhiji wrote to Patel as a sequel to this and the whole episode further aggravated the relations between the two.

And finally, how the same person looks upto Patel when he knows that he is helpless without him even to muster the support of the Congress Working Committee and his own guardian angel who anointed him as his successor.

On the morning of 10th May, V.P. Menon called on Patel and subsequently laid out his plan before Nehru and Mountbatten. The same afternoon, Nehru also rang up Patel repeating the substance of Menon's plan and asked his views on it. To this Patel, with his customary promptitude and clarity, replied, "There is no alternative but to accept this plan. Under it we lose only a fraction of India. Under the other plan we risk losing all of it." Nehru was relieved that Patel had approved. However, he was gnawed with the anxiety on two counts—acceptance by the Working Committee and more importantly from Bapu. He had informed Menon earlier that in this critical hour "Sardar will have to speak to Bapu." Patel knew that once he and Nehru had agreed, the Working Committee would fall in line. After much heart searching, Nehru had come to the view that only the Sardar could convince Bapu to accept the Partition Plan. He, the appointed heir of Gandhiji, did not have the courage to face the old man with the proposal. Deciding that discretion was the better part of valour, he used the Sardar to present the case to Gandhiji. The incident revealed another trait of Nehru. While he could and often was rash in his public statements, he was indecisive in private when left alone. On the other hand, Patel, who was cautious in his public utterances could be bold when the moment of decision came. He informed Nehru not to worry at all on this count. The rest is history. The Working Committee, as foreseen by Patel, fell in line, and the Congress gave its seal of approval to the Partition Plan.

Communalism and casteism, the bane of today's social and political scene, is not a new phenomenon as many would like to believe. After the general elections of 1952, when Congress, on the strength of its past services, sacrifices and achievements, with no national alternative in sight, swept the polls, the situation steadily deteriorated. Mahatma Gandhi had wanted the Congress to dissolve and convert itself into a party of national service and constructive work. But by then, the leaders had tasted power and they did not want to disband the organisation, that could churn out votes and secure them power and creature comforts. So the Congress remained, not an instrument of fight for freedom and justice but for perpetuating the rule of the leaders. The next elections in 1957 and 1962 saw the emergence of the forces of communalism and casteism. In almost all constituencies whether of Parliament or State Assembly, the candidates were chosen not on merit but on considerations of religion and caste politics. My uncle stood from the constituency of Modinagar in 1952 for the UP Assembly where the electorate were not from the so-called upper caste to which my uncle, being a Brahmin, belonged. But the sheer power of organisation of Shri Gandhi Ashram, the dedication of its workers and his own sacrifice and clean and simple image saw him through three times. But this was an exception. Almost, all other Congress candidates including Charan Singh and Kamlapati Tripathi invoked caste loyalties, while C.B. Gupta used organisational muscle and personal and group loyalties to win a seat. At almost all places where the electorate was chiefly Muslims, a Muslim candidate was put up. Nehru not only accepted it but approved it. His logic as he gave during the run up to 1937 elections is quoted from his own book, "Discovery of India."

"My tour was especially concerned with the general elections all over India that were approaching. But I did not take kindly to the usual methods and devices that accompany electioneering. Elections were an essential and inseparable part of the democratic process and there was no way of doing away with them. Yet, often enough, elections brought out the evil side of man, and it was obvious that they did not always lead to the success of the better man. Sensitive persons, and those who were not prepared to adopt rough-and-ready methods to push themselves forward, were at a disadvantage and preferred to avoid these contests. Was democracy then to be a close preserve of those possessing thick skins and loud voices and accommodating consciences?"

"The general elections in 1937 for the provincial assemblies were based on a restricted franchise affecting about twelve per cent of the population. But even this was a great improvement on the previous franchise, and nearly thirty million all over India, apart from the Indian States, were now entitled to vote. The scope of these elections was vast and comprised the whole of India, minus the States. Every province had to elect its Provincial Assembly, and in most provinces there were two Houses, and there were thus two sets of elections. The number of candidates ran into many thousands.

"My approach to these elections, and to some extent the approach of most Congressmen, was different from the usual one. I did not trouble myself about the individual candidates, but wanted rather to create a countrywide atmosphere in favour of our national movement for freedom as represented by the Congress, and for the programme contained in our elections manifesto. I felt that if we succeeded in this, all would be well; if not, then it did not matter much if an odd candidate won or lost.

"My appeal was an ideological one and I hardly referred to the candidates, except as standard-bearer of our cause. I knew many of them, but there were many I did not know at all, and I saw no reason why I would burden my mind with hundreds of names. I asked for votes for the Congress, for the independence of India, and for the struggle for independence. I made no promises, except to promise unceasing struggle till freedom was attained. I told people to vote for us only if they understood and accepted our objective and our programme, and were prepared to live up to them; not otherwise. I charged them not to vote for the Congress if they disagreed with this objective or programme. We wanted no false votes, no votes for particular persons because they liked them. Votes and elections would not take us far; they were just small steps in a long journey, and to delude us with votes, without intelligent acceptance of what they signified or willingness for subsequent action, was to play us false and be untrue to our country. Individuals did not count, though we wanted good and true individuals to represent us; it was the cause that counted, the oganization that represented it, and the nation to whose freedom we were pledged."

"That was the burden of my speeches, and only in that impersonal way could I fit myself into the election campaign. I was not greatly concerned with the prospects of particular candidates. My concern was with a much bigger issue. As a matter of fact that approach was the right one even from the narrower point of view of a particular candidate's success. For thus he and his election were lifted up to a higher and more elemental level of a great nation's fight for freedom, and millions of poverty stricken people striving to put an end to their ancient curse of poverty. These ideas, expressed by scores of leading Congressmen came and spread like a mighty wind fresh from the sea, sweeping away all petty ideas and electioneering stunts. I knew my people and liked them and their million eyes had taught me much of mass psychology."

I distinctly remember a rather funny incident during the 1952 elections. A senior student who took an active part during the 1942 Quit India Movement and had gone underground, stood for UP Assembly elections on the ticket of the Communist Party of India from one of the rural constituencies of Meerut District. He had striven hard with his dedicated communist cadres in door to door canvassing and was, in his own judgement, sitting pretty to win the election. But he did not reckon with the Nehru factor. As it happened, Nehru during his whirlwind tour of Meerut District, happened to address a meeting in the same constituency. The voters turned to the last man to have a 'Darshan' of their hero. Poor fellow, he did not know what hit him. Months of painstaking work was washed away by the Nehru tidal wave. Such was the magic of the man till about 1957. What a tragedy that he did not use his power over people to make 'men' out of them as the foundation of a great nation. Nehru's word was the law. The nation followed him blindly. But whither did he take the trusting millions? History is the judge.

The theme in subsequent elections remained the same—Congress and the higher cause. But the candidate's merit went by default. Later, Congress openly adopted casteism to win votes and finally resorted to the appeasement of Muslims to stay in power and label every other party as anti-Muslim and anti-lower caste. Nehru laid the foundations on which his unscrupulous followers raised their own vote banks. With every Congress win the country lost. The signs were clear in 1952 itself. Acharya Kripalani left Congress soon after. The tone and the tenor of the election campaign adumbrated the shadows of a murky polity. In 1952, the Congress far from being a vehicle for galvanizing the nation to rise to greater heights in the comity of nations degenerated into a machine to perpetuate power. Nehru the vote-catcher became synonymous with the bestower of power and privilege. Khadi and Gandhi cap became a passport to unmerited power and pelf. That was the time I came out of my trance and gave up wearing khadi and joined the Armed Forces. Nehru's pulling power and charisma was used by his inheritors, Indira and Rajiv too for their political aggrandisement.

Part II

5 Nehru After Independence

The events after the acceptance by Congress Working Committee of the Partition Plan are common knowledge and need not detain us here. However, certain events during these turbulent times throw some fresh light on Nehru's character traits. Even before the dawn of independence and his 'tryst with destiny' speech, preparations were afoot for ushering in of the new era. But the scale and nature of pageantry ill-matched with Indian simplicity. The civil lines approach was already at work. Scramble for big bungalows had already started. Alan Campbell Johnson in his book 'Mission With Mountbatten', recorded on 4th August, 1947:

"Having seen the draft schedule of arrangements for Independence Day in Delhi, I have come to the conclusion that they have too much British pomp and circumstance about them and lack some imaginative and informal act of identification with the Indian people." Austerity and simplicity were given a go-by.

The fury and the carnage of the divide and the large scale riots, followed by trans-border migration of communities have been well documented elsewhere. However, the problem was further complicated due to a rather warped view of Nehru on secularism and issues where minorities were concerned. According to him, the entire responsibility to keep alive cordial relations and observe restraint lay on the majority community. The minority could do no wrong. While the majority community must be restrained at all costs even under the strongest provocation there were no parallel demands on the minority. The Hindus considered this less than fair. All his actions clearly point out to this rather one-sided approach to the problem which left only bitterness among the migrating community. The problem at a different plane has still not been solved to the satisfaction of all the parties. Nehru constantly remonstrated with the Hindus to keep their cool, but there is no record of any attempt by him to discipline the local minorities or join issues with Pakistan to reciprocate by enforcing peace keeping measures within its territory. This approach was not acceptable to Patel who believed in fair play and handing out equal responsibility to both the communities to maintain communal harmony. Patel's role during the riots in Delhi is well-known, and but for his firm hand, the situation could have degenerated into an orgy of violence. Nehru's role was mainly one of an impulsive intruder, here and there, often clashing with the Sardar on whom as a Home Minister the whole responsibility devolved. Here is an example for the Sardar's foresight in the problem which even now bedevils us. The number of Hindus entering India from East Pakistan far outnumbered the Muslims leaving India for East Pakistan. The huge inflows into West Bengal virtually strangled its economy. Not prepared to put up with this injustice the Sardar during the Jaipur session of Congress in December, 1948, warned Pakistan. It should take back the refugees or surrender sufficient territory for their resettlement in an area contiguous to West Bengal. Patel had earlier written to Nehru offering yet another alternative, "a clear indication to Pakistan Government that if this migration continues we would have no alternative left except to send out Muslims in equal number".

Jawaharlal Nehru opposed it on rather flimsy moral grounds and possible international reactions, always the Achilles heel of Nehru, the international peacemaker. The Sardar had to yield. From then on till now it has been Pakistani infiltration into India as a one way street, causing so much concern to our state. The role played by erstwhile East Pakistan was followed by Bangladesh confirming the same trend in no less visible terms. Nehru's objections were no doubt sound in theory as he articulated these. "It would create communal trouble all over India. Every Muslim in India will feel an alien and in effect we would have established a Hindu state". Then again, "how would one pick out Muslims, who are undoubtedly citizens of India, to be sent to East Bengal? Neither international nor domestic law could justify this pushing out of our own citizens". But in real politics things do not always follow a logical course. Posterity bears witness to the fact that a bully understands only one language, that of force, or a threat. Patel's threat would have worked.

Thus restrained, Patel bowed to Nehru's wish at the time, though his reservations on the subject later proved prophetically true and his stand was vindicated in the long run. Patel then reasoned with Pakistan to take back its refugees and give Hindu Muslim co-existence a fair chance, both in India and East Pakistan. Nehru-Patel differences on this issue surfaced once again in 1950. Nehru made a token offer of Prime Ministership to Patel which the latter expectedly rejected. Nehru was already conscious of an undercurrent of grumbling among the majority of Congressmen and his cabinet colleagues who favoured Patel's strong approach and criticised his handling of the situation. He had "a feeling that I have largely exhausted my utility in New Delhi—from every point of view, my proposal appears to be justified". He wrote to Patel, "you would be there to guide them in any event". Patel, the realist, as mentioned, struck down the proposal, and stood solidly behind Nehru, the Prime Minister.

Negotiations were given a chance and Liaquat Ali Khan arrived in Delhi for a dialogue. After some talks it was agreed to have a Minority Commission in both the countries, though Azad had suggested this step for the two Bengals only and the Sardar had rejected it firmly stating, "I am quite sure the party will not accept it and the country will not swallow the bitter pill. We have conceded one Pakistan; that is more than enough". Shyama Prasad Mukherjee and K.C. Neogi left the cabinet in protest against this agreement, wildly cheered by frenzied crowds all over West Bengal. But the agreement was signed all the same. Nehru, not always thankful to him, now used the ailing Patel to fight the battle. One observer of the scene mentioned in `Hindustan Times'. "At this moment it was Patel who stole the scene . . . to M.Ps. he made one of the most moving appeals they had ever heard. . .assuring his whole strength and energy to making a success of the Agreement and vindicating the stand of the Prime Minister". The Sardar urged a fair trial of the pact and "secured support for the Agreement from quarters which refused to Nehru". It was not Nehru but the Sardar who urged to almost a hundred thousand reluctant Hindus to return to East Pakistan and the flow of Muslims back to West Bengal started. In Nehru's own words, "Vallabhbhai had been a brick during these days". And this was the man Nehru insidiously conspired against, for the latter to be dubbed as `anti-Muslim' and a `fascist'!

There was another area of discord, the disposal of evacuee property in India. According to Nehru the Muslims displaced from their old habitat in India, deserved a first right. But Patel felt that dispossessed refugees from Pakistan, Hindus and Sikhs, had a better claim on it.

And then an interesting aside on the much discussed payment of dues of Rs. 55 crore to Pakistan. How Nehru quickly changed his stand and went against the cabinet decision to which he was a party and let down his colleagues. Patel's reasoning on the release of Pakistani assets was already clear in his Calcutta speech.

"In the division of assets we treated Pakistan generously. But obviously we cannot tolerate even a pie being spent for making bullets to be shot at us. The settlement (on assets) is like a consent decree. The decree will be executed when all the outstanding points are satisfactorily settled".

"The Muslim Leaguers used to call Mahatma Gandhi as their enemy number one. Now they think of Gandhiji as their friend and have substituted me in his place, for speaking the truth. They believed that if they had Pakistan they would ensure full protection to Muslims. But have they ever sympathized with Muslims living in India?

"To Indian Muslims I have only one question. Why did you not open your mouths on the Kashmir issue? Why did you not condemn the action of Pakistan?. . .It is your duty now to sail in the same boat and sink or swim together. I want to tell you very frankly that you cannot ride two horses. Select one horse. Those who want to go to Pakistan can go there and live in peace.

"I appeal to the Hindu Mahasabhaites to join the Congress .. If you think that you are the only custodians of Hinduism, you are mistaken. Hinduism preaches broader outlook. I appeal to the RSS not to be rash and tactless. Do not be aggressive".

Patel had known through unimpeachable sources that being in financial straits, Pakistan would use this money to procure weapons and materials for use against India in the ongoing war in Kashmir. He had "no doubt that the payment would be converted into sinews of war against India" and had indicated that "not a pie" was to be given. S.P. Mukherjee, Ambedkar and Gadgil supported his stand. Based on the cabinet decision Patel issued a press statement on 12 January,. 1948, that "the settlement of financial issues cannot be isolated from that of other vital issues and has to be implemented simultaneously". And then proceeded straight to Birla House where Gandhiji stayed. Till then he was not aware of the latter's intention to go on fast unto death on this issue. On being informed about it Patel asked Gandhiji whether he had talked to Nehru on the subject, adding that "it was a Cabinet decision". Gandhiji replied that during his just concluded talk with Nehru his reply was, "Yes it was passed but we do not have a case. It is legal quibbling". The rest is history. The decision was revoked and money handed over to Pakistan to respect Gandhiji's feelings. But Nehru had once again let down his most valuable colleague.

This episode shows another example of the Sardar's maturity of judgement against Nehru's impulsiveness. And then the Randhawa episode. There was a dispute over Delhi's Sikh Deputy Commissioner, Randhawa. Azad and Nehru told Vallabhbhai "that Randhawa was not trusted by Muslims and should be transferred". "You have only to express your wish and I will execute it", Patel said to Nehru, but he added that the transfer would be "fraught with serious consequences". Replying that it was for Vallabhbhai with his "more direct sources of information" to decide, Nehru backed away. But not so soon. This is what Raj Mohan Gandhi has to say, "Nehru, Azad and the other Muslims attending the December 24 meeting had wanted Randhawa to be transferred and Patel had replied, 'Why don't you take charge?' I can't work like this. A significant proportion of Delhi's police were Hindu or Sikh Punjabis, including a number of refugees, several of whom had lost near and dear ones in Pakistan. They found it hard to sympathize with Muslims, and the Sardar did not press them to do so. He could not afford to lose their loyalty by putting too heavy a strain on it".

Gandhi understood this but found it difficult to tell Delhi's Muslims that there was a limit to the sympathy they should expect. Vallabhbhai's departure seemed to him a possible if hazardous way out. At the end of December or early in January—most probably on December 29 or 30—Gandhi said to Patel: "Either you should run things or Jawaharlal should". Vallabhbhai replied: "I do not have the physical strength. He is younger. Let him run the show. I will assist him to the extent possible from outside". The Mahatma reserved judgment.

In Nehru's scheme of things, the majority community

always had to take a second place to the pampered 'minority'. Those who asked for the promised land but missed it and stayed back in India were being given preference over those who opposed it. What an irony? Randhawa stayed and further slaughter of Hindus stopped.

Things would have been different if India had treated Pakistan more firmly and spoke with a single voice on issues of vital importance.

Sardar Patel's masterly handling of the 565 princely states is too well known to need repetition. But what was Nehru's contribution? Nothing but dithering and occasionally treading on Patel's toes and blundering into territory which legitimately belonged to the Department of States, directly under the Ministry of Home Affairs, under Sardar Patel, the then Home Minister. But this did not prevent Nehru from trespassing into Patel's territory. Gopalaswamy's handling of Kashmir was not the only snub Nehru offered to Patel which, beyond being clearly a case of impropriety hurt his self-respect too.

Nehru's interference in Ajmer, then a State, throws some light on this sorry development.

Mountbatten, with all the flamboyance, was a shrewd judge of men. He had told Gandhiji that without Patel the Government could not run, arguing 'Patel had his feet on the ground, while Nehru has his in the clouds'.

Towards the end of December 1947, after the riots in Ajmer, Jawaharlal Nehru sent his Principal Private Secretary, H.V.R. Iengar, to Ajmer for an on-the-spot study. He neither consulted nor informed Patel or any one in the Home Ministry, though Iengar, in a typical bureaucratic fashion did inform Shanker Prasad, Chief Commissioner of Ajmer, on his visit. During his stay, Iengar met delegates of the Advisory Council and other public representatives, while assessing the damage to the property. It was not so much the action of Iengar but the inquisitorial manner that jarred on the sensibility of the Chief Commissioner. Shanker Prasad had already issued a statement on the situation after the riots and this visit of Nehru's emissary almost amounted to a check on the activities of Patel and the civil administration. The hurt was further aggravated by the fact that Iengar was junior to Shanker Prasad. Understandably Patel was not amused. It was a clear trespass on his territory. Though Nehru might not have meant to supervise Patel, but he did resort to this strategem (unable to visit Ajmer himself). Nehru's intention was to convey "PM's regrets and Iengar as the eyes and ears of the PM". To the circles in Delhi, this surreptitious move appeared to show Nehru's lack of confidence in the Sardar. If only he could have informed Patel, there would have been no misunderstanding. This action of Nehru further reinforced the impression that there was no coordinated team work at Delhi. Inevitably, the Sardar wrote to Nehru on the subject showing his displeasure to which Nehru replied, "Am I not to send a personal representative to any place? That would make me a prisoner". But Patel's sane reply was "The question is not whether the Prime Minister was entitled to take this step or not, but whether I, as a Minister, was wrong in pointing out to him the inadvisability of the course he had taken". A number of points were made from either side and further bad blood was created forcing Gandhi to adjudicate in the matter, taking note of Nehru's complaint of 6th January, 1948, and Patel's reply of 12th January. While Nehru emphasised the pre-eminence of the Prime Minister, Patel stressed the importance of team work. Nehru's recorded reaction was, "the only alternative left is either for me or Sardar Patel to leave the Cabinet. If someone has to leave, I would prefer to leave". Patel's seasoned reply was: "If anybody has to go, it should be myself. I have long passed the age of active service. The Prime Minister is the acknowledged leader of the country and is comparatively young. I have no doubt that the choice between him and myself should be resolved in his favour. There is, therefore, no question of his quitting office".

It was a difficult piece of judicious dispensation for the Mahatma— who to be asked to leave and who to stay back. Patel was mentally prepared to quit. But true to his promise to Mahatma, he wanted to finish the onerous task of uniting all the States and his final gesture to the old man was to bring Kathiawad, Gandhi's home state, into the Union. He informed Nehru that he would be leaving for Bhavnagar on the morning of January 15. Patel also sent his resignation letter dated December 23 to Nehru.

And finally, Nehru's pathetic indecision on Hyderabad leading almost to a comatose state of mind in the nation's Chief Executive. While the British advised delay, the Sardar with his prescience could foresee a speedy outcome. Where others only saw difficulties he saw an opportunity to remove once and for all a cancer from the womb of the Indian mainland. Nehru as usual wrapped himself in eloquent inactivity and lofty indecision.

The chiefs of the defence forces were apprehensive about the shortage of troops required for internal security duties elsewhere in the country. This was reason enough to postpone the Hyderabad operation till after the monsoons. This view was conveyed by Menon to Patel and to the Cabinet Defence Committee. Patel's reply was sound and to the point.

"It is not, in the final analysis, the action of an Army which maintains law and order—look at the Punjab last August, when 55,000 men could not stop the massacres. It is rather the prestige of the Government backed by potential armed action which keeps the people in order. At the moment this prestige is sufficiently high to take action against Hyderabad and maintain order elsewhere at the same time. But if the Government delays action against Hyderabad much longer, then its prestige will fall so greatly that no amount of troops will be sufficient for internal security".

Once the green signal was given by Patel, it was decided on May 30 that the preparation for the invasion should proceed. Mountbatten still in India, and the chairman of the Defence Committee, made this note.

"Pandit Nehru said openly at the meeting, and subsequently assured me privately, that he would not allow any orders to be given for operations to start unless there really was an event, such as a wholesale massacre of Hindus within the State, which would patently justify, in the eyes of the world, action by the Government of India".

Patel was not prepared to give such an assurance. The double dealing of the Nizam was enough *casus belli* for firm and resolute action. The final countdown for Operation Hyderabad began on July 5 after Mountbatten's departure and the Sardar's return to Delhi. With Patel's unequivocal support the blockade of Hyderabad State had not only received final sanction but also became officially effective. The state virtually gave Patel his *casus belli* on a platter, when they hired gun runners flying from Pakistan airports into Bider and Warangal in Hyderabad. The Razakars and the communists came closer and in some cases raided the border villages and established their own rule. Towards the end of July, J.V. Joshi resigned from the Nizam's council and joined the Hindus residing mainly in the western districts of Hyderabad who were leaving the State in droves. There were also reports of attacks on Indian border villages and trains passing through Hyderabad as also assaults on foreign missionaries and molestation of nuns. There was a barrage of charges and counter-charges and the Nizam threatened to approach the United Nations and requested the President of the United States to arbitrate in the matter. Wisely the U.S. President refused. While Jawaharlal Nehru conscious of his promise to Mountbatten, prevaricated Patel was firm and decisive. The Cabinet and the new Governor General Rajaji were solidly behind Patel. Nehru conscious of his precarious position wailed to Mountbatten, "I am completely distrusted by large number of people here". Nehru later asked C.R. to order the Nizam to ban the Razakars and ask for the help of the Indian Army, to which the Nizam replied that the proposal was impracticable and there was no question of inviting the Indian Army. The choice was now narrowing down in favour of intervention. But Nehru still vacillated as described in Menon's note of September 8.

"The States Ministry pressed their view that we should occupy Hyderabad and put a stop to the chaos there. The Prime Minister was strongly opposed and was very critical of the attitude of the States Ministry. The Sardar left the meeting in the middle. The same afternoon the Governor General called in his room a meeting of the Prime Minister, Sardar Patel and myself".

The next day, the Cabinet Defence Committee decided that the border be crossed on 13th September, 1947, under the command of Lt. Gen. Rajendra Sinhji, GOC-in-C Southern Command, and an ultimatum was sent to the Nizam on September 10 declaring that further inaction by the Nizam would "force the Government of India to act on their initiative". The same night Jinnah died in Karachi. On the night of 12th September, K.M. Munshi rang up to say that he was about to be imprisoned by the Nizam, to which Patel's prompt reply was "We will intern their Agent General here" and further, "But you will lose the chance of martyrdom if they intern you".

That was a piece of joke that showed that the Sardar could retain his mental equanimity even in a crisis situation. After the exchange of a number of telegrams, aptly described by him as "a war of telegrams", Patel asked the Governor General to send a two line reply to the Nizam saying "Repeated denials cannot alter facts. I have nothing to add". But Nehru and C.R. wanted a longer communication stressing India's desire for peace before sending the troops. Patel having seen the text at 7.30 P.M. on 12th September expressed his disapproval and sent H.M. Patel and Menon to Rajaji at 10 P.M.

who debated with the Governor General for nearly three hours to work out the draft. But finally Patel's efforts bore fruits. The telegram was signed and the troops ordered to move before the Nizam changed his stand. `Operation Polo' the code name for the Hyderabad `Police Action' started to move before first light of 13th September inspite of General Bucher's last minute appeal for postponement. He feared that the State had acquired big aircraft possibly bombers. But the die was cast, thanks to Patel's levelheadedness and firmness of resolve. The 1st Armoured Division advanced along Sholapur-Hyderabad axis covering 186 miles; other units converged from the east along Bezwada-Hyderabad axis covering 160 miles, while minor skirmishes took place at a number of points on the border to cause confusion regarding the main blow. Everything was over by the evening of 17th. This was a tame-end to the bluster and threats of the Nizam. While it surprised Nehru, Vallabhbhai Patel merely heaved a sigh of relief when he found that Muslims in other parts of the country solidly supported his action. Patel wrote to Suhrawardy, "the Indian Union Muslims have come out in the open on our side and that has certainly created a good impression".

Now we come to Nehru's mishandling of the election of the first President of the Republic. This is apiece with his other infirmities, lack of organizational acumen and an autocratic insistence on laying the law.

In spite of his personal preference, Patel if approached by Nehru directly would have helped the election of Rajagopalachari, and if Nehru and Patel together had requested him, Prasad might have agreed to quit the contest. But Nehru's impatience and arrogance made it easy for Satyanarayan Sinha, the Government Chiefwhip, to prevent a satisfactory solution. Nehru insisted on an agreement regarding C.R.'s election in early October 1949 before his foreign visit. However Patel was not accessible, staying in Bombay for most of September seeking medical advice. Sinha who rooted for Prasad's election informed Nehru on 10th September that the general opinion was that it will not be possible for the PM to get Rajaji elected without the help of the Sardar. If Jawaharlal had shown the least amount of courtesy towards Patel and telephoned him of Sinha's facts, he would have easily obtained the Sardar's support without loss of face. But Nehru was not the man to accept his weakness in the organisation. He rode roughshod and wrote to Prasad, "I am told that rumours are afloat and some members of the C.A. are more or less canvassing. I feel this must be ended". And though he had not kept Patel into the picture for the last three months, he had the gumption to mention to Prasad that:

"I have discussed this matter with Vallabhbhai and we felt that the safest and best course was to allow present arrangements to continue . . .that is that Rajaji might continue as President . . .of course you would be a very welcome choice as president but that would involve a change and consequent rearrangements . . .I hope you agree. In this matter it would of course be fitting for you to suggest this, rather than for any other person".

Prasad, however, refused to yield to Nehru, writing back, "I am required to accept and act upon a decision which has been taken without even the courtesy of consultation, although it concerned me intimately. I am deprived of the chance of flattering myself with the thought that I have not been judged by you and rejected". He added that he was resigning from the Assembly, "and make myself free to carry out the decision that which you have taken" and ended up by saying that he should not be blamed for nursing the thought that he "deserved a more decent exit".

Taking diametrically opposite positions on the issue both now turned to the Sardar—Nehru for help and Prasad for justice. Nehru's entreaty to the Sardar, "it is for you to deal with the situation now" came a bit too late. Nehru admitted that his letter of 10th September

1949 to Prasad had been sent "without any reference to Vallabhbhai or consultation with him". Not only was he was brazen enough not even to offer a word of apology to Patel, but was presumptuous in taking Patel for granted, while misinforming Prasad at the same time. In the event Patel had no choice but to allow Prasad to do what he thought fit. On his return to Delhi at September end, Nehru requested Patel to convene a meeting of the Congress Parliamentary Party to seek the M.Ps' support for his stand in the election of C. Rajagopalachari. Patel had already warned Nehru that the M.Ps would not respect his wishes. The meeting was held on 5th October evening, a day before Nehru was due to fly to London. Nehru proposed Rajaji's name, but was repeatedly heckled and opposed by the M.Ps. Almost helpless he now looked to Patel for support. But the Sardar kept his counsels to himself and allowed the democratic process to proceed. One M.P. after another denounced the proposal to instal Rajaji in preference to Rajendra Prasad. It was ultimately Patel's large heartedness that he chastised some M.Ps. for using harsh words for Nehru and succeeded in deferring the matter till Nehru's return.

True to his form, Nehru again informed Patel in a hand-written note that since his leadership had been questioned, he would resign on return from London, and inform the Governor General to assume the Premiership. Patel, however, rejected the offer for what it was worth. He had amply demonstrated to Nehru that he should not lay down the law and take the democratic process for a ride. But he was noble enough to ask Nehru to forget all thoughts of resigning and carry out his visit to U.K. and U.S.A in good heart. Nehru tamely accepted this advice and did not speak of resigning after his return to Delhi. But he did not stop the mischief that he had already unleashed for sabotaging Prasad's election. He went to the extent of offering him the chairmanship of the Planning Commission. But Prasad was in no mood to oblige. Rejecting Nehru's offer, Prasad told him that his well-wishers would read his withdrawal as a surrender to "dictation" and a "betrayal". Seeing no possibility of success, C.R. finally abdicated in favour of Rajendra Prasad. Rajaji fully realised the nuances of the situation and Nehru's hamhandedness caused by Sinha's ill-advised action. But he did not bear any harsh feelings against Patel. His parting words before leaving Delhi were that the Sardar commanded "universal confidence" and embraced Patel openly before his departure for Madras on 27th January, 1950. Prasad, who along with his wife and sister, had called on Patel's residence at 1, Aurangzeb Road in the early morning of January 26, went with Patel and Maniben to Rajghat and later the same day, after the Republic was proclaimed, he was sworn in as the first President of the new-born Republic. Patel, the wise, had won a signal victory against Nehru, the impatient. But the age factor was to work in the reverse order. Patel had crossed 74 and was unwell, while Jawaharlal was robust and a mere 60.

Just as Nehru played a devious game on the election of Rajendra Prasad , he was to repeat this performance in the case of Purushottam Das Tandon, a stalwart of freedom fighter from the Hindi heartland.

Nehru's vanity and the mindset that could make him less than fair inspite of lofty posturing is revealed by his actions during the run upto the election of the Congress President in end 1950.

A successor to Pattabhi, the Congress president for the last 18 months, was to be chosen and the U.P. Congressmen strongly felt that Purushottam Das Tandon should stand again. Another candidate was Shankarrao Deo. There were preliminary parleys between Patel and Nehru in this regard in Dehra Dun on 5th July. Nehru while affecting his love for Tandon did not really wish him back. He considered him to be a Hindi enthusiast and too strong to be reined in. Unfortunately in Nehru's eyes Tandon was "a symbol of communal and revivalist outlook". He did not particularly appreciate his view on the problems related to the refugees. He also did not think very high of Shankarrao Deo for his advocacy of linguistic provinces and his insistence on a large Marathi-speaking State. While Nehru did not like either Tandon or Deo, both he and Patel did not feel comfortable with Kripalani either, the other possible candidate, who had been the Congress President in 1946-47. The other probable H.C. Mookerjee, a Bengali Christian and an unknown entity, was also not considered suitable. C.R. who had just joined the Interim Cabinet proposed to Nehru that the Sardar himself should take over. But Patel was adamant that the proposal should come from Nehru himself. Nehru somehow did not agree, and the Sardar let the matters rest there. All of a sudden on 2nd August, Nehru called on Patel and suggested Rajaji's name. Patel concurred saying that, "he is entitled to it", and remembering that he had never been a Congress President, he also said that, "I will speak to him, but I do not think he will agree". As things turned out, Patel was right. Rajaji did not agree. After many confabulations Tandon's name seemed to emerge as an acceptable candidate. Pant also pitched for Tandon. But there were other rumours now spread by Rafi Ahmad Kidwai and Mridula Sarabhai that Nehru himself might accept the chair. Patel gave a no objection certificate to this proposal and said as much to Azad "if he wants to become President, I will propose him and you and Rajaji will second him". Nehru now played foul and plotted against Tandon. He convened a meeting of some selected members of the working committee who were known Tandon baiters and expressed his views against his candidature. Patel was a notable absentee. It would have been much better if Nehru had consulted Patel and decided on a consensus candidate. But Nehru, the ever proud prima donna never considered the idea. He also wrote to Tandon conveying that "your election would mean great encouragement to certain forces in India which I consider harmful". Detailed correspondence on this issue and the chronology of this murky drama is given in a separate chapter "The Tandon Episode".

Prasad, the President of the Republic, had earlier set a precedent by refusing to vacate his chair and Tandon in a similar manner feeling that he was elder to Nehru and knew him for almost 50 years, refused to withdraw from the contest. His reply to Nehru as shall be brought out in a subsequent chapter, was correct, well reasoned and dignified. Tandon added:

"While you and I have agreed on and worked together on many vital problems, there have been some matters on which we have not seen eye to eye—the adoption of Hindi as the national language and the partition of the country being the chief among them.

"I assure you that the bitterest language you may employ against me will not succeed in making me bitter or abate my personal affection for you. I have loved you all these years as a younger brother, though my feeling is unobtrusive".

Patel was deeply affected by Tandon's letter while Jawaharlal, despite Tandon's candour made a public statement that, "it would not be proper for Tandon to accept the party presidentship, as long as I am Prime Minister", expressing the hope that "all decisions will be taken in consonance with the organisation's "old approach to political, communal and other problems". Without mentioning the name Nehru let it be known that he hoped for Tandon's defeat. There were many in the Congress who did not share Nehru's dislike for Tandon nor his hope that he would lose. Tandon had a strong following in the highly populated Hindi provinces and his integrity was above reproach. Knowing that Deo had not the slightest chance of humbling Tandon, Rafi, Nehru's adviser, counselled him to support Kripalani. All this while Patel was kept totally in dark of the developments, but when he came to know about it, he mentioned to C.R. that 'I have been shaken to the bones" and speaking of Nehru he said "how low he has stooped. I had better go to my Ashram". Rajaji similarly felt cheated that Nehru had kept his final choice of Kripalani "a secret from me". Patel and Rajaji however did not forget to remind Nehru that Kripalani's attacks on Nehru's views on Hindu-Muslim relations and the refugee problems were even more scathing than those of Tandon. But Nehru's mind was made.

Patel had ignored many slights in the past at the hands of Nehru, who had been lately showing critical interest in the day to day affairs of the Home and the States Ministry. Nehru now worked single-mindedly for Tandon's defeat, something that Patel did not relish . While Nehru and his coterie rooted for Kripalani, events took their own course. To all Congressmen it was clear that the Tandon-Kripalani contest was a mini show of the greater act, the Patel and Nehru duel. Kidwai, Nehru's henchman, and Mridula succeeded in convincing Deo to quit in favour of Kripalani. But the Congressmen from Maharashtra were not so amenable. Sensing the defeat of his candidate, Nehru now informed Patel on August 25 that Tandon's election would amount to a vote of no-confidence in him, threatening that in that event he would neither stay in the working committee nor in the Prime Ministerial chair. At this belated stage Patel did not have the heart to ask Tandon to quit, nor could he force the Congressmen to go against their conscience, just to defeat Tandon. But he did what he could. He entreated Nehru not to treat this affair as a prestige issue. In his heart he was certain that Nehru would not resign and mentioned as much to C.R. To Nehru he said, "I have known you for 30 years but I have not been able to enter your heart". The rest is history. In the polling on August 29, carried out at 24 locations, Tandon emerged as victor, polling 1306 votes against Kripalani's 1029 and Deo's 202. To add insult to injury, Tandon had won with a decisive majority in

Nehru's home province of Uttar Pradesh. Later Patel asked C.R. after the results, "have you brought Jawaharlal's resignation?" Patel did not expect it. Nehru as usual had changed his mind.

Mention has already been made of Nehru's election tours and speeches in the run up to the 1937 Provincial Assembly elections. Nehru had tasted blood. Mass adulation was the elixir of his life, but after Independence he had lost the moral high ground that he had occupied during the freedom struggle. The Congress had lost its vigour to serve and sacrifice. It was a party for power. Against Mahatma Gandhi's advice to Congressmen to disband the Congress and convert it into a Seva Dal to serve the poor and the down-trodden, the charm of power proved too strong to resist. Public disenchantment was not long in coming. But Nehru during his election tours, harped on old sacrifices and Congress legacy; the same way as his present successors do.

The themes of his election speeches in 1951 were more or less a replay of those of 1937. He dealt mostly with generalities incomprehensible to the masses and never once touched on the merit of the local candidate. The vote was sought in the name of Congress, the party in the vanguard of the national liberation movement. He never even once mentioned the rot that had started eating up into the vitals of this organisation. Like a gramophone needle stuck in a groove he kept on repeating the Congress sacrifice and asking vote for Congress. Confident of his mass appeal, Nehru played upon public sentiments and the strategy worked. It was a confidence trick played on the masses who trusted him sincerely. The campaign was a mockery of democracy which despite strong political overtones boiled down to the choice for or against Congress. The other parties i.e. the Socialists, the Communists, and the Kisan Majdoor Praja Party with the latest addition of Jan Sangh under Syama Prasad Mookerjee with enough ammunition did attack Congress on its dismal performance in the past, but they were never sure of replacing Congress. Time after time, Congress swept back to power, not on the vote of the intelligentsia but the gullible and the illiterates and always with a minority of the total votes cast. In spite of Congress winning almost everywhere more than half the electorate showed their disenchantment with the Congress. In view of this Nehru became even more indispensable to the Congress than ever before.

Just as Nehru had stepped into the British shoes soon after independence as shown in the opening lines of this chapter he carried his convictions on the composite Indian culture with even greater vehemence. There were many raised eyebrows among his Hindu cultural enthusiasts such as Dr. K.M. Munshi, Dr. Prasad and Purushottam Das Tandon. Even during discussions in the Constituent Assembly, Nehru's skewed approach on Indian culture was much in evidence. He had in his book, 'The Discovery of India' spoken of a composite Indian culture and the benign influence of the Muslim conquest on the Indian civilization. But here he propounded an astonishing new concept of our composite culture with strong influence of Islam and Muslim culture. A later day Muslim scholar, Prof. Mushirul Hassan, Pro Vice-Chancellor of Jamia Milia Islamia University, pronounced what had been evident to perceptive observers of the world history much earlier; that there is nothing like a Muslim culture. There are many Islamic countries but their cultures are so widely different from each other. The Saudi Arabian culture is entirely different from the Malaysian and the Indonesian. It is diametrically opposed to the Persian culture and has nothing in common with the Turkish. A culture is an emotional organism, born in the soil of the land and nurtured through centuries of growth and mutation. It draws its sustenance from the soil of that land. Nehru's avid advocacy of a Muslim culture was not only out of place but totally misconceived. It was only due to his pre-eminence in the Congress that had led to the unhappy provisions of Section 29 in our

Constitution. It was a beginning of the irrational and mischievous appeasement of the minorities. This section related basically to matters of education but Nehru gave it a cultural twist.

Each nation has its own culture as had been repeatedly pronounced in the Constituent Assembly. It is an irony that a stalwart like Dr. Rajendra Prasad, the Chairman of the Constituent Assembly and a profound student of Indian culture, was outvoted and outmaneuvered by Nehru and the Drafting Committee Chairman, Dr. B.R. Ambedkar, a persistent antagonist of the Congress-led freedom struggle, who had his own score to settle against Hindu nationalism!

6 Nehru as a Prime Minister

The Leader

Before independence, our leaders talked of freedom struggle as the struggle against our oppressors. There was the passion of a fighter, the clarion call of a crusader in their nationalistic rhetoric. After independence, all this had to change. Serious affairs of state had to be attended to, intractable problems demanded immediate and permanent solutions. This required shift of emphasis from words to deeds, from rhetoric to cool calculations. Schooled as Nehru and his colleagues were in the art of rabble rousing, they found themselves ill at ease with long hours of silent work; a sine qua non of serious effort at nation building. Nehru undoubtedly worked extra hours in the office to do justice to the testing task of national revival. But the lure of the fawning masses was too strong to resist. He developed the habit of addressing masses, attending functions, opening ceremonies and holding forth on almost any subject under the sun. This was not necessary. This time could have been more usefully devoted to serious task of national reconstruction. Mention of this has been made earlier. A leader is known by his deeds not words. Nehru led the path and his pack of followers outdid him. If one can calculate the total time spent by our leaders till today on unnecessary verbiage, it would run into aeons of man-hours. What a loss to the nation where words substitute deeds! This national trait had its genesis in Nehru's leadership. I vividly remember how we used to yearn to catch a glimpse or hear a word of Mahatma Gandhi or Sardar Patel. But Nehru was so easy to hear and so much to see. If only he could remember the wise words of Henry Ford, "You can't build your reputation on what you are going to do." And just sample the range of subjects our know-all Ministers can cover, from literacy drive to the profundities of literature, religion and philosophy, from agriculture to astronomy, from Ayurveda to aesthetics, from abstract art to architecture and archeology, from existentialism to economy, population control to potato harvesting, green to grey revolution; you name it and the pompous politician has the last word on it . Some mention of this had been made earlier, but the subject bears repetition. No function is complete without the presence of a Minister, even marriage and mundan ceremonies are not missed by these ubiquitous public servants. I remember two convocation addresses, one at Allahabad University in 1947 and the other at Delhi University in 1950. The latter was also attended by Mrs. Sukarno. A mention of this has been made earlier. Another one at Allahabad University addressed by Pandit G.B. Pant, was even worse, though, he meant well but what he said was nothing short of an insult to the intelligence of a premier educational institution like the hallowed Allahabad University. It was known then as Cambridge, Oxford or Harvard of the East. This august institution was known for inviting only the most distinguished intellectuals to its campus. We in India seem to have different priorities from the Western institutions. No wonder there is so much of politics in our blood. As a result the present day universities are a fertile breeding ground for quick fix *netas* rather than institutions for producing cultured and well rounded human beings. This trend of the politician among the academics like the proverbial cat among the pigeons was started, though inadvertently, by no less a person than Pandit Jawaharlal Nehru, our first Prime Minister.

Nehru's defenders often argue that he drew extra energy from the masses and drew sustenance and strength to carry out the onerous tasks of the state. Adulating crowds acted as a tonic on him. During my recent visit to the United States, I studied the life of all American Presidents in chronological order and their rating according to the 1982 historical census. The basis of this assessment was their popularity and performance. The best, the greatest and the most popular President of America, Abraham Lincoln had no pretensions to outward charm. People laughed at his ungainly sight and he was plagued by self-doubts during the critical years of Civil War when the Federal Armies were losing, one battle after another. He was the loneliest of men. Yet he retained his inner strength and steadfastness of purpose. He did not need the tonic of mass adulation.

As has been pointed out earlier, in just four years he achieved what no American President had been able to do. He abolished slavery and made a nation out of warring states. The spirit of Lincoln still inspires America. Great men are known to have inner strength. A leader who can perform well only under the mass cheering is as good as a gladiator in the arena or a cricket player amidst a friendly crowd. Greatness is based on more solid foundations than ephemeral and transient public applause.

Undoubtedly, Nehru derived sustenance and strength from the applauding crowd. However, it flies in the face of medical evidence. It is a moot point whether his 17 hours schedule in office tired him. He was certainly bleary eyed at times. In any case the chief executive of a nation does not have to slave it out for 17 hours. There is something called delegation and management by exception. In his early years in office, Nehru had a bounce in his gait and he is said to have been taking two steps at a time, founding the stairs, two at a time to his office. But later after the Chinese disaster, he was a different man. He grew weak. He could not stand just one political upset. One can only conclude from this how shallow must have been the reservoir from which he could draw his inner strength

After the humiliating defeat in the China war and his first major political reverse, Nehru was never the same man. His shoulders stooped and he suffered his first stroke at Bhubaneshwar. Compare this with Winston Churchil. Every war reverse steeled his bulldog determination to fight. Even the disaster at Dunkirk was turned into an opportunity by the British Prime Minister leading to his famous 'on the beaches' speech. Lincoln never despaired till he found the right general in U.S. Grant, who could defeat the Confederate forces. Nehru just could not stand one Chinese debacle. May be with the Chinese disaster everything that Nehru cherished and stood for went up in smoke. But if he had possessed resilience of character he would have certainly recovered, and though not in keeping with his character trait if he had the humility to accept mistakes and apply correctives for the future, things would have been different. But unfortunately Nehru was not in the habit of acknowledging his mistakes and seldom thought of mid-course corrections. His socialism, foreign policy, economic planning and plan priorities cried out loud for drastic corrections but Nehru, cocky as always, impatient of dissent and impervious to contrary advice persevered in his endeavours regardless. He had 'many miles to go' as he never failed to repeat to himself the famous lines from Robert Frost and he did cover many miles before eternal sleep overtook him. But the mileage covered was in the wrong direction and the sum total of advance to progress was inevitably small indeed. History is a harsh judge. But that is the unvarnished truth that we the nation shall have to live with.

Indo-Pak relations worsened after the partition and our tolerant policy towards Indian Muslims was not reciprocated by Pakistan against Hindus living in East and West Pakistan. Nehru always chided the Hindu for being chauvinistic in his approach against the timid minority as he considered the local Muslims. His bias speaks in a letter dated 30th June, 1950, to Patel where he blames even S.P. Mookerjee. He bemoans:

"I am far from happy about the situation in Bengal. While it is perfectly true that conditions in East Bengal are still abnormal and many incidents continue to occur there, the attitude of the East Bengal Government, from all accounts that we get, is fairly good and they appear to be in earnest to implement the pact. The general impression on foreign as well as our observers has been that the chief culprit at the present moment is the Calcutta Press as well as Syama Prasad Mookerjee. The Pakistan Press, more especially the West Pakistan Press, has behaved well. Recently some kind of a goodwill mission went to Western Pakistan and they had a wonderful reception wherever they went. They addressed vast gatherings all over Punjab and Sind. On our side, when Malik and Biswas went to Agartala, Malik was shouted down. Shankarrao Deo was also shouted down in Calcutta. All this makes foreign observers here think that the chief trouble is caused by some of our Press and by the Hindu Mahasabha propaganda. The Delhi Hindi and Urdu Press also continues to be very bad."

The Sardar who had a more balanced and sober view of matter replied, "In your letter of 29 June, you have referred to the satisfactory attitude of East Bengal Government. That attitude is of course matched by the equally satisfactory attitude of the West Bengal Government. The whole question is one of the attitude of the people. In that respect, I make bold to say that barring a few exceptions on our side— and I admit there are some big exceptions individually—our people have given and are giving the pact a fair trial, probably fairer than in East Bengal. We have been getting daily reports of incidents on the other side of the frontier. In the atmosphere which prevailed whether in East or West Bengal, we cannot afford to ignore even minor incidents which have the consequence of creating a vague sense of insecurity, fear or alarm. When people have lost their nerves, even small incidents acquire tremendous significance. I do not know whether you have read a letter from one Afgsaruddin Ahmed dated 10 June 1950. A copy was circulated by the DIB to Dharma Vira on 29 June 1950. That letter contains a survey of conditions both before and after the pact by a Muslim and can be taken to be fairly authentic. It confirms the many intelligence reports which we have been getting and also indicated that a great deal requires to be done in East Bengal before the general mentality of the people can approach that of ours in West Bengal. Unless this is done, any amount of goodwill and good intentions at the top in East Bengal is not likely to yield effective results." And again reassured Nehru saying:

"I share your anxiety about the situation in Bengal. At the same time, I do feel that a realization is growing that the pact is the last chance of securing a peaceful settlement of the whole matter. From what Diwakar tells me, it appears that the Bengal Press, particularly Suresh Majumdar and Tushar Kanti Ghosh, have now become converted to this view and mean to implement the Press code. It will be their headache to deal with Syama Prasad Mookerjee's utterances in accordance with that code. If they do not deal with them, we can then take them to task. I find no legal powers to deal with either Press or men like Syama Prasad Mookerjee. Before you left for Indonesia, I drew your attention to the Supreme Court decision in *Cross Roads* and *Organiser* cases. That knocks the bottom out of most of our penal laws for the control and regulation of the Press. The views which they have expressed in that judgment on the question of sedition make it doubtful whether we can do anything not only about the speeches of Syama Prasad Mookerjee but also those of the more extremist type. As you say, we have involved ourselves in so many legal and constitutional difficulties that we do not know how to overcome them. I sounded a note of warning and caution when these provisions were being debated in the Drafting Committee, but then we were led away by our idealistic exuberance." Patel a realist could be more balanced in stating that it takes two to do the tango"

Then on the Korean Invasion, the impulsive Nehru made a case which was not only defensive of a Communist country's aggression against its non-communist neighbour but was uncalled for. Patel wrote to Nehru on 3rd July, 1950.

"I have seen the statement on Korea. While it is satisfactory in its support of the UNO's recommendation, I feel that we need not have reiterated our foreign policy. Such reiteration implies that this step could be construed as a departure from that policy and we were being apologetic or on the defensive about it. After all, the step which we have taken fits in with our policy of supporting the UNO and invoking the various remedies mentioned in the Charter against aggression. Once we felt, as we did in the case of Korea, that an aggression had taken place, I do not think we can set any limits to our action to resist that aggression. We have to exhaust all the means laid down in the Charter. The question merely would be one of timing and effectiveness. When actual armed aggression takes place, it is doubtful whether negotiations and mediation alone can secure the objective of peace. Negotiations and mediation can avail us only if there is a cessation of hostilities. Otherwise we cannot match words against arms."

Nehru by nature impulsive and less than steadfast never really came to appreciate the Sardar's firmness and incisiveness of thoughts, which he mistook for rigidity and a fascist streak. Though he did not himself articulate these thoughts, he allowed his cronies to bandy these about. He also had a weakness for listening to tale carriers and interested rumour, often lacking veracity. Deep down in his heart, even though he was handed down the spectre of the realm by no less a person than

Gandhiji, he always looked upon Patel as a possible contender for power, little realising that old Patel had no such ambitions. In consequence, the tale carriers warmed upto their task with gusto and created many avoidable differences between the two. It was always Nehru who complained and it was always left to Patel to reassure him and remove the misunderstandings. Being elder to Nehru, the heir to the throne, but sworn by Mahatma to be loyal to him, Patel swallowed many a bitter pill. But he never wavered in his duty as a loyal lieutenant to the Prime Minister. To another such complaint after Bapu's death, Patel replied:

"My dear Jawaharlal,

Your letter of 26 March 1950 has surprised and distressed me greatly. From your letter it appears you have carried a weight of mental anguish and a burden and mental worry which, having regard to the relations which have existed between us, I would have expected you to unburden on me not only during the several meetings we have had but also, if necessary, at any special meeting which I would have been only too ready to have had. In fact I feel personally pained and hurt that you should not have thought me to be deserving of such confidence and should have permitted yourself to be upset by what obviously interested and malevolently disposed persons have been telling you or others and propagating with obviously a mischievous design.

"What you write about the unfortunate developments which preceded Bapu's death brings vividly to my mind the whole picture. But one thing in that stands out most prominently and it is the last conversation which I had with him and in which he expressed his considered opinion that both you and I should continue to collaborate in service of the country since the consequences of any separation would be disastrous to its interests. I have striven to my utmost to execute these last words of Bapu. I have according to my lights striven to strengthen your hands as much as I could, while giving expression to my views frankly and sincerely. I have given you my loyal support, often at times subjecting myself to considerable self-restraint. I cannot recall any time during the last two years when I have asserted myself against any determined course of policy which you have adumbrated. We have differed on some matters but have recognised that such differences were natural and have adjusted ourselves in order to evolve an agreed policy. It has, therefore, grieved me greatly to feel that I have been found by you wanting in the execution of Bapu's last message.

"This also brings me to the tragic developments which preceded Bapu's death. I warned him and you then of the terrible consequences that I apprehended of the developing serious situation. Unfortunately the tragedy could not be averted and [it] engulfed us. Certain persons even then interested themselves in creating an estrangement between both of us. They tried to poison your ears as well as Bapu's against me. After Bapu's death you wrote to me an affectionate and touching letter which I have prized all along and we resolved to devote ourselves jointly to the cause of our country. It appears that some persons have again found in the present troubled atmosphere and your own troubled state of mind an easy opportunity of creating an atmosphere of doubts, misgivings and conflicts . I am really sorry and distressed that you should have listened to their accounts and given credence to them without asking me even once for the authentic version. It is not, however, that aspect which bothers me so much as the parallel with the tragic situation which preceded Bapu's martyrdom. My mind is full of apprehensions about the end and consequence of it all, considering the highly emotional and explosive temperament of Bengalees and the surcharged atmosphere all over the country, affecting not only the towns but the villages which fortunately had been immune from the pernicious malady. I sometimes have the feeling that we are on the verge of a tragedy which might still be averted if we could act in time."

As Nehru proceeded in his tenure as a Prime Minister, he became increasingly intolerant and irascible. This trait was more visible in his treatment of small people in pubic. It is said that 'great men are known by the way they treat small people.' As is the practice today even in those days leaders with a VVIP status had to be kept away from the common crowds and a thorough police bandobast had to be organised. Although, there was no immediate threat to Nehru's security, his immense popularity ensured that, the police and the administration could take no chances. Nehru had a habit of changing at will his pre-arranged route or landing place, to meet the waiting masses and the police as part of their duty had to do their best to prevent the crowd from coming too close. This often infuriated Nehru. During one of his visits to Patna after he became the Prime Minister, he literally shouted at a policeman and stripping off one of his stripe badges in anger exclaimed:

"Yeh Lal Feete Wale Yahan Kya Kar Rahe Hain? Inhe Yahan Se hatao." (What are these red striped fellows doing here? Get them out of here.)

At another time in a similar outburst he shouted:

"Kis Bewaqoof ne Tumhe Lal Topi pahna diya?" (Which fool has given you this red cap?) Those days the police constables use to wear red turbans.

Mention has been made earlier regarding courtesy and humility in great people. Thomas Jefferson, one of the five most highly rated Presidents of America, was known as much for his modesty as for his versatility and tremendous mental abilities. An anecdote regarding his good breeding often talked about in the elite circles in Europe runs somewhat like this. When asked by the French Minister, soon after his arrival to Paris to relieve Benjamin Franklin, one of America's most popular representatives, "You replace Dr. Franklin, I hear."

Jefferson gave the felicitous reply,

"I succeed him; no man can replace him."

Contrast this with the irascibility and contumely displayed by Nehru in the Parliament and even outside. I always took Chou-En-lie's remarks about Nehru's arrogance with a pinch of salt. But in the light of my personal observations and facts recorded by others one has to just accept the substance in Chou-En-lie's statement.

Contrary to popular perception it was Patel, who was the patron saint of the Indian Civil Services and not Nehru who wanted to disband the whole lot. While Nehru wanted a pliant bureaucracy Patel insisted on a firm and independent one. He once remarked that a bureaucrat who is "Yes Man" is of no use to him. Once when needled by some Congress ministers who criticised the Civil Services, he remarked that these people were selected through an all India competition entirely on merit and on hard work. Even if they were dismissed from service, they would most certainly find a job anywhere. But he told the ministers that if they were dismissed, they would remain unemployed for the rest of their life. However, Nehru persisted in his distaste of the Indian Administrative Service.

Thus devaluation and humiliation of public servants had started in the time of Nehru, Patel, the father guardian, had left, the scene.

Another instance of Nehru's fiery temper was in evidence during one of his visits to the United States as described by one of the pilots of his aircraft. These two young pilots having parked Nehru's private plane at the parking lot at the New York airfield thought that they would not be needed for some time and as youth is impatient decided to go for a bit of shopping in the Manhattan streets of New York. Unfortunately, the unforeseen happened and Nehru suddenly realised that he wanted his shaving kit and to his dismay found that the box containing the kit had been locked and the keys were with the pilots who were not immediately available. Now Nehru hit the roof and raved and ranted on whosoever was available at hand. Members of his entourage tried to pacify him and offered him a different shaving kit. But Nehru was not the man to be soothed so easily. He demanded nothing but his own shaving kit. Even a new one was not acceptable. So he waited till the truant pilots returned to base cowering in their pants at the likely displeasure of the VVIP and certainly Nehru spared no words to chastise them. This was Nehru, the angry old man. Contrast this with the case of Lal Bahadur Shastri, the next Prime Minister. During 1965 operations against Pakistan at a forward airfield on the western front he accommodated, out of turn, a junior ground engineer officer of the Indian Air Force for a lift to Delhi to meet the latter's rather impetuous request to see his ailing wife. Shastri not only allowed him to travel without demur but had the courtesy to get up from his seat and ask this young officer about the health of his wife. Could there be a better example of humility in a Prime Minister? And Shastri was Nehru's successor and his chosen lieutenant.

On Nehru's burst of anger on people who could not retaliate, one has to recall Aristotle's famous words: "Anyone can become angry—that is easy, but to be angry with the right person, to the right degree, at the right time, for the right purpose, and in the right way—this is not easy".

Foreign Policy

Much before the dawn of independence and during the thick of the freedom struggle, blessed by Gandhiji and spurred by his own ambition, Nehru had mapped out a pre-eminent role for himself on the international scene. A Harrow boy with an exposure to international affairs, Nehru was also the obvious choice among many Congressmen of his genre to handle foreign affairs portfolio. Understandably, Nehru's self-portrayal of an international leader had all the colours and shades of Nehru, the man. Consequently, Nehru's foreign policy more than any other facet of our polity bore the imprint of the man. As a nascent republic emerging from the shadow of a colonial rule, an urge for independent status recognisable in real terms was but natural. Many years of struggle for freedom against a western power had led, as its natural consequence, to a desire to stay away from any tutelage or even a closer link to Western bloc. His admiration for Lenin and Soviet Russia only re-inforced this anti-West colonial stance. By then he had not realised, as he was to do later in 1962 that Communist countries could also wage wars of expansion and commit aggression the same way as Western colonial powers did. If he had studied Stalin's brand of nationalistic socialism carefully, the occupation after World War II of East European countries by an oppressive communist regime, he would have been warned well before it was too late. Between the two power blocs led by U.S.A. and U.S.S.R., he envisaged a role of an honest broker to bring the two together to some form of co-existence and understanding. This put paid to his desire to stride as a colossus on the international scene, courted by both the blocs, while holding a position of power out of all proportion to our national strength. He, however, overlooked the vital fact that a country lacking inherent economic and military power is ill-suited to play this role effectively. As a result, devoid of inherent strength on the home ground, his posture of peace and non-alignment turned out to be a mere exercise in demagogy. Attempting to please both the world powers, he fell between the two stools and got the worst of both the worlds. His attempt to position himself at a place of pre-eminence in international politics, largely on the strength of his idealism, served only a limited purpose. He did succeed to a degree at least in catching the imagination of the newly liberated nations by promising them a place in the sun. But such recognition was more a matter of media hype than a substantive acceptance of his role on important world issues. Here the old cold war equations ruled the roost. America, Russia and China went their own way and the backward countries made lofty gestures of world equality, only to be snubbed by powerful countries. Any help or aid that trickled to the developing countries was more a result of long term self-interest from the rich countries rather than any philanthropic concern for the weak, the underprivileged and the poor. The scenario persists even today.

Undoubtedly, some of the fundamentals of Nehru's foreign policy were sound and rightly dictated by the determinants of geography, history, an equitable social order and the alleviation of poverty. India's size, too, predicated its pre-eminence in the South Asian landmass. Other inputs for his foreign policy were anti-racialism, anti-colonialism and the desire to conserve scarce resources for development, rather than an arms build up, a natural corollary to any military alliance. These premises were unobjectionable. But there is much more to a nation's foreign policy than pious exhortations, and that is the realm of real politic. It was in this role of the self-appointed conscience keeper of the world that his foreign policy found itself strapped and it became synonymous with Nehru the man.

Coming back to Nehru, as confessed by himself later, the Russians initially called him "The Running Dog of Imperialism" while the Western powers dubbed his non-alignment phoney and viewed his credentials as a non-communist almost suspect. In his own words:

"We have sought to avoid foreign entanglements by not joining one ideological bloc or the other. The natural result has been that neither the Russians nor the Americans look on us with favour. Nevertheless, we intend cooperating with the United States of America and we intend cooperating, fully, with the Soviet Union."

Note the slant of "cooperating fully" with Soviet Union and just `cooperating' with United States of America. Can one really blame the Americans for considering Nehru's non-alignment less than genuine.

Nehru's experience was totally coloured by his aversion

to colonialism. His assumption regarding the whiteman's arrogance needed no justification. But this did not necessarily lead to the facile conclusion that his own judgement as a non-white was always to be superior to that of the whiteman. Nehru was firm in his belief that he was not to be dictated to by other countries howsoever powerful they may be.

While this assumption was incontrovertible in itself, Nehru was as arrogant as any Western diplomat and he was firm in his view that his judgement, read India's judgement, was better than others. As arrogance got the better of him, his policy stand and pontifications became like 'Sermons from the Mount' delivered from his own chosen moral high ground. Most of these were aimed at the Western leaders. On the Cold War also his position tilted heavily towards Russia and he was hectoring in his tone where America was concerned. This slant in Nehru's thinking was based on a simple premise nurtured in the European socialistic school of thought of the early 20s and 30s of the British School led by Harold Laski, as mentioned earlier. From this background, a holier-than-thou attitude to the capitalist West was but the next step. His preference for the Soviet Union and disdain for the 'immature' American led him to grant considerable rope to Russia while being unduly critical of America and the West. To him the revolutionary 'Egalitarian Russia' was less culpable than the Imperialist West, especially of the pre-war variety. His silence on the brutal suppression of the Hungarian uprising by the Soviet tanks as opposed to his downright condemnation of the Anglo-French support to Israel in its 1956 offensive against Egypt spoke volumes about his skewed perception.

As early as 1953-54, when Chester Bowles was the US Ambassador in Delhi, Nehru had his own hang ups about America. His radical and shrill leftist rhetoric never allowed him to see anything worthwhile on improving relations with the second largest democracy in the world. US was willing to help but Nehru often adopted a recalcitrant attitude. Dr. Rajendra Prasad, the President of India, often reminded him about the frequent US goodwill gestures. Here is a sample quote from his talk with Chester Bowles which he sent to Nehru: Bowles says,

"America is an independent country and we might lack in something but we are large-hearted people and we love independence. We, therefore, feel bad when America is equated with China or Russia. When civil war was going on in China during the last two years, what happened there? In India, China is cited everywhere as an example. I do not think that a new country has emerged in China during these two years; if indeed a new country emerges in this way, India could also change in a period of five years. To say that China has become a paradise in two years means that India also should become paradise." Bowles further emphasised that the so-called differences between America and India are being gradually removed." Dr. Prasad goes on to say:

"I mentioned to him about the U.S. grant of Rs. 25 crores for development work in 15,000 villages in India. It is hoped that these villages will be developed but I have my fears. He asked why. I said that Rs. 24,000 will be spent on each village covered by the programme. Fifteen thousand out of India's five lakh villages will be thus developed. What about the remainder? How to develop them? If we can find a way to continue this work of development of villages, it will be a big thing. He answered that this will put a model before the people and they will be encouraged to help in such venture. If the experiment proves successful, it would be a great thing for Americans respect success. I said, even so we have no means with us to develop the whole country to that standard."

"At the party, the U.S. Ambassador, Mr. Chester Bowles, told that Mr. Louis Fischer had met him after he met Nehru. After some time, Mr. Louis Fischer also called on me. He said that Mr. Bowles had told him that the

U.S. Government would give a grant of US $ 150 million (Rs. 95 crores) to India for the same purpose of development of villages."

The synergy between Nehru's personal ambition to emerge as an international colossus and the shape of our foreign policy is too obvious to be missed or wished away as an accident of history. An independent status, a niche for himself in the world history, the role of a peace maker and a balancer of two opposite poles was what Nehru desired for himself and our foreign policy was to subbserve that vision and concept. That the role was devoid of much substance, which only great and powerful nations can provide did not bother him, but it suited Nehru's temperament admirably. Nehru the idealist, as usual, triumphed over Nehru, the realist. In sharp contrast, China liberated two years after our freedom, worked quietly on the home turf, improved their military might and became a force second only to the United States and Soviet Russia. Mao had stated that "Power flowed from the barrel of the gun" not from empty words. Admittedly, initially, our priority of development over defence was incontrovertible, but later it became a fetish and as described in a later chapter paved the way for the Chinese Debacle in 1962.

A hesitation to condemn communist aggression initially in South Korea, later in Tibet and much later in Hungary made Nehru's non-alignment a lame duck proposition. At the other level his proclivity to view events in the Middle East through the eyes of the Indian Muslims and his espousal of Pan Arabism which was informed by a blind hatred of Israel, put our foreign policy options into a tight straitjacket. Initially non-recognization, and later open hostility towards Israel, further antagonised the world Jewry and a large section of money bags and opinion makers in America, which became a source of strong anti-India bias in days to come. It is indeed strange that the United States led by President Roosevelt during the war years, who so avidly championed the cause of India's independence to Churchill, later turned lukewarm and finally unfriendly towards independent India. History is yet to pronounce its verdict on our pro-Soviet tilt ostensibly forced on us due to our total dependence on Soviet veto to save Kashmir for us, against the so-called American support to Pak stand on plebiscite or merger with that country. But the cost in terms of loss of American support in the last four decades that could have transformed our economic and military status for the better has been heavy. The acid test of the success of any foreign policy is the gains that accrue to a nation in the field of diplomacy, winning of true friends and economic and social benefits. We seem to have a rather poor record on these counts. Our espousal of Pan Arabism came a cropper when Pan Arabism itself died in Nasser's own lifetime. The shortlived merger of Egypt and Syria was a non-starter from the very beginning. Jordan and Saudi Arabia never favoured the supremacy of Egypt. The infanticide of the United Arab Republic, a preudonym for Egypt-Syria entente, the socialist victory in Iraq under Saddam Hussain, the resurgence of Shiite Iran and the subsequent dispute between Iraq and Kuwait put paid to the demolition of the myth of a monolithic Muslim Middle East as a significant player in world politics. Our love for our distant cousins in the Middle East did not give us any economic benefits. In fact, we were the worst hit in the first oil shock of 1973. To be fair to Nehru, he once did argue the futility of ignoring the existence of Israel, but he seems to have recanted later, and official records are silent on any change in our anti-Jew bias. True to the Nehru legacy, we constantly failed to recognize Israel and the Muslim nations took us for granted. The earlier rebuff at Rabat and then the open support to the cause of Kashmir separation by the Organisation of Islamic States (OIS) does not really go to the credit side of our one way pro-Muslim Middle East policy. Among the three world powers, we had an indifferent Russia during the China war and a hostile United States during the

Indo-Pak conflict of 1965. At this juncture, even our Russian friends brought pressure on Shastri at Tashkent to return all the conquered territories to Pakistan. During the 1971 Indo-Pak war United States was openly belligerent and China hostile, forcing Indira Gandhi to sign a 20-year Peace and Friendship Treaty with USSR. Today, we stand alone. Even our neighbours are not friendly to us. Nehru who was never a great student of economics, did not use economic cooperation as an adhesive to forge regional alliances. He was too much of an idealist to realise that economic necessities often force political opponents to cooperate. The maxim "Politics divides while Economics unites" was lost on Nehru. Unfortunately, this is as true today as it was during Nehru's time. His absolute faith in total economic self-sufficiency which goes against the very *raison d'etre* of international trade and cooperation put the country in an economic time warp.

Nehru's conduct of foreign policy was more a result of his inner impulses than a result of cool foresight based on long term national interests. While ostensibly non-aligned, it had a definite pro-Soviet tilt, a result of Nehru's almost childlike fascination for communism and admiration for Lenin. At the operating level, the day-to-day functioning of the Ministry of External Affairs was far from perfect, to quote Neville Maxwell.

"India's foreign policy in the 1950s was thus the conception of Nehru himself, and its implementation the concern of Nehru and the senior officials of the External Affairs Ministry. Even there, in the early years Nehru tried to run the Ministry as if that were his only charge, often drafting even simple telegrams himself and not consulting his officials. Of the Indian Foreign Service in Nehru's day one perceptive observer wrote that 'it was not a good service—nothing like good enough for a country of India's importance.' There was not enough training or professional competence, not enough *esprit de corps,* and too much eagerness to please the boss. Nehru was too busy and too preoccupied to get to know the necessary detail, or to get to know the officers except for a handful of very senior ones or a few favourites. This encouraged sycophancy, personal ad hoc approaches, and a mixture of amateurishness and subjectivity."

Our foreign policy had never been on an even keel. To quote a Naval terminology, it always tilted portwards (left) and never stayed the course of enlightened national interest. From day one after independence, our diplomats never gave much attention to the country's economic interests. Our glamour boys never learnt the truth pronounced centuries ago by western diplomats that "Diplomacy is philanthrophy plus five per cent profit." Trade and commerce was anathema to our polished IFS cadre. Even as late as 80's, our business delegations abroad invariably complained of the lack of support from our foreign missions during their search for world markets or in getting commercial information and market intelligence. Only now with the liberalization and globalisation of trade has their outlook changed. In 1979, while I was doing an export orientation course at the Indian Institute of Foreign Trade, New Delhi, almost all the visiting speakers and the faculty staff informed us that the first step to explore the foreign market is to contact our local embassy, only to follow it up with a caveat that given the attitude of our diplomats it is easier said than done. During my visit to the USA in 1990 the one point which all our Indian community and almost all American friends brought to my attention was the tendency of the Indian diplomats to hold forth on almost any subject under the sun, pontificate on the greatness of our past and sermonise to anyone who had the patience to listen. The listen to speak ratio was 1:9. It should have been the other way around. Even Kautilaya had pointed out as early as in 300 BC that the "Rajdoot should keep his eyes and ears open and use the minimum of speech". But the voluble boys of the gilded service and our drawing room heroes seldom learnt this wisdom from their own country's past on which they took so much pride. Nehru, our first Minister of External Affairs who articulated our foreign policy and stayed its course for 17 long years, was the architect of this breed and their guiding spirit in the years to come.

Socialism

Though Nehru did show ambivalence on many issues of vital political importance, his devotion to socialism was complete. Mention has been made earlier of his Fabian social background and subsequent admiration of the Soviet phenomenon. He had a streak of impulsive radicalism untempered by any weight of learning or personal experience. Radicalism by definition is opposed to moderation, a virtue universally recognised in all religions, theosophic and philosophic thoughts. The age-old wisdom from our own Shastras and Upanishads, articulated by philosophic thinkers from Aristotle downward has held moderation as a virtue in all human endeavours and activities. In his own lifetime and much before Nehru's death, as early as 1920s, perceptive observers of Bolshevism in the West had started having second thoughts on socialism. In a letter Joseph Conrad wrote to Bertrand Russel, he had observed:

"The advent of international socialism is the sort of thing to which I cannot attach any sort of definite meaning, I have never been able to find in any man's book or any man's talk anything convincing enough to stand up for a moment against my deep-seated sense of fatality governing this man-inhabited world. After all it is but a system, not very recondite and not very plausible. As a mere reverie it is not of a very high order and wears a strange resemblance to a hungry man's dream of a gorgeous feast guarded by a lot of beadles in cocked hats. But I know you wouldn't expect me to put faith in any system."

In matters affecting future of states, leaders cannot take rigid stands or stick to facile and clear cut theories on social engineering. Pragmatism is the key word. As a student of physics, probably the most exact science known to man, I was often struck by the inaccuracies in our methods of analysis. There is a well known theory propounded by Heisenberg, a German born scientist, called the 'Law of Uncertainty' which shorn of all mathematical formulae, simply means that you cannot at the same time ascertain with precision the position and velocity of a material particle. You can be certain of one or the other but not of both. Similarly, the same matter say an electron at one time appear to be a wave and sometimes a particle. Scientists were not clear for a long time whether light as is commonly understood is a form of electromagnetic radiation or a source of energy in the form of waves or a series of energy packets. The more one unearths the mysteries of nature, the more chastened, humble and unsure one becomes. Cockiness is a hallmark of ignorance. When one cannot be certain on facts revealed by discoveries of physics, even less on medical research which pronounces different judgments with each passing day, how can one be certain about various isms in social science? In the light of such known facts, to accept socialism as a permanent creed would have been less than wise. To be fair to Nehru one did not expect of him much erudition, depth of thought or even hindsight on fundamental weaknesses of the socialist dogma. But Nehru, the knight in shining armour regardless of the sane advice to the contrary by his wise colleagues, galloped ahead with the reigns of the nation's destiny in his hands towards his socialist utopia. The experiment had developed cracks in his own lifetime and later collapsed completely in the country of its origin. Socialism was the creed of the radicals, a weapon to rouse mass frenzy against the established order. It was not a prescription for a country's progress. Masses can be irrational, even wicked, as earlier brought out. To plan a nation's destiny on mass appeal rather than sober and rational thought is the biggest sin a leader of men can commit. All leaders after Nehru, with the exception of Lal Bahadur Shastri, fell victims to this tempting monster. Populist rhetoric leads to populist politics, and since hatred rather than love is the strongest adrenaline known to man, which can whet the appetite of the mass frenzy, successive politicians adopted such populist postures. From socialism to social justice is but the next logical step. To serve their political ambitions the high priests of 'social justice' took out the Mandal genie from the bottle and pitted 'Dalits' against the 'priveledged'. These pseudo social reformers subtly transformed this social engineering with a desirable objective, into a caste war ranging the Scheduled Castes, Scheduled Tribes and Other Backward Classes (OBCs) against the Savaranas. And now the latest attempt to call Mahatma Gandhi, a Manuvadi and Harijan baiter! Populism leads to more populism, more hatred and violence, and the voice of sanity and reason is the first casualty. The war of haves against the have-nots is but the next step to sowing sectarian and caste hatred.

With so much uncertainties around, God be praised, there are still certain universal truths which have not changed with time. The fundamentals of human nature have remained unchanged over the ages. Men have not ceased to love or hate, to care for family or forgo the wish to own property. Yearning for excellence, the desire to rise above the herd, and a zealous determination to preserve one's freedom have endured. Except for the yearning for excellence the other traits are common even to the animals. See how even a parrot, well fed in a golden cage flies off to freedom at the first opportunity. Socialism and state controlled human systems attempted to deny these human rights. Nehru, the rationalist, forgot the fundamental lesson of human nature and introduced a system which, though not a true replica of the Soviet model, was equally harsh to snuff out the private enterprise at the cost of huge state undertakings that sucked in national wealth and gave back nothing in return.

A debate on socialism versus capitalism is too old to bear repetition. Nehru opted for the former, inspired as he was by the example of Soviet Russia and his own predilections towards Fabian socialism and the thought of Harold Laski. The pupil surpassed the master in the rigidity of his beliefs. During his own lifetime even before he became the Prime Minister, the enlightened Western thought led by social thinkers like Bertrand Russell, Laski, C.E. M. Joad and Aldous Huxley should have convinced him that a realignment of his paradigm on social justice through socialism was called for. The inefficiency of state enterprises lacking personal motivation, reward without excellence, lack of competition, an innate human desire for some kind of ownership of house or land should have been clear to any perceptive observer. Patel and Gandhi saw it, Nehru could not. He conceded only in mixing private enterprise with socialism.

The results are not difficult to see. Not wishing to make a complete volte face, he settled for mixed economy with state enterprises holding the commanding heights of economy and private enterprise, the 'pariah', being allowed to survive and fend for itself. Tatas and Birlas were dirty words in the socialistic lexicon. Debate after debate in the Parliament was devoted to heaping abuses and indignities on private enterprise and big business houses. The License-Permit Raj and the unholy nexus between politician, bureaucrat, and industrialist is too well known. In the state ownership of resources, means of production and profit, the coffers of the dispensers of power and privilege were filled, leading to a parallel economy, vitiation of the electoral process, and erosion of the very foundations of democracy and social justice, the goal of socialism which Nehru strived for. Nehruvian socialism, flawed from birth, has been a spastic child living on crutches of state money giving virtually nothing in return, except an indebtedness to the World Bank. It spawned a regime of corruption, retarded economic growth, fouled the breath of Indian polity, and released forces of violence and disruption. Socialism also meant that the core sectors of economy carry the Government on their back. It was a heavy burden indeed. It meant a total control of national economic activities by the bureaucrats. Such an economy would be, by its very nature, a high cost economy. Sooner or later the country's industry would have to compete with the industries the world over and face the global challenge. With a high cost bureaucrat driven economy no amount of borrowed capital, internal or external, could make it competitive. A Government meddling in all sectors of national production could do nothing well. Neither it would govern effectively which is its primary task nor produce cost effectively, the extra burden that it imposed upon itself. And the ultimate victim would be the tax payer, who was sustaining a Government that could not deliver value for public money on internationally comparable terms. But such mundane details were farthest from the mind of Nehru, the idealist. After almost four decades of groaning under the weight of Nehru's socialism, we have at last got the government off from our back and the individual enterprise is being promised a free play. That Nehru, the misguided messiah of socialism, led a gullible nation to economic disaster and moral decay, may be a harsh judgment on the man but truth is not always palatable. The doubting Thomases—and conscientious objectors—having been driven off the stage and sidelined long ago, the nation paid for its credulity and worship of the God that failed. The first two decades of the 20th Century and the years preceding, breaking loose from the complacency of the Victorian era witnessed a burst of new ideas in science, philosophy, politics and social engineering. Discovery of atom, theory of relativity, quantum mechanics and radio opened new vistas and spurred new thoughts. Socialism appeared to provide answers to all problems of humanity. Intellectual activity brimming with self assurance, seemed to have found all the answers for men and institutions, and spawned a generation of thinkers of exactitude, whose cut and dry solutions were accepted by the impressionable minds. Nehru was no exception and was swept away by the tide of the times. However, serious thinkers soon started having second thoughts. The Boer War and the First World War shattered the myth of the adequacy of the human institutions. Military adventurism and perversity of politicians deriving its sustenance from the magic word of patriotic nationalism, blurred the distinction between right and wrong. Perceptive observers like Bertrand Russell and his contemporaries saw through this facade of nationalism and socialism; how democracy and majority opinion was carefully manipulated by wily politicians leaving no sanctity to the 'Vox Populi'. Having imbibed the first flush of these thoughts, Nehru stopped growing and his mind fossilized at the level of the early Twenties.

He started airing his views on socialism as early as the Twenties during the numerous Congress meetings. Finding little support from his master Gandhi and his colleague Patel and a majority of Congressmen, Nehru persisted in his crusade. His association with Krishna Menon, who had spent much time with different brands of socialists in London, proved almost decisive. His enthusiasm for socialism and equality even surpassed his concern for liberty. To quote Giri Lal Jain:

"For Nehru, freedom was meaningful mainly if it paved the way for economic growth. He said so publicly again and again. Similarly, for him, democracy was meaningful if it facilitated movement towards economic and social equality. His was a commitment not so much to liberal democracy which prizes liberty more than equality as to democratic socialism which reverses the order of priorities. Nehru did not play havoc with the Constitution in his search for socialism. He was too imbued with the spirit of liberalism to do that. It could not occur to him that non-democratic means would be justified in the pursuit of socialism. But by emphasizing equality and, in the process, undermining the concept of the liberty of the individual, he created an atmosphere in which it became possible for his successors, Indira Gandhi foremost among them, to play with the Constitution and the constitutional arrangement. The emergency would have been inconceivable if demagogues, sired by Nehru, however unwittingly, had not prepared the ground."

The three pillars of Nehruvian order were secularism, socialism and non-alignment. We shall discuss the inadequacy of the concept of the secularism later. Again Giri Lal Jain:

"Socialism, however vaguely defined and implemented, was the linchpin of the Nehru system and that the system cannot possibly survive the disappearance of this linchpin. The linchpin has clearly disappeared. The collapse of the Soviet system and state and the opening of the Chinese economy to multinationals would by themselves have settled the issue. As it happens, the threat of bankruptcy as a result of the mismanagement of the economy since the very start of planning in the early fifties and more particularly in recent years has forced the Government of India to make a volte-face. It has abandoned all the dogmas and shibboleths of the Nehru-Indira Gandhi era. And the irony of it is that a Congress (I) government is presiding over this great reversal."

More on non-alignment under Foreign Policy and Chinese response under the chapter on 'Chinese Debacle'.

Nehru's reading of the socialist revolution in Russia is again as naive as it is hasty, and based on indirect knowledge and superficial factors. Here is an extract from 'Discovery of India':

"A study of Marx and Lenin produced a powerful effect on my mind and helped me to see history and current affairs in a new light. The long chain of history and of social development appeared to have some meaning, some sequence, and the future lost some of its obscurity. The practical achievements of the Soviet Union were also tremendously impressive. Often I disliked or did not understand some development there and it seemed to me to be too closely concerned with the opportunism of the moment or the power politics of the day. But despite all these developments and possible distortions of the original passion for human betterment, I had no doubt that the Soviet Revolution had advanced human society by a great leap and had lit a bright flame which could not be smothered, and that it had laid the foundations for that new civilization towards which the world could advance."

Contrast this with the observations of Bertrand Russell, the philosopher, on a personal visit to Russia during the days of the Revolution:

"For my part, the time I spent in Russia was one of continually increasing nightmare. I have said in print what, on reflection, appeared to me to be the truth, but I have not expressed the sense of utter horror which overwhelmed me while I was there. Cruelty, poverty, suspicion, persecution, formed the very air we breathed. Our conversations were continually spied upon. In the middle of the night one would hear shots, and know that idealists were being killed in prison. There was a hypocritical pretence of equality, and everybody was called 'tovarisch' but it was amazing how differently this word could be pronounced according as the person addressed was Lenin or a lazy servant. On one occasion in Petrograd (as it was called then), four scarecrows came to see me, dressed in rags, with a fortnight's beard, filthy nails, and tangled hair. They were the four most eminent poets of Russia. One of them was allowed by the Government to make his living by lecturing on rhythmics, but he complained that they insisted upon his teaching this subject from a Marxian point of view, and that for the life of him he could not see how Marx came into the matter.

"Never, in England, have I seen tramps who looked so abject as the mathematicians of Petrograd. I was not allowed to see Kropotkin, who not long afterwards died. The governing classes had a self-confidence quite as great as that produced by Eton and Oxford. They believed that their formulae would solve all difficulties. A few of the more intelligent knew that this was not the case, but did not dare to say so. Once, in a *tete-a-tete* conversation with a scientific physician named Zalkind, he began to say that climate has a great effect upon character, but instantly he pulled himself up short, and said:' Of course that is not really the case; only economic circumstances affect character.' I felt that everything that I valued in human life was being destroyed in the interests of a glib and narrow philosophy, and that in the process untold misery was being inflicted upon many millions of people. With every day that I spent in Russia my horror increased, until I lost all power of balanced judgement.

"I was amused by various small ways in which Bolshevik love of mass-production showed itself. The main meal of the day occurred at about four o'clock in the afternoon, and contained among other ingredients the heads of fishes. I never discovered what happened to their bodies, though I suppose they were eaten by the peoples' Komissars.

"It is ugly and brutal, but full of constructive energy and faith in the value of what it is creating. In creating a new machinery for social life, it has no time to think of anything beyond machinery. When the body of the new society has been built, there will be time enough to think about giving it a soul—at least, so I am assured. 'We have no time for a new art or a new religion,' they tell me with a certain impatience. I wonder whether it is possible to build a body first, and then afterwards inject the requisite amount of soul. Perhaps—but I doubt it."

On June 2, 1920, writing from a boat in River Volga, Russell observes:

"Last night, very late, our boat stopped in a desolate spot where there were no houses, but only a great sandbank, and beyond it a row of poplars with the rising moon behind them. In silence I went ashore, and found on the sand a strange assemblage of human beings, half nomads, wandering from some remote region of famine, each family huddled together surrounded by all its belongings, some sleeping, others silently making small fires of twigs. The flickering flames lighted up gnarled bearded faces of wild men, strong patient primitive women, and children as sedate and slow as their parents. Human beings they undoubtedly were, and yet it would have been far easier for me to grow intimate with a dog or a cat or a horse than with one of them. I knew that they would wait there day after day, perhaps for weeks, until a boat came in which they could go to some distant place where they had heard—falsely perhaps—that the earth was more generous than in the country they had left. Some would die by the way, all would suffer hunger and thirst and the scorching midday sun, but their sufferings would be dumb. To me they seemed to typify the very soul of Russia, unexpressive, inactive from despair, unheeded by the little set of westernisers who make up all the parties of progress or reaction. Russia is so vast that the articulate few are lost in it as man and his planet are lost in interstellar space. It is possible, I thought, that the theorists may increase the misery of the many by trying to force them into actions contrary to their primeval instincts, but I could not believe that happiness was to be brought to them by a gospel of industrialism and forced labour."

And finally he gives vent to his gut feeling about political process.

"Nevertheless, when morning came, I resumed the interminable discussions of the materialistic conception of history and the merits of a truly popular government. Those with whom I discussed had not seen the sleeping wanderers, and would not have been interested if they had seen them, since they were not material for propaganda. But something of that patient silence had communicated itself to me, something lonely and unspoken remained in my heart through all the comfortable familiar intellectual talk. And at last I began to feel that all politics are inspired by a grinning devil, teaching the energetic and quick-witted to torture submissive populations for the profit of pocket or power or theory. As we journeyed on, fed by food extracted from the peasants, protected by an army recruited from among their sons, I wondered what we had to give them in return. But I found no answer. From time to time I heard their sad songs or the haunting music of the balalaika; but the sound mingled with the great silence of the steppes, and left me with a terrible questioning pain in which accidental hopefulness grew pale."

To Nehru Lenin was a hero. Contrast this with Bertrand Russell's personal account on meeting the man.

"Lenin, with whom I had an hour's conversation, rather disappointed me. I do not think that I should have guessed him to be a great man, but in the course of our conversation I was chiefly conscious of his intellectual limitations, and his rather narrow Marxian orthodoxy, as well as a distinct vein of impish cruelty. I have told of this interview, as well as of my adventures in Russia, in my book 'Practice and Theory of Bolshevism'."

One reason always given by Nehru to defend his pro-Soviet bias was the need for Soviet veto on the question of Kashmir in our favour. To my mind this issue has been overplayed. We could have received assistance from U.S. when the chips were down, provided we had developed the right equation with America.

This tilt towards Russia was to colour all Nehru's thoughts and perceptions and subsequently foreign policy decisions. Instead of being equidistant from the two power blocs, he was always 'left of the centre' a phrase that later became official Congress ideology. In the bargain he got the worst of both the worlds. While being dubbed by Russia as the running dog of Imperialism he made conscious efforts to distance himself from America, a policy that provided avoidable distortions in our foreign policy. His unconscious tilting towards Russia was a reflex action of his socialistic upbringing. America favoured Pakistan and heavily armed them while we were let down by our friends during the Sino-Indian boundary dispute. Russia had declared that while India was just a friend Communist China was a brother. A man of masses Nehru's thoughts and actions were unconsciously aimed at securing a populist image. Inspite of his rhetoric Nehru did not always adhere to furthering the cause of socialism. Knowing fully well that all power flowed from Gandhiji he kept his peace with the old man and subordinated his ideals to his wish. In the case of election of Subhas Bose at Tripuri Congress and later the socialist party support, he was ambivalent in his stand. His one unwavering aim was always self-projection and personal gain. He let down the hard core socialists in Gandhiji's lifetime and later drove them to desperation and political wilderness. One by one they all left him. Jaya Prakash Narain, Dr. Ram Manohar Lohia and Acharya Narendra Dev, all great socialist leaders found him an unreliable customer. However, he cleverly used his radical mask to effectively neutralise the so-called 'rightists' within the Congress, and the diehard Gandhians who did not subscribe to his radical posturings. Dr. Rajendra Prasad, Sardar Patel and C. Rajagopalachari were made to look rightists and anti-progress in his socialistic rhetoric. He effectively used public enthusiasm for radicalism to brand them as "status quoist." As long as Gandhiji was alive, Nehru was neither a socialist nor a rightist but an ideologue of convenience with only one aim, that of promoting himself as the undisputed leader of Indian masses, next only to Gandhiji whose political heir he had become. It was a clever move and succeeded eminently. All tall leaders of any consequence were sidelined and consigned to political oblivion during Gandhiji's and later his own lifetime. Whoever were left were forced to leave the Congress for one reason or the other. His daughter played the same game of realpolitic to neutralise the organizational wing of the Congress calling it the 'Syndicate'. With her socialistic rhetoric of bank nationalisation and abolition of privy purses she gained political centrestage. The old guard was truly and fully vanquished. Self-projection and survival is a trait not new in Nehru's dynasty.

It is a rare historical example of doublespeak that an emerging leader used the crutches of his mentor's policy merely to pay lip service, differing from him in almost everything that mattered while he lived, and received his anointment as his political heir.

The hollowness of Nehru's socialistic masquerade is exposed by what happened to the country's economy during and after his rule. But even in the early stages, it was a convenient mask for creating a radical image for himself to the gullible masses, and create a constituency amongst the younger Congressmen. In one of his speeches, he thundered that he would form a united front of all mass organisations against imperialism. The Indian princes were his obvious and convenient 'windmills' to be tilted at.

He reviled them as props of the alien power. To him the 1935 Act was 'a new charter of slavery to strengthen the bonds of imperialist domination and to intensify the exploitation of our masses'. Nehru prejudged the issues as always. Even Gandhiji did not agree with this assessment of Nehru and more certainly the Sardar, the realist, was not too comfortable with these ideas. It was even rumoured that Gandhiji had parted ways with Nehru and that he felt that his life's work was harmed 'more by Nehru's words than the repression of the British Government!' Though Gandhiji denied this later, there was some element of truth in this rumour. However, at the time of the Congress session when it came to the question of selecting members for the Working Committee, Nehru brought in ten leaders from the Congress Right

Wing and only four from his own platform. This sent a shock wave amongst his socialist friends. Nehru had always given an uncertain support to the Congress Socialist Party and this was the proverbial last straw.

While the Congress had rejected Socialism as a creed, Nehru was advocating it. It was an act of indiscipline, straight and simple. But Nehru, the great survivor, wriggled out of this embarrassment. He protested that his utterances were more mild and did not harm the cause for the struggle of freedom.

To quote Michael Edwardes:

"Nehru's popularity with the masses, already high, increased with every tour. The crowds who attended his meetings understood him even less than the majority of Congress when he talked about socialism, but they knew exactly what he meant when he castigated landlords and factory owners. It was not long before those he attacked began to be alarmed and their fears were passed on to the right-wing Congress leaders. At the end of June 1936 six members of the Working Committee offered their resignations. The list was headed by the names of Vallabhbhai Patel, Rajendra Prasad and C. Rajagopalachari, a formidable triumvirate. Patel, the shrewd and subtle lawyer from Gujarat, Prasad, an orthodox Hindu and believer in pure non-violence, and Rajagopalachari, a Brahmin from Madras, an intellectual with a cold reserve and a gift for biting sarcasm. In the tragi-comedy of Nehru's life these men were among the Eumenides."

"He offered his resignation once again, pleading that his health had suffered because of the opposition inside the Working Committee. As usual with the letters between Nehru and Gandhi there is an air of unreality, as if they were always intended for publication........" The reason "he gave to himself and the public was that with the outbreak of the Spanish civil war he saw the coming of a world conflict and could not weaken the Congress movement in the face of it. Nehru the internationalist, escaping from the problems that surrounded him into the wider and more amenable reality of 'foreign policy', was not an entirely new persona but it was one that would be more frequently assumed in the future. Wearing it, Nehru could ignore the parochial politicians and what he believed to be their petty concern with narrow domestic problems—let small men get on with small matters. It was an escape which hardly damaged the struggle for freedom but after independence Nehru's preoccupation with foreign affairs was to lead to an abdication of decision on internal matters to just those parochial politicians he so despised."

While Nehru continued with his Janus-faced personality on socialism, ambivalence on principles and dichotomy in thought and action the crunch came when a move was set about to form a Congress Socialist Party within the Congress umbrella. Nehru shied away although the Congress Socialist Party members formed one-third of the delegates at the 1934 Session.

The earlier hurts and subsequent slights finally forced the socialists to leave the Congress after independence.

But the right wing within the Congress whose guiding spirit was the more realistic Patel, frustrated this socialist namby pamby. Thwarted thus, Nehru considered resigning but later changed his mind in 'public interest' as he so conveniently put while in effect it was just the opposite. There was a limit to which Gandhiji could tutor Nehru. He could not stop his attack on the Congress 'Right wing' which to Nehru appeared autocratic.

Mention has been made earlier of the differences in approach to the Indian princes between Sardar Patel and Jawahar Lal Nehru. Inspired by his anti-colonial rhetoric, Nehru never really liked the princes whom he considered to be the stooges of British Imperialism. Socialism further aggravated his dislike for these rulers whom he considered autocratic despots wallowing in riches. That was all very well. But there are limits where such prejudices should be replaced by reason and fairplay. Patel had stood strongly against the abolition of privy purses which he called dacoity. It was a breach of faith with the princes, who had willingly surrendered their states on the promise of a reasonable pension and financial compensation, called the privy purses. With Patel no more on the scene to restrain Nehru, his socialistic rhetoric and pique with the princes prompted him to renew his efforts to abolish the privy purses. So much so that Dr. Rajendra Prashad, the then President of India, had to intervene to persuade the impetuous Nehru to abandon this approach. His letter of 4th June, 1954, is reproduced below:

"My dear Prime Minister,

Please refer to your secret letter dated the 25th May, 1954, enclosing a draft of a letter which you propose to address to Princes. When you saw me while leaving Simla on the 30th May, I mentioned to you that I was looking into the matter from the point of view of finding out the financial implication of the suggestions you propose to make to the Princes. I have since then got all the necessary figures. It seems from the tabular statement enclosed that the total amount of Privy Purse payable to all the Rulers to whom such purses have been allowed and whose number is 283, comes to Rs. 5,39,82,346. Out of these, 24 Princes get amounts above Rs. 5 lakhs each and their total Privy Purses comes to Rs. 3,21,26,000. According to your suggestion, the voluntary contribution and investment which they can make, if they all accept your suggestions, will be Rs.48,18,900 by way of contribution and a similar amount by way of investment. Those getting a Privy Purses between Rs. 2 and Rs. 5 lakhs number 31 and the total Purse comes to Rs.90,41,635. Their contribution and investment would be Rs. 13,56,244 and Rs.9,04,163 respectively. The amount payable to those whose Privy Purses are below Rs.1 lakh comes to Rs.63,82,688 and their number is 181. Assuming that they agree to the same rate of voluntary contribution and investment as in the case of those getting Rs.1 to Rs.2 lakhs, their contribution would be Rs.9,57,403 and investment Rs.6.38,268. Thus the total amount of contribution, if all the Princes accept your suggestions in their entirety, would come to Rs.80,97,350 and the amount of investment would come to Rs.70,04,533. When we consider that the contribution has to be distributed among the various States and to be reserved for development purposes, the amount available for such distribution does not appear to be of much consequence in the context of the demand for development purposes. The investment of a little over Rs.70 lakhs, when we are aiming at Rs.150 crores at the least, will also appear to be insignificant.

"The question, therefore, naturally arises whether it is worthwhile raising this controversial question in this form and whether it is not desirable to leave it to the Princes themselves to do their duty in view of the very earnest appeal which you have made to the people at large. The first letter that was addressed by you in September last has not, as far as I am able to judge, received any encouraging response, even from those who have cared to reply. My fear is that although this is in the form of an appeal, those who are opposed to a voluntary cut will take it to be a command and will raise the objection that the Government is going back upon the covenants under which the Privy Purse was fixed. If the suggestion had proceeded from any considerable section amongst them we could have hoped for a better response. I know your idea is not to impose anything on the Princes but to enable them to play their part in the national reconstruction and thus to assuage to some extent the hostile feeling that may be existing against them. I am afraid they will not be able to claim any credit, nor will they be entitled to do so, as the suggestion has not emanated from them, and I doubt if they themselves will look upon the proposal from that angle at all. If the amount recoverable had made any significant contribution to the solution of the financial situation, it might have been worthwhile raising this question even at the risk of being misunderstood or misinterpreted; but as I look upon it, even if the proposal is accepted in its entirety, however reluctantly it may be, the contribution will not be a significant one and we shall only be giving a handle for raising a controversy."

This reined in Nehru, but his daughter later used the same rhetoric against the old guard in the Congress to defeat the 'Syndicate' in 1969 to win a personal battle and settle scores by abolishing privy purses along with nationalisation of fourteen private banks. Like father, like daughter, socialism used for personal ends!

Secularism

The concept of secularism in its ideal form implies that religion should not be allowed to interfere in the political decisions or affairs of the state. The meaning of the word secularism as given in Chambers 20th Century Dictionary is, "Pertaining to the present world or to things not spiritual; civil, not ecclesiastical; lay, not concerned with religion; not bound by monastic rule."

In simple terms, it means that the state which aims to be secular should function with no distinction or discrimination to individuals or institutions based on their religions. By the same logic it should not lean to or protect any religion and should disregard it in making any political decision. The trend to treat minorities differently from the majority, to keep them under the constant fear of the majority and thus, assume the halo of a patron saint, with less than noble reasons, and to treat minorities as a potential vote bank for election is a dangerous undertaking. This trend was unconsciously, set by Nehru himself but was adumbrated much earlier during the partition days; mention of which has been made earlier. This was to have far-reaching consequences in the fragmentation of the Indian polity. Having accepted partition, one would have thought that the question of

Muslim separatism was finished once and for all. Those who subscribed to the Two Nation Theory, had left this mainland for good, but that was not to be. Congress still kept alive the apprehensions of the Muslim minority which stayed back in this country, and in so doing, they purposely painted the Hindu organizations as communal. Thus, the threat from the so-called Hindu communalist was kept alive to keep the electoral arithmetic favourable to the Congress. Nehru and the Congress knew well that Hindus never vote as Hindus, since they do not think in terms of religion while dealing with political matters. In fact, their's was a true spirit of secularism. While the silent majority of the Muslims also thought on these lines, a few leaders with vested interests with a view to legitimise their leadership assumed the role of their guardians by stoking the fires of separatism and fear of the majority community. They played into the hands of power seekers and the Two Nation Theory in its new incarnation of Muslim appeasement still bedevils our polity. Nehru had no reason to encourage such a trend but he did exactly that and from there all our present problems flowed. It is no one's case that the minorities should not be protected, but there the matter should end.

Now, it is no more Muslim separatism. Even amongst the Hindus, one caste is pitted against the other by the followers of their messiah, Dr. Ram Manohar Lohia, who have left no stone unturned to sow the seeds of caste hatred, and fragmented the Hindu society not only on caste lines but also along the forward and the backward community. Dr. Lohia wanted social justice for the downtrodden but did not pit one caste against the other. Social justice to him would mean improvement in quality of life, education, better economic opportunities and gradual levelling up of differences between sections of society by a smooth and harmonious process of development through consensus and cooperation, not through confrontation, hatred and class war. What we see today is the logical culmination of the vote bank politics started in Nehru's time. He may not have meant or anticipated the present outcome, but will history ever absolve him of the consequences of his actions. Nehru's brand of secularism was a precursor to many later distortions and the beginning of a pro-Muslim bias dating back to early February, 1950. This caused many differences with Sardar Patel and a majority in the Congress Party. A letter by Nehru to Patel quoted below illustrates the point.

"So far as the party is concerned, it is not only getting out of touch with Government's policies and activities, but is also drifting away further and further from my own approach to these problems. I think the biggest issue in India is the Indo-Pakistan issue. This stretches from Kashmir to East Bengal, although the problems are different. I think that war between India and Pakistan will have dangerous consequences and should be avoided, unless it is forced upon us. At the same time circumstances demand that our policy towards Pakistan should be clear and firm. The party has repeatedly made it clear by its speeches that it disapproves of much that we have done in regard to Pakistan. Now this is a very vital matter and I entirely disagree with many of the criticisms made by the party."

Expressing his inability to understand the party line he explained:

"I cannot do this as Prime Minister, more especially because the views of the party are not in line with my own. There is a constant cry for retaliation and of vicarious punishment of the Muslims of India, because the Pakistanis punish Hindus. That argument does not appeal to me in the slightest. I am sure that this policy of retaliation and vicarious punishment will ruin India as well as Pakistan. We have set going a chain of action and reaction and unless one breaks out of that chain, we can never overcome these troubles."

And finally his usual offer to resign knowing fully

well that Patel would not accept it, since he too had, like Nehru's lines from Frost, his promises with Bapu to keep.

"I am quite convinced that I would serve the cause of our country much better today in a private capacity than in the public office that I hold. If I can be of any real use in the Bengals at present, then that would be a great service indeed. I want to try that. I also want to put an end to this constant bickering in the party and our rubbing each other in the wrong way from time to time. Even from other points of view about the future what I suggest has great value."

The fact that if Hindu lives could, with impunity, be sacrificed in Pakistan with no retaliatory threat in India to their co-religionists it would only encourage Pakistan to fresh excesses of violence against the helpless Hindus, never crossed Nehru's mind. To him Hindu lives lost in Pakistan was not a high price to pay for sustaining his brand of secularism. This meant ensuring full safety for Muslims in his secular India with no visible concern for safety of Hindus in Pakistan. His secular ideals stood out in utter disregard of the ground realities, where one religion was threatened with destruction, while the other had to be saved at all costs. To Nehru facts did not matter, ideals did.

The members of Congress Party felt that while Hindus were being massacred in Pakistan, Nehru was mollycoddling the Muslims in India according to his "terms of settlement". This infuriated Nehru and he made fresh efforts to explain the rationale of his policy, anchoring it on long term ideals rather than immediate acts of provocation by Pakistan. He elaborated:

"The whole Bengal problem and the Indo-Pakistan issue have many facets—political, economic, communal, national and international. Of these, the communal aspect has great importance.

"Indeed the whole problem is in the nature of a communal problem. We have long stood for discouraging and putting an end to communalism. That has been the Congress policy and it has been repeated and affirmed by Parliament. We talk of a secular State. That of course simply means any normal State today, leaving out the abnormality of Pakistan's Islamic State. We adopted our policy regardless of what the Muslim League or Pakistan might say or do, because we thought that was the only policy, both from the idealistic and the practical and opportunist points of view. Any other policy could only lead to disruption and disaster. Certain organisations, notably the Hindu Mahasabha, adopted an exactly contrary policy, that is contrary to ours, though exactly similar, in reverse, to Pakistan's. I find that progressively we are being driven to adopt what is essentially the Pakistan or the Hindu Mahasabha policy in this respect. It may be that the circumstances were too strong for us. I do not think any circumstance can be strong enough to upset a long-term policy which we consider essential. I am quite convinced that old policy of ours was the only right one and is the only right one in present circumstances. That was the Gandhian approach to the communal problem. It meant an attempt not only to protect the minorities but to win them over and thus demonstrate the rightness of our policy. If we do not adhere to that policy, then inevitably other consequences follow. It is no good at all for us to follow two contradictory policies at one and the same time. That is the worst way out of a difficulty."

And he went on to say:

"The position today is that while Pakistan has followed and is following an intensely communal policy, we are tending to do the same and thus completely playing into the hands of Pakistan. Hindus in Pakistan are terrified and want to come away. There is no doubt that Muslims in India are also full of fear. There is hardly a Muslim in West Bengal or even in Delhi and many other places in India who has a sense of safety. Certainly they have no sense of future well-being and progress. That is no doubt partly due to circumstances beyond our control. But partly also it is due to our own wavering policy and to the thought in the minds of many of us that Muslims are aliens in India, not to be trusted, and to be got rid of as soon and as tactfully as possible."

He then advocated a tough policy towards Hindu organisations. His outburst is recorded below.

"I think we have taken up far too lenient an attitude towards those in India who encourage this communal feeling of hatred and violence. The Hindu Mahasabha talks about Akhand Bharat, which is a direct incentive to conflict. War is openly talked about. As a Government we seem to be fading out of the picture and people publicly say that our Government has contradictory policies and, as a result, no policy at all. The belief that retaliation is a suitable method to deal with Pakistan, or what happens in Pakistan, is growing. That is the surest way to ruin for India and Pakistan and for vast numbers of human beings in these two countries. That surely is not a way to protect minorities."

This was an echo of the words and arguments that his 'secular' friend Maulana Azad was prompting Nehru to use in his complaints to Gandhiji against Patel's handling of the situation of Muslims in Delhi, in particular, and against Hindus in general. This further exacerbated the differences between Nehru and Patel, and then Nehru returned to his differences with Patel and told him:

"In these circumstances, the fact that you and I pull in different directions, and in any event the belief that we do so, is exceedingly harmful. Our Governmental machinery is suffering because of this and senior Government officers have the temerity to criticise Ministers of Government in private even to some extent in semi-public. It is clear that such a situation must be ended as rapidly as possible.

"The matter is far too important for a decision by individuals. It involves national policy. The party of course must have a say in the matter. But ultimately it is for the Congress organisation to decide, whether it is the Working Committee or the AICC. The Working Committee is meeting soon. Personally I think the matter is important enough for the AICC to have an emergency meeting. I wish we could have a full session of the Congress, but that is not possible for some months. A clear line must be laid down and followed rigorously and loyally.

"There should be no doubt in the minds of the people and the party and Government officials what our policy is and how it should be carried out. Any weakness in it on the part of a Government official will have to be sternly met."

Patel's reply reflects the words of a strong man bereft of any namby pamby idealism, but sincere in the extreme, trying to remove Nehru's misunderstandings. This was the letter that Patel was forced to write to Nehru on 28th March, 1950, and had been reproduced in the earlier Chapter under 'Nehru The Prime Minister'.

The following inescapable conclusion emerges from the above correspondence. That Nehru's idealism and his policy towards Pakistan under the shadow of his concept of secularism was far off from the ground realities. That the Congress Working Committee did not endorse his views. That in spite of Nehru's Rashtriya Swyamsewak Sangh (RSS) bashing prompted by some of his lieutenants of the so-called 'secularist' mould, the latter was found perfectly innocent of any wrong doing, when detailed investigations were carried out. That our foreign policy which Nehru considered his exclusive preserve and of which he considered himself an expert had been found lacking, since Pakistan did not play ball. The unchallenged expert blundered from the very beginning in his approach. His premature encomiums for Communist China and alienation of Nationalist China were already causing concern in Western countries more importantly United States of America. Later his antipathy to Israel which was born out of Muslim appeasement sounded less than convincing or even well reasoned. History proved how wrong he was in all this and how the nation had to pay a very heavy price for a presumptive and straitjacketed foreign policy leaving us no room for maneuver. All because his secularism, in real terms, amounted to looking at India and the world from the eyes of the Indian Muslims. It was an unmitigated minorityism not secularism or even 'realpolitik'.

Nehru had a blind spot regarding the RSS who, he suspected for Mahatma Gandhi's murder. It was banned in February 1948, being considered a fascist organisation, often compared to Hitler's Nazi party. Gandhiji's fast for the release of Pakistani assets had definitely infuriated a section of the Hindu fringe of RSS extremists, and those celebrated his death. Taking cognisance of this 'indulging in dangerous activities", as Patel was to put it, he endorsed the ban. But Patel, differed from Nehru in his assessment of the RSS, particularly Nehru's tarring the whole organisation with same broad brush, based on his opinion that 'Bapu's murder was not an isolated business but a part of a much larger campaign organised chiefly by the RSS."

But Patel informed Nehru in his letter dated 27 February, 1948:

"I have kept myself almost in daily touch with the progress of the investigation regarding Bapu's assassination case. I devote a large part of my evening to discussing with Sanjeevi (head of intelligence and I.G. of Police, Delhi) the day's progress and giving instructions to him on any points that arise.

All the accused have given long and detailed statements... It emerges clearly from these statements that the RSS was not involved in it at all. It was a fanatical wing of the Hindu Mahasabha that hatched the conspiracy and saw it through."

Though Nehru stood mute when violence broke out against Hindu Mahasabha, RSS and the Brahman community to which Godse, Gandhiji's assassin belonged, Patel was firm in his instructions to Kher to deal firmly with the law-breakers.

It will not be out of place here to dwell a little on the varying perceptions of secularism by Nehru, Gandhi and Patel, especially the latter.

A conference was held at Lucknow towards end-December, 1947, organised by Mussalman-e-Hind consisting of 70,000 Muslims and attended by Maulana Azad. The tone was set by the fiery speeches delivered by Muslim leaders, such as Dr. Syed Mahmud of Bihar. Even to the sceptic it was a reiteration of the same logic and arguments that Muslim League had used before August 15. Dr. Syed Mahmud, a Nationalist Congress Muslim, fumed: "I can tell Hindus and Sikhs that Muslims may be finished in India, but they should know that they also in that case would not survive."

Nehru let all this pass. He neither castigated Dr. Mahmud nor disapproved the presence of his friend Azad at such a forum. Patel was not the man to gloss over the event or sit silent. It were the speeches made at the conference that forced him to put the records straight and clear himself of the suspicion that he was anti-Muslim and pro-Hindu.

Patel's secularism differed from that of Gandhiji and Nehru. It was against an unqualified compromise and appeasement of minorities. He did not subscribe to the give-in-to-win policy that amounted to endless concessions to win over the Muslims. He treated Hindus and Muslims alike and believed in plain speaking to both the communities. He told the Hindus "to forget the past, because it is a manly virtue to do so—in India every Muslim should feel that he is an Indian citizen and has equal right as an equal citizen."

In the same breath, he could also tell the Muslims, "there is no place here for those who claim separate representation.... For a community to think that its interests are different from that of the country in which it lives is a great mistake".

He, therefore, advised them to realize that "the future of a minority— any minority—is to trust the majority", that they should "make friends with others and create a change in the atmosphere. You will then have more than your quota, if you really feel for the country in the same manner as the other people."

Continuing in the same vein, Patel mentioned:

"I am a true friend of the Muslims, although I have been described as their greatest enemy. I believe in plain speaking. I do not know how to mince matters. I want to tell you frankly that mere declarations of loyalty to the Indian Union will not help you at this critical juncture. You must give practical proof of your declarations. I ask you why you do not unequivocally denounce Pakistan for attacking Indian territory with the connivance of Frontier tribesmen. Is it not your duty to condemn all acts of aggression against India?... In the recent All-India Muslim Conference, why you did not open your mouth on Kashmir?... In the Constituent Assembly, one of the Lucknow Muslim Leaguers pleaded for separate electorates and reservation of seats. I had to open my mouth and say that he could not have it both ways. Now he is in Pakistan".

Patel, therefore, advised the Muslims:

"Those who want to go to Pakistan can go there and live in peace. Let us live here in peace to work for ourselves."

Earlier he had reminisced:

"Today, I think of those days when in this city of Lucknow the foundation of the two-nation theory was laid. It was said Muslim culture and tradition were not akin to those of the Hindus. The Muslims were a separate nation."

He continued:

"Muslim Leaguers call me their greatest enemy. Formerly they used to call Mahatma Gandhi Enemy Number One.

Now they think Gandhi is their friend, and have substituted me in his place. But I too speak the truth... I want to say a word as a friend of the Muslims and it is the duty of a good friend to speak frankly. It is your duty now to sail in the same boat (with the Hindus and others) and sink or swim together. I want to tell you very clearly that you cannot ride on two horses. You select one horse, whichever you like best."

It was a catharsis of all the pent up impulses and his concern for the unity of the nation that made Patel to make this profound and historic statement even if it was to be unpalatable to some of the vested interests and mischief mongers. After hearing this speech Mountbatten was moved to make his famous observations, describing Patel as:

"'a very stern realist' and who, he thought, had 'the courage to rise above popular sentiment.. (when) the interests of the country demanded a different line'".

Patel's Lucknow speech was a bombshell exploding on the faces of Khalq-uz-Zaman and other members of the League who had supported the formation of Pakistan but due to their inability to move out stayed back and were now sporting the label of Nationalist Muslims. Here was Patel holding a mirror unto these Nationalist pretenders, showing them their true colours. Azad, Hafiz-ul-Rehman and others of his ilk complained to Gandhi about Patel. Nehru stayed neutral. But the plaintiffs had the tacit support of his socialist friends, only to elicit the following reply from the wise old man:

"I know the Sardar... His method and manner of approach to the Hindu-Muslim question, as also to several other questions, is different from mine and Pandit Nehru's. But it is a travesty of truth to describe it as anti-Muslim. The Sardar's heart is expansive enough to accommodate all."

Gandhiji had by now realised that Patel was too masterful and nobody's yes-man. Patel's differences with the Congress policies arose from the latter's surrender at Simla in 1945 and acceptance of parity between the

Caste Hindus and the Muslims and the "assumption that the Muslim League was the sole representative of the Indian Muslims."

Subsequently, during the deliberations of the Constituent Assembly, it was Patel's astute stage management and behind the scene strategy that ultimately forced the so-called Nationalist Muslims to abandon their plank of separate electorates for the Muslims in favour of joint electorates without reservation. However, Patel made a generous comment in the Constituent Assembly saying:

"It is upto the majority community, by its generosity, to create a sense of confidence in the minorities, and so also it will be the duty of the minority communities to forget the past and to reflect on what the country has suffered owing to lack of the 'sense of fairness' which the foreign rulers thought was necessary to keep the balance between community and community."

To the Muslims, he advised:

"If the minorities have honestly come to the conclusion that, in the changed conditions of this country, it is in the interest of all to lay down real and genuine foundations of a secular State, then nothing is better for the minorities than to trust the good sense and sense of fairness of the majority and to place confidence in them... In the long run it would be in the interest of all to forget that there is any thing like majority and minority in this country, and that in India there is only one community."

Later, Govind Ballabh Pant was to echo the Sardar's sentiments thus:

"Let not the lesson of history be lost. It is a lesson which should burn deep in the hearts and minds of all minorities that they can find their protection only from the people in whose midst they live; and it is on the establishment of mutual goodwill, mutual trust, cordiality and amity that the rights and interests not only of the majority but also of the minorities depend. This lesson of history, I hope, will not be forgotten... There is the unwholesome and to some extent, degrading habit of thinking always in terms of communities and never in terms of citizens."

It fell not to Nehru, the woolly headed secularist, with a pro-Muslim bias but to Patel to utter these famous words which should be etched for all times to come in the memory of our secular India. He said:

"A minority that could force the Partition of the country is not a minority at all."

We have already defined secularism earlier in this chapter but certain aspects can bear repetition. The Hindu ethos never associated state with religion. Kings had their religion and their priests, but there was no coercion to the laity to conform to one or other form of worship. This diversity in the system of worship and philosophic thought was based on the inherent tolerance in the teachings of our saints which for ever precluded the possibility of a state controlled religious regime. Though ancient Indian polity drew its sustenance from Dharma, which meant ethical conduct and virtuous living, it did not press adherence to any 'panth' or religious denomination.

But with Islam it was different. The Prophet was also the head of the State and he had to lay the foundations of a worldly state where his writ could run. Thus, the system of the king as the religious head persisted in Islamic countries. The Quran later enjoined the faithful to obey the king. It prescribed the rules of government and the Ummah made certain that the state was run on the Quranic ideals. Gen. Zia-Ul-Haq's Nizam Mustaffa was the modern version of this primal rule. It would, thus, be clear that while secularism came naturally to the Hindu psyche, to the Muslim it was against the basic tenets of their religion. Giri Lal Jain elaborates a profound thought.

"As for secularism, supposedly the third leg of the Nehruvian tripod, two points have to be made. The first is the usual one, which is that Hinduism is tolerant and, therefore, secular. This is valid and it is sheer dishonesty or naivete' to suggest, as is being widely suggested these days, that Hinduism can admit of theocracy. That is a Muslim privilege which no one else can appropriate."

And then he describes the real secular content of Hindu progress:

"The dominant concern of Hindus over the last 200 years has been with achievements in the secular realm—education, trade, industry, equality with the British before independence and with the West since independence. The upsurge I have been speaking about, in fact, relates wholly to the secular realm. This does not mean that our spiritual-religious heritage has no place in this scheme. But it does mean that Hindus have recognized once again, as they did in the past, that the secular realm has to be secured if a culture and a civilization has to flourish. Swami Vivekanand emphasized the importance of secular achievements and so did Sri Aurobindo."

Talking of secularism of Hindu culture he makes a point:

"It is not being Semitized and it cannot be Semitized as a result of a deliberate design on the part of some individuals or groups. But from being a confederation of ways of life, it has had to move towards being a federation. To put it differently, the small society has had to give way to larger ones as small economies and polities have had to give way to larger ones. Only a secular and modern intelligentsia could have presided over these changes. The task would have been beyond the reach of traditional elites. That is the true significance of secularism. It may be called the 'midwife of Hindu nationalism."

Nehru heavily influenced by the proximity of Azad and Kidwai and his own mis-reading of the Hindu psyche considered any assertion of Hinduism or 'Hindutva' or even an indirect suggestion to the Muslims to demonstrate their loyalty to the mother country as a communal act. Nehru's concept that "minority communalism was not very dangerous" , inevitably led to the corollary that majority communalism was. Therefore, in his scheme of things while one could wink at the minority's need to stress their identity and resort to aggression and communal posturing, the majority was to be restrained at all costs. Any stirings of its civilizational identity, even if not threatening the minority was an unpardonable act, and was to be resisted by all the might of the State. In the long run, this could only incite the minority to violence against the majority community where the end losers will always be the minority. Most members of the Congress resented Nehru's interpretation of communalism in its anti-Hindu overtones. An interesting light on the subject was thrown during the election of Purushottam Das Tandon, as Congress President as has been mentioned earlier. Durga Das's record of events is an eye-opener. How Nehru not only denounced Tandon for his views, since he did not conform to his own, and how inspite of holding out threats of resignation from the Congress Working Committee and Government, Nehru had to suffer the humiliation of being thwarted. This case shows the re-enactment, as it were of repeated charades of Nehru almost till his death, threatening to resign and the ever fawning array of sycophants and hangers-on entreating him to refrain. As usual a more than obliging Nehru always changed his decision and never left his chair.

"When Islam came to India" declared Nehru at the Azad Memorial lecture on 20th February, 1959:

"In the form of political conquest it brought conflict; it encouraged the tendency of Hindu society to shrink still further within its shell. Hence the great problem that faced India during the medieval period was how these two closed systems, each with its strong roots, could develop a healthy relationship.

"The philosophy and the world outlook of the old Hindus was amazingly tolerant. The Muslims had to face a new problem, namely, how to live with others as equals. They came into conflict with Christiandom and through hundreds of years the problem was never solved.

In India, slowly a synthesis was developed. But before this could be completed, other influences came into play."

But GiriLal Jain has a counter question:

"Typically, Nehru skirts inconvenient issues. He does not tell us why the Christian-Muslim encounter did not lead to a synthesis despite the common Semitic origins of the two faiths, or how Hindus and Muslims could move towards one if both were truly closed systems, or why Hindus shrank into their shell before the onslaught of Islam since they had not faced a hostile civilization earlier. He also uses the wrong concept of tolerance in relation to Hindus and Hinduism in place of the proper one, which is 'comprehensive' or 'all-embracing' or 'total'. Hindus were 'amazingly tolerant' because their *dharma* (worldview) provided for every possible expression of the human spirit and indeed they so remained in spite of their decline for centuries for the same reason.

And then he avers:

"Finally, it is a pity that there does not exist the slightest awareness, either among Hindus or Muslims, that Muslims need the rise of Indian civilization as much as Hindus, if not more. Indeed, such is the grip of the misrepresentation of Hindutva in anti-Muslim terms that its proponents, including some leaders of the Bharatiya Janata Party, themselves, speak of it defensively."

Jain further adds:

"It is inconceivable that Nehru was not sensitive to Muslim resistance to modernization and secularization. Indeed, it can safely be assumed that he left them alone in respect of their Personal Law and did not seek to bring them into the orbit of a common civil code precisely because he was aware of the depth of their opposition, though that is clearly an essential part of a modern polity based on the principle of equal citizenship. Perhaps he expected that their attitude would change in course of time under the pressure of forces unleashed by the spread of education, economic development and the democratic political process. If he ever spelt out his views on how the Muslims would come out of their ghetto psychology after independence, it has still not been made public."

"This brings me to the point I made earlier regarding Nehru's lack of confidence in his ability to persuade Muslims to get out of the psychological and cultural ghetto of their own making and join the mainstream brought forth, in his view, by the process of modernization. It does not follow that Nehru's secularism was phoney; but it does mean that it was lame. To borrow the Chinese phrase, it did not walk on two legs. It wobbled on one, though Muslims provided him a crutch in the shape of electoral support which facilitated his and the Congress party's stay in power."

With Nehru's ambivalence on secularism and socialism serving as a backdrop, his secularistic rhetoric in true poetic justice went up in flames on his death. Michael Edwardes in his well written book, "Nehru: A Political Biography" (Vikas Publications 1971) describes his funeral rites thus:

"To the sound of muffled drums the body was placed on the pyre. Hindu priests began the magical rites for the dead, holy water from the River Ganges was sprinkled, a small group of leaders filed past, each placing a piece of sandalwood on the pyre. The Indian flag was replaced with a white scarf and flower petals. Sanjay lit the pyre and the body of Jawaharlal Nehru, socialist, agnostic, prophet of Indian secularism went up in flames like that of a Hindu king."

"The whole affair had appeared to many as a display of bizarre incongruities. Nehru's Will, written ten years before his death, had laid down that no religious ceremonies should be associated with his funeral. Among those who placed a final piece of sandalwood on his pyre were such Muslims as the Vice-President of India, and Sheikh Abdullah, the Kashmir leader."

"Yet none of these contradictions was without its point or its relevance to Nehru's own life and personality. The Eurasian overtones of the funeral, those elements of east and west which some saw as being in execrable taste, had been as much a part of the living Nehru as they were of his death. The Muslims who willingly took part in a Hindu ceremonial represented not only the special place the Muslim world had occupied in Nehru's political life but also his antecedents, for his family background had been significantly influenced by the pre-British Muslim rulers of India the Mughals."

The three pillars of Nehruvian order were: socialism, secularism and non-alignment. Regarding secularism we have seen how ill-defined it was. It was based on a flawed reading of history and total incapability to comprehend both the Hindu psyche and the Muslim thought. And Nehru blundered. But Nehru took a synergetic view of non-alignment and secularism. One view was bad enough, the twin mix proved too potent a potion and spelt disaster in both the fields.

The *sine qua non* of Nehru's scheme of secular thought was firstly, subsuming the Hindu content of our cultural identity, considered by him to be backward looking, obsolete and full of distortions, and secondly a process of progressive assimilation of two alien influences, the Islam and Christianity, which to him appeared more catholic and egalitarian. Nothing could be farther from the truth. Islam and Christianity with all their virtues were not content with enriching themselves and staying where they were born. Their essential creed was to spread the gospel, by persuasion and inducement if possible, and force, if necessary. While Christianity mainly resorted to the first two in good measure, Islam used the third. Proselytising was an essential part of both. However, Hinduism never left its domain, to conquer and convert. It had the tolerance to absorb all that was good in others and the magnanimity to accept dissent within. Such a religion was branded by Nehru as 'backward and inward looking.' Today's elite blindly follows this concept of Nehru and his historical thought. Even the mention of a Hindu identity of independent India was an anathema to Nehru who constantly harped on our composite culture.

What is Hinduism or Hindutva? What does it mean to be a Hindu? Hindu and Hinduism is not a world body or a religious form of any persuasion. It is a feeling and thought; it is the heart-beat and the music note of our world view and philosophy of life; it is the fragrance of this ancient land of Bharat; the idiom of thought of our people, the constructive urge of our sages and the proclamation of our rich cultural inheritance along with the definition of our Vedic consciousness. Hindu and Hinduism is but the modern edition and the essence of the proto and ancient Indian thought enshrined in the Upanishads. It encompasses all forms and variations in the modes of religious worship. It embraces monotheism, polytheism and even atheism. It allows for a choice of gods and form of worship and even concepts of cosmology and cosmogeny. And most importantly, the concept of 'Vasudhaiv Kutumbkam' (the world as a family with fatherhood of God and brotherhood of man). It teaches the universality of human values and respect for all religions. Such a value system cannot be inimical to any religion or coercive in its preachings or practice. Nehru who did not know Hindi and Sanskrit had not read even one page of our *shlokas,* the spiritual text of the Shastras nor even an elementary treatise of the *Bhagvad Gita*.

An unusual event occurred in our secular India on 15th January, 1996, at Aligarh where the Mili Parliament, a Muslim body meant to preserve the pristine purity of Islam, passed the following resolutions:

"That the present secular system cannot ensure the protection of the legitimate political rights of the Muslims;

"That Muslim MPs of all political hues are lackeys of the Hindus;

"That Muslims should support only those leaders who lead the Namaz in the mosques;

"That secular democracy is a constitutional fraud, while secularism and democracy are both unIslamic and 'Haram';

"That Muslims should prevent formation of an unIslamic system of governance;

"That the Muslim Ummah should strive to destroy all systems of falsehood and injustice and replace these by just order;

"That separate electorates for Muslims based on proportionate representation is the need of the hour. (This issue had been rejected even in pre-partition India when Gandhiji threatened to go on fast to forestall British deviousness in dividing India on the basis of communities and castes by a demand for separate electorates for Muslims, Sikhs and Hindus and so on. This very same issue resurfaced during the discussions in the Constituent Assembly, strongly supported by Dr. Ambedkar, the so-called Messiah of the Dalits; but was given a quiet burial after prolonged discussions under Patel who silenced all opposition.);

"That other autonomous States should be formed in the country and that a self-defence based security system be introduced in the country to help only the minorities during riots. (In other words issue arms to the Muslim minorities to protect themselves against the Hindu majority)."

All this happened in everyone's sight and hearing and not a whiff of protest was raised by our so-called secularists who lose no opportunity in castigating Hindu self-assertion as communalist. The policy of minority appeasement, started in Nehru's time, has reached its logical climax today when the minority appetite feeds on what it is offered. The genesis of this trend lies in the Nehru mindset and the JNU thought.

In spite of Nehru's treating Muslim minorities more

equal than the others this is how the vicious seeds of separatism took roots and today we are hearing the echo of the same sounds that were raised in pre-partition days.

Economic Planning and Policy

Nehru's economic policy should have caused no surprise to perceptive observers, who had grasped the essence of the observations he had made in his book, *"The Discovery of India"*. Enthused by the unfolding of the technical developments, a sequel to the industrial revolution in the west he was overwhelmed by the Bolshevik revolution and its socialistic rhetoric. This is how he proposed to engineer the relative positions of the big machine and the small scale industry. He wrote:

"Is it possible to have two entirely different kinds of economies in a country—one based on the big machine and industrialisation, and the other mainly on cottage industries? This is not conceivable, for one must overcome the other, and there can be little doubt that the big machine will triumph unless it is forcibly prevented from doing so. Thus it is not a mere question of adjustment of the two forms of production and economy. One must be dominating and paramount, with the other as complementary to it, fitting in where it can. The economy based on the new technical achievements of the day must necessarily be the dominating one. If technology demands the big machine as it does today in a large measure then the big machine with all its implications and consequences must be accepted. Where it is possible, in terms of that technology, to decentralize production, this would be desirable. But, in any event, the latest technique has to be followed, and to adhere to out-worn and out-of-date methods of production, except as a temporary and stop gap measure, is to hamper growth and development.

"Any argument as to the relative merits of small-scale and large-scale industry seems strangely irrelevant today when the world, and the dominating facts of the situation that control it, have decided it in favour of the latter. Even in India the decision has been made by these facts themselves, and no one doubts that India will be rapidly industrialized in the near future. She has already gone a good way in that direction. The evils of unrestricted and unplanned industrialization are well recognized today. Whether these evils are necessary concomitants of big industry or derived from the social and economic structure behind it is another matter. If the economic structure is primarily responsible for them, then surely we should set about changing that structure instead of blaming the inevitable and desirable developmental technique."

How did Nehru intend to change the economic structure? In his own lifetime, he could not do so. The very concept of the commanding heights of economy and the state production, occupying the main national space and allowing the small and cottage industries to a subsidiary role where these would be forced to occupy whatever little space and wherever it was available. The concept was flawed from its birth. The small scale and private industry was to be a poor cousin to rely on it's own resources. Had Nehru studied his economics correctly and observed the development of the American economy, he would have known better. A few home truths. Firstly, the State has no business to enter the market, except as a referee to ensure fairplay, and secondly even amongst the so-called big machine and the small industry, the contribution of the latter to the generation of employment, the lynchpin of Gandhian thought, was much more. It was much more to the medium and small industry than to the big corporate giants that the huge army of unemployed could look for succour. There is no lord and serf relationship between the two. The big has its own problems. Heavy overheads, indirect command, delayed decisions, lack of resilience to market changes and nimbleness in managerial responses, and above all, the lack of what is called 'street-smartness'. The small too has its own shortcomings. Lack of resources for high capital investment, market research and somewhat inadequate research and development facilities. Since Nehru was not a realist or even a pragmatic thinker, he failed to grasp the nuances of the economic order that would best suit the Indian conditions. He rigidly stuck to his theory of generation of wealth based on the big machine, and constantly sneered at Mahatmaji's cottage industry and *gram swaraj,* as so much mumbo jumbo. He hoped that by the mere process of percolation, the benefits of wealth would somehow reach the poor below. He forgot his concept of social justice in his enthusiasm for the big and the beautiful. In the process, he fell between two stools; accumulation of wealth and equity of distribution. Unprofitable public sector undertakings (PSUs) produced little wealth and since he could not forge an instrument of distributive justice, he could neither produce much national wealth nor enrich the lowly and the wretched of the earth. He blindly followed the grand Soviet pattern of New Economic Plans (NEPs) in the form of his own Five Year Plans. These were highly capital-intensive and were intended to produce the essential infrastructure for an economic take-off, and rapid industrial development, a task in which they completely failed. Today, India is the largest undeveloped country, for its size, in the world. Despite our liberalization policy and open invitation to foreign investors, there is direct foreign investment is not all that forthcoming in the infrastructural areas, the essential sectors of our economy. Nehru's first foundation stone to support his economic edifice collapsed at birth. It was kept alive on artificial respiration with a heavy drain on the taxpayer. Inspite of the private and small sector, as in the United States, providing almost 75 percent of the total employment generation, in our country it was always called an untouchable. This is in keeping with our socialistic rhetoric. Nehru's state control of the means of production led to the 'Licence and Permit Raj' as has been pointed out earlier. Far from being an instrument of social justice, his socialism and its synergic economic order led to the creation of flabby monoliths, not only of the state but also monopolistic business houses, which festered like gangrene on our social order and led to the unholy nexus between the big business patrician and the ugly politician. The highest patriotic achievement came to be an account holder in a Swiss Bank. The ramifications are there today for everyone to see. As Nani Palkhiwala, so aptly states, in 'The Last Decades', we blundered along all the possible wrong directions till we struck the right path of liberalization. Gandhiji's concept of 'Gram Swaraj' envisaged the village as an independent economic unit with self-sufficiency, as far as possible in local resources, local artisans and enough expertise to conduct its economic activities locally in order to fulfil all the requirements of its population. This did not mean a total isolation of the community from the winds of industrial change, but it certainly ensured availability of employment to all working hands, the weavers, the spinners and the craftsmen near their homestead, inculcating thereby a spirit of self-reliance in the village folk. It would also prevent, as a main plank of the Gandhian thought, the mass exodus of the village population to the cities in search of jobs. This could also prevent the pauperisation of the villages and overcrowding of our cities, resulting in huge slums and squalors in urban centres. Even the western world today realises the soundness of this concept of 'providing jobs at one's own place' to prevent mass migration, unnecessary clogging of roads and unbearable pressure on civic services. Gandhiji had said that after him Jawaharlal would speak his language. Nehru had no intention of doing so. My uncle, Vichitra Narain Sharma, had been to jail the same number of times spanning nine years just as Nehru had done during the freedom struggle. He was the true follower of this concept of Mahatma and had provided large scale employment to lakhs of workers all over the country through a vast network off cottage and village industries under his constructive programme through the dedicated institution of Gandhi Ashram which was later affiliated to the Khadi & Gramodyog Commission. He constantly reminded Nehru about the need to prevent the pauperisation of villages and follow Gandhiji's concept. Nehru hardly listened. Innumerable letters sent to him by this indefatigable man remained unanswered.

Nehru would make full use of the disciplined cadre of Gandhi Ashram workers to brighten the electoral prospects of his Congress candidates during the three successive general elections from 1952 to 1962. My uncle himself got elected thrice to U.P. Assembly and received ministerial office in cabinet rank all these 15 years upto 1967 i.e. even after Nehru's death. But all his pleadings and remonstrances to Nehru for the cause of cottage and village industries elicited no response. Nehru was by now truly and fully under the spell of Mahalanobis model of development and the big machine. He had no time for these 'primitive and archaic concepts' as a prescription for development. We know today that the credit for generating the largest volume of employment even in America goes to the medium and small scale industries and not to the corporate giants. Cottage industries are not known in America but they had their roots in the Indian soil. They were not inimical to the big machine but had a symbiosis with the small, medium and the large scale sectors. It is not due to any grand design or positive efforts on Nehru's behalf that our traditional skills and crafts are still alive. It is like our ancient culture and heritage that refuses to perish away. Indian handloom, handicrafts and cottage items are much coveted in the West, not only as anti-deluvian museum pieces, but a throbbing reality of the present day Bharat. Nehru like many foreign invaders of the past tried his best to wipe out this legacy, but the enduring spirit of India prevailed. Our hand skills and crafts are in their present state of perfection not because of Nehru, but in spite of him.

The steel frame of the Indian Government, called the Indian Civil Service, later renamed the Indian Administrative Service, was by its very nature not attuned to the developmental process and projects took a very long time to materialise. The committed bureaucracy of Indira Gandhi's time was another evil progeny of the same system. The crushing State control of production further aggravated the situation. It would have been much better if the State had confined its activities to the essential tasks of human resource development, such as education, health welfare and social security and not indulge in generating power and making steel. The four decades lost to the cause of socialism not only ruined our economy but led to a fiscal deficit which is the largest in the world for a country of our size. Nehru started this process of living on borrowed money and the coming generations and those still unborn will carry a debt burden at birth. Our future generations have been consigned to indebtedness due to the profligacy of their ancestors, who lived on borrowed wealth to the extent that the debt servicing today accounts for an almost impossible percentage of our national revenue. The execution of the production and control of goods and services was left to the politicians and bureaucrats, who became a law into themselves. Gandhiji's concept of power meant service to the poor and downtrodden. As Peter Drucker puts it, "Rank does not confer privilege or give power. It imposes responsibility." This lesson in management was completely lost on our politicians and bureaucrats who used their position to feather their own nests with successive slogans of "Garibi Hatao' and such populist cacophony. The poor became poorer while the coffers of the rich and the mighty swelled their Swiss accounts. That was our socialistic economy ushered by Nehru.

Instead of "Garibi Hatao", the *garib* himself was removed to the limbo and political oblivion.

Enough has been said elsewhere about the absence of correct priorities in the Nehruvian order. National character and discipline was something to which Nehru merely paid lip service, but never really enforced. A tiny city state like Singapore which started on the path of its economic reconstruction much later has achieved a near miracle. Their leader Lee Quan Yew (LQY) did not possess the sophistory of Nehru but he had no illusions about what he had set out to achieve. A decade after Nehru, on 18th May, 1974, when the Nehruvian order of socialism and the commanding heights of state enterprises was a holy cow, this is what that man had envisioned for his country and had largely achieved. In an interview with J.R.D. Tata, thanking him for establishing the first Technical Training Institute in Singapore, he replied to the latter's query in achieving so much in so little a time. Here are some extracts:

"LKY—I am happy that despite our small size, we are able to create a significant impact. I think the clarity in our thinking is helping us. We are clear, irrespective of the criticisms we invite, that there must be political stability in our country and total discipline among our people. We know that what happens when law and order collapses, as indeed they did in the Sixties.

"We are too small a country to risk experiments in liberalism, and we are determined to establish discipline as the central unifying and stabilising factor in our country. In this area, there will be no experiments and compromises.

"We will allow the technology and the capital of the world to pour into Singapore; indeed, we will have to search for foreign technology and foreign capital. But this must not mean that our identity as Singaporeans should be allowed to be erased. This is all the more so as we are a multiracial society and, therefore, the discipline has both the political and economic value."

LKY's message was going down to all levels of society. Contrast this with what happened in our country in Nehru's own life- time and later during his daughter's rule leading to emergency for the wrong reasons. LKY further explained:

"But at the end of the day, it is the leaders, the bureaucrats, the policy-makers who must demonstrate this discipline in their lives. Enforcement must be reinforced by example. All of us must be perceived by the people of Singapore to be impartial and to be incorruptible. We attach great importance to our bureaucracy —our Chinese 'mandarin culture' is important. It is our backbone. It must win, not just demand, the respect of our people.

"We go all out to ensure that our civil servants are paid salaries quite close to those paid by the private sector. This alone will not guarantee efficiency or honesty, but it will mean that we can recruit the best talents available, and we can demand from them the highest standards of honesty and efficiency.......

"Having established the base of political stability, having created an efficient and honest bureaucracy, we can then allow the forces of free enterprise to work.

"I would like to elaborate this point rather carefully. We must allow forces of creativity to enrich our country and we must provide incentives to all who really put their hard work, who take great risks and who have ideas to sell.

"Take the Indian community in Singapore. I do not think you can say of them that, intellectually, they are superior to the Indians back in their own country, but they flourish here because the environment we provide them ensures political stability, an honest bureaucracy, and an economy based on incentives. I think this explains why so many Indians have been able to make such a useful contribution to the economic life of Singapore.....

"We in the government of Singapore come into the economic picture not to run the economy, but to make it run. Only where the private sector cannot deliver the goods, say, in housing, do we come in. There is no question of the command economy, or commanding the heights of the economy. Even when the State starts certain industries or services, we try to hand them back to the people of Singapore."

Contrast this with Nehru's obsession of state control of economy and its pre-eminence in economic planning. Even during the writing of his book, 'The Discovery of India," he had worked out his blueprint of socialism as has been pointed earlier. JRD articulated the current wisdom of Indian Government and its stifling effect on economy, a situation that called for correct priorities.

To JRD's query whether the system will work in India, LKY replied:

"It does work in Singapore. We have been giving tax incentives on a liberal scale—in fact, we have been giving tax holidays for a period of seven to ten years. We have control over the private sector, but not a whole regime of controls. The result is that our tax revenues are actually going up every year, and we ensure that every year a sizable portion of this tax revenue goes in creating jobs for the people and subsidies for the poor.

"Simultaneously, there are provident fund schemes which make it possible for our employees to make their own savings, supplemented by the savings provided by their companies, even to own their houses. People must learn to save for their future.

"I do not want the State to take the responsibility of evolving a whole network of social security systems, but at the same time we want to create conditions under which savings by individuals are raised to the maximum. I believe our savings rate today is one amongst the highest in the world, and while right now only 30 per cent of our workforce have private housing, it is our goal to provide housing to at least 80 per cent of our people within the next decade."

JRD: Was it possible that a developing country.. in

the world can come to have very high rates of growth? L.K.Y.: "Why not? I think you will soon hear of one country after another in this part of the world showing rate of growth in their national incomes." And again, in regard to the population growth in our country and the query raised by J.R.D., L.K.Y. replied:

"I am afraid, we have to then seek another solution rather fast. As I told you, you cannot go on, year after year, with a 3 or 3.5 per cent rate of economic growth, virtually cancelled out by a 2.2 per cent rate of population growth. At this rate, while so many countries of South East Asia have doubled their per capita income in 9 to 12 years, you will require almost 35 to 40 years only to double your per capita income.

"Time is running out; your people are too talented to allow this situation to continue. Your young men and women are emigrating on a large scale. You should provide them an economic environment which permits them to give their best to their country.

"I think I can take the liberty of telling you that in the framing of our foreign policy, we have put very high hopes on India as a major achiever. We would like India to emerge as a powerful economic nation, so that with the Chinese economy now in a total spin, India could emerge as a counterpart of Japan in this region. We therefore have a selfish motive in wanting India to emerge, as early as possible, as a major economic power in world politics."

JRD: Where does India come into the picture?"

L.K.Y.: "As I told you before, I have no right to pass any judgement about your country, but I do say that your country is not doing justice by not allowing the talents of the people of India to secure its rightful reward. I know your country has enormous problems, but I also know that she has enormous potentialities.

"For example, if your country is temporarily in the grip of socialism that can neither achieve economic growth nor make an impact on the poverty of the people, why can't one of your Federal States be made to serve as a model? Let the Central Government agree that it will permit such an experiment in a mixed economy in that particular State. Let the people of India see its achievements, and then the other States will want to follow."

This is what Patel had suggested to one of his socialist friends. To try out his socialist system in one and private enterprise system in another part of the country and see which one succeeds. "We have seen this repeatedly not only in our own country, but in so many of our adjoining countries, that a concrete achievement immediately serves as a magnet to motivate others. I think this can be a practical solution." LKY's reply is as prophetic as it is revealing.

On mixed economy, Nehru's dream child to have the best of both the possible worlds, which never survived the harsh realities of existence, LKY had this to say:

"Since you have brought up this point about the mixed economy, do you think what is prevailing right now in India approximates to a mixed economy? I do not think so. It is not our business to pass strictures on the economic policies of other countries, but I must say that to an outsider like myself, your socialism is not based on incentives but on controls.

"It is a socialism in which the politicians and the bureaucrats dominate the economy, with business at their mercy. It is a socialism in which the principal goal is to ensure that the State commands the dominating heights of the economy: it is not a socialism in which the creation of the right economic environment is the first priority.

"You are not going to solve the problem of poverty with this type of socialism. Your government is right in insisting that there must be specific schemes for the poor. Indeed, in this respect, our country has ambitious schemes to provide subsidised housing and subsidised education to our people. How are you going to do all this by establishing an economy in which all power is vested in the politicians and in the bureaucrats? I honestly do not see the poor coming into the picture in your socialism."

Regarding our low growth, LKY had this to say:

"This is precisely the point. I cannot believe that with your 3.2 per cent growth, matched by your 2.2 per cent of population growth, you have the conditions of solving the poverty of the people of India. You must have a faster rate of economic growth, combined with a 'shop floor socialism'—let the people see for themselves the new houses that come up, the new schools that come up. I think that is effective message of modern socialism."

On the resources for the shop floor socialism, he said:

"I think it comes from rapid economic growth, in which you have to ensure that the drive and dynamism of the market forces result in the creation of wealth, which you then distribute to the poor at large in the shape of subsidised housing, subsidised education, subsidised medical treatment, and so on.

"We know that our people are not going to wait for seven to eight decades to see this. We have, therefore, to ensure that resources are released, not by having a confiscatory rate of taxation, not by having a whole system of controls; in fact, resources are released by the very process of economic growth."

LKY's prophecy has been eminently vindicated as one after another South East Asian countries crossed the economic sound barrier on which our great socialist country is still stuck, thanks to the Nehruvian order which was partially jettisoned only four years back. And that is not the end of a bad dream. There are again whisperings of reverting to the old order. Malaysia, Thailand, Indonesia, way behind us upto as late as 1956, are far ahead today in the race of economic progress. So much about Nehru's legacy of economic planning.

Nehru's advisers continually harped that unless you produce wealth, all you can distribute is poverty. We did produce but not enough; and all our plan targets failed. Nehru could not ensure social justice either. The poor became poorer and then we started borrowing. The system being inefficient and exploitative, the money borrowed gave no returns. Instead invested as it was through the same exploitative machinery of the politician, bureaucrat and business combine into unproductive ventures, the balance sheet turned red. Soon nemesis caught up with us and this country was deep in a debt trap. While talking big on socialism, the one obvious fact which never struck Nehru, the Chairman of the Planning Commission, was the heavy rate of taxation and unwieldy non-plan expenditure and cost of governance. This is what Dr. Rajendra Prasad, our first President, wrote to Nehru on 2nd June, 1957:

"Now we have embarked upon a very much bigger programme in the Second Five-Year Plan. It is therefore worthwhile considering how things should be so arranged as to enable the people to derive the best from the projects.

"I believe there are inspecting agencies both at the State and the Government of India level to be continuously assessing the efforts and the results thereof and keeping the field workers on the alert so that their sloth and complacency are not allowed to cause frustration. If there is no such agency, I would suggest that immediate steps should be taken to have such an agency at both the levels. But apart from the inspecting agency, the actual field workers also require to be brushed up and enthused, so that they may do their best. Unless this is done, I am afraid not only will the country be deprived of a great part of the advantage expected of these projects, but the very heavy investment which is being made at such sacrifice by the people may fall in jeopardy.

"We have embarked upon a scheme of heavy taxation which is considered necessary for financing the Second

Five-Year Plan. I do not know what steps have been taken to introduce economy and reduce expenditure on the administrative machinery of the Government. While it is true that there has been increase in the field activity of the Government as the result of the adoption by us of the ideal of a Welfare State and socialistic pattern of society I believe there is still room for economy and economy at all levels, in the Central as well as in the State Governments. From time to time enquiries have been held, but I do not know to what extent economy has been introduced in governmental expenditure. The people may be better reconciled to further taxation if they are told that side by side the Government is also reducing the expenditure on administration. The bigger the Department, the greater the room for economy. This should be treated as a matter of the same urgency as the question of raising finance by taxation. I believe that the deficit, to cover which the taxation proposals were originally conceived apart from the capital expenditure intended to meet the demands of the Plan, could have been reduced, if not altogether eliminated, by measures of economy. This can be enforced best if a Minister or a senior departmental officer is deputed to go into the details and all the Departments are not only advised but also are willing to cooperate in introducing economy. The Indian proverb is that it is small drops which ultimately fill the tank and if leakages are allowed even drop by drop the tank can be emptied. So in matters of expenditure no item should be considered too small to deserve attention. If a slogan in favour of economy is raised and it is impressed on everyone dealing with public funds to economise to the utmost, the results can be seen even at the end of the current year." And then another reminder on the poor execution of Nehru's grandiose plans on ground:

"For example, many of the canals and distributaries have not been completed, and water which should have been utilised has not been used. This is the position in a very much aggravated form in regard to the Hirakud Project, worse still in the Tungabhadra Project. The efforts of the Government of India and the Planning Commission to increase agricultural production are not backed to the extent expected or necessary by the State Government. There is no coordination in their work and there is a general lack of enthusiasm even in the Community Project and National Extension Service Block areas. For example, improved seeds even where available are not supplied in time. Beds are not prepared timely for raising seedlings; chemical manures are not supplied at the right moment; loans are delayed and so on and so forth. The result of all this is a shortfall in the expected yield, and it is difficult to be sure about the actual production and to base any conclusions thereon. The state of uncertainty creates conditions which are conducive to hoarding, rise in prices and the like. There is a general sense of insecurity created which further aggravates the situation.

"Again, for example, out of 6.30 million acres the State Governments were expected to bring under irrigation under the First Five-Year Plan, only 4 million acres have been actually irrigated. I was told by the Food Minister that in Bihar, while the number of tubewells has increased nearly three or fourfold during the last five years, the area irrigated by these tubewells has not increased to anything like the extent expected. As a matter of fact, the calculation is that while in 1952-53 the average area actually irrigated by a tubewell came to about 200 acres, in 1955-56 it was something like 60 acres per tubewell. All this shows that the amount invested in these big projects as well as in these tubewells is, for some reason or other, not being utilised to the best advantage, and although water is available for irrigation, it is not being used, with the result that the investment is to that extent suffering a dead loss, the equipment is undergoing deterioration, and the increase in the crop is not available. All this may be due either to some defect in the execution of the Plan or want of coordination."

Nehru under the advice of his economic mentor Mahalanobis midwifed the steel mills, Heavy Engineering Corporation and giant public sector undertakings. These like the proverbial white elephants guzzled up scarce public funds and taxpayers' money to produce more losses. To a lay economic observer, it is a truth that cannot be hidden by any government subterfuge, that Rs. 35 lakh crores invested in public sector undertakings even if they could give a mere 5% return on investment, a very meagre amount by any standards of business management, the amount so earned in 50 years would have been enough to finance all the poverty alleviation programmes of our socialist government. A succint observation on the legacy of Nehru and Mahalanobis, the product of London School of Economics, by Jay Dubashi is worth quoting:

"Ever heard of something called HEC? The letters stand for Heavy Engineering Corporation, a huge, ailing government-owned company that has been put on sale and will come under the hammer . . ., if there is a buyer foolish enough to buy it.

"HEC is not an ordinary company. It was supposed to be the core of the Nehru-Mahalanobis model when it was founded as a kind of mother unit to make machines for other factories. It was as much a symbol of Nehruism as the farm collective was a symbol of Stalinism in Soviet Russia. When HEC closes down . . . it will mark the end of Nehruism good and proper, just as the fall of the Berlin Wall on November 9, 1989, marked the demise of Stalinism."

Mahalanobis was neither an engineer nor an economist and knew little about machines, just as Stalin knew little about farming. But he was a clever man with figures, who could spin out a plausible tale for the likes of Nehru and others, who too were neither engineers nor economists.

Mahalanobis hijacked India's five-year plans with the help of fancy models that led to expensive and useless plants like HEC at Ranchi. It was his models and plants, backed to the hilt by persons like Manmohan Singh, that messed up the Indian economy for 40 long years and brought the country close to bankruptcy.

Manmohan Singh now sings another tune but his old friends have not forgiven him. They gang up together from time to time and issue statements, criticising this and that, and pouring scorn on the reforms. I am not a great admirer of the reforms myself, but I was not an admirer of Mahalanobis either.

Somebody had to clean up the mess he and his men left behind and the present government is doing it. They are, of course, not doing a good job of it, but something is better than nothing, until there are fresh brooms to sweep the whole thing clean.

But I do not understand with what face these leftists can criticise the reforms, or the attempt at reforms. They themselves were at one time in full charge of the economy and what did these so-called eminent economists do? Among gentlemen who issue learned statements from time to time, one is a past member of the Planning Commission, another a former chief economic adviser to Indira Gandhi.

These men were all over the place—they ran the Planning Commission; they ran the finance ministry; they had the eye and the ear of the Prime Minister, no less; they ran public sector undertakings, including units like HEC; they recruited their own kind for organisations and agencies advising the government; and they occupied key positions in the World Bank and the International Monetary Fund. They doled out licences, cooked up Budgets year after year and begged funds from Washington, London and Paris.

And what did they do with all the power they had? They ran the economy into the ground, and made India the laughing stock of the world.

But for these worthies, India would have been a leading nation in South Asia, with incomes closer to those of

Spain. There would be fewer slums and no starvation deaths. What credibility do these people have, that we have to put up with their views, amounting to diatribes, on foreign debt and Enron, on budget deficits and inflation?

It was during their regime that inflation soared from 5 per cent in the Fifties to 8 per cent in the Eighties, and growth was frozen at 3 to 4 per cent, among the lowest in the world.

They were not, of course, alone. They had friends elsewhere —in Africa, in Latin America, not to speak of Britain and China. They wrought havoc there too, before they were found and bundled out. The London School of Economics, where most of them studied and taught, not only destroyed the British economy but that of half the world, before the virus was isolated and destroyed.

These are also the men who were responsible for peppering the country with HECs in the name of self-reliance. India will be building more steel plants in the next five years than it did in the last 50—and without a single HEC. It is good that HEC is finally being put to sleep. But so should the Planning Commission which should be turned into a mausoleum for P.C. Mahalanobis as a kind of warning to future generations."

This is as fitting a requiem for the Nehruvian model of economic planning as one could wish for and it sizes up truly the so-called economists of "The London School of Economics", a breed that under the patronage of Nehru and his dynasty has played havoc with economy of the nation.

Nehru's socialism and economic planning brought little more than scarcity of goods and poverty to the rural and toiling masses. The urban lower and middle classes fared no better. Continued inflation progressively robbed them of their purchasing power. Nehru saw all this but could do little to turn round the march of socialism and bring relief to the suffering masses. Election after election, he made promises to remove poverty and asked for votes in the name of Congress and thereby played a confidence trick on the gullible masses. India continued sliding down on the poverty scale. Once exasperated with shortages, Nehru blamed the blackmarketeers and hoarders. It was they, he said, who were creating artificial shortages and caused suffering to all. Once he even exclaimed that if he could just catch one hoarder or a blackmarketeer, he would have him hanged from the nearest pole. Nothing like this ever happened. I still remember that in Nehru's seventeen years of undisputed reign not one blackmarketeer was hanged nor any hoarder punished. The parallel economy continued to grow and Congressmen developed vested interest in shortages of essential commodities and through their infamous nexus with the traders amassed huge fortunes. Today's 'Sugar Scandal' is a latter day example. What an achievement? We had to beg for food from United States, the very country that we always abused on our socialist fora. Nehru thought big but his actions resulted in small gains. In South Asia, we were the first country to gain freedom. Other South East Asian countries followed later. But thanks to our socialist planning, these small countries have overtaken us.

True to Nehru's legacy of "borrow and live beyond your means", even though ostensibly the purpose may be development, our economic planners have been constantly increasing our national indebtedness. The present scenario should be a good example, being the true acopalypse of the Nehruvian model of economic planning. Our national debt based on the Rupee value at 1992 level in early 1996 stood at Rs. 410,000 crore and the interest burden at Rs. 36,000 crore. To meet this mounting interest burden, the Government true to its old doctrine kept on borrowing and the national debt kept on increasing at the same pace. The inability to control the Governmental spending, ultimately led to a situation when we have to borrow just to meet the interest burden which has been caused, inter alia by borrowing at high interest rates.

In 1992, the average rate of interest on total Government loan was 7.6%. In 1995, this rose to 8.8%, a fairly high interest rate by any standard. The interest debt payment in 1992 was Rs. 27,000 crore. If we had kept the old interest rate unchanged, the interest burden would have amounted to only Rs. 31,200 crore. But due to high interest borrowing this rose to Rs. 36,000 crore, leading to an increased interest debt burden of Rs. 4800 crore in addition to Rs. 4200 crore still needed to service the old interest burden. This was clearly a case of self-infliction of indebtedness although the Government kept on claiming that it had pruned high interest loans.

Even if it is assumed that the Government could do little about the inherited debt burden, the least it could do would have been to control the interest rates. It failed in this task. What is even more serious is that it reduced investment from Rs. 25,600 crore in capital investment in 1992, to Rs. 20,800 crore in 1995, leading to a reduction of Rs. 4,800 crore. The loan was thus used neither for interest payment nor capital investment. It led neither to reduction of revenue expenses nor a search for low interest loans. The Government's sole effort was directed towards controlling debt by reducing capital investment without any attempt at reducing Governmental expenditure.

The Government during Manmohan Singh's time had been claiming that the revenue expenses had been kept at Rs. 56,000 crore for the last four years with only a marginal increase. This expense mainly consisted of Rs. 6300 crore as revenue expense on development and Rs. 325,00 crore for defence and remaining other heads. But a closer look at revenue expenses reveals that the Governmental expenditure of Rs. 6300 crore in 1992 had gone upto Rs. 7100 crore. As opposed to this the developmental expenditure had been reduced from Rs. 325,00 crore to Rs. 313,00 crore. Thus an increase of Rs. 800 crore in administrative expenses had been matched by Rs. 1200 crore reduction in developmental expenses while the total revenue expenses remained around Rs. 56,000 crore. This is clearly a case of increased Governmental spending and reduction in developmental expenditure. This was certainly not the aim of our planned economy. If we could just control the Governmental expenditure, we would have needed less loans. In fact, the loans had been taken primarily to meet the increased Governmental spending as has been mentioned above. Thus in view of these figures, the Government's claim of keeping debt burden under control seemed farcical. Tutored on the same fundamentals this is the fitting contribution to the Nehru legacy by our present day planners from the London School of Economics and Harvard Business School, who claim credit for the liberalisation and reforms. Chidambaram followed the lead.

The miraculous transformation of Malaysia from an economy based on just three items i.e. rubber, tin and palmoil into a multifaceted prosperous economy in just fifteen years is an example of what can be achieved through wise and dedicated leadership. There was no magic formula but two simple objectives that they followed. A purposeful Government and clear priorities. Nehru with all his pomposity and rhetoric could not follow these simple ground rules in his seventeen years of undisputed reign.

Linguistic Provinces

One of the blunders, though, not wholly of Nehru's making but to which he was an accessory was the creation of the linguistic provinces. The demand for linguistic provinces was heard even before independence. But then only a hurried note was taken of the local aspirations to help the general struggle for freedom. After independence, a more reasoned consideration of the issue should have been undertaken, subsuming any narrow political considerations of populist rhetoric. To understand the genesis of this problem, let us step back a little to the years 1948-49.

The boundaries resulting from the integration of princely states into newly formed states were being worked out. At that time speedy integration was more important than rationalisation, though, the demand for re-organization was certainly legitimate, but for different reasons. The linguistic element finally entered into this exercise only in the year 1949, articulating as it did, the interests and ambitions of the landlords and the well to do. A Commission of Enquiry was set up in 1948 to settle this issue. The Commission's view was that things should be allowed to remain as they are at least for the time being. The erstwhile provinces from the British India would contain existing major linguistic groups as also certain minority groups which could not be segregated so soon. But where the Commission stood firm was the fact that the creation of linguistic states would not inspire national consciousness through linguistic patriotism. On the other hand, this could definitely act as a setback to development of national consciousness and the adoption of a national language as its inevitable sequence. A committee was, therefore, appointed to look into the matter and in the typical Congress fashion allowed to procrastinate on the matter. The committee consisting of Nehru, Patel and Pattabhi, obviously considered the need for national unity more important than the demands of the concerned states. But the matter was left unsettled.

After the 1952 elections, the demand for separate linguistic states for Tamil and Telugu speaking people took roots not based on any rational logic but on the personal differences of the two Chief Ministers, Shri C. Rajagopalachari and T. Prakasam, the latter popularly known as the Lion of Andhra. They were also heading the two linguistically based Congress Committees that comprised the state of Madras. Nehru abdicated his right as the Prime Minister to stand firm against this division. He did not even ask for a plebiscite on this issue, but left the decision to the two interested parties thereby negating any possibility of objectivity and fairplay.

The Andhra Provincial Congress Committee comprising Telugu-speaking population of the erstwhile Madras Presidency demanded division of the state on a linguistic basis. Likewise, the Tamil Nadu PCC justified such a decision on the basis of the election manifesto. Nehru initially firmly refused to consider such an arrangement, but later somewhat relented in the face of an emotional outburst when a respectable Telugu leader, Potti Srimarulu: threatened to go on fast to support the creation of a Telugu-speaking Andhra State. Nehru, while reassuring the Cabinet that he would not succumb to blackmail finally yielded ground when Srimarulu died while being on fast. He not only capitulated but later personally attended the inauguration of the newly created State of Andhra Pradesh in October 1953. The message was loud and clear. Pressure and blackmail would work where reason failed. Other special interest groups read the message clearly. Nehru's appeal for reason fell on deaf ears, though, theoretically he stuck to the logic that the demarcation was justified on administrative than linguistic reasons; nobody listened to him and linguistic pressures kept building up leading to the formation of the States Reorganization Commission. Nehru's shift in stand was typical of his political style that could be termed as protean. On a visit to Belgaum he was greeted by black flags demanding a Kannada-speaking state including parts of Mysore, Bombay and Hyderabad. Nehru always unduly sensitive to public reactions was not the leader to stand firm on matters of principle of national concern unlike Patel; it was not in him to educate the errant masses. He was too conscious of his popularity to risk public disapproval. He appointed a Commission but did his best to delay any decision it might recommend. Inspite of his persistent exhortations on the need for national unity, the Commission intent upon validating regionalism, acted in a lackadiasical manner and the sordid process continued.

The 1948 Commission had rejected the argument

that multiplicity of languages in one unit was a guarantee against narrow nationalism. But the new Commission appointed rejected this view. It said:

"In states having more than one developed language, there has been no marked tendency in the past to develop a sense of loyalty to the state. There was never any noticeable Madrasi sentiment when that state was a composite one. On the other hand, such loyalties as did develop within the area were based on languages. The idea that multilingual states will weaken the loyalty to language groups does not seem to be justified." Examples from Europe were quoted in support. The Pandora's Box was thus opened.

The Commission delivered its report in October 1955, where- in the number of states were to be reduced to 16 with three Union Territories. The moment the report was made public, discontent, agitation, trouble and violence spread in Orissa, Bengal and Bihar. The real centre of violent dissent was in Bombay and Punjab. Bombay had two linguistic groups—Marathi and Gujarati. There were large scale riots in Bombay in January 1956. The Central Government, as usual, was dazed into inaction. Indecision gripped Nehru and interim arrangements were made for the division of the state into two linguistic states with Bombay remaining a Union Territory. Finally, in 1960, it was decided that Bombay was to go to the Marathi-speaking state of Maharashtra and become its capital while a separate Gujarat state was created with its capital at Ahmedabad. Following these happenings, the Sikhs too demanded a separate state and the Sikh population was angry at the suggestion of merging of Himachal Pradesh with Hindi-speaking area in Greater Punjab. In the event a compromise was reached wherein the Hindu areas were to be centrally administered and both Punjabi and Hindi were to be made the official languages of Punjab state. This was a temporary reprieve and the issue for a Punjabi Suba later surfaced in Nehru's own lifetime and later the state of Punjab was to be created along with Haryana and Himachal Pradesh out of the erstwhile Punjab. The States Reorganization Bill was finally passed by the Parliament in November 1956 and the original proposal of 13 States and three UTs came to become 14 States and seven Union Territories. Undoubtedly, Nehru had much to do with the indecision of the Government. The report of the Commission shook everyone and there were many Congress leaders who advised that the report be kept in cold storage at least for 25 years. The Chief Ministers of Bengal and Bihar even suggested a merger of their States to put an end to this linguistic madness. But Nehru had already put the burning matchstick into the haystack of this madness as early as October 1955, saying in a broadcast that "no decision is irrevocable in a democracy." This was a visible olive branch for linguistic groups to agitate and achieve their ends. Nehru's problem emanated from his weakness to listen to everyone and give them the impression that there was substance in their argument which he was prepared to consider. He justified his prevarication to his distaste for dictatorship and imposing unpalatable decisions. This was one failure of his leadership. His stand on vital national issues was more like that of a moderator of debaters of rival arguments than a practical politician. He dithered and delayed even on issues on which he held strong ideological convictions. By the mid-1950s, this became Nehru's technique. Gandhiji no longer alive, there was no one to turn to for support or guidance. Unable to take decisions, he procrastinated and allowed the events to overtake him and run their course. Patel too was dead and there was no one to counsel and stand firmly by him in his hour of need. He would accede even to unreasonable demands which became irresistible, protesting nevertheless to keep the records straight.

The language issue inevitably led to national language controversy, more of which later. The seed was sown by people who could not see beyond their sensitive noses.

Linguistic states bred further factional hostility and provided an edge to the old controversy over the issue of a national language. The Constitutional provision of 1950 guaranteeing equal status to fourteen regional languages and a prominent place to English for fifteen years only temporarily appeased the fears of non-Hindi states. In 1955, the Official Language Commission was appointed for introduction of Hindi in ten years. In 1957, a report stated that only two out of its 25 members had reservations on substitution of Hindi for English. This stiffed the back of non-Hindi provinces in South. And English continued to rule the roost.

This is how Nehru used his official and moral authority to once and for all crucify the issue of national honour, our national language, the fingerprint of our cultural identity.

National Language

Nehru's love of English and his leftist leanings spawned a generation of leftist historians who rewrote Indian history in English and put the evidence of the history on its head. To quote Prof. Ramesh Chandra Mazumdar one of these luminaries:

"If we have to choose one single factor which helped more than others in bringing about a great transformation in India in the 19th century, we can, without hesitation, point to the introduction of English education."

English language did not enlighten the world. There are many other languages which can claim such credit. Every culture gains by interaction with a new culture. We gained from Arabic and Persian. What we gained from English language was an exposure to the winds of change sweeping the Western world. Even if there had been no English the genius of our people would have gained its knowledge from the past and present. Sanskrit and Prakrit have enough storehouse of knowledge of our own which we ignore in our blind pursuit for English speech and thought. It is a moot question whether in this process we gained or lost. The richness of our ancient knowledge is now being discovered by the Western world. We could have certainly added the knowledge of English and the modern Western thought to our existing mass of knowledge. We learnt astronomy and mathematics from the Arabs, philosophy from the Persians and many profound thoughts from the Chinese. The motivations behind Macaulay's introduction of English in our country were not wholly philanthropic. The British rulers needed to have a class of clerks and middle level executives to help the administration of the white man. In doing so, they blanked out the good things of our culture by painting it as semi-barbaric. The result was a permanent enslavement of our minds to the British Rulers and their ways of life. Subsequent events eminently demonstrate the purpose of introducing English in India as explained by T.B. Macaulay to his countrymen. The cretinous legacy of Macaulay persists even with greater force today.

The argument that very little scientific literature is available in Hindi is untenable. Even if it be so, for an advanced student of science, German language is more useful and in some local universities this study is encouraged. Similarly, for advanced study in literature, French is as rich as English. For Western Philosophy, one could with equal logic learn German, which the British themselves do in order to understand European philosophic thought. But the language spoken within the country has no relationship to these forays into foreign literature for specific knowledge. The point here is not merely of acquiring knowledge from outside countries for the benefit of our country. It is one of acquiring a national symbol, a medium of expression that unites this country as one civilizational entity. Israel, Germany, Japan, France, Italy, Russia, China have their own national languages. In fact, the Israelies, one of the most scientifically advanced people, speak Yiddish and Hebrew, the oldest language known to man, almost as old as Sanskrit. So much for the nonsense of lack of scientific vocabulary in Hindi. Given the national will any language can acquire the vocabulary it needs. No one stops us from learning any language to enrich our knowledge of science or any other field of knowledge.

The grounds for adopting Hindi were discussed at length by our Constitution makers and have not changed with times. Within the Union of India, we need a symbol of national unity. Every large country has minor dialects and even multiplicity of local languages; but they still have one national language. How is it that after almost five decades of freedom, we have not been able to shake off the burden of English and adopt our own national language. That Hindi is the only language spoken by the largest number of people in the largest number of states is an undisputable fact. If a Tamilian or a Keralite can learn English with ease why can he not learn Hindi, whose Sanskrit base is a common source of many words in his own language. To our eternal shame, we take pride in communicating to our own countrymen in a foreign tongue. Nehru, the Western Oriental Gentleman (WOG) never really made any sincere effort nor did he muster enough political will to implement Hindi.

No nation is worth its spirit and soul which does not have its own vehicle of cultural articulation that its national language provides. Except for countries like USA, Canada and Australia, where the British immigrants formed a major part of their ethnic structure, there are few great countries which use a language imposed by its conquerors. The Moslems and the Moghals brought Arabic texts and used Persian as their court language, replacing Sanskrit and its local variants. The British brought their own language and allowed Urdu to stay as the local language of courts and land records. Once they left, it was inevitable that the country should reclaim its own national language. The Constitution enjoins upon the Government to adopt Hindi as its official language. Nehru's westernised upbringing baulked at the very idea of switching to Hindi. He used specious arguments, such as lack of scientific vocabulary, difficulty in international communications and diversity of local Indian languages as an excuse to stonewall the adoption of Hindi. The dragon's seeds of linguistic jingoism had been sown as a natural consequence of the lingistic provinces, as has been discussed earlier. Thereafter, to reconcile recalcitrant local language enthusiasts was not easy. Love of English by the leftist litteratti and their intolerance of Hindu culture translated itself into a movement to denigrate Hindi. The argument that Hindi as advocated by the enthusiasts was too Sanskritised and difficult for comprehension by the average Indian people is as fatuous as it is mendacious. It was no one's case that Hindi should be only Sanskrit oriented. To the extent that Sanskrit was the mother of all languages, as acknowledged even by Western philologists, the Sanskrit origin of Hindi was inevitable. But the spoken and written Hindi has an equal measure of words from Persian and Urdu, its progeny. Thus, the case against abstruse Hindi falls flat on its face. Nehru, the Harrowian pupil, stood passive, often lending support to the anti-Hindi lobby. The *raison-d'etre* and justification for Hindi is lucidly brought out by Dr. Rajendra Prasad, the first President of India, in his letter given at Appendix 'A'. Thereafter, he repeatedly reminded Nehru of the Government's obligations to introduce Hindi. Here is a letter dated 27th February, 1954, seven years after independence.

"My dear Prime Minister,

"The Constitution provides that the official language of the Union shall be Hindi in Devanagari script but that it will come into use for the official purposes of the Union after 15 years from the commencement of the Constitution. It is also provided that during this period the President may by order authorise the use of the

Hindi language in addition to the English language for any of the official purposes of the Union. At the expiration of five years from the commencement of the Constitution, and again at the expiration of ten years, a Commission shall be constituted to make recommendations as to the progressive use of the Hindi language for the official purposes of the Union and the restrictions on the use of the English language.

"More than four years have elapsed since the Constitution came into force, and within the next nine or ten months the Commission contemplated by the Constitution will have to be appointed. It may not be possible to introduce Hindi for the purposes of the Union without some preparatory steps being taken in advance. I have no information about any steps that may have been taken by any of the Ministries of the Government of India for the introduction of Hindi for any purpose whatsoever. As the adoption of Hindi for all purposes except those for which there is a special provision in the Constitution is contemplated at the end of fifteen years, it is desirable, and infact absolutely necessary, to introduce it gradually and progressively so that the requirement of the Constitution may be fulfilled when the time arrives. I would, therefore, suggest that immediate action be taken for the gradual and progressive introduction of Hindi within this year, so that when the Commission is appointed, it gets the results which may have been achieved, the difficulties which may have been experienced, and any other relevant matters, to enable it to make its recommendations in the next year.

"I understand that in some of the States, Hindi has already been adopted as the official language for those States. They are, I believe, Uttar Pradesh, Bihar, Madhya Pradesh, Rajasthan and Madhya Bharat, which cover practically most of the area, of which Hindi is the language.

"I would suggest that the following steps be taken which may be considered for immediate and long-term implementation of the Constitution:

"I. *Immediate Steps*

"(a) In each Ministry of the Government of India there should be at least one officer of a rank entitling him to authenticate orders and directives issued by the Government of India who possesses a working knowledge of Hindi. It would of course be desirable to have a person who may be competent to prepare drafts in Hindi and also to check the accuracy of drafts of translations made by others. But if there be any serious difficulty in getting officers of that rank for every department, working knowledge may be insisted upon. By a person with working knowledge I mean a person who is not able to prepare his own drafts or to write the language correctly but is able to read the drafts prepared by others intelligently and sign the document after understanding its contents. It should be the duty of such officer not only to do such work as may be required in the department to be done in Hindi but also to see to it that Hindi is progressively introduced within his department so that progress may be judged and the area covered known from year to year.

(b) I presume some correspondence or communication is received by every department in the Hindi language. I do not know how such correspondence is dealt with, and if any replies that go from the various departments are in Hindi, I should suggest that, to begin with, all communications received in Hindi by every department of the Government of India should be dealt with or at least replied to in Hindi.

(c) To enable the department to use Hindi even in a limited way, there should be the requisite staff of clerks, stenographers, typists, etc., and such staff should be employed in every department.

(d) Government should make out a programme of gradual replacement of English by Hindi, and each department should see to it that the targets fixed for each year are reached.

(e) Correspondence with States which have already adopted Hindi as their language should, at any rate in respect of those matters in which work in the Central Secretariat will be done through Hindi, should be through the medium of Hindi.

(f) Arrangements should be made on a graded scale for enabling the employees in the Central Secretariat from the highest to the lowest to learn Hindi in their spare hours, and encouragement should be given for learning it by the award of prizes and, after two years, by making promotions dependent upon proficiency in the language.

"II. As a *long-term* measure for making Hindi the State language, I would suggest the following:

"(a) Hindi should be made a compulsory subject for examination for every candidate who appears at any competitive examination for the All India Services—Administrative, Police, Forest, Education, etc. In order that candidates from Hindi-speaking areas may not have an additional advantage, the marks obtained in Hindi at the examinations should not be counted for determining the place occupied by a candidate amongst the examinees, but passing or securing a minimum number of marks in that language should be made obligatory for every candidate selected.

(b) During the period of training for the Administrative and other Services of candidates, who have passed a competitive examination, an examination in Hindi of a fairly adequate standard should be insisted upon.

(c) Encouragement to those already in service whose language is not Hindi should be given by the award of prizes, etc., as was the case formerly during the British time.

"I suggest that steps on the above lines be taken from now onwards, so that from the 1st April next the use of Hindi for some purposes, which may be determined with special reference to the requirements of each department may begin. It may be that action has already been taken in some respects or in some departments. If so, I shall be obliged to be furnished with detailed information with regard thereto.

Yours Sincerely
Rajendra Prasad"

Inspite of such irrefutable logic and compelling evidence, apart from reasons of national pride, Nehru continued to obstruct adoption of Hindi as a national language. How should one describe this attitude on the part of the first Chief Executive of India? Sheer cussedness in a man described as a rationalist by many of his admirers.

Atal Bihari Vajpayee made history in 1977 when as India's Foreign Minister, in his first formal address to U.N.General Assembly , he spoke in Hindi. This is what Jagat Mehta, the Foreign Secretary at the time, had to say about its impact:

"Never before had I come across the power of Hindi, with richness of vocabulary expressing with sophistication and necessary ambiguities, on the vast range of international problems."

To the Cassandras still doubting the legitimacy of Hindi to be accepted as the national language the following incident should be an eye-opener:

Time 10 A.M. onwards; date 26th January, 1996; place Rajpath during the Republic Day Parade.

The ceremonial parade of our military might and cultural diversity, the vigour of our youth and the soul of our nation in various contingents, pageants and tableaux was on display. The commentry on this unique spectacle was conducted both in Hindi and English by competent announcers. But even to the meanest intelligence the Hindi broadcast seemed to resonate so well with what was being presented, the sound mingled so naturally with the sight that even the sceptic and the diehard was moved beyond measure and we all felt proud of our country. The words vibrated to the spirit and soul of the land that is Bharat. But the English version though well pronounced not only sounded discordant but almost alien and intrusive. English just does not empathise with the soul of India. It is about time our English enthusiasts take Hindi more seriously. To refit a French saying in this context "Ill faut que vous voyez la parade de notre jour de la Republique pour avoir une ide bien exact de la beaute et le harmonie de notre langue". (It is necessary that you should see our Republic Day parade in order to have a very exact idea of the beauty and the harmony of our language.)

Appendix A

Extracts from an article by Dr. Rajendra Prasad, published in the "Harijan" dated 5 December and 12 December, 1948.

A State Language for India

(I)

"When the Muslims came to India and became its rulers, they used their own language for governmental and administrative purposes but otherwise they let Sanskrit and provincial languages alone. The language of Islam is Arabic. It is the language of the Holy Quran, the Hadis and a great part of the religious lore of the early Muslims. But Arabic was not the language of the Muslim rulers of India who adopted Persian as they were more familiar with it than with Arabic. Arabic in India thus has remained more a language of the learned priests and *alims* rather than of Muslims as a body. Persian became the court language and was for that purpose studied on an extensive scale not only by the Indians who had embraced Islam but by Hindus also. The Persian language and literature have of course been very largely influenced by the Arabic language and literature but so far as India was concerned, it was more Persian than Arabic which was adopted. Persian had become so prevalent that it was adopted as the official language for administrative purposes even by a large section of ordinary people just as we see today many Indians carrying on their private business in English. I have seen the accounts and records of some zamindars kept in Persian language till so late as the nineties of the last century.

"When the English came they used their own language for administrative purposes and gradually replaced Persian by English and all those classes that had used Persian during the Muslim period and had continued to use it by sheer inertia till many years after the British rule had been established also gradually displaced Persian and adopted English in its place. The result has been that English has now been accepted for some years past as the language not only for governmental and administrative purposes but also by business firms and others. This was inevitable because ever since English was adopted as the medium of instruction it has gone on spreading until it became the medium not only for all higher education in the universities but also in lower forms of schools. Only during recent years when the national movement grew and gained strength that Indian languages began to be considered as media of instruction in schools and today several universities have decided to adopt them although no university has yet completely done so.

"What the Muslim rulers or the English did in India is what has been done everywhere all the world over when one nation has conquered another or established its rule over another country. Now that foreign rule has ceased, the desire has naturally been expressed that all our transactions should be in our own language but as I have said above there are several languages prevalent in different parts of the country and it is necessary, therefore, to have one language for all-India purposes. There is no question of forcing any language of any one part of the country on others and thus establishing a sort of linguistic imperialism any more than there is any question of establishing or enforcing a government or administration on any part of the country not acceptable to it. It is here that the difference arises between the common language that will be now accepted by the country as a whole on the one hand and Persian or English on the other."

"Let us look at the same question from another point of view. Are our universities which are not unnaturally adopting provincial languages as media of instruction within their respective jurisdictions to grow independently of each other without any intercourse and without any relationship? In what language are our research journals to be published? Are they to be in our provincial languages or in the common language? If the former, how are the students, teachers and research workers in other linguistic areas to profit by the work done in one area unless they know the various languages? If they are to be in the common language, then all the research workers must possess a pretty high standard of proficiency in that language. How is that proficiency to be attained unless the common language is studied with diligence and its study holds out prospects of preferment? The English language has been studied with great success in India because proficiency in that language was a *sine qua non* for material success in every department of life during the British rule.

Any attempt to reconcile conflicting claims is always a difficult task but it has to be faced."

(II)

"The need and implication of a common language for India being established, the question that arises next is what language can be that common language. It is suggested in some quarters that English has already acquired that position and there is no reason why it should not be continued and why it should be displaced by any Indian language. It is true that English is at the present moment doing what such a common language is expected and intended to do. It has also the advantage of having a rich and flexible vocabulary and it is understood over a large part of the world and has acquired an international status and utility which it would be difficult for an Indian language to acquire. With all this advantage, however, English has not taken root in this country and once the state patronage, which it has been enjoying is withdrawn, it will cease to make that widespread appeal which it does today. Besides, any foreign language will be exotic in all parts of the country and no part of the country as a whole can acquire it in a way in which it knows its own language. So English will have to be studied and its study kept up by an artificial state help: it will never take root and will never be the language of the masses of any part of this country whereas any Indian language will be the language of, at any rate, some part of the country and will be the language of all the classes and masses of that part of the country. It will also have affinity with a number of other provincial languages and thus easily assimilable by the people in those provinces also. Our choice must, therefore, be confined to an Indian language. It does not mean that we shall have to cease learning English altogether. For all international purposes English will have to be studied. It will also have to be studied for the rich heritage it has got in the shape of its vast stock of literature—scientific, philosophic and literary. But then it will have to be studied by a few and the intensity of its study will also depend upon its utility for the particular use to which it has to be put. Even today many Indians learn other foreign languages for enabling them to study scientific and research journals and for other similar purposes.

"Among the Indian languages the choice will naturally fall on the language which is most widely known and understood, and Hindi or Hindustani, by whatever name we may call it, is the obvious choice. It has a good literature, it has capacity for development and it is allied to all the languages of Northern India and can be easily learnt by people speaking and knowing any of them. Even the South Indian languages have a large admixture of words of Sanskrit origin, particularly Telugu, Kanarese and Malayalam."

And finally, the conclusions that are arrived at are as follows:

"[1. A common language for all-India purposes is necessary.
2. That common language will have to be studied on a fairly extensive scale by people all over the country whatever their own language may be.
3. That language cannot be English but will have to be an Indian language.
4. Of Indian languages Hindi or Hindustani is best fitted for this purpose.
5. But Hindi or Hindustani will have to give up the policy of boycott of words of foreign origin and to make its door open for entry of words from other languages.
6. These additional words must come in the first place from the various provincial languages and from dialects. Even words of purely foreign origin may not be altogether excluded.
7. In view of the above the controversy between Hindi and Hindustani is futile.
8. With all the additions to the vocabulary that can be made with the help of other languages there will still remain the need for coining a large number of words to express modern ideas very largely of a technical nature and the source from which these additional words have to be derived is Sanskrit.]

Uniform Civil Code

The landmark judgment of Supreme Court of 10th May, 1995, and its direction to the Government of India asking it to work towards implementing a uniform civil code, reminds one of the ills of omission and commission as early as 1954 when Nehru moved the Hindu Civil Code Bill. Article 44 of the Directive Principles in the Constitution urges the state to "secure for its citizens a Uniform Civil Code." Parliament can amend the Fundamental Rights for implementing the Directive Principles of State Policy so long as the amendment does not touch the basic features of the Constitution and nothing prevents it from enacting legislation to enforce them. Nehru who scoffed at Hindus for their antiquated religious customs and beliefs could and did have the courage to enact the Hindu Marriage Act (1955), the Hindu Succession Act (1956) and the Hindu Adoption and Maintenance Act (1956); in fact, the whole gamut of Hindu Code Bill; though, strongly opposed by no less a person than the then President, Dr. Rajendra Prasad. However, where Muslims were equally concerned, he could not muster enough courage to amend the Muslim Personal Law in a similar manner. Was he afraid of the Muslim reaction or their vote bank slipping away from his hands should he venture on such a course? With the support of all his Muslim friends, surely, he should have been in an unassailable position to get the legislation through. While he would harangue and berate into submission the Hindus forming 80% of the population, he baulked at touching his favoured community and the vote bank of Muslims.

The Supreme Court judgment spelt out that successive Governments till date have been wholly remiss in their duty of implementing their Constitutional mandate enshrined in the Directive Principles of the State Policy. The Supreme Court further averred that a Uniform Civil Code was imperative both for the protection of the oppressed and the promotion of national unity and solidarity. The first step towards the Uniform Civil Code was to rationalise the Personal Law of the Minorities "to develop the religious and cultural amity."

While taking the Hindus for granted, Nehru preferred to use his socio-political discretion in such sensitive matters as the Muslim Personal Law and treated it as a holy cow. Dr. Rajendra Prasad's letter given below notwithstanding, it was only the Hindu Code Bill that was affected and the Muslims remained outside the pale of a Uniform Civil Code. Did it not amount to segregating the minorities and instilling in them a feeling of a separate identity and a tacit admission of the Two Nation Theory the very thing he opposed all his life? This is what Dr. Rajendra Prasad had to say:

"All our social reform movements and the moral fervour behind them are so far generally confined to the Hindus. We have always allowed the Muslim and the Christian communities to have their own way. This may be a good example in toleration; it may perhaps reflect the hope that the reform amongst the Hindus may give rise to a healthy emulation in the minds of other denominations also. But political self-interest has so far come in their way, and orthodoxy amongst the Christians and the Muslims and other denominations is as hopeless and hard as the orthodoxy amongst the Hindus—only, the former is stronger and never discredited. Sometimes the criticism is heard that the Government is partial to the Hindus in the sense that it throws its whole weight on the side of social reform amongst Hindus and helps that community to overcome its weakness, but when it comes to any social legislation for overcoming the social defects and antiquated moral standards of non-Hindus, the Government has thought it fit to follow a policy of non-intervention and non-interference. This is bound to weaken the nation as a whole, and thereby weaken the forces of moral and spiritual reform started in the Muslim and Christian countries of the world. It is sometimes a wiser course to allow social reform in the minority communities to grow spontaneously from within instead of using the weight of the enlightened sense of the majority community for quickening the pace of reform amongst them. It is safe to wait for some time at least."

In a whole decade, after the introduction of the Hindu Code Bill, Nehru the uncrowned Caeser and darling of the masses could not muster enough political will to give effect to one of the Directive Principles of the Constitution. Had he done so, most of our present day problems of Muslim minorities, and the trend of minority appeasement and vote bank politics would not have arisen at all. To the so-called 'secularly enlightened' in the Congress and the self-professed leaders of Moslem faith such a measure would be tyrannical to the minorities. When this question came up in the Constituent Assembly, Dr. K.M Munshi stood up to refute this objection. This is what he said:

"A further argument has been advanced that the enactment of a civil code would be tyrannical to minorities. Is it tyrannical? Nowhere in advanced Muslim countries the personal law of each minority has been recongised as so sacrosanct as to prevent the enactment of a civil code. Take for instance Turkey or Egypt. No minority in these countries is permitted to have such rights. But I go further. When the Shariat Act was passed, or when certain laws were passed in the Central Legislature in the old regime, the Khojas and Cutchi Memons were highly dissatisfied.

"They then followed certain Hindu customs; for generations since they became converts they had done so. They did not want to conform to the Shariat; and yet by a legislation of the Central Legislature certain Muslim members who felt that Shariat law should be enforced upon the whole community carried their point. The Khojas and Cutchi Memons most unwillingly had to submit to it. Where were the rights of minorities then ? When you want to consolidate a community, you have to take into consideration the benefit which may accrue to the whole community and not to the customs or a part of it. It is not, therefore, correct to say that such an act is tyranny of the majority. If you will look at the countries in Europe which have a civil code, everyone who goes there from any part of the world and every minority has to submit to the civil code. It is not felt to be tyrannical to the minority."

When asked as late as 1954 in Lok Sabha, why a Uniform Civil Code as mentioned in the Constitution has not yet been legislated, Nehru gave the same halting half truth that the time is not yet ripe for such a legislation. The same answer as for the abrogation of Article 370. The high priest of secularism could not comprehend that in a secular society, State laws have to rise above religion and must apply to all religious communities in equal measure. This pandering to obscurantist Muslim opinion led to an incongruous situation which even Nehru, the self-proclaimed rationalist, could not miss; the Muslims would accept the Indian Penal Code for criminal offences when it suited them, such as in the case of theft and adultery. The punishment prescribed in Quran and Shariat for theft is cutting of both hands and for adultery stoning to death. Why did the Muslims not accept the Laws of Shariat and Quran on these issues ? Rather they preferred the Indian Penal Code which is more lenient. But in matters of divorce and inheritance they just chose to be governed by the Shariat. Nehru, the ever accommodating Prime Minister, condoned Moslem fundamentalism and aquiesced meekly. The situation continued till again under pressure of the obscurantist Moslem clergy, his grandson following in his footsteps, reversed the verdict of the Supreme Court in the Shah Bano Case by bringing in a legislation in Parliament, to appease the orthodox Muslims in order to secure Muslim votes. Secularism of some sorts indeed? It had to befall the Supreme Court to remind the cavalier Government that they were found remiss in not implementing Article 44 of the Constitution regarding the Uniform Civil Code. To even the most obtuse it should be clear that civil code is different from religious practices and does not infringe on the freedom of worship or observance of a religion as guaranteed by the Constitution. It only deals with the secular and more mundane matters of marriage, divorce and inheritance. The Supreme Court rightly pointed out that those elements of the Muslim society who wanted a division of our country on religious lines and desired to undertake the task of social reconstruction on the basis of religious books, demanded a separate nation and got it from their British masters. Pakistan was thus created and this country partitioned. Those, who on the basis of religion and Quran wanted to build a nation and society, had gone to Pakistan. Those who stayed back had their choice and are deemed to have implicitly accepted the underlying principle of the Indian polity that there will be no social reconstruction on the basis of any religious books. Since India is a secular country, it cannot be run on the text of religious books. The Supreme Court further averred that the two-nation theory was anathema to the Indian Constitution makers. But Nehru not only turned a Nelson's eye to this fundamental spirit of our nation and the Constitution by procrastinating any state action to implement Article 44. That was Nehru's faith in our Constitution. The first Prime Minister of India in seventeen long years could not implement one essential item that could integrate different sections of our society into a nation with a Uniform Civil Code.

Nehru's motivations were not necessarily philanthropic nor in the long term national interest of ensuring a common national identity for this country which should have included all Muslims. His actions, deliberate and inadvertent, encouraged a separate Muslim identity in the Indian polity whose thoughts and actions were not always co-terminus with the national ethos. By instilling a sense of insecurity in the Muslim minds and thereby encouraging a ghetto mentality and posing as their champion, he berated and denounced the so-called Hindu majority as communal, hoping to create a permanent Hindu-Muslim schism and vote-bank for the Congress and thus succeeded in dividing the polity on religious lines. His successors perpetuated this game of Muslim appeasement and perfected it into a fine art, ready to use it against any party which tried to talk of national sovereignty and integrity or even suggest that there should be no discrimination in favour of any minority. The Muslims, Nehru ensured, were more equal than others and deserved a special status. Hence, his stand on Article 370, and the Uniform Civil Code. His secularism was only meant for the Hindu majority. The Muslims were outside its pale. The dragons seeds were thus sown by the great secularist and soon enough the wrath of the angels was upon us. That the Muslims have never been fully integrated in the Indian society inspite of their own silent majority wishing it, remains true and the seeds of another partition have been sown.

Concern for Minorities

Nehru ignored the reality that a large number of Muslims remaining in India were the same who had raised the slogan of Pakistan but could not migrate there for one reason or the other. But this inability to reach the haven of their religious faith did nothing to diminish their ardour for that promised land. They were just not the minority wishing to assimilate themselves into the national mainstream, for whom Nehru spent so many sleepless nights. His constant upbraiding of the Hindu majority for being inimical to this 'innocent' minority was not supported by any evidence of the loyalty of this minority to their new home. This was the contentious issue on which Nehru found himself isolated from his colleagues. To be fair to Nehru, his efforts to instill confidence and champion the cause of Hindu-Muslim unity, was not yet influenced by a desire to benefit from the Muslim vote-bank. During his term, the Congress was strong enough on its own past record, not to need any such props; but the same was not true of his own successors who carried out the same policy for less than honest motives. At that point of time, Muslim ethos did not show any sign of being nationalistic; rather it had a definite streak of pan-Islamism transcending national boundaries. To quote Giri Lal Jain, a perceptive observer of Indian political scene, from his last work just before his death and published posthumously "The Hindu Phenomenon":

"Jinnah could call Indian nationalism, as espoused by the Indian National Congress, 'Hindu nationalism' on the ground that the Congress was a Hindu body, which it was, by virtue of its ethos if not by that of its ideology and composition, and pit 'Muslim nationalism' against it. But he could not possibly overcome the obstinate fact that Islam, on the one hand, does not admit of nationalism and, on the other, does not help overcome local and even tribal loyalties.

"Thus, while Jinnah could bring Muslims together on an anti-Hindu platform and force the country's partition, he could not lay the foundations of a Pakistani nation. It is not surprising that Pakistan continues to 'define' itself in anti-India and anti-Hindu terms. It could not possibly overcome its essentially transient character and disruptive role and it has not. The military muscle it has acquired, thanks to US bounty and Soviet stupidity, has inevitably increased its capacity for mischief but not its ability to define itself in terms of itself.

"No political party has succeeded in making Muslims partners in the common enterprise of building a secular and democratic India. Muslims, as a community do not, and indeed cannot, accept secularism as a legitimate doctrine for the public domain. For them the public domain is not separate from the all-encompassing religious realm. This problem haunts the entire *ummah* and not only its Indian constituent: it is first and above all a community of believers."

As mentioned earlier in this book, Nehru's reading of history never came anywhere near the Indian identity of the Hindu phenomenon, since by self-confession, he came to India from the West and approached Indian spiritual essence and history as British authors did who saw it through their own coloured glasses. Much more objective research on the subject has since been carried out by later day historians including French and German Orientalists. Nehru was handicapped by a lack of knowledge of Sanskrit and other Indian languages. Educated at Harrow and deliberately westernised by his father who had a sneaking admiration for the white-skinned rulers and was devoid of his Indian roots, Nehru's thinking was not deep enough. He was influenced by the current trends in British thought which no less a person than Bertrand Russell himself, considered to be too superficial. He had missed the essence of the Indian culture, in spite of his rather romantic view of our past. While this aspect has been discussed at many places earlier in this work it bears repetition, since it has been reinforced by Giri Lal Jain, a known secularist and admirer of Nehru, in his latest book mentioned earlier. Consider this piece, which, re-emphasises the hollowness of Nehru's concept of a synthetic culture.

"Nehru's intellectual background led him to take a synthetic (aggregationist) view of Indian culture, though on a more careful reflection, it should have been possible for him to recognize, on the one hand, its integral unity founded on yoga, of which the Veda itself is a fruit, and, on the other, its capaciousness on the strength of the same boundless yogic foundation which placed no limit on the freedom of the human spirit. Inevitably this synthetic view of Indian culture led him—especially in view of the Persianized cultural background of his own forebears and of the Kashmiri Pandit community in the plains and, indeed, in the valley itself —to accept the theory of a Hindu-Muslim cultural synthesis. The fact of partition must have provoked some doubt in his mind."

"But, by then, it was too late for him to review and restate his basic position, even if he were so inclined. No political leader in his position could afford to do so. And if it was too late before partition, it was certainly worse after independence when he was charged with the task of covering up the wounds inflicted by the

Muslim League in the hope that the cover-up would allow the healing process to take over in course of time. All that makes it truly remarkable that he allowed himself to say as much as he did. Three of his speeches deserve attention in this regard."

"In view of his bitter experience of events leading to partition, it is inconceivable that Nehru could be so naive as to believe even vaguely that educated Muslims could possibly regard themselves as 'sharers and inheritors' of the cultural heritage he was speaking about. In fact, it would be reasonable to infer that he said what he did precisely because he knew that the opposite was true." Disillusioned of his pipe-dream of a cultural synthesis of Islam and Hinduism, Nehru was left with no choice but to settle for a harmonious co-existence of the two. This was Nehru's concept of secularism; vague and wide off the mark.

Nehru was particularly and unduly critical of the distortions that had crept into the Hindu religion. Being a student of history, he should have known better. Insistence on form, rather than substance, has been the common bane of all old religions. Christianity began by protesting against the irrational and the obsolete in the older religion of Judaism. Islam, the more recent one, was the more aggressive and revolutionary. While Christianity was born out of an attempt to reform old practices of Judaism Prophet Mohammad, born in the barrens of Arabia, had little available religious literature, except his own godly inspirations. Consequently he leaned heavily for precedents on Judaism and Christianity. Both were monotheistic. Mohammad deprecated the worship of many gods, a practice prevalent at Mecca and announced his own new faith. He wavered once, recanted and again under the influence of angel Gabriel pronounced his faith in a formless one God, Allah. Though there were no idols to be worshipped the believers even till date revere the black stone at Mecca. They still have mazars, dargahs and tombs of saints and Sufis, where Chaddars are offered in worship. There are no such instructions in *Quran*.

To a discerning observer of the development of Christianity into a full-fledged religion it would be evident that even as early as the time of Nicaea there was a marked difference in the current Gospel from the simple teachings of Jesus of Nazareth. The teaching of Jesus was a new 'prophetic teaching' which began with Hebrew prophets. It had no place for priests, consecrated temple or the altar. It contained neither rites nor ceremonies and at the centre of its sacrifice was "a broken and contrite heart". The only organisation was that of the preacher and his sermon. Even in the 4th century A.D. Christianity, though based on the teachings of Jesus, had already become a priestly religion with which the world was familiar for millenia. The ritual, centered on the altar and the worship on the sacrifice by a consecrated priest of the Mass, developed soon into an organisation of deacons, priests and bishops. This Christianity then adopted cults uncannily reminiscent of those of Bel-Marduk, Amman or Serapis, already known to the world. Similarly, in later Judaic faith, where idol worship was forbidden, the 'Arc of Yahveh' or 'Arc of the Lord' was a sacred totem of worship and treasured by the Jews. So much so that the tent carrying the Arc was even carried to the battlefield. Likewise, Talmud and Tora were the religious books cherished, preserved and kept at sacred places in the synagogues, just as Guru Granth Sahib is kept in all Gurudwaras.

Thus we shall see that there are minor and understandable deviations from the highly theoretical concept of an invisible monotheistic entity which an average and less learned man cannot easily comprehend. Monuments and places of worship are common in each religion. Similarly, in the latest religion of Sikhism which started as a movement towards removing certain distortions that had crept into Hindu religion had its own places of worship. Gorgeous Gurudwaras were constructed for religious congregations. Although there are no idols, the *Guru Granth Sahib,* the holy book is kept and read by the devout. All talk of the Nirankari essence of God but indulge with vigour and reverence for the worldly and grand construction of Gurudwaras. Seen in this manner, outward physical form, in one way or the other have been added to the original concept of the formless God in almost all religions. And what is a temple after all, if not a place of worship just like the mosque, the church, or the synagogue. The presence of idols in it serves only as a means of concentration on the infinite and 'nirankar swarup' of God through physical symbols that man can easily comprehend. It is no one's case that all was right with the Hindu rituals and worship. But it did not lead Ramakrishna Paramhans or Swami Vivekanand to denigrate the Hindu worship of God. On the other hand, Nehru's impatience with and disdain for the Hindu form of worship persisted throughout his life. He was not so severe on the Muslims for similar aberrations on their part. It is altogether a different matter that his last rites were performed according to the Hindu religious traditions. One only wishes that he had the patience to study the teachings of Swami Ramakrishna and Vivekanand. Gandhiji was much more realistic in this regard, and was a devout Hindu to the core.

While Nehru lived in a world of his own secular 'make-believe', and completely ignored the ground realities of those days in post-partition India regarding Muslim separatism it was left to Patel, the strong man, to nip this mischief in the bud. Further, the religious basis for Pakistan was not lost sight of . On Patel's insistence and cold logic, Mr. Ahmed Said, a local Muslim leader, wrote the following letter to Nawabzada Liaquat Ali Khan:

"As some of my messages were kept unreplied, I would not have taken the liberty to encroach upon your time as I know how terribly busy and worried you are at present. But I do think that in the interest of Muslims of the minority provinces I must write to you. The recent statement by the Prime Minister, Mr. Khuhro, in which he said that Sind is an Islamic Government has caused a certain amount of difficulties for the Muslims in the minority provinces. If they are going to form theocratic Governments in Pakistan, there will be every justification for Hindus to form a Hindu Raj in the rest of India and, therefore, I would request you to make a definite declaration on this question or advise His Excellency Quaid-i-Azam to make some announcement including the following points:

1. that formation of Governments in Pakistan will be on a secular basis and not on a religious basis;
2. a declaration about the protection and rights of minorities in Pakistan; and
3. an expression of disappointment and regret at what happened in Western and Eastern Punjab with an assurance of protection and fair treatment to those who had left their homes and property if they come back to Western Punjab; so that on the basis of reciprocity, Muslims in minority provinces may hope to receive the same protection."

This was a sequel to an attempt by Pakistan to recruit Army Officers from Aligarh Muslim University. Aligarh was always a fortress and stronghold of Muslim League before partition. While the significance of this sinister move of Pakistan was lost on Nehru, the ever alert Patel acted with perspicacity. He wrote a letter to Pantji, later the Chief Minister of Uttar Pradesh.

"We have received information that the Pakistan Government have sent, or are sending representatives to recruit army officers from among Aligarh University students. I should be glad if you would kindly order immediate enquiries into this matter and send an official report. I feel that if the report is substantiated, we could presume that the university authorities are giving facilities for such recruitment, and on that account, we shall have to reconsider our attitude to giving this university a grant.

"I also feel that, if the report is correct, you should detain the representatives concerned, because this would in effect amount to suborning the loyalty of Indian nationals."

This no nonsense letter is in sharp contrast to the pussyfooting style of Nehru on any matter dealing with Muslims in India. A similar earlier letter by Patel on 7th July, 1947, to Govind Malaviya is equally revealing:

"The point that you have raised in your letter about those who have in the past worked for, or had sympathy for Pakistan choosing to stay in India for future service has not escaped our attention. Such people will be given no option. I have noticed in my experience during the last 10 months that the Muslim personnel of the services are thoroughly disloyal to Government, and it was impossible to run any administration efficiently or even tolerably fairly. Their full energy was concentrated in disruptive activities inside the organisation. There was no discipline, and they were not afraid of doing anything contrary to rules. We have therefore taken care to see that all such elements in the services go over to Pakistan.

"After 15 August, the service rules and regulations will be strictly enforced and no disloyalty will be tolerated. The oath of loyalty to the Indian Government will first be administered to all, and anyone found to have any other sympathy or loyalty with any outside agency or organisation will have to leave service. You may therefore rest assured that proper action will be taken to see that all such people are weeded out from here."

And finally, the Sardar's stern warning to Indian Muslims in 1948, after the partition, is equally forthright.

"In the recent All India Muslim Conference, why did you not open your mouths on the Kashmir issue? Why did you not condemn the action of Pakistan? These things raise doubts in the minds of the people."

Patel roared:

"In free India, there is no room for divided loyalties."

Could one ever imagine Nehru, the eternal Hamlet, ever administering such a warning in the interest of the security and integrity of our new state. His breed today in the Congress is even weaker and it is unimaginable to think of any Congress leader who does not blindly pursue the Muslim vote-bank politics to the utter disregard of our country's defence and national integrity, when threatened by Muslim separatism.

After Mahatma Gandhi's death, under Nehru's benevolent guidance, the public outrage was deliberately directed to serve Nehru's anti-Hindu and pro-Muslim bias. Public anger was cleverly directed towards the Hindu Mahasabha, a favourite whipping boy of Nehru, and a whispering campaign and media onslaught was carefully mounted against Hindu organisations. To rebut this charge and to put the facts in the proper perspective, Ashutosh Lahiry of Hindu Mahasabha had to issue the following public statement with a copy to Dr. Rajendra Prasad, the President of India.

"We repudiate the calumny that the Hindu Mahasabha's activities have helped to promote and to aggravate communalism in the country. Excepting that the Mahasabha confined its membership to Hindu community alone, there is nothing in the Mahasabha programme or activities which can be called communal in the sense that it ever claimed for the Hindus anything which it sought to deny to non-Hindus. In fact in the Bilaspur Resolution of the Hindu Mahasabha, the Mahasabha guaranteed to the minority community its share in the governance of the country according to its population ratio. Under the Mahasabha conception of Hindu Rashtra, Moslems would get unrestricted right to share in the political power, along with the Hindus, in accordance with their numerical strength, besides full liberty to develop their religion, culture and language. The ideal of Hindu Rashtra, therefore, did not differ in any respect from the ideal of the

Congress which swore by principles of nationalism but which at every stage surrendered to communalism and strengthened the Muslim League and the communal element in the country by successive concessions to the communal demands, quite contrary to their professions. In fact the fight of the Hindu Mahasabha has all along been for upholding principles of nationalism and democracy and against surrendering to forces of communalism."

If the statement has a familiar ring to the utterances of some present day stalwarts, the fact cannot be helped. He went on to say:

"People ask why Hindu Mahasabha is again returning to politics. Since the 15th of August 1947, and particularly since the suspension of our political activities, the attitude of the Congress, the dominant political party, towards the Mahasabha has been one of superciliousness and malicious misrepresentation and a campaign of slander has been carried on to create and strengthen prejudice in the public mind against the Mahasabha. Our workers are most anxious to serve the people in the political field and we cannot shut them out indefinitely from their right to serve according to their own light. The Mahasabha has a distinguished record of public service, and we cannot allow this great organisation to be throttled out of existence by such baseless campaign of lies and slander, coming from our political opponents."

And then he chastised the Congress for its autocratic attitude.

"In consequence of this totalitarian and monopolistic political ambition of the Congress, there is a steadily growing opposition to Congress administration throughout the country which has been further aggravated by misrule, maladministration and unprecedented corruption in every department of public administration. The Congress leaders defend their new policy on the plea of danger to internal peace and security, and necessity of meeting all subversive movements. Strangely enough, any opposition to the will of the ruling party, however constitutional it might be, is now being misrepresented as subversive."

"I may recall that the Hindu Mahasabha was founded by revered leaders like Pandit Madan Mohan Malaviya, Lala Lajpat Rai and Swami Shraddhanand of hallowed memory, at a time when Moslem onslaughts in Malabar, Kohat, Saharanpur and in other places brought home to them the need for an organisation for safeguarding and defending Hindu interests, which they could not do as members of the Congress, because the Congress belonged to both Hindus and Muslims. From that time onward the aggression on the Hindus had gone on increasing with the tacit consent of our Congress leaders by virtue of their policy of appeasement. The members of the Hindu Mahasabha and of the Congress had worked together side by side without any differences till the year 1937, when the Congress adopted a resolution banning all members of communal organisations from becoming office-bearers of the Congress. The Hindu Mahasabha was thus shut out from Congress."

While Nehru never tired of castigating the Hindu organisations like the Rashtrya Swayamsevak Sangh and Hindu Mahasabha, he turned a Nelson's eye to the activities of Muslim communal organisations like Jamait-e-Islami. Dr. Rajendra Prasad was not so blind. In his letter to Dr.K.N. Katju dated 23rd September, 1953, he records his observations on 'Jamait-e-Islami':

"I heard part of the questions and answers given in Parliament and the impression left on my mind was that the Prime Minister thinks that it is a religious body and it does not have much politics about it. I did not hear all that you said and I can quite appreciate that in giving a public answer you have to be cautious. I have read the note with great interest and it seems to me that it is not only a religious body but much more than that. In Islam, I believe they do not make any distinction between religion and politics and its whole tenor is to take the two together or side by side. That appears to be the modus operandi of this organization also which aims at establishing Islamic rule in India as that is the only rule which can be called God's rule and no Muslim can submit to any rule except God's rule. That being so, it is quite intelligible how it cannot appreciate a secular State and is as much opposed to it as to any other rule which is not according to Islam as conceived by this organisation. It is, therefore, not quite accurate to think that it is a religious body and has not much to do with politics."

Further evidence of Nehru's Janus-faced personality of bending over backwards to Muslim minority during partition is brought out from the following extract from Dr. Prasad's writings on 16th August, 1948:

"There is, however, another aspect of the question which may not be ignored. The Government of India and the Provincial Governments have not been able as yet to resettle and rehabilitate more than two million of non-Muslim town dwellers, traders, business people, professional men, etc., who migrated from Western Pakistan to India. These refugees are becoming impatient and it is becoming a very delicate and serious problem how to deal with them. Further there is not only no migration of non-Muslims from India to Pakistan but there is a steady stream of non-Muslims still coming to India from Western Pakistan, particularly Sindh. This stream would become more voluminous if more transport were available, and there are several lakhs of such people anxiously awaiting:

. . ."if what is stated in the newspapers is correct, then many of the permit-holders will be shifting with their families, which means at least 30,000 or 40,000 Muslims returning to India per month on this basis. Every permit carries with it the necessary promise that the permit-holder will be treated on his return to India as a national of India and in the same way as any other national. There is also the further implication that these returning Muslim refugees will claim to be rehabilitated and resettled in India just as other refugees and on the same footing. They will certainly be entitled to claim back possession of their houses and lands which they left behind when they migrated. I wonder if the Government of India or the Provincial Governments will be able to fulfill these expectations which are not only natural but also implicit in the permits granted to returning refugees."

"Mahatmaji was indeed anxious that conditions should be created when Muslims could return, but he was no less anxious and emphatic that the non-Muslims should also return to their homes and lands in Pakistan. Of the latter there is no sign or indication in any foreseeable future and even the holy Id had been utilised by Mr. Jinnah for rallying the Muslims of the world against the so-called enemies of Pakistan, who are no other than India and Indians. We shall be taking a very heavy responsibility if we allow and encourage this one-way traffic to continue."

Nehru was not the man to act strongly on this issue. He allowed events to take their own course, piously hoping that good sense will prevail on Pakistan. This 'one-way traffic' continued despite Prasad's warning. Patel died two years later and the chickens of Nehru's action or rather inactions came home to roost. Today in spite of being called a minority, India houses the largest Muslim population in the world, even more than Pakistan. In comparison, non-Muslims in Pakistan is a threatened species and a vanishing breed indeed.

Corruption

At the dawn of independence and the end of my teens the future looked rosy. Then a student of the Allahabad University, Muir Hostel, alongwith many others of my generation, I too was carried away by the greatness of the moment. Nehru's "Tryst With Destiny" seemed real and we all waited for a golden era to be ushered. Disappointment was not long in coming; first, by the carnage of the partition and second, by the mediocrity of thought of those who were guiding our destiny.

News of corruption and scramble for power started trickling in Nehru's own time. When I left the holy Sangam in July, 1948, the ominous signs of the times to come were already there. Nehru's socialistic rhetoric still held sway over the masses. But the concentration of all powers of economy and the production of wealth in the hands of the state apparatchic, ensured that wealth and economic power would be shared between the triumvirate of the elected leaders who made rules, laws, regulations and controls; the bureaucrat fraternity who advised and executed, and the heads of industry who were to produce under their dictates. The State came to the market place for producing and distributing every thing from bread and butter to electricity and locomotives. All this had nothing to do with the poor for whom the Mahatma showed so much concern. By laying the foundation of socialism and state control of economy, Nehru created a fountain head of corruption. Most Governments are corrupt and venal, some more so, but the socialist governments are the most corrupt, since there is no one to point the accusing finger. Very little was known outside the Iron Curtain, and later the Bamboo Curtain of what all went on inside there. Now we all know how pervasive was the state corruption in both the Red states. The Russian economy is in a shambles and the Chinese by a skilfull timely rescue act have just about averted a disaster. The Chinese who are always preemptive and quick to learn have taken the path of economic re-construction and growth under state control. We are still trailing behind, late starters as we were in the liberalization process. From the very beginning of his charge, Nehru wanted quick results and aimed at the spectacular, not substantive, the pedestrian not profound. He seldom thought of building national character first, but preferred to invest in big dams, and steel mills which he called the temples of modern India. Lacking character, the leaders even in Gandhi's time had started showing their venality. Starting from Krishna Menon's

Jeep Scandal, the Mundhra deal, Dharma Teja, K.D. Malaviya's oil scandal and Pratap Singh Kairon's highhandedness and his corruption ridden sons, the tale was unending. Nehru closed his eyes to all. See no evil, that seemed to have been his motto. When someone reminded him of Kairon's misdeeds, he shot back, "What if some national money is misused, but he works and produces results." This venality in politicians was not a subject for public discourse. But his son-in-law Feroze Gandhi embarrassed him in the Parliament and brought the skelton of the awkward Mundhra deal tumbling out from the closet, and in the wake of public uproar, T.T. Krishnamachari, the then Finance Minister, was reluctantly asked by Nehru to resign. Nehru, though himself financially honest, did little to bring to book the corrupt leaders, and hereby lies a precedent which his worthy daughter so well emulated. And thus corruption became the way of life with almost all politicians. Probity in public life was given a quiet burial. The lady when cornered on this issue by the insistent opposition remarked non-challantly that corruption is a world-wide phenomenon. So what's new? Famous last words. Nehru and his dynasty sowed the winds. The deprived masses are now reaping the whirlwind. The politicians, of course, are basking in the sun of their ill-begotten gains. In the land of Vedas, Yudhishthir, Harish Chandra and Mahatma Gandhi, corruption has now reached gargantuan proportions. The Nadir was to be reached when in April, 1995, T.N. Seshan won a national award for honesty, implying thereby that in this great country of ours no other than him does have even this elementary human virtue. What a national shame!

A common tactic to deflect criticism regarding corruption among Congress leaders and, the ministers by the conscientious leaders, within or outside the pale of Congress culture, was to use the socialists or the radicals to shout down and silence such objectors. Nehru used this technique to encourage the radical camp within the

Congress and even the Communists to start a whispering campaign, branding Sardar Patel, his sole equal, as a fascist. The charges were, of course, baseless as Nehru well knew, but allowed the criticism to continue. We all know the Sardar died a poor man. Indira Gandhi perfected this art by using her shouting brigade and other vocal ministers and Members of Parliament to do her bidding to silence the critics of corruption rampant in her time. The family heritage was duly passed on to Rajiv Gandhi, who used his own new set of imperial guard, with loud speakers in their lungs, to silence the opposition. And the game continues to this day in one form or the other to deflect the attack on mega scandals and stonewalling any attempt to bring the guilty to book. The latest in the series is the episode of the opposition demand for appointment of a Parliamentary Committee to investigate the security scam. The request met with a stout refusal. It may be the prophetic last nail in the coffin of ministerial accountability and probity in public life. There has been a series of scams in the last five years ending with Hawala and Housing scams, where Supreme Court itself had to indict ministers and bureaucrats for criminal offences, corruption and misuse of power.

A later day apologist of Congress ministerial corruption made a strong case in an English national daily that the chattering middle class, always bent upon criticising everything under the sun, should look into their own backyard first before pointing an accusing finger at the politicians. His logic reduced to its absurd simplicity, was that those living in glass houses should not throw stones at others, and rather than indulging in this dubious pastime they should first improve their own value system and correct themselves by shunning all corrupt practices. This miracle pre-supposes the existence of a magic wand which can remove corruption in higher places in one single movement once corruption in the hoi polloi disappears. How simplistic indeed! The writer obviously forgot the

Law of Gravity. Corruption, like water, flows from top to bottom rather than upwards. The Indian public is used to emulate their leaders, and follows them, a profundity stated by many of Nehru's colleagues in his own lifetime. But Nehru remained unmoved and ignored all such warnings. There is no record of any effort by him or his government to bring out a systematic reform in the polity to remove corruption. The results are for everyone to see.

The Tandon Episode

Nehru had a known dislike for anyone who stood staunchly for his Indian identity or philosophy, based on our rich cultural heritage, preservation of Hindi language and the best of our old traditions. On many issues, he had basic differences with P.D. Tandon, a candidate for Congress presidentship in the second half of 1950 at Nasik Session. To Nehru, Tandon's election was an anathema. Not so to Patel, who had a more balanced approach on the subject. In fact, as events moved the inevitable task of a peacemaker between the two camps fell on his shoulders. Nehru gave out his views in his letter to Tandon on 8 August, 1950.

"The problem that troubled me, however, was somewhat different. You were one of the candidates for the presidentship and there were some other old colleagues. Most of these are friends of old standing, you the oldest of them. I need not tell you of my affection for you and my high regard for your integrity, Nevertheless, I have been troubled and distressed in mind. It has been our misfortune during the past two or three years or so to have drifted apart to some extent. I am referring not to our infrequent meetings but rather to the way our minds had been functioning. Probably you think that much that I say or do is wrong. For my part, I have often read your speeches with surprise and distress and have felt that you were encouraging the very forces in India, which, I think, are harmful." And then warmed upto the matter in his mind.

"Your presiding over the refugee conference recently held in Delhi also distressed me because that refugee conference gave expression to views which struck me as excessively intolerant, communal and impractical. We are all interested in helping and rehabilitating the refugees and it may be that we have not done as much as we should have done. But that should not lead us into wrong directions. I think the major issue in this country today, if it is to progress and to remain united, is to solve satisfactorily our minority problems. Instead of that, we become more intolerant towards our minorities and give as our excuse that Pakistan behaves badly. What happens to Pakistan is not my primary concern. But I am most intimately concerned with what happens to India, and this progressive decline in some of the basic things of life is distressing.

"Unfortunately, you have become to large numbers of people in India some kind of a symbol of this communal and revivalist outlook."

To this Tandon replied with his characteristic firmness and candour but mincing no words.

"I agree that the Congress is in bad way and that steps have to be taken to prevent its utter collapse. Our whole social life is going to pieces and the Congress is a sample of the grossly low ethical standard spreading all round. The soul of the country has to be saved. I wish you could take up this great work which is so much above the Prime Minister's routine task—highly important as it is." And then coming to Nehru's allegations, he says:

"You have referred to some of my speeches about which you have read and to my presiding over the refugee conference. I ask you to believe your eyes and ears more than newspaper or other reports. You seem to connect me with narrow communalism and what you call revivalism. While you and I have agreed on and worked together on many vital problems, there have been some matters on which you and I have not seen eye to eye—the adoption of Hindi as the national language and the partition of the country with its consequential issues being the chief among them. It is a failing even with great persons to take their own geese for swans, their own aptitudes for fundamental principles. But I ask you to look at the matter with some detachment. It is possible that others may be right and you may be wrong. In any case why should it be necessary to attribute narrowness to others who differ from you!" And finally, he holds the bull by the horn saying:

"Obviously you have the Hindu-Muslim question in mind when you speak of communalism. You were present at the last political conference of our province when I spoke for about an hour and a half as president. I expressed then clearly my views on the Hindu-Muslim question in general and on the cultural relationship between the two communities in particular. I have never deviated from the views then expressed. I do not recognise any Islamic culture or any Hindu culture. I do not recognise that there is any book in the world which has said the last word on what man should be. Neither the Veda nor the Quran is the last word for me in human thought. Muslim divines take umbrage at my expressing this view and say I am anti-Muslim. I thought you at least would rise above that outlook. The old-world Pandits of Banaras also dislike my views and attack me freely in their organs—the daily Hindi *Sanmarg* is an exponent of their views. My leading thought in politics is an all-round unity in the country as far as it can be achieved with unavoidable and necessary diversities being kept within proper limits. I have openly advocated Hindu-Muslim marriages and, as you know, caste orthodoxy has played little part in my life. I am, therefore, surprised at your connecting me with a communal outlook."

Regarding revivalism, Nehru's euphemism for the Hindu upsurge, he says:

"Revivalism is a confusing expression. It may mean renaissance and it may mean reactionarism. I would revive today some of the great spiritual standards that out country stood for in the past. I regard them as precious legacies. At the same time I reject strongly the irrational dogmas that surround both Hinduism and Islam in action—though such dogmas may be laid down by the religious books sacred to Hindus or Muslims. I hold that all religious precepts have to be weighed by the intellect and not one of them can be accepted merely on the authority of a book."

Coming to the prickly issue of refugees, Tandon made his stand clear that it was not a Hindu-Muslim or communal question.

"The question of refugees stands on a footing different from that of the Hindu-Muslim relationship. It is a human question. It has assumed intensity because of our national action in bringing about partition. To have sympathy for the cause of refugees is natural both for you and me. I feel that we must do much more for them than we have done hitherto and that, apart from Providence, you and I and the leaders of public opinion in our country are responsible for the miseries of the refugees. It was, therefore, in the ordinary course of public life that I accepted some months ago an invitation, pressed with earnestness by Dr. Choithram Gidwani and Lala Achintram, that I should preside over the proposed refugee conference. I am responsible for what I said. I suggested a capital levy which would bring in a few *arabs* (thousands of millions) of rupees, not crores, for the purposes of rehabilitation. This is perhaps a heroic remedy. But I feel that it is practical and deserves earnest and fearless examination. Thirty crores or so a year cannot solve this big problem."

And he concludes by putting ranks and appointments in a proper perspective.

"I do not like some of your opinions and administrative acts. I wish you could take a more balanced view in some matters and a sterner attitude in others, but that cannot affect my personal emotion towards you or those connected with you, for it is a part of my being.

"The presidentship of the Congress or the prime ministership of the country are great and attractive positions but are, after all, small things in a proper valuation of our duties or of what contributes to our happiness. Looked at in a world perspective the country itself becomes a small affair. Even before our eyes the importance of individual countries is dwindling in the world drama. Perhaps with returning sense or what you may call revivalism of the old concepts, the world itself may appear to many as not the be-all and end-all of existence.

"I have learnt to see things with a somewhat impersonal outlook. I try to adhere to truth as I conceive it. In expressing it I wish to avoid causing pain but I am conscious that my views sometimes create misunderstanding and I am not always able to remove them."

Nehru's reasoning as usual is confused and out of focus, in contrast to Tandon's clear, precise and forthright approach. Patel in a letter to Jawaharlal on 27th August, 1950, gives a better picture of what had transpired. In the spirit of a sane elder colleague, (it deals with Nehru's dislike for Tandon and his veiled threat to reign), he writes:

"Prior to yesterday's talk, the only talks I had with you when Tandonji's question was discussed at some length, were two—one at Dehra Dun and the other here the day you called an informal meeting of the Working Committee. We had some correspondence as well. During these talks and this correspondence the farthest that the mention of your resignation went was in your letter of 11 August in which you said, 'As I have told you, I may find it difficult to continue as a member of the Congress Working Committee or even of Government.' In my letter of the 12th in reply I tried to point out to you that any apprehensions on this question were premature and that the Nasik Congress, and not the presidential election, should be the test.

"As regards your correspondence with Tandonji, your letter of 8 August, a copy of which you sent me, makes no mention of any intention to resign if he were elected. It is confined to the necessity of explaining your opinion in some form or the other.In fact, in your last letter to Tandonji dated 13 August, of which the latter sent me a copy, you said you would like to talk to him about the various matters or write to him. In the meantime you had issued your statement to the Press, and the correspondence which passed between us about Tandonji and the talks which I had with Rajaji left me with the impression which Rajaji shared that you would wait for the Nasik Congress and would not take any decisive step till then. It was for this reason that your letter of the 25th came to me as so much of a shock. Between my last letter to you dated the 12th and your letter of the 25th, I have never been consulted by you on this issue, and there was, therefore, no occasion for me to be enlightened about any change in your attitude or preference.

"Regarding Tandonji, apart from my preference for him from among the candidates that are standing, the difference between your approach and mine is only this, that I am in favour of giving him a chance, and if he does not adjust himself to such decisions as the Nasik Congress might take naturally he has to go. There can be no question of your going out; on the other hand you condemn him right now and feel that his election itself would mean a defeat of your policy, etc. I hold that the latter is not an issue, since past decisions and policies of the Congress bind all presidential candidates, and the President is as much bound by it as any ordinary member of the Congress. This seems, strangely enough, somewhat similar to Kripalani's own view, as would be clear from the attached copy of his statement published a couple of days ago.

"As regards candidates, you and I both agreed at Dehra Dun that Kripalani was out of the question. I strongly favoured Tandonji on personal grounds and disfavoured Shankarrao Deo. You disfavored Tandonji and were prepared to accept Shankarrao on the principle of "lesser evil." I have throughout held that your condemnation of Tandonji was unfair and premature. I was not taken into confidence when recently your preference seems to have changed from Shankarrao to Kripalani. As I wrote to you yesterday, I refused to believe it at first; even now I am amazed as personally I regard Kripalani as having taken in the past, with reference to the points you hold against Tandonji, a more destructive and critical role against you than Tandonji has ever done. His speeches and writings in the Press will amply confirm it."

Nehru had never asked for Patel's cooperation or advice in the matter. He had also held out the threat to pull out of the Central Working Committee and the Government in the event of Tandon's election and expressed the same in his following letter.

"Developments since then have confirmed it and made it perfectly clear to me that if Purushottam Das Tandon is elected, then I have no further place in the Congress executive, and consequently also as Prime Minister. It is not Tandon personally that I object to. But he has become [a] symbol of something which I consider exceedingly harmful to the Congress and the country. His election thus would have meant, whether consciously done or unthinkingly, support of these very ideas and forces.

"On my way back from office late this evening, I dropped in at Rajaji's place. In the course of our conversation he mentioned that you did not think that I would act up to what I had said in the event of Tandon's election. That, in fact, I would adjust myself to the new situation. I was a little surprised to learn this for I had thought that I had made myself perfectly clear. It was this conversation that led me to think that I should write to you so that there might not be any misapprehension left. I am absolutely clear in my mind that, in the event of Tandon's election, I should treat it as a vote of no-confidence in me by Congressmen or at any rate by those who vote in the presidential election. As a result of this, I cannot function in the Congress Working Committee or other executives. As a further consequence, I cannot continue as Prime Minister.

"Apart from the logic of this, I am certain that I shall have no heart in holding on to my present position. That would not be fair to myself or to the Congress or the country. There is far too much self-delusion and hypocrisy in our public life. We say one thing and then quietly ignore it and act in a contrary way. We pass fine resolutions and then forget them. I know I am myself guilty of this in common with others. I do not wish to add to this self-delusion and I think I shall be much happier as a free man, not bound by office of any kind." And again Nehru reiterates his decision to quit office.

"I cannot possibly continue to function as I have done when I receive a public slap on my face and an expression of Congress disapproval of what I stand for. The resolutions that the Nasik Congress [passes] will no doubt be important but they cannot get over this patent fact. There is no point in my being Prime Minister in these circumstances. I shall be frustrated and disheartened and totally ineffective.

"The question of my resigning early or late is a minor matter. The point is that I cannot avoid it. To avoid it is to be false to myself and the Congress.

"As it is I feel increasingly incapable of effective work."

As things happened, Tandon with the support of Patel and others, won by a thumping majority. Yet what do we see? Inspite of his intention to resign, as would happen many more times later, Nehru stuck to his position as Prime Minister. Nehru's statements on personal matters and position of power were never the last word. How does this episode show up, the man, Nehru? A man of firm resolve? A man who would stake his personal position for principles or a man who just could not live without power?

The Thimayya Episode

It would not be incorrect to mention here, the less than high esteem in which Nehru held uniformed soldiers in general, and competent and independent minded generals in particular. The case of open confrontation between Gen. Thimayya and the then Defence Minister V.K. Menon is well known. Thimayya, the then Chief of Army Staff, developed strong differences with Menon not only on matters of defence but also appointments to higher Army ranks, subjects which fall exclusively within the sphere of the Army organization and functioning. The politician has no business to interfere. But Menon, spoiled as he was by Nehru's indulgent attitude, often crossed the sacred line that divides the civilian control of armed forces and strictly Army matters. The matters came to boil on a specific issue on Army appointments and Thimayya not only strongly disagreed with Menon but offered to resign. We in the Army at that time were only aware of the distant rumblings of this incident. Every soldier in uniform stood solidly behind Thimayya. Nehru realised the gravity of the situation and tried to persuade Thimayya to accept the Defence Minister's judgment. Thimayya, however, was not the man to back out of a position which he considered not only correct but also in national interest. Here was a great soldier standing for what was right. Thimayya offered his resignation. Even as a young officer, Thimayya had shown no less patriotism than some of the so-called freedom fighters. As early as Moti Lal Nehru's time when Menon was not even heard of, Thimayya along with other Army officers went over to Moti Lal Nehru's residence at Allahabad and expressed his desire to resign and join the freedom struggle. The wise old man had then told

Thimayya, "The contribution you are making is a difficult one. Nothing would please the British more than your resignation. For 30 years we have fought for Army's Indianisation. We are now winning the fight. If you give up, we shall have lost it." He, therefore, advised these officers to show patience and wait till Independence when their services will be needed by the country. These were prophetic words and even before Independence after the signing of the Partition Plan, large scale riots broke out in erstwhile Bengal and Punjab and soon Thimayya was sucked in the whirlpool of events in Punjab where he did a commendable job in restoring normalcy in the riot-torn areas and mete out justice with a firm and even hand.

Later anticipating the dawn of independence, Thimayya expressed himself with candour to the effect:

"We Indian officers felt the excitement of great expectation, we knew that we had made a good showing in the war. We no longer lacked confidence. We knew, also, that the British Raj was irrevocably finished. We were impatient for the day when the Indian Army would finally serve its own country under its own leaders."

General Thimayya was the only Indian in the Indian Army to have had the distinction of commanding an infantry brigade in the Second World War in Burma. It was the same brilliant tactician who played a master stroke by posting tanks atop the famous Zoji-la pass, something unheard of in the annals of military fighting in this sub-continent and thus, frightened the Pakistani invaders out of their positions in the fight for the Valley. Earlier, Hannibal, the Carthaginin had crossed the Alps with an army of elephants to defeat the Romans and later Napolean followed the same route with a ragged army and heavy artillery to rout the Austrian forces in the plains of Lombardy. Thimayya by the skillful use of infantry and armour had, earlier, thrown the enemy back from Uri and Tithwal and had threatened Muzaffarabad. He then commanded the next phase of operations in

Kashmir and his success owed not a little to his magnificent leadership. It was to be Thimayya's misfortune to serve as the Chief of the Army Staff to a vitriolic, egoistic and a known communist Defence Minister, who was not only a conceited politician and a scheming Machiavelli, but a favourite of the Prime Minister himself. And matters were not helped by Lt. Gen. B.M. Kaul, an upstart political general, fishing in troubled waters, trying his game of one upmanship against Thimayya. Coming back to the incident, when Nehru realised that Thimayya had the solid support of the entire Army he changed track but advised caution to the great soldier. He sweetly talked him into withdrawing his resignation while he said that he would speak to V.K. Menon to reconsider his stand and accept his proposals.

But Nehru was not the man known to honour his words. After returning Thimayya's resignation, he said nothing to Krishna Menon. On the other hand, to add insult to injury, he gave a long sermon in the Parliament about the supremacy of civilian leadership over the soldier, however high his rank. The unsuspecting Thimayya was thus shortchanged and taken for a ride. Not only were Thimayya's proposals over-ruled, but he was made to eat an humble pie in public and Nehru administered a mild rebuke to the "truant soldier" and Krishna Menon had the last laugh. That was Nehru.

Thimayya's able handling of the Hindu-Muslim riots during the partition brought him approval and praise from every political quarter. He had the power to enforce strict discipline in using troops from the same region against the rioters who happened to belong to the same community. This from his own confession:

"I had already proved that army discipline was strong enough so that, for example, Moslem troops could be used against a Moslem mob. If Hindu and Sikh troops had been given the responsibility of protecting the Moslem minority in India, and if Moslem troops had the chance to safeguard the minorities in Pakistan, the conflagration could have been prevented."

Thimayya's apolitical character had never been in doubt. But Nehru, ill-advised by the remaining British officers during the partition days, regarded that a soldier's natural inclination was to grab political power. He was thus extremely sensitive to the ambitions of outstanding generals. In a way, Thimayya's ability proved his disqualification. This is clear from the fear that both Nehru and Krishna Menon showed against his harboring any political ambitions. There was never any fear that General Thimayya was anything more than a soldier. The same was not true of Lieutenant General B.M. Kaul. Thimayya just did not have the making of a political general. He had once mentioned:

"My experience taught me that a country's armed services should be an instrument, but never an arbiter, of national policy." The history of countries whose military men were not taught to be apolitical shows what disruptive influences they sometimes can be. Admittedly, the Indian Army originally was divorced from politics because the British feared another sepoy mutiny. The effect on the jawan, however, was to make him think of himself as a servant of India rather than as someone in a group separate from his countrymen. Even more important, he learned regard for his country as whole, and not just for the district from which he came. As a result the jawan became a valuable citizen."

It was against such a General that Menon's mendacity was directed against the background of the politician's usual suspicion of a soldier's ambitions. The shabby treatment meted out to Thimayya speaks poorly not only of Menon from whom such a behaviour was not unexpected, but that Nehru could stoop to such depths could not be imagined.

Before we close this sorry episode it will not be out of place to place on record the bonafides of Menon narrated by no less a person than Maulana Azad, Nehru's close friend:

"There was one other person responsible for the change

in Jawaharlal. An Indian named Krishna Menon had lived in London since the early Twenties. Jawaharlal had met him first in the late Twenties and had found in him one who professed great admiration for Jawaharlal's views. We all like our admirers but perhaps Jawaharlal likes them a little more than others. Sometime later, in the early Thirties, the Labour Party sent a delegation to India led by Miss Ellen Wilkinson. Krishna Menon was attached to the delegation and visited India.He had also been taking an interest in the activities of the India League in London. During this period, his contacts were mainly with people who were regarded as communists or fellow-travellers."

"Jawaharlal was impressed by him and requested me to grant some money. I did so and placed the matter before the Working Committee. Gandhiji and Sardar Patel told me frankly that they did not like my action but they would say nothing since I had paid the money in good faith.They however asked me not to make any further payment. They pointed out that Indians in London were sharply divided in their judgment about Krishna Menon.He had some supporters but there was a strong body of opponents who brought all kinds of charges against him. The general impression I got was that his conduct was not above reproach. I could not therefore trust him fully. Later events proved that Gandhiji and the Sardar were right in their suspicion of Krishna Menon. He was, to take a charitable view, unreliable and had little concern for the way public funds were spent. Most people took an even worse view and regarded him as downright dishonest."

Such was the man on whose advice Nehru publicly humiliated one of the greatest soldiers of our time.

to Jawaharlal. An Indian named Krishna Menon had lived in London since the early Twenties. Jawaharlal had met him first in the late Twenties and had found in him one who professed great admiration for Jawaharlal's views. We all like our admirers but perhaps Jawaharlal likes them a little more than others. Sometime later, in the early Thirties, the Labour Party sent a delegation to India led by Miss Ellen Wilkinson. Krishna Menon was attached to the delegation and visited India. He had also been taking an interest in the activities of the India League in London. During this period, his contacts were mainly with people who were regarded as communists or fellow travellers.

Jawaharlal was impressed by him and requested me to grant some money. I did so and placed the matter before the Working Committee. Gandhiji and Sardar Patel told me frankly that they did not like my action but they would say nothing since I had paid the money in good faith. They however asked me not to make any further payment. They pointed out that Indians in London were sharply divided in their judgment about Krishna Menon. He had some supporters but there was a strong body of opponents who brought all kinds of charges against him. The general impression I got was that his conduct was not above reproach. I could not therefore trust him fully. Later events proved that Gandhiji and the Sardar were right in their suspicion of Krishna Menon. He was, to take a charitable view, unreliable and had little concern for the way public funds were spent. Most people took an even worse view and regarded him as downright dishonest.

Such was the man on whose advice Nehru publicly humiliated one of the greatest soldiers of our time.

Part III

7 Nehru and the Media

Indian media and the media hype has the dubious distinction of making instant heroes, out of men of straw. In true business fashion, they churn out the most saleable product. There are numerous examples of political mediocrities, ruthless manipulators and publicity-hogging individuals of even yesterday and today who, deflated of the media gas, would crumble into a heap of disposable waste. There are any number of ex-bureaucrats, police persons, and self-appointed crusaders, who, when the media hype burns out due to sheer fatigue and a sense of 'deja-vu', will look like the cinders of the meteoric burnout and consigned to the dustbins of history. True history is more than sensational and instant news. Our print media did a very desirable and commendable job of informing, inspiring and sustaining the freedom struggle and thereby made many heroes. Gandhi, Nehru and Patel did not need media; the media needed them. Of these, Gandhi and Patel stood on solid personal achievements. They sat, planned, and to quote modern business language, orchestrated the corporate Congress efforts and planned the future strategy. Nehru, the travelling salesman of Congress, sold it to the masses and in communicating to the youthful hearts of which he was un-disputed King, he adequately conveyed the message of freedom as desired by his master Gandhi. He was an instant media success. His good looks. enthusiasm, sincerity and Gandhi's blessings were enough. His real worth, however, mattered little to the adoring crowds. But his honeymoon with the print media lasted even for almost a decade and a half after independence and this was a sign of a lack of maturity and sound judgment in our print media. Almost, all Congress leaders of freedom struggle basked in the after glow of their exertions in their Jail terms. Most cashed on it and became Ministers in the Government, little remembering Gandhi's advice to disband the Congress and turn it into a voluntary service organization. But the media gave them enough leeway and showered unquestioning accolades even on the less deserving ones. Many who left the Congress and the Government were quickly forgotten by the press. Nehru retained a larger than life picture in the national newspapers and almost a sycophantic adulation from all. It is amusing to know that a few years after independence, so hypnotised was the press with Nehru, that it failed even to mention, let alone criticise many a faux pas that he made. His lecture at Patna in August, 1954, after the burning of the National Flag there by the students and unleashing of police terror, so critically commented upon by Jaya Prakash Narain went unreported in the press.

Till the end of his life he remained the hero to the press despite all the blunders he had made. Truly newspapers do not form the substance history is made of. Few newspapers would have dared to touch Einstein's 'Theory of Relativity', Milton's 'Paradise Lost', or the plays of Shakespeare, Bernard Shaw or Ibsen. No really great men have been truly recognised by the current press. Conversely, Nehru with so much of print footage to his credit will occupy a very small place in the history of our country, leave alone the World History. To do that one needs force of character, substance, unflagging zeal, a sense of mission and utter honesty of purpose. One doubts if Nehru had these in any substantial measure. Mention has been made earlier of the Patna incident. It is interesting to note how Nehru's nearly dictatorial and high-handed measures and utterances were blacked out by the press. The incident is revealing. Here is a sequence of events as recorded in Dr. Rajendra Prasad's correspondence during his Presidential years concerning the events mentioned earlier. This is what Jaya Prakash Narain had written to Nehru on 30.8.1955.

"Yesterday I was at Ashram deep in the interior of Gaya and had no intention whatever to go to Patna and seek to meet you. But a young man brought an urgent letter yesterday from my friend Babu Baldev Sahay, to whom more than to anyone else are the people of Patna beholden for rising to defend their rights and liberties and the cause of justice and humanity, so urgently called me, I could not resist. (Baldev Babu by the way is a loyal Congressman and has no political axe to grind. He is one of Patna's foremost lawyers and was Advocate General in the first Congress Ministry.)

"There are two common public apprehensions. One, that the disrespect shown to the national flag on the 15th August by some young men may be played up to screen the events of the 12th and 13th August. (Your own public statements, among other things, help to create this apprehension.) Two, the Bihar Government, which has so completely identified itself with its Police, may so arrange your Patna programme that you may get only one side of the picture.

"As for the first, while it is certainly a serious matter that the nation's flag should be dishonored, it is far more serious that a situation should be created in which young men, particularly students, should be driven to such behaviour. Merely condemning or haranguing the boys will never do; it will only push them into the arms of I shall not say of communism but nihilism. The boys surely acted wrongly, but in my considered judgement their fault is being exaggerated. Whatever they did was in a fit of anger, and which one of us has not misbehaved when angry. I have no doubt in the boys' patriotism and I do admire their spirit of revolt against injustice and barbarity.

"Moreover, and this is being conveniently forgotten, the 12th and 13th of August came before the 15th and not after. However grievous be the wrong committed by the boys—and people may try to teach them patriotism by wholesale condemnation—that had nothing to do with the far more grievous wrongs committed by the custodians of people's welfare. A judicial enquiry is being held into those wrongs, and the powerful machines of the Government are moving to see that truth and justice are denied. The people do not expect you to take sides.

"I do not know how your programme will be fixed, but you should visit at least the B.N. College and meet the important members of the public concerned and the students' representatives. If you allow me I should like personally to meet you, preferably as early as possible."

Again another letter dated 31.8.55:

"This morning, I wrote you a letter for a transcript of your speech. After that the local authorities allowed me to listen to it at the Patna Station of AIR. As I sat listening I could not withhold the tears from my eyes. I do not know why I should have wept instead of getting angry. But that is how I felt. It was obvious that you have not read my statement, or if you had, you did not consider it worth notice. I had never imagined that you would allow yourself to be so completely captured by one-sided,untrue and interested versions. Do you think that there is no honest men left in this country than your Chief Ministers? If you rely entirely on their versions, I am afraid you will shut yourself completely from public opinion. The British were at war with the Indian public, so they relied entirely on their police. But why should you or Shri Babu consider the statements of trustworthy, upright citizens, who are not interested in politics, to be untruthful? Why should the statement of the police be given more weight than that of university teachers? Why should Jayaprakash Narayan's statement be considered unworthy of note? By the way, I shall again beg you to read my statement.

"What you said about casteism and the castes—you deliberately mentioned Rajputs and Kayasthas—shows how one-sided is the view which you have taken of the situation. I am not a Congressman, but I am aware that the standards of the men in power cannot but set the standards of public life. The depths to which Congressmen have fallen here are unimaginable. If you had not come here and made the kind of speech you did, I would not have suggested this. But I do suggest now that you ask Dhebarbhai to come over here for a few days and find out things for himself—things which are not likely to come up before the Enquiry and in which the Enquiry cannot be interested. In your speech you condemned everyone wholesale—Patna citizens, the Press, etc. I too stand condemned and all others who did their best to control the situation and restore normalcy. Your Congressmen were hardly in the picture during the stormy days, to make up for which they have been issuing a spate of statements abusing all and sundry.

"This letter will become too long if I do not stop now. But I shall not rest till you have the truth and the public gets justice. I had and have no desire to enter into any controversy with anyone, particularly with you. But your last night's speech has given such encouragement to the guilty men that I shall be failing in my duty if I did not raise my voice. I have decided to issue a Press statement tomorrow from Gaya. I hope you will not mind it and take it as a personal affront. This is a public issue and there is a great conspiracy afoot to cover up the truth, to cow down justice-loving citizens, to buy up inconvenient persons, to fabricate falsehood. All this is much more dangerous to the future of the country than an outburst of youthful anger.

"The records of your speech are being sent in the ordinary course to the Delhi AIR. If you give them a word they can send me a transcript. I shall be obliged.

The reports of your speech as published in the local Press have been so edited and framed that the reader gets a very different idea of what you actually said. This is the effect of your lashing out at the Press for performing its bare duty.

"Excuse me for the length of this letter."

Another letter dated October 22, 1955:

"I had your letter of September 5 in time, but deliberately delayed replying in order to allow for enough time to lapse for me at least to take a more detached view.

"A few days after your letter came I saw in the Press your remark made at Rewa that my approach was 'wrong from beginning to end.'

"What I had feared had obviously happened. You were angry at me and my statement. I should have never thought that there would ever be need for me to tell you what opinion I hold of you. How can I have but the highest regard for you, and have I not many times shouted from the house-tops, as it were—much to the annoyance of my socialist friends—my opinions of you. I had heard that even Attlee wondered at Rangoon how an opposition leader should so praise his country's Prime Minister. (Attlee was present when I made those remarks about you.)

"But do not even the best amongst men go wrong sometimes? In my humble judgment your Patna performance was an instance in point—not only the words you spoke but also the manner and the temper. In no democratic country would any person have dared speak in that manner, nor the audience allowed him to do so.

"When I went to see you at Patna, I had not known much about your speech. I was not present at the meeting and those few whom I met before leaving for the Raj Bhavan, including Prabhu who had gone to hear you, said that the sound arrangements were bad and you were not very audible. They could tell me only a few things about what you had spoken. In any case, I was not going to see you to discuss your speech, and my mind was full of other things. When I left you that night I had no cause to be dissatisfied with our talk.

"It was quarter-to-twelve when I reached back home. Prabha was sitting up for me and she was the first person who gave me a shock. She as you know has nothing to do with politics and, apart from the admiration she has for you, she is also deeply attached to you on account of Kamalaji. She said she had heard your whole speech on the radio after I had left for the Raj Bhavan to meet you. "Bhai bahut kharab bole" was her brief comment. We were soon joined by two inmates of my Ashram who had also heard you on the radio. They gave me a detailed report. I cannot describe the distress that I felt. I went to bed saying to myself that I should read your speech in the papers next morning and then write to you. But the papers seemed to have had their wind up—thanks to your angry words. They had put as fine a face on your speech as possible. Many people came to see me by then—by no means all socialists—and the terrible effect that your speech had produced began to be borne upon me. For the first time I heard that crowds leaving a meeting of yours went back not only sullen and discontented, but deeply wounded and with angry abuse on their lips.

"It was then that I tried to get in touch with you. Raj Bhavan said you had already left; and when after annoying delays I got through to the Air Station I was told that you were already in the plane. Then I sat down and wrote you a short letter, the one that did not apparently reach you, asking for a transcript of your speech. At the same time I contacted the Bihar authorities, and was ultimately enabled to hear you on Patna Radio. I have already written to you how deeply affected I was and how I felt impelled to make a public statement. I do not regret having made that statement. I claim that thereby I have done you a service.

"There have been reactions to my statement. I am enclosing a sample—an excerpt from Shree Babuji's speech at Muzzaffarpur. It made me very sad to read that speech. I cannot say what you will think of it. Let me say only this that I have no desire whatever to enter party politics. In fact, had not friend Lohia created an unfortunate situation, I would have even given up my membership of the PSP by now.

"As for my approach, it may be wrong from beginning to end. But let me say that I yield to none in the love of country or of the virtue of discipline. But in my view, much that happens from the people's side in our country is in the nature of a reaction to what the Government and the authorities do. The people of this country are generally quiet-natured, submissive and peace-loving. I have heard it from many district authorities that the apparatus of law and order is more often than not responsible for disturbances, including thefts and robberies. The students in particular are being very badly handled. The unseemly wrangles that are rampant in educational institutions, the falling standard of teaching and of public life, the whole aimless and futile system of education; and added to all these, the uncertainties of gainful employment—all these conspire together to drive the youth to frustration and confused irresponsible behaviour.

"Secondly, I feel that the right approach to the misbehaviours of the people is not denunciation and punishment but rectification of the deep lying causes of those misbehaviours. Very little attention, I am afraid, is being paid to this aspect of the problem.

"Police firings—to give a relevant but yet not so important an example—have been a common occurrence since the dawn of our freedom. Judges have often inquired into these incidents and their findings have not always upheld the police. But it had not yet occurred to our rulers to try to discover if there is not something basically wrong with the system of law and order itself. Some day this will have to be done, for that system is patently wrong.

But in the meanwhile many more people will have to suffer.

"Lastly, I wish you earnestly to consider if the attempt to cast out violence from international affairs can ever succeed without casting out violence from intra-national affairs. It is not only charity that should begin at home. Further, you are so anxious to have nuclear weapons banned, But is not the Lathi or the rifle the mother, as Vinobaji said the other day, of the hydrogen bomb? All of you, i.e., those who are in power today, belong to the Gandhi family. I think it should be your duty now to think whether it is not possible to maintain peace in this country without taking any human life.If serious thought were given to this problem it should not be impossible of solution."

These letters reveal the deep anguish and the heart cry of a man, one of Nehru's most ardent admirers. Jaya Prakash Narain, J.P. as he was later called, was even more popular than Nehru among the Indian youth during the 1942 'Quit India' movement on account of his daring escape from the Hazaribagh Jail. He was a socialist by conviction and not, like Nehru, a radical for convenience. In spite of being a socialist, he was nearer to Gandhiji in his thoughts and actions than Nehru, Gandhiji's own heir. Unlike Nehru, he believed in development from grassroot levels like Gandhiji, and did not think much of Nehru's big machine and the trickle down theory. Later, he was to move the youth of this country into a movement for total revolution to re-write the rules of the political grammar in the Indian polity. At the time, when he was writing these letters, he had no reason to feel any thing but admiration for Nehru. He was soon disillusioned. Earlier, Nehru had encouraged a whispering campaign against Patel branding him as a fascist, knowing fully well that this was a traversty of truth. His own actions now showed his real authoritarian face which the Press did everything to hide. Nehru had not only acquired the ways of British rulers so soon after independence but had also inherited more than the usual measure of their arrogance.

If only during the years after independence and Nehru's own lifetime, our media had been more critical, well informed and objective, most of our ills mentioned earlier, need not have set their roots in the Indian polity. A nation gets the Government it deserves. So also, a people get the press they deserve, since it is they who make or unmake the media. The media survives on people's patronage and their appetite. In Nehru's time our media failed, and logically enough, Nehru too failed the nation in many ways that he could.

8 The Kashmir Crisis: Lost Victories

Before we come to Nehru's role in Kashmir after independence, it would be appropriate to briefly take note of the situation in Kashmir prior to the partition plan. Nehru, as has been mentioned earlier, did not take kindly to the princely order. His attitude to Maharaja Hari Singh was no different and the undercurrent of Moslem discontent against the Hindu King thinly garbed in nationalistic shibboleth was voiced by leaders of the National Conference. One of these, Sheikh Mohammad Abdullah (SMA), who had developed close relations with Jawaharlal Nehru, Maulana Azad, Khan Abdul Gaffar Khan and other such leaders came to occupy a pre-eminent position in the organization. The first demand for secession too on behalf of the National Conference was articulated by Sheikh Abdullah.

Launching his 'Quit Kashmir' movement on May 10, 1946, the Sheikh, now the leader of the National Conference, made a speech on May 17 reinforcing his earlier stand.

"The tyranny of Dogras has lacerated our souls. It is time for action. You must fight slavery and enter the field of `Jihad' as soldiers. Every man, woman and child will shout `Quit Kashmir'. The Kashmiri nation has expressed its will. I ask for plebiscite on this question."

The Maharaja, thereafter, on May 20 got the Sheikh arrested alongwith other leaders of National Conference. Nehru, however, demanded the immediate release of the Sheikh, and in a gesture of defiance to challenge the authority of the Maharaja proceeded to cross the boundary into Kashmir. The Prime Minister prohibited Nehru's entry and he was arrested. There was considerable public turmoil and relations between the Maharaja and Nehru, never cordial, reached almost a point of no return. Obviously, Sheikh Abdullah provided Nehru another excuse to settle scores with the Maharaja. The Congress Working Committee, however, took a more sober view, and asked Nehru to return. The Sheikh was also later released after he offered an apology of sorts to the Maharaja dated September. 26, 1947, wherein he wrote:

"I assure your Highness that myself and my party have never harboured any sentiment of disloyalty towards your Highness' person, throne or dynasty. I assure your Highness the fullest and loyal support of myself and my organization. Not only this, but I assure your Highness that any party within or without the State, which may attempt to create any impediments in our efforts to gain our goal, will be treated as our enemy and will be treated as such".

The other Moslem leaders and the Muslim Conference voiced slightly different views on the matter. But both demanded independence with or without the Maharaja as the head of the State. Earlier, on September 25,1946, the Mirwaiz Moulvi Yusaf Shah had thundered:

"The Hindu capitalists want to get the State into their grip, but I warn that if the Government of Jammu and Kashmir gets terrified at the might of the Congress and strikes an unholy alliance with the National Conference fascists, it will have to face the terrific opposition of the Muslims. And this sinister alliance will be smashed to pieces. The Muslims of Kashmir have warded off Pt. Nehru's invasion in 1940,1945 and 1946. Now he is again out to make a fresh attempt and it is the duty of the Kashmiri Muslims particularly and all the well-wishers of the country to smash up this onslaught". And then later on May 10, 1947, Chowdhary Hamidullah Khan, President of the Muslim League, voiced similar aspirations for independence:

"If Kashmir has to keep itself aloof from carnage and bloodshed, it should lose no time in adopting a strong and bold policy. His Highness the Maharaja Bahadur should declare Kashmir independent immediately. A separate Constituent Assembly to frame the Constitution for the State according to the wishes of the peoples, should be established at once. His Highness the Maharaja Bahadur will receive the cooperation of Muslims in carrying out this policy. The Muslims form 80% of the population. They are represented by the Maharaja Bahadur as the first constitutional ruler of independent and democratic Kashmir".

The forces and actors in the Kashmir drama were the National Conference of Sheikh Abdullah, influential mainly in the valley and blessed by Jawaharlal Nehru; its foe, the Muslim League; Mirwaiz Moulvi Yusuf Shah, a wild fanatic leader and common enemy to both; Muslim Conference, ideologically closer to Muslim League advocating independent status for Kashmir and finally the Maharaja, a symbol of Dogra domination, distrusted and disliked both by Nehru and Sheikh Abdullah.

The coming events in Kashmir and Nehru's mishandling were adumbrated in the earlier crisis in Junagadh, so aptly handled by Patel. To go back a little.

While the process of negotiation and merger of the States into the two dominions was going on, interesting developments were afoot. The prize for the two dominions was Kashmir. Jinnah was certain that in the eventuality of India insisting on a plebiscite of the Hindu people for the merger of Junagadh State with Nawab as the Muslim head, into the Indian dominion, he would insist on the same yardstick being applied for Kashmiris in case the Hindu Maharaja with his Muslim subjects deciding to join India. In such a situation, plebiscite in Kashmir could return to centre stage the logic of the Two Nation Theory and the option to accede to Pakistan would mean a vote for Islam, the motive behind his game plan. However, the gullible Nehru on September 30 announced that though India questioned the accession of Junagadh to Pakistan and the propriety of the Nawab's action, he would accept the general elections, plebiscite or even referendum in Junagadh. Patel, however, was more sagacious. He would not have committed himself to such a course. Mountbatten picking on Nehru's words to Liaqat, re-assured him that when the occasion came, Nehru would apply the same principle to the other States too.

"Pandit Nehru nodded his head sadly. Mr. Liaqat Ali Khan's eyes sparkled. There is no doubt that both of them were thinking of Kashmir."

Patel, however, insisted that a plebiscite in Kashmir would be subject to a similar one in Junagadh. Now, Jinnah was not prepared for such a contingency. Patel's gambit completely flummoxed Jinnah and finally he agreed that no plebiscite need be held in Junagadh. After this faux pas by Nehru, Patel functioned almost independently in dealing with the States and took all control of the policy regarding the States, only keeping the Cabinet informed. This chapter was finally closed with the accession of Junagadh, where on September 24, a brigade of Indian troops took possession of the State.

Jawaharlal Nehru completely under the spell of Sheikh Abdullah could not develop an objective and statesmanlike approach to Kashmir and the problem that could be posed by the Muslim majority for the Kashmiri Pandits later. We know the problem now; of a people rendered homeless in their own country. Nehru, himself a Kashmiri Pandit, as early as August 1945 had declared at the National Conference session at Sopore that "Sheikh Abdullah's National Conference was the real national organization of the people of Kashmir, so that if the Kashmiri Pandit community did not join it, no weightage and safeguard would be able to protect them."

The Maharaja's hesitation in making up his mind to join one of the two dominions i.e., India or Pakistan was a fatal blunder. He was toying with the idea of complete independence; an impracticable proposition under the Partition Plan. Allen Campbell Johnson (ACJ) writes in his book:

"When he got there he found the Maharaja politically very elusive, and the only conversations that took place were during their various car drives together. Mountbatten on these occasions urged him and his Prime Minister, Pandit Kak, not to make any declaration of independence, but to find out in one way or another the will of the people of Kashmir as soon as possible, and to announce their intention by August 14 to send representatives accordingly to one Constituent Assembly or the other. He told them that the newly created States Department was prepared to give an assurance that if Kashmir went to Pakistan this would not be regarded as an unfriendly act by the Government of India."

It is generally not known that Mountbatten, while reassuring Nehru and Patel an even hand in persuading the Maharaja to join either Pakistan or India, was in fact, egged on by the British Government, coercing the Maharaja into joining Pakistan. Unknown to Nehru, this game was being played by Mountbatten, a person so well trusted by Nehru. Nehru's gullibility and a flawed assessment of the man he was dealing with came to force with a hammer like blow. Failing in his attempt, Mountbatten finally made a forceful plea in the presence of some British officers and the Prime Minister, Pandit Kak for a merger with Pakistan. The Maharaja avoided the meeting. Mountbatten hoped to play on the Maharaja's feelings against Nehru, arising out of the latter's known hostility to him and the subsequent shabby treatment meted out to the Maharaja. The Maharaja, however, was too shrewd and entered into a standstill agreement with Pakistan while keeping the independence option open. Pandit Kak, stridently anti-Nehru, was openly for merger with Pakistan. The Muslim Conference too, keen to consummate the merger with Pakistan passed a resolution on July 19, 1947, to this effect. Very little of this subterranean play of forces was known to Nehru, who was by now fully incharge of the Kashmir affairs, to the exclusion of Sardar Patel whose legitimate domain it was.

Another sidelight on Nehru's myopic vision on Kashmir and a lack of timely action was the case of the Gilgit lease. Here Pakistan was quicker on the ground than the fumbling Government of India. Gilgit and the areas around, managed by the Gilgit Agency was obtained on lease by the British Indian Government in 1935 for 60 years. Due to reasons of its strategic importance, the Agency was administered by the British directly; this with a view to keep surveillance on the activities of the Soviet Union and the happenings in Sinkiang province of China. Mountbatten in April 1947, with Nehru agreeing to the proposal, recommended the return of the area of the Gilgit Lease to the Maharaja to which Lord Listowel, the Secretary of State for India, agreed. However, there was no written formal order to this effect. With the transfer of power on August 15, the lease stood lapsed and the Political Department of Government of India asked the Maharaja on June 3, 1947 to immediately take over the region of Gilgit and assume its administration. Brig. Gansara Singh, appointed the Governor of Gilgit by the Maharaja, reached Gilgit on July 30, 1947, and found that he was too late. One Major Brown commanding Gilgit Scouts had already taken charge of the administration and achieved a fait accompli. Although, he was arrested later on November 1, the damage had been done. The Gilgit Scouts revolted and demanded merger with Pakistan and two weeks later, the Pakistan Government formally posted a Political Agent there, thus completing the annexation of the Gilgit Lease area and bringing it directly under their control. An extremely important strategic piece of territory was thus handed over to Pakistan at a silver platter. Nehru and the Government of India were too slow and too late.

We all know about the standstill agreement offered by General Janak Singh, the Prime Minister of Kashmir, to both India and Pakistan to ensure continuation of existing arrangements till the final option of accession to either dominion was exercised. While Pakistan Government accepted the proposal, the Government of India procrastinated. Thus, as of August 15, 1947, Pakistan had a standstill agreement with Kashmir while India had none. The Radcliff Boundary Commission Award, ready on August 13, 1947, was kept confidential by Lord Mountbatten till August 18, 1947, to avoid any disturbances prior to the independence day celebrations of each country. But once Pakistan came to know about District Gurdaspur, which includes the only passage from India to Kashmir, being given to India, they were greatly agitated. Through Gurdaspur also lay the access to Pathankot, the gateway to Jammu and thereafter to the Kashmir Valley. Pakistan had two shorter and better communication lines from Rawalpindi and Sialkot to Kashmir compared to the one that India had, from Pathankot through a dusty track via Jammu. Thwarted in their effort to get back the territory of Kashmir, this strategic advantage to Pakistan enabled her to slap down an economic blockade against Kashmir while India watched helplessly. A few essential commodities, however, were sent by the Government of India through air. To the meanest intelligence, it would have been clear that trouble was brewing and sooner or later a confrontation with Pakistan over Kashmir was inevitable. Nehru, however, did not prepare for this contingency. On the other hand, Patel the farsighted did, though he was not directly dealing with Kashmir. He immediately ordered on a war footing the improvement of this 112 km. fair weather track from Pathankot onwards to Jammu. Inspite of the problems of communal trouble and attempts from Pakistan to disrupt, the job was completed in record time before the commencement of hostilities. This track later became our only lifeline to the Valley. Had he been given a free hand in Kashmir, it is almost certain that Patel would have obtained the accession of Maharaja to the Indian Union just as adroitly as he had done in the case of Junagadh and other States within the Indian landmass. But this was not to be. The situation worsened. And now from the records.

"Alongside this blockade an all out effort was made by Pakistani agents to create communal trouble inside the State just as it had been created in India before and after partition. The State of Jammu and Kashmir was absolutely free from outbursts of communal frenzy when Punjab on both sides of the border was having a full dose of it. Lakhs of refugees from Pakistan were in Jammu and Kashmir territory and were passing to India on foot, unmolested by Muslim residents of the State, but the situation completely took a turn for the worse soon after Jinnah got news about the rejection of his several requests to the Maharaja for accession. Muslims of the Jammu province were excited to create communal trouble inside the State and Jammu became a seat of communal killings."

Pakistan prepared feverishly for the invasion of Kashmir. Rumblings of this were conveyed to the Maharaja who still prevaricated. On the night of October 21-22, 1947, Pakistan struck. Pathans and irregulars led by regular officials under the command of Major General Akbar Khan advanced along Rawalpindi-Muzaffarabad-Srinagar road. The first Indo-Pak conflict had begun. From then onwards, events moved very fast. Failure to blow up the Krishna Ganga bridge in time for want of dynamite led to the fall of Muzaffarabad on October 23, 1947.

The story of the invasion by Pak troops, subsequent advance and the loss of precious time, plunder and rape at Baramula, with the respite it gave to the beleaguered garrison is all too well known. This allowed the Indian Air Force to fly in reinforcements in time for the defence of Srinagar and block any further advance. All this is history and need not detain us here. Nehru as described earlier in a manner reminiscent of a Greek tragedy, wailed in his All India Radio broadcast on Pakistan's perfidy. The same way as he was to do later on China.

It was a cry of desperation and not a clarion call to the nation for firm resolve and determined action. To quote from Bible:

"If the trumpet giveth an uncertain sound, who shall prepare himself to battle."

Not a Churchillian bull headed determination to fight on land, air and the sea beaches, but a whimper of protest. Contrast this with Patel's reaction. He did not speak; he acted.

Patel took quick and bold decisions to hold the situation firmly under control. He ordered planes to be diverted to the Delhi-Srinagar route and got wireless and telegraph communications established between Pathankot and Jammu. Mehar Chand Mahajan, a judge of the Punjab High Court, was to be the next Prime Minister of Maharaja Hari Singh. He was virtually ordered by Sardar Patel to report on duty forthwith, having been sanctioned eight months leave from the High Court. This is what Patel had communicated to Maharaja Hari Singh on September 21, 1947:

"Justice Mehar Chand will convey to you personally the gist of our conversation on all matters affecting the interests of Kashmir. I have promised him full support and cooperation on our behalf."

One man who was bounden in his resolve to oppose the Maharaja and seek his own fiefdom in Kashmir was Sheikh Abdullah. He was the founder of the Muslim Conference in 1930 and later changed the name of this body in 1938 to National Conference. He was frequently in and out of the jail alongwith his colleagues; the final release being on September 29, 1947, as mentioned earlier. While Vallabhbhai had misgivings about the Sheikh, Nehru had his own reasons for disliking Maharaja Hari Singh who had imprisoned him in June, 1946, during his entry into Kashmir. Patel, however, showed understanding and dealt with the Maharaja in a more sympathetic manner.

The Maharaja, ill advised as he was, dithered between asking for Indian assistance or opting for independence, till the situation went out of control. Srinagar was threatened. The only way he could get assistance from India was by acceding to the Dominion.

On October 26 at 3.00 PM, a crucial meeting took place at Nehru's house attended by Patel, Nehru, Baldev Singh, Abdullah, Mahajan, Kashmir's Deputy Prime Minister, Batra and Menon. The Sheikh and Mahajan instantly recommended that military help be sent to Srinagar. Nehru was rather hesitant and Mountbatten seemed to concur with his policy to wait and watch. Nehru with all his love for Kashmir, as usual, prevaricated. Almost forcing the stout Hindu Mahajan to explode that if India did not help, Kashmir would be forced to accept Pakistan's assistance on Jinnah's terms. This annoyed Nehru and he asked Mahajan to leave. Sardar Patel, however, had more sense. As the Kashmir Premier was about to leave the Sardar took him aside saying, "Of course Mahajan, you are not going to Pakistan."

Even before the Maharaja had made his impassioned appeal Patel's mind was clear. The only reply to Pakistan's attack on Kashmir was to be an immediate despatch of Indian forces. Patel's clear headedness and firm resolve carried the day, despite Nehru's indecision. Menon was ordered to return at once to Kashmir and inform the Maharaja that Indian Army would be there to help. However, this firm decision of Patel did not completely outsmart Mountbatten, and with Nehru's assistance he got two of his own suggestions accepted; one was, Hari Singh's accession to be a pre-requisite before the despatch of the troops; and second, the commitment to hold a plebiscite after normalisation of the situation. This part was to be included in the instrument of accession. Patel had his misgivings on both these counts. To him the Pak invasion of Kashmir was enough of a *casus belli* to warrant use of force by India and he hoped that Kashmir's accession would lead to greater difficulty for Pakistan in securing Hyderabad's accession. Regarding the plebiscite, Patel felt that the principle of reciprocity in this regard was sound. In the event, he yielded to Mountbatten's suggestion with a feeling at the back of his mind that a large number of British officers in their individual capacity were still as much part of the Indian Military services as that of Pakistan. Patel also agreed to Nehru's condition to allow Abdullah a position of authority in Kashmir; this with a view to enlist Muslim support against the Pak attack. But regarding plebiscite Patel never really intended to accept it as a permanent feature of the instrument of accession. This "enfant terrible" midwifed by Mountbatten and Nehru today hangs like the proverbial sword of Damocles over our heads. Despite Patel's exertions to the contrary, Nehru, the hesitant Hamlet, succumbed to Mountbatten's pressure, and all our sorrows and sufferings in Kashmir flow from this original sin. Patel was right in his objections, Nehru was wrong.

Travelling all night, Maharaja at last reached Jammu on the morning of October 26, almost despairing that he had lost Kashmir. He was woken up by Menon and informed of the decision of the Indian Government to send military force provided he signed the Instrument of Accession, which the Maharaja promptly did. The Maharaja, however, gave a written request for prompt military assistance, while agreeing to make Abdullah the "Head of Administration" or Prime Minister.

In a recently published book by Prem Shanker Jha titled "Kashmir 1947--Rival Versions of History" the author gives at Appendix-I page 135, a statement of Field Marshal Sam Manekshaw, recorded in Delhi on December 18, 1994, where the latter had stated, "Nehru talked about United Nations, Russia, Africa and God almighty, every body, until Sardar Patel lost his temper. He said `Jawaharlal do you want Kashmir or do you want to give it away?' (He (Nehru) said `Of course, I want Kashmir'. Then he (Patel) said `please give your orders'. And before he (Nehru) could say anything Sardar Patel turned to me and said `you have got your orders'. I walked out and we started flying in the troops at about 11 or 12 O'clock." The meeting referred to by Sam Manekshaw was held at the Viceregal Lodge at about 10 a.m. on the morning of October 26, 1947, presided over by the Lord Mountbatten and attended by Nehru, Patel, Baldev Singh, V.P. Menon and Sam Manekshaw. This was after Manekshaw along with Menon had brought the Instrument of Accession duly signed by Maharaja Hari Singh in the wee hours of October 26, 1947.

Regarding the exertions of Sardar Patel during Kashmir crisis many records exist, including his correspondence published by Durga Das. On October 27 Patel was at the Willingdon airfield to see off one air sortie after another take off for Srinagar, while awaiting the return of Menon alongwith the Instrument of Accession duly signed. Patel, the man of action, believed in abiding by the famous saying from the Bhagvad Gita, in letter and spirit.

"Yuddhaya Krita Nishchaya" (Resolved in Battle). He, however, had a hidden anxiety regarding the news from Kashmir, while Jinnah was likewise waiting at Lahore for a similar report from Kashmir regarding its accession to Pakistan. The latter was even gloating over his coming victorious journey to Srinagar which he hoped the tribesmen would have occupied by October 26-27. His Private Secretary, Khurshid Ahmad, was already in Srinagar. At mid-day on October 27 when he heard the Indian troops had landed at Srinagar, Jinnah's hopes went up in smoke and disappeared into the thin air. This was the reward of the Sardar's masterly handling of the situation. The Sheikh, never an admirer of Patel, grudgingly admitted this after Patel's visit to Srinagar.

"Events took a decisive turn. The Sardar did not lose even one minute. He studied the situation and said that the enemy must be driven back. Major General Kulwant Singh and several hundred soldiers were flown to Srinagar the next day. Taking over from Major General Sen, Kulwant Singh freed Baramula on November 8.

The town bore terrible marks of the raiders' arson and pillage, loot and rape."

In Pakistan Chaudhri Muhammad Ali was to rue later that "Had the tribal *Lashkar* been more disciplined and had it not indulged in plunder on its way, it would have been in occupation of the Kashmir valley on October 26."

Another example of Patel's firm handling and lack of any direction from Nehru is available in the observation of Dr Gadgil.

"In the last week of October 1947, Patel took out a map and pointing to the Jammu-Pathankot area, said that the 65-mile road between the two towns had to be made capable of carrying heavy army traffic within eight months."

Patel had known that it was no cakewalk and there will be long and gruelling days ahead. Gadgil, Minister for Works, had his reservations on the task and pointed out rivers, rivulets, hills and mountains which could not be clearly seen at the map that could impede the task. To this, Patel had a short and curt reply: "You have to do it".

A force of 10,000 workers was brought from Rajasthan through special trains. Aided by floodlights they worked whole nights. Labour camps, dispensaries, mobile cinemas were all established and commandeered into operation and the 65 miles track was completed in time.

After the decision to help there is not much record of Nehru's exertions to expedite the pace of re-inforcement or the conduct of military operations. Almost all military commanders involved in these operation could testify to this.

The operations of the Indian Army in J & K are well documented and need not detain us here. However, the closing stages, need some mention.

Briefly summarised, the 'Operation Easy' under Major General Yadunath Singh commenced on the night of November 6-7 with the advance of a brigade group each on either side of the Rajauri-Bhimbergali Road, on November 8, 1948. Rajauri column captured Ramgarh Fort on November 9. The advance continued towards Mendhar, feinting towards Kotil to mislead the enemy. The brigade on the left of the road encountered stiff resistance, while only light opposition was met by the brigade on the right. By shifting of a two battalion force to the right on November 18, the advance continued. By speed and surprise, the enemy was completely outmaneuvered on the ground, while the Indian Air Force resorted to some dummy airdrops. Finally the last height, Point 5982 and Topa Ridge leading to Punchh, were captured on November 20, 1948. By 14.00 Hrs. the same day, the beleaguered garrison linked up with the relief column and the siege of Punchh was lifted. Pakistani troops had been given a bloody nose. The deception plans had worked admirably and the enemy troops were completely routed. Pakistani losses were 363 killed and 633 wounded alongwith many prisoners. Thus, Indian troops had liberated 1300 square kms. of the State territory. The Engineers following the advance completed the track upto Punchh via Bhimbergali, thus breaking the isolation of Punchh and linked it with the rest of the country. This was the high tide of our operations in Jammu and Kashmir. Unfortunately, instead of consummating the offensive into victory by liberating the complete areas, aggressed upon by Pakistan, Nehru, under the advice of Lord Mountbatten, decided to refer the question to the United Nations. Earlier, Mountbatten had advised Nehru to accompany him to Lahore to hold talks with Jinnah and Liaqat. To this Patel had objected saying, "For the Prime Minister to go crawling to Jinnah when we are the stronger side and in the right would never be forgiven by the people of India". Patel's objection was too strong to be turned down, and due to Nehru's illness, just at the time the visit was postponed. Patel, however, consistently expressed his strong views against any reference to the United Nations till the entire territory was cleared of the invader. But Kashmir being Nehru's direct charge by now, Vallabhbhai did not insist beyond his brief. Without reference to Patel, Nehru announced by end December the decision to go to U.N. despite Gandhiji's reservations. Nevertheless, it was due to Gandhiji's personal intercession that the wordings of India's complaint were changed and a reference to an independent Kashmir as a possible alternative to merger with the Dominion of India or Pakistan was removed. Patel's prophetic warning was later justified by the events. To India's complaint Pakistan retorted with the counter-charges regarding Junagadh and the alleged genocide of Muslims in India. The British official policy was, as always, tilting towards Pakistan. Their representative showed a definite pro-Pakistan bias and his efforts made the Security Council view the Pakistani case to be stronger than ours. The simple issue of removal of aggression by Pakistan was turned into an 'India-Pakistan problem.' Despite a praiseworthy performance of Gopalaswamy in the debate at U.N. he was outmaneuvered by Pakistan's Foreign Minister Zafrullah Khan who emerged with a distinct advantage. Winter had set in. In the State of Kashmir only the valley could be cleared but a large chunk of mountainous territory remained in Pakistani hands. This was to be later called Pak Occupied Kashmir (POK).

While the enemy was still in retreat, on January 1, 1948, India invoked Article 35 of the UN Charter.

There were two issues before the UN, first whether or not to recognise the fact of Pakistan's aggression in Kashmir and bring about a cease-fire. The second was the holding of a plebiscite which clause was unfortunately incorporated into the 'Instrument of Accession' by Nehru under Mountbatten's pressure. While India's stand was clear Pakistan was using every weapon in its armoury to delay and obfuscate the issue to gain sufficient time so that by the time the cease-fire agreement was signed, they could grab enough territory and speak from a position of strength. The UN Resolution of January 17, 1948, required both India and Pakistan to cease hostilities at once. Another Resolution dated January 20, 1948, called for the formation of a United Nations Commission for India and Pakistan (UNCIP) of five members to investigate the situation on the spot and assist the two countries to restore normalcy in Kashmir and subsequently bring about a plebiscite that would decide the issue of accession. The UNCIP in consultation with the two countries made out its plan on August 13 which called for a cease-fire and simultaneous negotiations for a truce with the explicit condition that all the Pathan tribesmen and other Pakistani officers be withdrawn first, and subsequently, Indian forces be asked to pull out. After all this was done India and Pakistan should start preparing for a plebiscite. The U.N. Resolution of August 13 1948, is given at Appendix B and the assurance given to India by UN Commission at Annexure-1 to this Appendix. While India accepted the above plan, Pakistan demurred hoping to use the regular troops in greater strength to occupy more territory before the onset of winter to achieve a position of advantage in subsequent negotiations. However, as events turned out, Pakistan suffered one repulse after another. The case of relief of Punchh has been described earlier. With the fall of Dras on November 15 and Kargil on November 23 in the North, Pakistani troops were no longer in a position to threaten Leh or for that matter any other territory in Ladakh. Once the message became clear that more delay would cost them more loss of territory, Pakistan decided to cut its losses and decided to accept the UNCIP's plan of August 13, 1948. Indian offensive was on its tide while Pakistan's ground situation looked gloomy. Thus, destiny wrote a sad chapter in Kashmir. Those who refuse to take advantage of a winning situation are bound to repent for all times to come. Thus finally, on January 1, 1949, the cease-fire came into effect.

And now we come to Nehru's role in this sordid

affair. Was his decision to call a halt to military operations a wise step? Contrast this approach to the timings of cease-fire by Pakistan. Pakistan deliberately indulged in delaying tactics hoping for a favourable ground situation to prevail before accepting the cease-fire. But what forced Nehru to accept the cease-fire when the enemy was on the run. Pakistan repeatedly refused a cease-fire waiting for the situation to improve and, thus regain lost ground. This did not happen. The steamroller of the Indian onslaught forced the invaders back, and to cut further losses Pakistan on August 13, 1948, accepted the cease-fire proposal. What compulsions did Nehru have to stop an offensive which was so well succeeding on the ground. To quote Shakespeare:

"There is a tide in the affairs of men.
Which, taken at the flood, leads on to fortune;
Omitted, all the voyage of their life
Is bound in shallows and in miseries;
And we must take the current when it serves,
Or lose our ventures."

The Pakistani offensive had lost momentum, they were retreating, and the Indian offensive was on its tide. Given a few more days, the invaders would have been driven back from the valley and the aggression completely wiped out with the liberation of Kashmir. This was not to be. Nehru's decision to call a halt to the offensive was even worse than Hitler's halt orders at Dunkirk. In the latter case, at least, his Panzers were fighting on a foreign soil in France and Belgium . In our case, it was our own country and he allowed the enemy to stay. History never forgives those who refuse to learn from it. Here was a student of history who learnt nothing from it. Once Kashmir had acceded, it was an integral part of India. Does any sane person allow a criminal who has trespassed into his house, allow him to remain and rest there and run to a third party for arbitration. Nehru left half of Kashmir in Pakistani hands, even though he had enough strength to evict him. He left the occupied territories in the permanent possession of the aggressors; the enemy lording it over the territory aggressed upon. The trespasser was allowed into our house not even as a tenant but as an owner. Thus, the problem of Kashmir was frozen for posterity. More of this later.

With the cease-fire coming into effect on the night of 1st/2nd January, 1949, Pakistan's attempt to grab Kashmir and of India to liberate it, came to an end. Alistair Lamb in his book , 'Crisis in Kashmir ' is credited with the view that India might have won the plebiscite in Kashmir if it was held in 1948 itself. Kashmiri people, fresh with the memory of Pakistani blockade, subsequent attack and repression let loose, the heinous crimes and rape perpetrated by the tribal invaders, would have definitely opted for India. But there were two contervailling factors in this dynamics. First, the risk of losing so much rich and valuable territory, the prize being the valley. Secondly, an electoral victory for Sheikh Abdullah would not by itself mean union with India. But on a closer look, these risks appear more imaginary than real. Firstly there was almost no possibility of Kashmiri people, after what they had gone through at the hands of their own co-religionists, to exercise the Pakistan option. Secondly, given an astute leadership in India such as that of Sardar Patel, Sheikh Abdullah could have been tamed. With Nehru alone the risk was there. One is reminded of a famous saying of Earl of Montrose, which General Montgomery, the famous victor of the Battle of El-Alamien against Rommel, used to carry in his caravan:

> "He either fears his fate too much,
> or his deserts are small,
> who dare not put it to the touch,
> To win or lose it all".

A certain amount of risk is inherent in all bold ventures

and here there was not even a calculated risk. But Nehru was not the man to take bold decisions or known for his cool nerves. Only the Sardar could do it. But he was not handling Kashmir. He was being scrupulously kept out of it by Nehru who felt strangely possessive about Kashmir. Nehru could react and fume in the public and parliament and indulge in surcharged rhetoric but in moments of bold decision he developed cold feet. He was indecisive to a fault . So a chance to solve the Kashmir problem once and for all was allowed to slip by.

Even subsequently, Nehru's stand on the issue of plebiscite was always defensive, giving an impression of weakness in India's stand. The substantive points in the UN Resolution of plebiscite was the prior vacation of territories illegally occupied by Pakistan, which he never emphasised in diplomacy, nor threatened militarily to liberate. Thus, with the exception of Soviet Russia, the world view influenced by the Pakistani propaganda always considered Pakistan as the injured party. Nehru's second failing was his undue insistence on retaining Article 370, a temporary provision, and stonewalling all public opinion to the contrary. This article is reproduced at Appendix 'C'. Thoroughly under the influence of Sheikh Abdullah, he did nothing to abrogate it, thus , leading to far-reaching consequences in the State and the present sorry pass. Coming now to the political developments as the act was being played out on the international scene, events did not wait in Kashmir after the accession of the State. The Maharaja appointed Sheikh Abdullah as the head of the administration and later on March 4, 1948, as the Prime Minister with a Council of Ministers to serve him. The Sheikh was handed over all powers of the government, so much so that as someone put it, "Where the Maharaja was required to be consulted, he was bullied; and where he was needed to be informed, he was ignored".

In all such actions, the Sheikh had the tacit support of Nehru, despite a sullen and disillusioned Patel. As if the happenings at the United Nations were not enough the Maharaja was provoked and insulted by the Sheikh. Humiliated to the extreme he expressed his exasperation at the turn of events in the following words:

"There is an alternative possible for me and that is to withdraw the Accession and that may kill the reference to the UNO because Indian Union will have no right to continue the proceedings before the Council if the Accession is withdrawn. The result may be a return to the position the State held before the Accession".

Later, in his complaint to the Home Minister regarding the arrogance of the Sheikh he wrote on April 20, 1948:

"I refer to the wild and baseless allegations that are being made against me that I left the capital at the dead of night and removed truckloads of furniture and other belongings. I would ordinarily have dismissed these allegations but, to my great regret and profound shock, they have found expression in some of the utterances of my present Prime Minister".

In another letter of May 6, 1949, he wrote:

"Nor would it be fair on my part to conceal from you my own feeling that while Sheikh Abdullah has been allowed to depart from time to time as suited his inclinations from the pledged and written word, to act consistently in breach of the loyalty which he professed to me prior to his release from jail and the oath of allegiance which he took when he assumed office, and to indulge openly along with his colleagues in a campaign of vilification and foul calumny against me, both inside the State and outside, I should have had to be driven from position to position each of which I thought I had on the advice of the State's Ministry". And what happened to all these complaints? Patel was helpless since Nehru held the Kashmir cards close to his chest. The Maharaja was not only humiliated but forced to abdicate. To soften the blow he was asked to issue a legal proclamation on June 9, 1949, giving all his powers to Yuvraj Karan Singh, whom the Sheikh manipulated at will.

On adoption of the Indian Constitution on January 26,1950, the earlier 'Instrument of Accession' of October 27, 1947, became an integral part of India's Constitution and the Maharaja's jurisdiction lapsed de jure. Many things happened almost simultaneously at this juncture. While on the one hand political and constitutional issues needed to be resolved, on the other the Praja Parishad agitation gained momentum and to add to all this the appetite of Sheikh Abdullah to be the independent ruler of Kashmir was further whetted by the political events. This is the time the Delhi Agreement between Sheikh Abdullah and Nehru was announced in the Union Parliament on July 24, 1952 and on August 19, the Constituent Assembly of the State also approved it. The Sheikh's less than covert ambitions for seeking independence and unlimited powers for himself and his cabal and his ability to exploit India's difficulty with regard to plebiscite gave him further advantage. Soon after this declaration, Sheikh Abdullah moved the State Constituent Assembly to abolish the institution of hereditary monarchy on August 21, 1952, and re-named the Maharaja as 'Sadar-e-Riyasat' who was to be elected by the State Legislature for five years and was to be recognised by the President of India and hold office at his pleasure. The public opinion in India, in general, and Jammu, in particular, was against the appeasement of the Sheikh at the cost of national interest. The Sheikh on June 10, 1952, not only invited the wrath of the Jammuites by his open denouncement of Dogra kings but in his speech in the Constituent Assembly openly denigrated the Maharaja's rule.

"The people, under the guidance of National Conference, have sacrificed their lives, have gone to jails, and have lived in narrow cells inhabited by serpents and scorpions. Hundreds of womenfolk have been dishonoured, hundreds made to crawl on their bellies and thousands rendered martyrs by shedding their blood". This was nothing but a travesty of truth

The agitation in Jammu was led by the Praja Parishad. The main plank of agitation was, "Ek desh mein do vidhan; ek desh main do nishan; ek desh mein do pradhan nahin chalenge" ("In one country, two constitutions; in one country, two flags; in one country two prime ministers cannot be allowed"). This agitation gathered momentum as Jana Sangh strongly supported the feelings of Jammuites against the so-called Delhi Agreement which they said sounded as a sellout and reacted in the following words:

"Sheikh Abdullah has secured the most unreasonable of his demands without conceding anything substantial. Every concession that Nehru has secured is limited by a proviso which almost nullifies it. This is not likely to gain Kashmir for India but will certainly endanger the security and development of Jammu and Kashmir".

Syama Prasad Mookerjee, the President of Jana Sangh, reached Jammu on May 11, 1953, and was arrested on orders of Jawaharlal Nehru. He was to die subsequently in custody one month later and the whole nation rose in indignation at Nehru's virtual surrender to the separatist movement in Kashmir. The martyrdom of Syama Prasad Mookerjee, a great patriot, moved the nation beyond expectation. His body was flown to Calcutta and given the biggest funeral ever in Calcutta. Not only was Nehru criticised and the Delhi Agreement condemned inside and outside the Parliament, the country started suspecting Abdullah of insincerity and his future intentions of secession. He was allowed to amend and alter the provisions of Delhi Agreement at will and that too with Nehru's indulgence. It was too late when Nehru got wise to the Sheikh's treachery and he wrote to Abdullah on 6 and 7 August 1952, stating that the latter's actions had made his own position in the Parliament indefencible. On June 28, 1953, Nehru said:

"To me it has been a major surprise that settlement arrived at between us should be bypassed or repudiated. That strikes at the root of all confidence. My honour is bound up with my word".

Abdullah remained unfazed. He avoided Nehru. He was secretly harbouring a paranoia of an independent Sheikhdom in Kashmir. At last Nehru lost faith in Abdullah, and on April 10,1952, the Sheikh shed even his pro-Nehru veneer and at Ranbirsingh Pura he condemned the Indian press and the Indian government accusing them of communalism. On July 13,1952, in his speech on 'Martyrs Day', he denounced the interference of the Central Government in the affairs of Kashmir which he said would not be tolerated. On May 3,1953, the American Ambassador, Adlai Stevenson after his meeting with the Sheikh at Srinagar expressed his doubts about the intentions of Abdullah and the *New York Times* in its issue of July 5, published a map, showing the valley as an independent state. True to form the Sheikh thundered at Mujahid Manzil:

"A time will, therefore, come when I will bid them goodbye". And again on July 13, 1953, "It is not necessary that our State should become an appendage of either India or Pakistan". This even to the most gullible was a demand for complete independence. On 7 August, 1953, Bakshi Ghulam Mohammad, the Deputy Prime Minster, alongwith a majority of his colleagues accused Abdullah of causing uncertainty in the public mind which forced the Sadar-e-Riyasat to summon an immediate cabinet meeting. The Sheikh ignored the advice and proceeded to Gulmarg instead, where he was finally arrested on August 8, 1953.

How does this turn of events reflect on Nehru's ability to judge a person? He was being betrayed by the same person whom till yesterday, he trusted and supported all along against the better judgement of his colleagues, specially Sardar Patel. Subsequently, when Sheikh Abdullah's anti-India tirade and pro-independence stance became clear even to the dullest intelligence he was arrested and Bakshi Ghulam Mohammed was sworn in as the Chief Minister of Kashmir.

And now the charade of Article 370, a temporary provision with the ultimate aim of fully integrating

Kashmir with the rest of India at the earliest. To quote from the records of the Parliamentary proceedings in zero hour on November 27, 1963, a member asked the Prime Minister (who had gone for a holiday in Kashmir) regarding his address there to a special delegation, where Nehru had mentioned:

"That Article 370 of the Constitution will disappear by getting eroded gradually. The member persisted. 'But after resigning from his office the Ex-Prime Minister of Kashmir, Bakshi Ghulam Mohammed, has said that Article 370 of the Constitution is a permanent provision, and that Kashmir's destiny is tied up with it . I want to know, which of these two statements is correct and what is the Government of India's position via-a vis these two statements'".

Nehru replied:

"What the Hon'ble Member has said about my statement is correct. What Bakshi Ghulam Mohammed has said on different occasions, I cannot comment on that without going through the records. He might have laid some emphasis that Article 370 should remain and had given some indication that gradually it was changing. *Vakya yeh hai ki usme koi bahut zyaadaa jaan rahi nahin hai*—the reality is that there is not much life left in it".

Nehru then mentioned the necessity of retaining some good parts of the J & K provision, such as not allowing outsiders to buy land in Kashmir and that changing these old things would not be good. He insisted that these were not germane to the issue:

"But has there been some change in the Government's thinking since the Prime Minister's statement (in Srinagar)", the Member continued, "which has led Bakshi Ghulam Mohammed to say that Article 370 is a permanent provision and there is no question of removing it".

Nehru's reply was, 'The answer to that has just been given by the Home Minister". Incidentally the Home Minister had said in a written reply. ("Article

370 of the Constitution occurs in Part XXI of the Constitution which deals with *temporary* and *transitional* provisions. Since this Article was incorporated in the Constitution, many changes have been made which bring the State of Jammu and Kashmir in line with the rest of India. The State is fully integrated to the Union of India. Government are of opinion that they should not take any initiative now for the complete repeal of Article 370. This will, no doubt, be brought about by further changes in consultation with the Government and the Legislative Assembly of Jammu and Kashmir State. This process has continued in the last few years and may be allowed to continue in the same way.")

Nehru reemphasised this reply and the line of reasoning, saying:

"Our view is that Article 370, as is written in the Constitution, is a *transitional,* in other words a *temporary* provision. And it is so. You can see how much change has come about in so many things since it was enacted. And that is continuing to happen. The Home Minister has just mentioned two or three things in which changes have recently been made. I do not regard it as permanent."

"Article 370, as the House will remember, is a part of certain transitional and provisional arrangements. It is not a permanent part of the Constitution. It is a part so long as it remains so. As a matter of fact, as the Home Minister has pointed out, it has been eroded, if I may use the word, and many things have been done in the last few years which have made the relationship of Kashmir with the Union of India very close. There is no doubt that Kashmir is fully integrated."

The tall stalwart, an ex-I.C.S. and an eminent Parliamentarian, H.V. Kamath, rose to say "Not fully".

"No", "I repeat that it is fully integrated". Nehru stoically maintained. Within seconds he did a volte face and said that he was merely giving his opinion and mentioned some good things in the Article 370. Typical of his protean style, Nehru's words on any subject were never his last. Could the utterances of such a Prime Minister even in Parliament on issues affecting a nation's integrity, be taken on their face value? Nehru continued, "So we feel that this process of gradual erosion of Article 370 is going on". He then closed the debate by reminding the House in Hindi that. "Some fresh steps are being taken and in the next month or two they will be completed. We should allow it to go on. We do not want to take the initiative in the matter and completely put an end to Article 370. The initiative, we feel, should come from the Kashmir State Government, and people. We shall gladly agree to that". Mark the word "The initiative should come from Kashmir State Government, and people".

This was the olive branch for the future but meanwhile the Centre cannot and will not enact something vital, that sustains the unity and integrity of the country unless the local government and the people wish it. This argument was used with deadly repetition when it suited Nehru. Be it the case of implementation of Hindi as a national language which could now only be done if the people from South wished it. If it was to be the policy in tribal areas, it will be the tribals who will decide. It was quite another matter that Dr. Verrier Alwin, Nehru's adviser on Tribal Affairs, a Christian, could ordain that the tribal areas be thrown open to Christian missionaries but remain always sealed against Hindu priests to preserve the pristine isolation of the tribals. The Hindu influence could corrupt. But the Christian proselytisation was an altogether different matter. Today, thanks to Nehru almost all the population of North-East tribal areas is Christian. The same fatuous argument was used against introduction of uniform civil code provision under Article 44 of the Constitution; the people concerned in this case are Muslims. The minority must wish it. The Centre can only sit and watch hopelessly. Coming back to Article 370, it was a strategam to clothe the Centre's incapacity to do its duty in the garb of pompous principles. Article 370, it was emphasised, was the umbilical cord which bound Kashmir with India and through which provisions of the Indian Constitution could be extended to the territory of Kashmir. It was the link to serve a temporary purpose till the State is totally integrated within the Indian Union. That the Article is a temporary provision is evident from its very title which reads: "Article 370 Temporary provision with respect to the State of J & K".

Remember that such an important matter concerning Home was being handled not by the Home Minister, Sardar Patel, but by N. Gopalaswamy Ayyanger, an earlier Prime Minister of J & K for six years with effect from 1937. Subsequently an aide to Nehru and later promoted to the rank of a Minister, dealing with the delicate problem of J & K. The discussions on Article 370 in the Constituent Assembly are revealing when on October 17, 1949, two years after the invasion of Kashmir, N. Gopalaswamy Ayyangar moved Article 306 A (since then repealed). A member asked, "why this discrimination please?"

Gopalaswamy replied, "The discrimination is due to the special conditions of Kashmir. "(And we must recall that this discussion was taking place on 17 October 1949—within just two years almost to the day of the all-out invasion of Kashmir by Pakistan forces and "Mujahideen"; that a tenuous cease-fire had been declared just nine months earlier.). "That particular state is not yet ripe for this kind of integration. It is the hope of everybody here that in due course even Jammu and Kashmir will become ripe for the same sort of integration as has taken place in the case of other States. At present it is not possible to achieve that integration". A similar special treatment was not given to the Maharaja of Baroda by Sardar Patel, who in any case would not have countenanced the special provisions in the case of J & K too, if he was allowed by Nehru. He mentioned inter alia the earlier war in Kashmir, where a large part of the State was still under Pak occupation and the discussions were too close to the date of cease-fire, and said:

"We are entangled with the United Nations in regard to Jammu and Kashmir and it is not possible to say now when we shall be free from this entanglement".

"Till a Constituent Assembly comes into being, only an interim arrangement is possible and not an arrangement which could at once be brought into line with the arrangement which exists in the case of other states".

"Now if you remember the viewpoints (sic) that I have mentioned," he summed up, "It is an inevitable conclusion that, at the present moment, we could establish only an interim system. Article 306 is an attempt to establish such a system".

Just as Defence, External Affairs and Communications, subjects which are Centre's responsibility in other States can be extended to Kashmir through the concurrence of the State Government, the other parts of the Constitution can also be similarly extended. The State Government in either case had a veto power to accept or reject the introduction of these provisions within their territory. This was a patently undemocratic action to single out a State in this manner. But Gopalaswamy Ayyangar kept on harping on the nature of the provisions of Article 306 A and Article 370.

"At present, the legislature which was known as the Praja Sabha in the State is dead. Neither that legislature nor a Constituent Assembly can be convoked or can function until complete peace comes to prevail in that State. We have, therefore, to deal with the Government of the State which, as represented in its Council of Ministers, reflects the opinion of the largest political party in the State. Till a Constituent Assembly comes into being, only an interim arrangement is possible and not an arrangement which could at once be brought into line with the arrangement that exists in the case of the other states. . ."

"Clause (b) (ii) refers to possible additions to the List in the Instrument of Accession, and these additions could be made according to the provisions of this Article with the concurrence of the Government of the State. The idea is that even before the Constituent Assembly meets, it may be necessary in the interests of both the Centre and the State that certain items which are not included in the Instrument of Accession would be appropriately added to the List of that instrument so that administration , legislation and executive action might be furthered, and as this may happen before the Constituent Assembly meets, the only authority from whom we can get consent for the addition is the Government of the State. That is provided for." Amply satisfying the desirability of full and final integration, he said, "Now, it is not the case, nor is it the intention of the members of the Kashmir Government—whom I took the opportunity of consulting before this draft was finalised—it is not their intention that the other provisions of the Constitution are not to apply. Their particular point of view is that these provisions should apply only subject to such modifications of exceptions as the particular conditions of the Jammu and Kashmir State may require. I wish to say no more about that particular point at the present moment".

But Sheikh Abdullah, who was privy to this so-called Delhi Agreement and was staying in Delhi at that time hoping to derive maximum autonomy out of an obliging Nehru, had other views. Today, history is being repeated by his son, Dr. Farooq Abdullah.

The Sardar had reluctantly acquiesced to the usurpation of Kashmir portfolio by Nehru, a subject legitimately falling under the Department of States of the Ministry of Home Affairs. He did this to avoid unpleasantness. However, he did feel concerned when without consulting him Nehru brought in Gopalaswamy Ayyangar as a minister without portfolio to help him in dealing with Kashmir and the duo started muddling up things. He mentioned the same to Nehru without mincing words. Nehru flared up and replied on December 23, 1947.

"Gopalaswami Ayyangar has been especially asked to help in Kashmir matters. Both for this reason and because of his intimate knowledge and experience of Kashmir he had to be given full latitude. I really do not see where the States Ministry (the Sardar's Ministry, that is) comes into the picture except that it should be kept informed of steps taken. . . ."

"All this was done at my instance and I do not propose to abdicate my functions in regard to matters for which I consider myself responsible. May I say that the manner of approach to Gopalaswami was hardly in keeping with the courtesy due to a colleague?"

The Sardar immediately wrote back:

"Your letter of today has been received just now at I p.m. and I am writing immediately to tell you this. It has caused me considerable pain. . .Your letter makes it clear to me that I must not or at least cannot continue as a Member of Government and hence I am hereby tendering my resignation. I am grateful to you for the courtesy and kindness shown to me during the period of office which was a period of considerable strain."

The matter was soon in Gandhiji's lap to bring the two colleagues together.

From the records kept by V. Shankar, ICS, personal secretary to Patel, and the correspondence of Sardar Patel, published by Durga Dass, it is clear that Nehru had finalised the draft of Article 370 in collusion with Sheikh Abdullah without even consulting Patel and then proceeded abroad leaving Ayyangar to hold the baby during his absence through debates in the Constituent Assembly. In an earlier exchange of letters, Nehru had shown his irritation with Patel over their differences on 23 December, 1947.

"I am sorry that what I wrote to you gave you pain. I am myself very unhappy about the trend of events and the difficulties that have arisen between you and me. It seems that our approaches are different, however much we may respect each other. If I am to continue as Prime Minister, I cannot have my freedom restricted and I must have a certain liberty of direction. Otherwise it is better for me to retire. If unfortunately either you or I have to leave the Government of India, let this be done with dignity and goodwill. On my part I would gladly resign and hand over the reins to you." This was answered at noon the next day.

"I have no desire to restrain your liberty of direction in any manner nor have I ever done so in the past. . .The question of your resignation or your abdicating your functions does not arise at all. I am at one with you in that the decision may be taken with dignity and goodwill and I will strain every nerve to help you in doing so but you will not, I am sure, want me to continue long as an ineffective colleague."

And yet Nehru was using the same colleague with whom he differed so much and often quarrelled, to get his draft passed in Parliament. Shanker records in *My Reminiscences of Sardar Patel,* Vol 11, pages 61-64:

"In the Congress party, there was a strong body of opinion which looked askance at any suggestion of discrimination between the Jammu and Kashmir State and other States as members of the future Indian Union and was not prepared to go beyond certain limits in providing for the special position of Jammu and Kashmir. Sardar was himself fully in accord with this opinion, but due to his usual policy of not standing in the way of Pandit Nehru and Gopalaswami Ayyangar who sorted out problems in their own light, he had kept his own views in the background. In fact, he had not taken any part in framing the draft proposals with the result that he heard the proposals only when Gopalaswami Ayyangar announced them to the Congress Party. . .The announcement was followed by a storm of angry protests from all sides and Gopalaswami Ayyangar found himself a lone defender, with Maulana Abul Kalam Azad an ineffective supporter. Metaphorically, the situation may be succinctly described by saying that both Gopalaswami Ayyangar and his proposal were torn to pieces by the Party".

"Later in the evening Sardar received a telephone call from Gopalaswami Ayyangar explaining the genesis of the proposals he had put before the Party and describing the scenes that he had painfully witnessed. He felt that only Sardar could intervene to save the situation and appealed to him to come to his rescue. Sardar heard him and lapsed into silence."

Loyal to his absent colleague, Sardar tried to defend what he himself was convinced was indefensible. He convened a meeting of the Congress Executive. As Shanker recalls:

"The meeting was one of the stormiest I have ever witnessed, barring the Party meeting which discussed the proposition relating to Rajaji becoming the first President of Indian Republic. The opinion in opposition to Gopalaswami's formula was forcefully and even militantly expressed and the issue even brought in the sovereignty of the Constituent Assembly to draw up the Constitution without being tied down to the apron-strings of the Kashmir State Constituent Assembly. In such a situation even Maulana Azad was shouted down. The Party was in uproar. The Sardar had to plead that because of the international complications a provisional approach alone could be made leaving the question of final relationship to be worked out according to the exigencies of the situation and the mutual feelings and confidence that would have been by then created."

Once the Sardar had taken charge, all opposition to the Draft was silenced. Ayyangar later under pressure from Sheikh Abdullah was prepared to make substantive changes in Nehru's documents in favour of the Sheikh. But the Sardar stood firm and said. . .

"I do not at all like any change after our Party has approved of the whole arrangement in the presence of

Sheikh Sahib himself. Whenever Sheikh Sahib wishes to back out, he owes no duty to India or to the Indian Government or even on a personal basis, to you and the Prime Minister who have gone all out to accommodate him. In these circumstances, any question of my approval does not arise".

And later sensing his disquiet, Patel told Shankar:

"So you are annoyed with me for having accepted Gopalaswami's formula'. I queried that if he felt that way, why did he not indicate his mind earlier. He said, `I was deeply concerned at the situation. Gopalaswami had acted under Panditji's advice. If Jawaharlal were here I could have had it out with him. But how could I do so with Gopalaswami who was only acting under orders? If I did, people would have said that I was taking revenge on his confidant when he was away. Gopalaswami had appealed to me for help. How could I have let him down in the absence of his chief".

But to others, the Sardar was more forthright and told them, "Jawaharlal Royega".

Barely two years later on 24 July, 1952, after the Sardar's death, Nehru made a detailed statement on Kashmir in Parliament dealing with all the issues including the slow progress of integration of the State of Kashmir and mentioned that "Sardar Patel was all the time dealing with these matters". Stressing again the temporary nature of Article 370, he obfuscated the issue and involved the Sardar in the decision making, the very man who opposed it tooth and nail. He said:

"This came to an end in November, I think of 1949 when we were designing our Constitution in the Constituent Assembly. Well, we could not leave everything quite vague and fluid there. Something had to be stated in our Constitution about Jammu and Kashmir State. *That problem had to be faced by Sardar Patel.* Now, he did not wish to say very much, he wanted to leave it, we all wanted to leave it in a fluid condition because of these various factors, and gradually to develop those relations. As a result of this, a rather unusual provision was made in our Constitution relating to Jammu and Kashmir. That provision is now in Article 370".

Later referring to this speech of Nehru, Shankar remarked, "When I was working as his (Ayyangar's) Joint Secretary in July 1952 the self-same Article came in for criticism in the Lok Sabha. In defence, Pandit Nehru took the stand that the Article was dealt with by Sardar in his absence and he was not responsible for it. I met Gopalaswami the same evening as he was walking on the lawn of his residence. I questioned the bonafide of Pandit Nehru's stand. Gopalaswami's reaction was one of anger and he said, `It is an ill-return to Sardar for the magnanimity he had shown in accepting Panditji's point of view against his better judgement' He added, `I have told Jawaharlal this already".

A year later on 8th August, 1953, Nehru realised his earlier blunder and ordered the arrest of Sheikh Abdullah. "Jawaharlal Royega" were the prophetic last words of the Sardar and the chicken came home to roost. How does all this murky episode show up Nehru, the Prime Minister. He goes on a foreign trip when an important constitutional provision is being debated in the Parliament, a provision vital to the security and integrity of the country. And then on his return he puts the blame for the sponsorship of his misconceived handiwork on the very colleague who against his better judgement defended him. Is this the stuff leaders are made of, less than truthful, less than loyal? Who says that Nehru was not an honourable man? His dynasty inherited most of his qualities. Thus, we see that Article 370 midwifed by Nehru and Sheikh Abdullah did not really secure the integration of Kashmir with the Indian Union but encouraged the Sheikh to carve out an independent fiefdom for himself. It did not allow the benefits of equality, liberty and freedom from feudal oppression and economic development to reach the people of Kashmir but kept them in a permanent state of serfdom under their feudal lords. The fruits of economic aid and enormous resources poured into the State were cornered by a few self-seeking politicians, while the people remained poor, illiterate and steeped in misery. The discontent kept simmering. The rigged elections of the National Conference and Indian National Congress coalition in 1987 proved to be the proverbial last straw, and the youth of Kashmir, frustrated, unemployed, long suffering from inequities, while their feudal rulers prospered, said "enough is enough". The cult of the Kalashnikov was the inevitable consequence. The seeds of alienation of Kashmir were sown as early as July, 1952, when Nehru announced in the Union Parliament the Delhi Agreement leading to the incorporation of Article 370 in the Constitution of India. Later in 1957 some top leaders of the National Conference, Mir Qasim, G.M. Sadiq, G.L. Dogra and D.P. Dhar split the party and formed the opposition group, called the Democratic National Conference, (DNC) which subsequently increased its strength as more members of State Legislature joined it. This was a healthy trend as it started functioning as an effective check on the almost unchallenged authority and power of the National Conference. It was a healthy democratic development of checks and balances. Three vital points on the agenda of the Democratic National Conference were the extension of the jurisdiction of the Supreme Court to J & K state, holding of elections under the auspices of the Union Election Commission, and abrogation of Article 370, which confers a special status on the state. Democratic and perfectly legitimate, these demands needed no perceptive Prime Minister to accede to willingly. Nehru, the democrat, would brook no opposition to his preconceived Kashmir policy and his obsession to keep Kashmir a separate entity. He warned the leaders of DNC of a so-called danger from the north and forced them to drop the demand. This was in 1960 when Chinese threat was being perceived as more than the so-called hallucination of the Army authorities. Would a loosely tied up State subserve the defence needs of the Centre better than an integral territory with freedom of movement of men and resources and a populace solidly behind the national authority. Nehru let go another splendid opportunity of integrating Kashmir with the Indian Union.

While discussing the Kashmir fiasco in the preceding pages, the focus has been only on the events leading to the enactment of Article 370, the linchpin in the process of integration of Kashmir into the Union of India. For reasons more than academic a detailed look on this controversial provision is necessary. For the readers' benefit this has been reproduced at Appendix'C'.

The rootcause of alienation of the Kashmiri people and separatist trends in the politics of that unhappy State is the continued presence of Article 370 in the Constitution of India which ensures a special status for the State as against the other States of the Indian Union. The tremors of this historical act of Nehru have shaken the historical, social, economic and political foundations of the State and dealt a deadly blow to the unity of India while leading to deleterious effects on our polity. The consequences, if the Article is not abrogated, may be even more far-reaching. There is little doubt that vested interests of the Sheikh and his successors have been the prime beneficiaries as also the *raison d'etre* of this Article. The isolation of the State from the rest of Indian polity was not for its good health but to create a territory where the laws of natural justice, development and fairplay would not prevail. In consequence, the few power elites and their brokers have filled their coffers and kept the poor poorer. The beneficial laws of our Constitution such as the Wealth Tax, Gift Tax, Urban Land Ceiling Act, the right to buy property and inter-marry with other Indian nationals have not been allowed to operate in Kashmir. The Central Government under this Article can besides Defence, Communication and Foreign Affairs, make laws even on items featuring in the Union and the Concurrent List. But these can be applied only with the concurrence of the State. This amounts virtually to granting the State a veto on what it wishes to be introduced in its territory. The position is not the same in regard to the other states where the Union Parliament is free to make laws in respect of both the lists in any State within the Indian Union. However, under fair weather and with adroit political handling, some provisions of the Indian Constitution have been extended to the State from time to time. The process started after the Delhi Agreement of 1952 which enabled such an exercise. Some of these worth mention are Article 356 and the jurisdiction of the Supreme Court, Central Election Commission and the Comptroller and Auditor General. But there are still large areas mentioned in the Concurrent List and the residuary powers that have been left untouched in the State. One of these is Article 352 which gives the President the power to declare national emergency and another one, Article 360 regarding financial emergency which cannot be imposed in Kashmir, just as Article 365 enabling the President to suspend constitution of the State is not similarly applicable. Kashmir has its own Constitution by virtue of Article 370, unlike other states which have a uniform Constitution as enshrined in part IV of the Indian Constitution. Inevitably, a number of discrepancies and avoidable problems, such as the right to hold property, citizenship and freedom of settlement for the Indian citizens, have arisen. An Indian national has no right to settle or buy property in this State. While an average citizen of India can claim only one citizenship, the one in Jammu & Kashmir can have two—citizenship of India and that of the State. Those outside Kashmir cannot vote. What is most galling is that a woman of Jammu & Kashmir origin if married to an Indian who is a non-citizen of the State loses claims to property, both her own as well as that inherited from her parents. Such unreasonable, archaic and legally unsound laws, which are incompatible with the fundamental principles of our Constitution, have a field day in Kashmir. The State has its own flag and emblem, unknown in any other State of India. Many financial frauds have been perpetrated in the State in the absence of a close scrutiny by the Central Constitutional authority. Considerable wheeling dealing which started from the time of Sheikh Abdullah continued till the times of his worthy successor Dr. Farooq Abdullah where the State laws on property sale and puchase were flouted with impunity, with no checks and balances available to monitor the happenings within the State. In the case of the renewal of lease to Nedous Hotel in March 1988 and the Karal Sangri Hill in 1985, according to Jagmohan, ex-Governor of the State, the State exchequer was defrauded of crores of rupees which belonged to public. Corruption and nepotism were rampant and selective patronage to persons, plans and projects had a free run in the valley with total disregard to financial probity and public interest. The Urban Land (Ceiling and Regulation) Act, 1976 prevalent in India has not till now been extended to Jammu & Kashmir. It beats human intelligence as how such a provision could detract from the special status of Jammu & Kashmir. The underlying motive for non-extension of the above provision could only be the less than noble intentions of the ruling class, so that, under the shelter of Article 370, there shall flourish a politically corrupt oligarchy. The Anti Defection Act was not extended nor adopted fully in the State. It is the Leader of the Legislature Party and not the Speaker who can adjudicate on matters of defection. The situation is virtually tantamount to all powers of governance, political activities distribution of party tickets and nomination of Ministers being centered in the party chief who heads the Government. It is he who takes decision on the propriety of his own acts or those of a Minister in the Government or a Member of his Legislature Party. Such a provision was enacted in the Constitution of Jammu & Kashmir by 18th Amendment

Act, 1987. It stipulates that "If any question arises as to whether a member of the House has become subject to disqualification under this schedule, the question shall be referred for the decision of the Leader of the Legislature Party to which such member belongs and his decision shall be final". If this is not constitutional dictatorship what else is? The infirmity imposed on a woman citizen of Jammu & Kashmir after her marriage to an Indian citizen can have serious implications. Not only does she lose her property rights as mentioned above, but also suffers certain other disabilities, such as admission to Government aided colleges—Medical or Engineering. It is a mockery of justice when a person who is a citizen of India, by virtue of being a citizen and permanent resident in Jammu & Kashmir, forfeits his or her rights for admission to the Medical College funded by the Union Government, after marriage with an Indian citizen. The case of migrants from the West Pakistan after the partition who have been settled in Jammu & Kashmir for more than the last four decades and have still not been granted the basic human rights is some thing to which our so-called conscience-keepers and custodians of human rights such as the PUCL have turned a Nelson's eye. These unfortunates cannot cast their vote in the panchayat, municipality or the state elections, nor get admission to State colleges or secure state loans. These are the `nowhere' people residing in our country, who have left their homes for no fault of theirs and are unable to secure even elementary justice in their new homeland. It is not incidental that most of these people are Hindus. The plight of these unfortunates is the hidden sting of the infamous Article 370 and its consequences.

An argument that has often been touted for the retention of Article 370 is the need to maintain a special identity for Kashmir and its people and to preserve its cultural heritage. Is such a plea not applicable to the remaining states of our country, such as Andhra Pradesh, Tamil Nadu, Gujarat, Maharashtra, Punjab, West Bengal, Sikkim,

Nadu, Gujarat, Maharashtra, Punjab, West Bengal, Sikkim, Nagaland, Meghalaya, Tripura, Rajasthan to mention just a few. These have their own clear and distinctive culture and history. Why then Article 370 has not been applied to these States? How is it that Article 370 finds its rationale in the one and only one Muslim majority State of Kashmir? Jinnah had raised the ghost of two-nation theory. Does this Article then not amount to a shameful homage to Jinnah's theory and an effort to validate it? Jawaharlal Nehru along with Gandhiji and Patel denounced the two-nation theory during the pre-partition days, what 'compelled' Nehru to perpetuate it in Kashmir by introducing Article 370 and ensure its existence against all opposition in the country.

Article 356, a provision under which President's rule can be imposed in any State within the Indian Union, cannot be enforced in the State of Jammu & Kashmir without the consent of the Governor who himself is an appointee of the President. In other words, the President has to seek the permission of his own appointee to order what he considers right in national interest. Take another instance. If the Governor of Jammu & Kashmir decides to become a Sadar-e-Riyasat, then again Article 356 cannot be introduced without his consent. The situation really boils down to the fact that the elected Government of Jammu & Kashmir can defy the President of India should it so desire, virtually placing the State Government in a position superior to the Head of the Indian State.

Defence is a subject under the Union, but the State of Jammu & Kashmir can refuse the building of cantonment at any site or refuse to allot land for Defence purposes if that becomes necessary and defy the needs of national security. In other words, a subject as important as Defence, can be subverted by a recalcitrant State Government which wishes to obstruct the plan of the Government of India in respect of any concrete measure that it may deem necessary for the defence of the State..

Kashmir, through Article 370, they usually forget that the State is not a homogeneous entity. There are Buddhists in Ladakh, as different from the Muslims of the Valley as the Hindus of Jammu. The nomad Gujjars, Bakarwals and the Muslims of Kargil as also Nubra valley are likewise vastly different from the valley people. The Nubraites are of a different Aryan Afghan Turkoman blood, distinct from the ethnic group in Srinagar Valley.

We come to a very anomalous position regarding electoral representation at the level of the State Assembly and the Parliament. The total area of Jammu and the remaining parts of Jammu & Kashmir excluding the Valley is 70%, larger than the Valley, representing only 40% of the total State population. While one million people in the valley elect one Member for the Parliament, it is 1.4 million people from Jammu who have the same privilege. In other words per unit of population in Jammu sends less number of Members of Parliament than the Valley. Similarly, out of a total of 76 seats for the State Assembly, 42 come from the Valley while Jammu provides only 32 seats. This position is due to the fact that while in Jammu 90,000 people elect one M.L.A. to the State Assembly, in Kashmir only 73,000 people elect one—again a gross distortion of voting rights between Jammu and the Kashmir Valley. To accommodate the aspirations of the Valley people three new Districts were created in 1979, on an ad-hoc basis, while three districts recommended by Wazir Commission (1981-83) for Jammu have not been created till date. With such a step-motherly treatment against Jammu and favouring the Valley, let us have a look at the distribution of Plan funds to the two parts. While Jammu with its two million tourists, mainly to the Vaishno Devi shrine contributes the lion's share to the State exchequer, only half a million tourists visit the valley contributing almost one-fourth of the share of Jammu's contribution to the State resources. As against this, huge funds amounting to 90% of the total allocation this, huge funds amounting to 90% of the total allocation to the tourist sector, goes to the Valley alone. Huge expenses on projects such as a cable-car at Gulmurg and the Srinagar Golf Course have gobbled up Rs. 50 crore. But their poor cousin, the Dogri Art Gallery in Jammu with its rich collection of antiques, paintings and museum pieces gets nothing. The injustice does not end here. Jammu with a total area of 26,293 sq. kms. has only 3,500 kms. of roads while the Valley with an area of only 15853 sq. kms. has been gifted with 4900 kms. of road network. This leads to a situation in which Jammu has only 18% of its area covered by roads, while the Valley has 40% of its area so covered. The situation of Ladakh is even worse than Jammu. That is the fair treatment under the State control, and sheltered from the Centre's eye—thanks to Article 370 that has been bestowed selectively by the State Government! Privileges, pelf, resources and funds have flowed into the Valley out of all proportion to its size and population and against the stronger and better justified demands of Jammu & Ladakh. That is where Article 370, midwifed by Nehru and Sheikh Abdullah and nursed by Farooq Abdullah and his successors, under the approving eye of Nehru and his successors has taken the State today. Could there be a bigger mockery of justice, fair play and constitutional propriety?

Mr. Jagmohan, who as the Governor of Jammu & Kashmir had a ringside view of the realities in Kashmir observes in his book "My Frozen Turbulence in Kashmir":

"The primary task in Jammu & Kashmir is not the circulation of the fake coin of autonomy and fooling the people in the name of cultural entity, but to eliminate poverty, hunger and disease and carry out balanced development by stressing the commonality of the deprived and the underprivileged. Unless backwardness is eradicated, there would be no real freedom and democracy. Even Kashmiri culture would stagnate. Abrogation of Article 370 would, in fact, help in removing poverty and

Kashmiri culture and enhancing the cultural personality of the State as a whole. No culture can advance in isolation. It requires cross fertilisation. It requires the 'stimulus of contact'." And later he observes:

"In a similar strain, expressions like `historical necessity' and `autonomy' are talked about. What do these terms mean in practice? Does historical necessity mean that you include, on paper, Kashmir in the Indian Union on the one hand at a huge cost and give it back, in practice, on the other hand, on a golden platter? And what does autonomy or the so-called pre-1953 or pre-1947 position imply? 'You will send and I will spend; you will have no say even if I build a corrupt and callous oligarchy and cause a situation in which Damocles' sword of secession could be kept hanging over your head?'"

Thomas Jefferson of whom a mention has been made earlier, the prime architect of the American Constitution, and the author of the Bill of Rights, has this to say about the sanctity of laws and institutions. "Laws and institutions must go hand in hand with the progress of the human mind. We might as well require a man to wear the coat that fitted him as a boy, as civilized society to remain for ever under the regime of their ancestors". Surely, there is nothing sacrosanct about the Article 370 which a Central government with the necessary political will and concern with the territorial integrity of this nation, cannot abrogate.

But it is the holy cow that must be preserved. Judged on the issue of Article 370 alone where would Nehru's place be in the Valhalla of great nation builders? Misdeeds of politicians do not lie innocently buried under the soft sediments of history, but like the dragon's seeds, have the power to erupt into myriad sprouts of venom and discord that spread disaster and destruction on the land that they feed on. The seeds of separation sown in Kashmir are now bearing fruits of secession and separatism, striking at the very roots of our national integrity. Kashmiri separation fanned by armed support of Pakistan and separation fanned by armed support of Pakistan and the culture of Kalashnikov is playing havoc with the secularist fabric of Kashmir while self-proclaimed secularists like Kuldip Nayyar, I.K. Gujral and others of their ilk sit silently and watch. They may yet have a weapon of defence, 'Kashmiriat' like their earlier cliche of "Punjabiat'. Has one ever heard of `Uttar Pradeshiat', `Madhya Pradeshiat' or for that matter 'Rajasthaniat'. This is how these secular disciples of `Nehruism' which they would prefer to call `Nehruiat' are contributing to the integrity of our country and the sanctity of its geography.

Nehru sired and midwifed Article 370 and nursed it advancing specious arguments for its retention inside and outside the Parliament, till the hand of fate removed him from the political scene, a sad and weary man. His successors perpetuated the blunder, the so-called secularists, blind to the integrity of the nation.

Mercenaries from across the border are spreading violence and mayhem in this once peaceful paradise. Despite its strategic importance, Kashmir is not secure and this integral part of the India is fast turning into an impossible strategic liability, endangering the neighbouring areas, and putting a question mark on the secular fabric of India. Nehru's admonitions to Kashmiris to throw their lot with Muslim leadership of the National Conference has come true, but in a different way. The same Muslim leaders turned upon these helpless Hindus forcing them to flee their homes and live like refugees in their own country. Patel had prophesied 'Jawaharlal Royega'. The man has passed away. So has Nehru. The dead have no problems. Nehru should have none. But the living ones have. Kashmiri Pandits today are certainly crying their hearts out and we the nation are silently watching.

The recent disaster at Charar-e-Sharief and its earlier rehearsal at Hazratbal, aborted partly by the Indian Army is a result of two developments adumbrated in Nehru's own lifetime. First is the use of holy places for political purposes, in the present context, read their

The second was the acquiescence by the leaders of the so-called secular Kashmir of Nehru's days to allow this to happen. Nehru knew that his earlier partner Sheikh Abdullah always used Hazaratbal shrine for his political speeches and anti-India tirade. Nehru could, but did nothing to prevent this. Sixties were not the same as seventies. Kashmir was much more peaceful then. A firm decision at that time would have prevented the misuse of the holy places for such anti-national purposes. If the Sheikh could be arrested later, surely the law of the land could have been applied to prevent the earlier misuse of the holy shrine by him. It did not even run counter to the Article 370, wherein Indian Laws could be enforced in the J&K territories. Why did Nehru the secularist allow such a thing to happen? Charar-e-Sharief is but the logical outcome of the original sin committed by Nehru. If Patel the stout hearted had lived even a few years more there would have been no Kashmir Problem.

Appendix B

United Nations Security Council, Resolution of August 13, 1948

Resolution of the Commission of August 13, 1948:

The United Nations Commission for India and Pakistan. Having given careful consideration to the points of view expressed by the representatives of India and Pakistan regarding the situation in the State of Jammu and Kashmir; and

Being of the opinion that the prompt cessation of hostilities and the correction of conditions the continuance of which is likely to endanger international peace and security are essential to implementation of its endeavours to assist the Governments of India and Pakistan in effecting a final settlement of the situation;

Resolves to submit simultaneously to the Governments of India and Pakistan the following proposal:

Part I: *Cease-fire Order*

A. The Governments of India and Pakistan agree that their respective High Commands will issue separately and simultaneously a cease-fire order to apply to all forces under their controls in the State of Jammu and Kashmir as of the earliest practicable date or dates to be mutually agreed upon within four days after these proposals have been accepted by both Governments.

B. The High Commands of the Indian and Pakistani forces agree to refrain from taking any measures that might augment the military potential of the forces under their control in the State of Jammu and Kashmir.

(For the purpose of these proposals forces under their control shall be considered to include all forces, organized and unorganized, fighting or participating in hostilities on their respective sides).

C. The Commanders-in-Chief of the forces of India and Pakistan shall promptly confer regarding any necessary local changes in present dispositions which may facilitate the cease-fire.

D. In its direction and as the Commission may find practicable, the Commission will appoint military observers who, under the authority of the Commission and with the co-operation of both Commands, will supervise the observance of the cease-fire order.

E. The Government of India and the Government of Pakistan agree to appeal to their respective peoples to assist in creating and maintaining an atmosphere favourable to the promotion of further negotiations.

Part II: *Truce Agreement*

Simultaneously with the acceptance of the proposal for the immediate cessation of hostilities as outlined in Part I, both Governments accept the following principles as a basis for the formulation of a truce agreement, the details of which shall be worked out in discussion between their representatives and the Commission.

their representatives and the Commission.

A

1. As the presence of troops of Pakistan in the territory of the State of Jammu and Kashmir constitutes a material change in the situation since it was represented by the Government of India before the Security Council, the Government of Pakistan agrees to withdraw its troops from that State.

2. The Government of Pakistan will use its best endeavour to secure the withdrawal from the State of Jammu and Kashmir of tribesmen and Pakistani nationals not normally resident therein who have entered the State for the purpose of fighting.

3. Pending a final solution, the territory evacuated by the Pakistani troops will be administered by the local authorities under the surveillance of the Commission.

B

1. When the Commission shall have notified the Government of India that the tribesmen and Pakistani nationals referred to in Part II, A, 2 hereof have withdrawn, thereby terminating the situation which was represented by the Government of India to the Security Council as having occasioned the presence of Indian forces in the State of Jammu and Kashmir, and further, that the Pakistani forces are being withdrawn from the State of Jammu and Kashmir, the Government of India agrees to begin to withdraw the bulk of its forces from that State in stages to be agreed upon with the Commission.

2. Pending the acceptance of the conditions for a final settlement of the situation in the State of Jammu and Kashmir, the Indian Government will maintain within

with the Commission are considered necessary to assist local authorities in the observance of law and order. The Commission will have observers stationed where it deems necessary.

3. The Government of India will undertake to ensure that the Government of the State of Jammu and Kashmir will take all measures within its power to make it publicly known that peace, law and order will be safeguarded and that all human and political rights will be guaranteed.

C

1. Upon signature, the full text of the truce agreement or a communique containing the principles thereof as agreed upon between the two Governments and the Commission, will be made public.

Part III

The Government of India and the Government of Pakistan reaffirm their wish that the future status of the State of Jammu and Kashmir shall be determined in accordance with the will of the people and to that end, upon acceptance of the truce agreement, both Governments agree to enter into consultations with the Commission to determine fair and equitable conditions whereby such free expression will be assured.

Annexure I to Appendix B

Summary of assurances given to India by United Nations Commission during the course of discussions and correspondence

(i) Responsibility for the security of the State of Jammu and Kashmir rests with the Government of India.

(ii) The sovereignty of Jammu and Kashmir Government over the entire territory to the State shall not be brought into question.

not be brought into question.

(iii) There shall be no recognition of the so-called Azad (Free) Kashmir Government.

(iv) The territory occupied by Pakistan shall not be consolidated to the disadvantage of the State of Jammu and Kashmir.

(v) The administration of the evacuated areas in the north shall revert to the Government of Jammu and Kashmir and its defence to the Government of India who will, if necessary, maintain garrisons for preventing the incursion of tribesmen, and for guarding the main trade routes.

(vi) Pakistan shall be excluded from all affairs of Jammu and Kashmir in particular in the plebiscite, if one should be held.

(vii) If a plebiscite is found to be impossible for technical or practical reasons, the Commission will consider other methods of determining fair and equitable conditions for ensuring a free expression of the people's will.

(viii) Plebiscite proposals shall not be binding upon India if Pakistan does not implement Parts I and II of the resolution of 13th August, 1948.

Article 370 of the Constitution of India

Temporary Provisions with respect of the State of Jammu and Kashmir

1. Notwithstanding anything in this Constitution:

(a) the provisions of Article 238 shall not apply in relation to the State of Jammu and Kashmir;

(b) the power of Parliament to make laws for the said State shall be limited to

Government of the State, are declared by the President to correspond to matters specified in the Instrument of Accession governing the accession of the State to the Dominion of India as the matters with respect to which the Dominion Legislature may make laws for that State; and

(ii) such other matters in the said Lists as, with the concurrence of the Government of the State, the President may by order specify.

1. *Explanation:* For the purposes of the Article, the Government of the State means the person for the time being recognised by the President as the Maharaja of Jammu and Kashmir acting on the advice of the Council of Ministers for the time being in office under the Maharaja's Proclamation dated the fifth day of March, 1948.

(c) the provisions of Article (1) and of this Article shall apply in relation to this State;

(d) such of the other provisions of this Constitution shall apply in relation to that State subject to such exceptions and modifications as the President may by order specify:

Provided that no such order which related to the matters specified in the Instrument of Accession of the State referred to in paragraph (i) of sub-clause (b) shall be issued except in consultation with the Government of the State;

Provided further that no such order which relates to matters other than those referred to in the last preceding proviso shall be issued except with the concurrence of the Government.

(2) If the concurrence of the Government of the State referred to in paragraph (ii) of sub-clause (b) of clause (1) or in the second proviso to sub-clause

referred to in paragraph (ii) of sub-clause (b) of clause (1) or in the second proviso to sub-clause (d) of that clause be given before the Constituent Assembly for the purpose of framing the Constitution of the State is convened, it shall be placed before such Assembly for such decision as it may take thereon.

(3) Notwithstanding anything in the foregoing provisions of the Article, the President may, by public notification, declare that this Article shall cease to be operative or shall be operative only with such exceptions and modifications and from such date as he may notify.

Provided that the recommendation of the Constituent Assembly of the State referred to in clause (2) shall be necessary before the President issues such a notification.

Part IV

9 The Chinese Debacle

Much has been written on our Chinese policy and Nehru's role in it. Detailed accounts, official records and military memoirs have highlighted different aspects of this unfortunate episode. What shall concern us here is mainly Nehru's role as a Prime Minister in the entire sordid drama from 1950s till the final catastrophe in November, 1962. Patel's warning regarding Chinese intentions and Nehru's reply thereto are by now history. However, to refresh public memory which is proverbially short, a copy of Patel's letter dated November 7, 1950, alongwith a note prepared by States Ministry working under him and Nehru's note dated November 18, 1950, are reproduced below in original.

New Delhi
7 November 1950

My dear Jawaharlal,

Ever since my return from Ahmedabad and after the Cabinet meeting the same day which I had to attend at practically 15 minutes' notice and for which I regret I was not able to read all the papers, I have been anxiously thinking over the problem of Tibet and I thought I should share with you what is passing through my mind.

2. I have carefully gone through the correspondence between the External Affairs Ministry and our Ambassador in Peking and through him the Chinese Government. I have tried to peruse this correspondence as favourably

to our Ambassador and the Chinese Government as possible, but I regret to say that neither of them comes out well as a result of this study. The Chinese Government have tried to delude us by professions of peaceful intentions. My own feeling is that at a crucial period they managed to instil into our Ambassador a false sense of confidence in their so-called desire to settle the Tibetan problem by peaceful means. There can be no doubt that during the period covered by this correspondence the Chinese must have been concentrating for an onslaught on Tibet. The final action of the Chinese, in my judgment, is little short of perfidy. The tragedy of it is that the Tibetans put faith in us; they chose to be guided by us; and we have been unable to get them out of the meshes of Chinese diplomacy or Chinese malevolence. From the latest position, it appears that we shall not be able to rescue the Dalai Lama. Our Ambassador has been at great pains to find an explanation or justification for Chinese policy and actions. As the External Affairs Ministry remarked in one of their telegrams, there was a lack of firmness and unnecessary apology in one or two representations that he made to the Chinese Government on our behalf. It is impossible to imagine any sensible person believing in the so-called threat to China from Anglo-American machinations in Tibet. Therefore, if the Chinese put faith in this, they must have distrusted us so completely as to have taken us as tools or stooges of Anglo-American diplomacy or strategy. This feeling, if genuinely entertained by the Chinese in spite of your direct approaches to them, indicates that even though we regard ourselves as friends of China the Chinese do not regard us as their friends. With the Communist mentality of "whoever is not with them being against them," this is a significant pointer, of which we have to take due note. During the last several months, outside the Russian camp, we have practically been alone in championing the cause of Chinese entry into the UNO and in securing from the Americans assurances on the question of Formosa. We have done everything we could to assuage Chinese feelings, to allay its apprehensions and to defend its legitimate claims in our discussions and correspondence with America and Britain and in the UNO. In spite of this, China is not convinced about our disinterestedness; it continues to regard us with suspicion and the whole psychology is one, at least outwardly, of scepticism, perhaps mixed with a little hostility. I doubt if we can go any further than we have done already to convince China of our good intentions, friendliness and goodwill. In Peking we have an Ambassador who is eminently suitable for putting across the friendly point of view. Even he seems to have failed to convert the Chinese. Their last telegram to us is an act of gross discourtesy not only in the summary way it disposes of our protest against the entry of Chinese forces into Tibet but also in the wild insinuation that our attitude is determined by foreign influences. It looks as though it is not a friend speaking in that language but a potential enemy.

3. In the background of this, we have to consider what new situation now faces us as a result of the disappearance of Tibet, as we knew it, and the expansion of China almost up to our gates. Throughout history we have seldom been worried about our northeast frontier. The Himalayas have been regarded as an impenetrable barrier against any threat from the north. We had a friendly Tibet which gave us no trouble. The Chinese were divided. They had their own domestic problems and never bothered us about our frontiers. In 1914, we entered into a convention with Tibet which was not endorsed by the Chinese. We seem to have regarded Tibetan autonomy as extending to independent treaty relationship. Presumably, all that we required was Chinese countersignature. The Chinese interpretation of suzerainty seems to be different. We can, therefore, safely assume that very soon they will disown all the stipulations which Tibet has entered into with us in the past. That

throws into the melting pot all frontier and commercial settlements with Tibet on which we have been functioning and acting during the last half a century. China is no longer divided. It is united and strong. All along the Himalayas in the north and northeast, we have on our side of the frontier a population ethnologically and culturally not different from Tibetans or Mongoloids. The undefined state of the frontier and the existence on our side of a population with its affinities to Tibetans or Chinese have all the elements of potential trouble between China and ourselves. Recent and bitter history also tells us that communism is no shield against imperialism and that the Communists are as good or as bad imperialists as any other. Chinese ambitions in this respect not only cover the Himalayan slopes on our side but also include important parts of Assam. They have their ambitions in Burma also. Burma has the added difficulty that it has no McMahon Line round which to build up even the semblance of an agreement. Chinese irredentism and Communist imperialism are different from the expansionism or imperialism of the Western Powers. The former has a cloak of ideology which makes it ten times more dangerous. In the guise of ideological expansion lie concealed racial, national or historical claims. The danger from the north and northeast, therefore, becomes both communist and imperialist. While our western and northwestern threat to security is still as prominent as before, a new threat has developed from the north and northeast. Thus, for the first time, after centuries, India's defence has to concentrate itself on two fronts simultaneously. Our defence measures have so far been based on the calculations of a superiority over Pakistan. In our calculations we shall now have to reckon with Communist China in the north and in the northeast, a Communist China which has definite ambitions and aims and which does not, in any way, seem friendly disposed towards us.

4. Let us also consider the political conditions on this potentially troublesome frontier. Our northern or northeastern

approaches consist of Nepal, Bhutan, Sikkim, the Darjeeling [area] and tribal areas in Assam. From the point of view of communications, they are weak spots. Continuous defensive lines do not exist. There is almost an unlimited scope for infiltration. Police protection is limited to a very small number of passes. There, too, our outposts do not seem to be fully manned. The contact of these areas with us is by no means close and intimate. The people inhabiting these portions have no established loyalty or devotion to India. Even the Darjeeling and Kalimpong areas are not free from pro-Mongoloid prejudices. During the last three years we have not been able to make any appreciable approaches to the Nagas and other hill tribes in Assam. European missionaries and other visitors had been in touch with them, but their influence was in no way friendly to India or Indians. In Sikkim, there was political ferment some time ago. It is quite possible that discontent is smouldering there. Bhutan is comparatively quiet, but its affinity with Tibetans would be a handicap. Nepal has a weak oligarchic regime based almost entirely on force; it is in conflict with a turbulent element of the population as well as with enlightened ideas of the modern age. In these circumstances, to make people alive to the new danger or to make them defensively strong is a very difficult task indeed and that difficulty can be got over only by enlightened firmness, strength and a clear line of policy. I am sure the Chinese and their source of inspiration , Soviet Russia, would not miss any opportunity of exploiting these weak spots, partly in support of their ideology and partly in support of their ambitions. In my judgment, therefore, the situation is one in which we cannot afford either to be complacent or to be vacillating. We must have a clear idea of what we wish to achieve and also of the methods by which we should achieve it. Any faltering or lack of decisiveness in formulating our objectives or in pursuing our policy to attain those objectives is bound to weaken us and increase the threats which are so evident.

5. Side by side with these external dangers, we shall now have to face serious internal problems as well. I have already asked [H.V.R.] Ienger to send to the E.A. Ministry a copy of the Intelligence Bureau's appreciation of these matters. Hitherto, the Communist Party of India has found some difficulty in contacting Communists abroad, or in getting supplies of arms, literature, etc., from them. They had to contend with the difficult Burmese and Pakistan frontiers on the east or with the long seaboard. They shall now have a comparatively easy means of access to Chinese Communists and through them to other foreign Communists. Infiltration of spies, fifth columnists and Communists would now be easier. Instead of having to deal with isolated Communist pockets in Telengana and Warangal we may have to deal with Communists threats to our security along our northern ad northeastern frontiers where, for supplies of arms and ammunition, they can safely depend on Communist arsenals in China. The whole situation thus raises a number of problems on which we must come to an early decision so that we can, as I said earlier, formulate the objectives or our policy and decide the methods by which those objectives are to be attained. It is also clear that the action will have to be fairly comprehensive, involving not only our defence strategy and state of preparations but also problems of internal security to deal with which we have not a moment to lose. We shall also have to deal with administrative and political problems in the weak spots along the frontier to which I have already referred.

6. It is, of course, impossible for me to be exhaustive in setting out all these problems. I am, however, giving below some of the problems which, in my opinion, require early solution and round which we have to build our administrative or military policies and measures to implement them.

(a) A military and intelligence appreciation of the Chinese threat to India both on the frontier and to internal security.

(b) An examination of our military position and such re-disposition of our forces as might be necessary, particularly with the idea of guarding important routes or areas which are likely to be the subject of dispute.

(c) An appraisement of the strength of our forces and, if necessary, reconsideration of our retrenchment plans for the army in the light of these new threats.

(d) A long-term consideration of our defence needs. My own feeling is that, unless we assure our supplies of arms, ammunition and armour, we should be making our defence position perpetually weak and we would not be able to stand up to the double threat of difficulties both from the west and northwest and northeast.

(e) The question of Chinese entry into UNO. In view of the rebuff which China has given us and the method which it has followed in dealing with Tibet, I am doubtful whether we can advocate its claims any longer. There would probably be a threat in the UNO virtually to outlaw China in view of its active participation in the Korean war. We must determine our attitude on this question also.

(f) The political and administrative steps which we should take to strengthen our northern and north-eastern frontiers. This would include the whole of the border, i.e. Nepal, Bhutan, Sikkim, Darjeeling and the tribal territory in Assam.

(g) Measures of internal security in the border areas as well as the States flanking those areas, such as UP, Bihar, Bengal and Assam.

(h) Improvement of our communications, road, rail, air and wireless, in these areas and with the frontier outposts.

(i) Policing and intelligence of frontier posts.

(j) The future of our mission at Lhasa and the trade posts at Gyangtse and Yatung and the forces which we have in operation in Tibet to guard the trade routes.

(k) The policy in regard to the McMahon Line.

7. These are some of the questions which occur to my mind. It is possible that a consideration of these matters may lead us into wider questions of our relationship with China, Russia, America, Britain and Burma. This, however, would be of a general nature, though some might be basically very important, e.g. we might have to consider whether we should not enter into closer association with Burma in order to strengthen the latter in its dealings with China. I do not rule out the possibility that, before applying pressure on us, China might apply pressure on Burma. With Burma, the frontier is entirely undefined and the Chinese territorial claims are more substantial. In its present position, Burma might offer an easier problem for China and, therefore, might claim its first attention.

8. I suggest that we meet early to have a general discussion on these problems and decide on such steps as we might think to be immediately necessary and direct quick examination of other problems with a view to taking early measures to deal with them.

Yours,
Vallabhbhai Patel

The Hon'ble Shri Jawaharlal Nehru
New Delhi

EXTRACTS

A NOTE BY THE STATES MINISTRY ON NEW PROBLEMS OF INTERNAL SECURITY CAUSED BY CHINESE OCCUPATION OF TIBET

Soviet Russia now feels that India will be more swayed by the influence of China than of Russia and Mao Tse-tung will make a better leader for the Indian masses than even Stalin can. It is with this object that the Peking Liaison Bureau was established last year, that Mao Tse-tung has been given a dominating voice in the affairs of India and the Far East and that the Indian Communists have been told by numerous Communist publications, as well as by the Cominform, in clear unambiguous words, to follow the China way to victory. If therefore the occupation of Tibet by the Communist forces gives to world Communism any strategical and tactical advantage of furthering the cause of Communism in India, all such advantages will be exploited legally and illegally to the fullest extent without any consideration for international conventions even though the Chinese Government may continue to remain superficially in the friendliest terms with the Indian Government. And the occupation of Tibet by the Chinese Communists does open up vast possibilities for creating internal disorders and disruptions within India.

Up till now India's northern frontier from Ladakh in the west to the Sadiya Hill Tracts in the east has been free from any dangers of external invasion or from even any subversive movements fostered by external forces. With Tibet as a weak and autonomous country, giving many facilities to India which no other independent country would give, India could rightly feel absolutely secure about its northern frontier and this sense of security was reflected in the past in all the policies followed with respect to this northern frontier and actions taken for its security in these areas and on the understanding that no danger would come to India from the north very little security measures have been taken which in the altered circumstances will be found to be completely inadequate.

With an aggressive Chinese Communist Government in Tibet, intent on furthering the creed of International Communism in India and holding the belief that world Communism and so Communism in China can never be safe unless India becomes a Communist country and following the basic Communist creed that the International proletariat (which in other words means the Soviet and the Chinese Governments) must assist the peoples of all colonial countries (which include India) in their fight for national liberation (which in India means the overthrow of the Nehru Government), every method will be adopted to disrupt the integrity of India and what will be more opportune and easy than to foster trouble in these frontier areas where India's administrative control is not strong and where her cultural influence is less.

With China on India's long unguarded frontier, the Indian Communists will be in a good position to get help by way of supply of arms, by the infiltration of trained agents and by direct contact with the Chinese Communists. The Indian Communists have been badly mauled during the last two and a half years and they are passing through a difficult period and there is definite information that they are wanting direct guidance from foreign Communists. So far attempts to make such contacts have to a great extent been countered by Governmental action, but with China strongly entrenched in Tibet it will be extremely difficult to stop this contact. With the commencement of trouble in the frontier areas where India's armed forces will have to be moved, more Telengana struggles will be launched in India itself so as to dissipate India's armed forces by wide dispersal.

PRIME MINISTER NEHRU'S NOTE ON CHINA AND TIBET DATED 18 NOVEMBER 1950

[The note was obviously forwarded to Sardar Patel as it answered indirectly some of the matters raised in the Sardar's letter of 7 November, 1950.]

The Chinese Government having replied to our last note, we have to consider what further steps we should take in this matter. There is no immediate hurry about sending a reply to the Chinese Government. But we have to send immediate instructions to Shri B.N. Rau as to what he should do in the event of Tibet's appeal being brought up before the Security Council or the General Assembly.

2. The content of the Chinese reply is much the same as their previous notes, but there does appear to be a toning down and an attempt at some kind of a friendly approach.

3. It is interesting to note that they have not referred specifically to our mission [at] Lhasa or to our trade agents or military escort at Gyangtse etc.

We had mentioned these especially in our last note. There is an indirect reference, however, in China's note. At the end, this note says that "As long as our two sides adhere strictly to the principle of mutual respect for territory, sovereignty, equality and mutual benefit, we are convinced that the friendship between China and India should be developed in a normal way and that problems relating to Sino-Indian diplomatic, commercial and cultural relations with respect to Tibet may be solved properly and to our mutual benefit through normal diplomatic channels." This clearly refers to our trade agents and others in Tibet. We had expected a demand from them for the withdrawal of these agents etc. The fact that they have not done so has some significance.

4. Stress is laid in China's note on Chinese sovereignty over Tibet, which we are reminded, we have acknowledged, on Tibet being an integral part of China's territory and therefore a domestic problem. It is however again repeated that outside influences have been at play obstructing China's mission in Tibet. In fact, it is stated that liberation of Changtu proves that foreign forces and influences were inciting Tibetan troops to resist. It is again repeated that no foreign intervention will be permitted and that the Chinese army will proceed.

5. All this is much the same as has been said before, but it is said in a somewhat different way and there are repeated references in the note to China desiring the friendship of India.

6. It is true that in one of our messages to the Chinese Government we used "sovereignty" of China in relation to Tibet. In our last message we used the word "suzerainty." After receipt of the last China's note, we have pointed out to our Ambassador that "suzerainty" was the right word and that "sovereignty" had been used by error.

7. It is easy to draft a reply to the Chinese note, pressing our viewpoint and countering some of the arguments raised in the Chinese note. But before we do so we should be clear in our own minds as to what we are aiming at, not only in the immediate future but from a long-term view. It is important that we keep both these viewpoints before us. In all probability China, that is present-day China, is going to be our close neighbour for a long time to come. We are going to have a tremendously long common frontier. It is unlikely, and it would be unwise to expect, that the present Chinese Government will collapse, giving place to another. Therefore, it is important to pursue a policy which will be in keeping with this long-term view.

8. I think it may be taken for granted that China will take possession, in a political sense at least, of the whole of Tibet. There is no likelihood whatever of Tibet being able to resist this or stop it. It is equally unlikely that any foreign power can prevent it . We cannot do so. If so, what can we do to help in the maintenance of Tibetan autonomy and at the same time avoiding continuous tension and apprehension on our frontiers?

9. The Chinese note has repeated that they wish the Tibetan people to have what they call "regional autonomy and religious freedom." This autonomy can obviously not be anything like the autonomy verging on independence which Tibet has enjoyed during the last forty years or so. But it is reasonable to assume from the very nature of Tibetan geography, terrain and climate, that a large measure of autonomy is almost inevitable. It may of course be that this autonomous Tibet is controlled by communist elements in Tibet. I imagine however that it

is, on the whole, more likely that what will be attempted will be a pro-communist China administration rather than a communist one.

10. If world war comes, then all kinds of difficult and intricate problems arise and each one of these problems will be interrelated with others. Even the question of defence of India assumes a different shape and cannot be isolated from other world factors. I think that it is exceedingly unlikely that we may have to face any real military invasion from the Chinese side, whether in peace or in war, in the foreseeable future. I base this conclusion on a consideration of various world factors. In peace, such an invasion would undoubtedly lead to world war. China, though internally big, is in a way amorphous and easily capable of being attacked on its sea coasts and by air. In such a war, China would have its main front in the South and East and it will be fighting for its very existence against powerful enemies. It is inconceivable that it should divert its forces and its strength across the Himalayas. Any such attempt will greatly weaken its capacity to meet its real enemies on other fronts. Thus I rule out any major attack on India by China. I think these considerations should be borne in mind, because there is far too much loose talk about China attacking and overrunning India. If we lose our sense of perspective and world strategy and give way to unreasoning fears, then any policy that we might have is likely to fail.

11. While there is, in any opinion, practically no chance of a major attack on India by China, there are certainly chances of gradual infiltration across our border and possibly of entering and taking possession of disputed territory, if there is no obstruction to this happening. We must therefore take all necessary precautions to prevent this. But again, we must differentiate between these precautions and those that might be necessary to meet a real attack.

12. If we really feared an attack and had to make full

provision for it, this would cast an intolerable burden on us, financial and otherwise, and it would weaken our general defence position. There are limits beyond which we cannot go, at least for some years, and a spreading out of our army on distant frontiers would be bad from every military or strategic point of view.

13. In spite of our desire to settle the points at issue between us and Pakistan, and developing peaceful relations with it, the fact remains that our major possible enemy is Pakistan. This has compelled us to think of our defence mainly in terms of Pakistan's aggression. If we begin to think of, and prepare for, China's aggression in the same way, we would weaken considerably on the Pakistan side. We might well be got in a pincer movement. It is interesting to note that Pakistan is taking a great deal of interest, from this point of view, in developments in Tibet. Indeed it has been discussed in the Pakistan Press that the new danger from Tibet to India might help them to settle the Kashmir problem according to their wishes. Pakistan has absolutely nothing in comon with China or Tibet. But if we fall out completely with China, Pakistan will undoubtedly try to take advantage of this, politically or otherwise. The position of India thus will be bad from a defence point of view. We cannot have all the time two possible enemies on either side of India. This danger will not be got over, even if we increase our defence forces or even if other foreign countries help us in arming. The measure of safety that one gets by increasing the defence apparatus is limited by many factors. But whatever that measure of safety might be, strategically we would be in an unsound position and the burden of this will be very great on us. As it is, we are facing enormous difficulties, financial, economic, etc.

14. The idea that communism inevitably means expansion and war, or to put it more precisely, that Chinese communism means inevitably an expansion towards India, is rather naive. It may mean that in certain circumstances. Those

circumstances would depend upon many factors, which I need not go into here. The danger really is not from military invasion but from infiltration of men and ideas. The ideas are there already and can only be countred by other ideas. Communism is an important element in the situation. But, by our attaching too great importance to it in this context, we are likely to misjudge the situation from other and more important angles.

15. In a long-term view, India and China are two of the biggest countries of Asia bordering on each other and both with certain expansive tendencies, because of their vitality. If their relations are bad, this will have a serious effect not only on both of them but on Asia as a whole. It would affect our future for a long time. If a position arises in which China and India are inveterately hostile to each other, like France and Germany, then there will be repeated wars bringing destruction to both. The advantage will go to other countries. It is interesting to note that both the UK and USA appear to be anxious to add to the unfriendliness of India and China towards each other. It is also interesting to find that the USSR does not view with favour any friendly relations between India and China. These are long-term reactions which one can fully understand, because India and China at peace with each other would make a vast difference to the whole set-up and balance of the world. Much of course depends upon the development of either country and how far communism in China will mould the Chinese people. Even so, these processes are long-range ones and in the long run it is fairly safe to assume that hundreds of millions of people will not change their essential characteristics.

16. These arguments lead to the conclusion that while we should be prepared, to the best of our ability, for all contingencies, the real protection that we should seek is some kind of understanding of China. If we have not got that, then both our present and our future are imperilled and no distant power can save us. I think on the whole

that China desires this too for obvious reasons. If this is so, then we should fashion our present policy accordingly.

17. We cannot save Tibet, as we should have liked to do, and our very attempts to save it might well bring greater trouble to it. It would be unfair to Tibet for us to bring this trouble upon her without having the capacity to help her effectively. It may be possible, however, that we might be able to help Tibet to retain a large measure of her autonomy. That would be good for Tibet and good for India. As far as I can see, this can only be done on the diplomatic level and by avoidance of making the present tension between India and China worse.

18. What then should be our instructions to B.N. Rau? From the messages he has sent us, it appears that no member of the Security Council shows any inclination to sponsor Tibet's appeal and that there is little likelihood of the matter being considered by the Council. We have said they [we] are not going to sponsor this appeal, but if it comes up we shall state our viewpoint. This viewpoint cannot be one of full support of the Tibetan appeal, because that goes far and claims full independence. We may say that whatever might have been acknowledged in the past about China's sovereignty or suzerainty, recent events have deprived China of the right to claim that. There may be some moral basis for this argument. But it will not take us or Tibet very far. It will only hasten the downfall of Tibet. No outsider will be able to help her and China, suspicious and apprehensive of these tactics, will make sure of much speedier and fuller possession of Tibet than she might otherwise have done. We shall thus not only fail in our endeavour but at the same time have really a hostile China on our doorstep.

19. I think in no event should we sponsor Tibet's appeal. I would personally think that it would be a good thing if that appeal is not heard in the Security Council or the General Assembly. If it is considered there, there is bound to be a great deal of bitter speaking

and accusation, which will worsen the situation as regards Tibet, as well as the possibility of widespread war, without helping it in the least. It must be remembered that neither the UK nor the USA, nor indeed any other power is particularly interested in Tibet or the future of that country. What they are interested in is embarrassing China. Our interest, on the other hand, is Tibet, and if we cannot serve that interest, we fail.

20. Therefore, it will be better not to discuss Tibet's appeal in the UN. Suppose, however, that it comes up for discussion, in spite of our not wishing this, what then? I would suggest that our representative should state our case as moderately as possible and ask the Security Council or the Assembly to give expression to their desire that the Sino-Tibetan question should be settled peacefully and that Tibet's autonomy should be respected and maintained. Any particular reference to an article of the Charter of the UN might tie us up in difficulties and lead to certain consequences later, which may prove highly embarrassing for us. Or a resolution of the UN might just be a dead letter, which also will be bad.

21. If my general argument is approved, then we can frame our reply to China's note accordingly.

18 November 1950 J.Nehru

One does not need any more convincing evidence of Sardar Patel's foresight and prescience and an equally fumbling and incoherent approach of Nehru to the problem of our northern borders in general and China in particular. If only Patel's warning could have been taken seriously by Nehru, history would have been different.

Patel's prescription and preventive steps to be taken against China is a masterpiece of statesmanship and the higher direction of Defence. He is clear, precise and decisive, while Nehru the eternal Hamlet is unsure and hesitant. A look at Nehru's note shows that it is not only wholly unsatisfactory but is no better than the whimpering of a pusillanimous man completely blind to facts and unsure of himself. It is not a satisfactory reply to the points raised by Sardar Patel. In the same vein the Sardar's advice on handling the Korean situation is clear and practical. He advocated no half measures nor a meak hearted approach to the problem. This has been discussed earlier under Nehru's foreign policy. To my mind, a vital fact which no politician or historian has mentioned and which has defied defence strategists to this date, while few have grasped the full significance of this prophetic letter of the Sardar whrein he recommended a bold and firm response to the Chinese in Tibet. This was not mere bravado but a result of deep insight Patel displayed in strategic matters of national security. Patel knew something which failed politicians and defence analysts had to see. The nuclear angle. It is the repetition of a similar situation and thought which prompted Mac Arthur, the ablest military commander of the United States, to ask the permission of President Truman, to be allowed to use a nuclear attack against Chinese troops in Korea. This was the only time that China had not yet acquired a nuclear bomb and Patel's thoughts were the same. China did not then possess a nuclear device. Indian troops had performed magnificently in Kashmir against Pakistan. In Tibet, a well timed and properly organised show of strength by the disciplined Indian troops, even though in smaller numbers than the Chinese, who were much more numerous but still used to guerilla tactics, thus far, would have effectively checkmated any offensive Chinese intentions. The strong world opinion against Chinese aggression in Tibet would have taken care of the rest. Russia was noncommittal. America would have definitely supported us, since at that time, they were opposing the Chinese as would be evident from the subsequent events later in Korea. *London Economist* had mentioned:

"Having maintained complete independence of China since 1912, Tibet has a strong claim to be regarded as an independent state. But it is for India to take a lead in this matter. If India decides to support the independence of Tibet as a buffer state between itself and China, Britain and the U.S.A. will do well to extend formal diplomatic recognition to it." But this was not to be. We stood hypnotised while China quietly gobbled Tibet. What is the record of parliamentary debates on Tibet?

On September 4, 1959, Atal Bihari Vajpayee rose up in Parliament and moved a resolution to refer the Tibetan issue to the United Nations. Nehru, in line with his reasoning given in his note of November 18, 1950, reproduced earlier, opposed this move. There was more justification for referring this issue to U.N. than there was in the earlier case of Kashmir which was not only ill-timed but against national interest. Referring to the genocide in Tibet after the escape of Dalai Lama, Vajpayee added:

"Suppose, India does not refer the question to the United Nations; some other country may raise it. I would like to know what will be our policy in that case? We cannot prevent other nations from raising that issue. What shall be the policy of our Government? All our attempts for a peaceful solution of the Tibetan tangle have failed. In spite of the best wishes of our Prime Minister, the Chinese communist leaders are not prepared to heed to the voice of wisdom, reason and justice. On the contrary they are branding India as imperialist and also the Indian people. India relinquished its extraterritorial rights that accrued to us from the Britishers. The other day, our Prime Minister objected to the boundary line between India and China being called as the McMahon Line. He said, he disliked, I think because the very name McMahon smacks of British imperialism. As Shakespeare has remarked, there is nothing in the name. But, it showed how deep our feelings are against imperialism. But, then, the Chinese communists are branding us as imperialists."

"When the Government of India has decided to raise the issue of China's recognition and admission into the United Nations, in spite of all that is being done and said against India by the Chinese Communists, I think it is but proper that the Tibetan issue should also be raised by our Government in the forthcoming meeting of the General Assembly of the United Nations. Government will have the benefit of knowing the wishes of the House in this matter, and I am sure my resolution will get wide support and Government will accept it and will discharge the moral duty to the people of Tibet as a free nation."

Nehru's reasons for rejecting the resolution were less than convincing. While expressing sympathy for Tibetans, Nehru said that there was little that he could do to directly influence the situation. Rambling in his usual style, mixing facts with opinion, he continued:

"So far as this question of Tibet is concerned, we may look at it from many points of view: historical, cultural and other contacts with India, China, etc. It is a long and chequered history and one need not go into it. When a country has had a long and chequered history, it supplies enough material for any party to support any claim. The Chinese claim that Tibet was subject of their sovereignty or suzerainty. I do not know what word they use—for hundreds of years."

Mind you, the forum is Parliament and Nehru is discussing a vital issue of facts and then goes on to say:

"The Tibetans claim that they were independent for many periods except when they were forced into some kind of subservience. Now, really this may be interesting to the historical students, but it does not help us. It is a fact, of course, that for a period of 40 years or so, for all practical purposes, ever since the Manchu Dynasty fell or a little after that, Tibet was practically independent; even so China never gave up her claim. But in effect it was independent."

But in the same breath he gives a different view and expresses difficulties.

"As I said, it does not help us very much. Of course,

if this question arose in the International Court of Justice at The Hague— of course, it will not; such questions do not arise there because nation States do not take them there and China, anyhow, has nothing to do with the International Court of Justice at The Hague, they might consider all these questions."

"I know that, sometimes, it is difficult to feel friendly when one hears things that irritate, that anger, when we see that our people have not been treated even courteously, when we receive communications from the Chinese Government, which are singularly lacking in even ordinary politeness. All that is irritating. But, then, it is easy enough for anyone to get angry and irritated. It is necessary for people who hold responsible positions not to allow themselves to be irritated, certainly to maintain the dignity of the country and the continuity of our policy too."

Later, he admitted his failure to read the Chinese mind and still underplayed the Chinese threat.

"We have got to deal with these difficult problems, these border incidents. If anyone asks me, as they sometimes do, what do the border incidents indicate, frankly, I do not know what might be in the minds of the other party: whether it is just local aggressiveness or just to show us our place, if I may use a colloquial phrase, so that we may not get uppish, or whether it is something deeper. I do not know."

And then Nehru goes off at a tangent and declares:

"The two or three main considerations that are internationally considered: Tibet has not been considered as an independent country. It has been considered an autonomous country but under the suzerainty or sovereignty of China."

Is Tibet independent or a suzerain? India's position was as indecisive as the conflict between the above two words and thus fate of Tibet hung in balance. The question was never answered satisfactorily and Tibet as a country disappeared from the map of the world.

Vallabhbhai who had noted in June 1949 that "Tibet has long been detached from China" would have treated the views put up by Vajpayee differently, and acted in a decisive manner as suggested by him earlier. But non-embarrassment of China was the cornerstone of Nehru's foreign policy, even now. Time justified Patel's apprehensions that Tibet's autonomy would shrink. The Dalai Lama was forced into exile in 1959. The attack on India that Vallabhbhai feared and Jawaharlal had ruled out took place three years later. Nehru was Prime Minister still but Patel had been dead for twelve years.

Once confronted with the enormity of the Chinese deception on Tibet and their true intentions, Nehru flinched from facing unpleasant facts. Even his able Ambassador to China concluded his report, in less than accurate terms, of the appraisal of the Chinese, possibly afraid of hurting Nehru's feelings, who had fervently espoused the Communist Chinese cause. There is a Chinese proverb that 'He who treads lightly goes far.'

Nehru rushed with hobnailed boots into territories where angels fear to tread and met his nemesis. Nehru's weak-kneed response to the Chinese invasion of Tibet has also been described elsewhere. Few of us know that after Pakistan had signed a mutual security pact with United States in 1954, an Act in conformity with the US global strategy of containing communist Russia, Eisenhower, the then US President, had offered military assistance to India 'proportionate' to her size, importance and strategic potential. While offering this assistance, he had China in mind. Nehru, however, spurned the offer and chose to befriend China which had already violated the independence of Tibet. China now returned the compliment with demands on Indian territory. It was during this time that General Thimayya reminded Nehru that the vast road network being constructed by the Chinese near the Indian border in Aksai Chin and the East was not meant to promote Sino-Indian friendship or offer a toast to India's health. Nehru lost his temper and threw the file at Thimayya telling him not to talk nonsense. It was an ostrichlike attitude on the part of the chief executive of the Indian nation. Belatedly, realising that our border areas were not properly mapped, survey parties were sent somewhat late to map these far-off places. My younger brother as late as May, 1960, had to proceed to Ladakh at a rather short notice to carry out the first survey work in the Galwan and Nubra Valley areas, then administered by Brigadier R.S. Garewal with a brigade group. These troops were composed of a few regular battalions and some local militia. The Chinese diplomatic position on the border had been consistent, in as much as they did not wish to commit themselves in the western sector, where they had already built up a lifeline highway in Aksai Chin to link up their Sinkiang Province with Tibet. However, they were prepared to accept McMahon Line as the natural boundary between India and China. What do the records say?

The Chinese Prime Minister Chou-En-lai was firm on his position regarding Aksai Chin which he considered, formed a part of the Chinese jurisdiction for a long time. Through Aksai Chin, right across its heart ran the famous road that China had taken years to build and completed only in 1950. It connected the outlying region of Sinkiang through Tibet to the mainland China. But Chou-En-lai conceded that even this could be debated. While he was confident of his stand regarding the Eastern boundary and was prepared for a compromise, Nehru insisted that both the boundaries should be finalised in a comprehensive agreement. The Chinese position as stated by Chou-En-lai was briefly enunciated in the following manner.

"As you are aware, the 'McMahon Line' was a product of the British policy of aggression against the Tibet Region of China and aroused the great indignation of the Chinese people. Jurisdically, too, it cannot be considered legal. I have told you that it has never been recognized by the Chinese Central Government. Although related documents were signed by a representative of the local authorities of the Tibet Region of China, the Tibet local authorities were in fact dissatisfied with this unilaterally drawn line. And I have also told you formally about their dissatisfaction. On the other hand one cannot, of course, fail to take cognizance of the great and encouraging changes: India and Burma, which are concerned in this line, have attained independence successively and become states friendly with China. In view of the various complex factors mentioned above, the Chinese Government on the one hand finds it necessary to take a more or less realistic attitude towards the McMahon Line and, on the other hand, cannot but act with prudence and needs time to deal with this matter. All this I have mentioned to you on more than one occasion. However, we believe that , on account of the friendly relations between China and India a friendly settlement can eventually be found for this section of the boundary line."

The above statement is crucial to the understanding of the border issue.

The Indian side read Chou-En-lai's message in ambiguous terms. There could have been no outstanding problem in settling for McMahon Line as the eastern boundary between China and India. But mutual suspicion and the India's reading of Chinese territorial expansion created further misunderstanding. While China could and did after two years settle its border with Burma on the McMahon Line as the boundary, the Indian side could be dealt in a similar manner, but in 1959 the Indians could not be reassured of the Chinese intentions as articulated in Chou-En-lai's letter. It is somewhat surprising that inspite of the clear signals from China, we could not finalise the McMahon Line as the boundary between the two countries. The Chinese basically wanted a readjustment and did not wish to group all the issues together even on McMahon Line they were prepared go for an adjustment here and there but the Indian stand was rather obdurate insisting on the sanctity of the McMahon Line. The Indian response was anchored on the following propositions:

(a) Territory south of the McMahon Line cannot be ceded.

(b) McMahon Line was not negotiable.

(c) No negotiation for any specific section of the border was to be accepted except as part of a total package for the entire border; the feeling being that China may not agree to piecemeal negotiations of the border.

(d) The Indian claim in the central and western Himalayas would be as unalterable as the question of the McMahon Line.

The above premises led to the following two policy stands of the Government of India:

(i) That the complete boundary with China was an accomplished fact and could be based on the 1914 agreement as well as on the de facto situation, which were effective only in the northeast since 1951, and was to be applied to the western sector as well.

(ii) Since an obdurate policy against negotiations may show India in a less than favourable light because of Nehru's earlier ideology insisting on peaceful negotiations to resolve the dispute, this refusal to negotiate had to be somewhat covered up.

Though the above was the ultimate effect, Nehru and his advisers may not have seen these trends adumbrated in clear cut terms. Nehru entered into long correspondence basing his arguments on geography as also 'the sanction of specific international agreements between the then Government of India and the central Government of China'. He also quoted extensively from an earlier treaty of 1842 between Maharaja Gulab Singh and the Tibetans in Kashmir, while the McMahon Line derived its legitimacy from the Simla Convention. Nehru, even though, agreeable to Chou-En-lai's proposals to maintain status quo till the settlement of the dispute, stated inter alia his intentions to exercise India's sovereign right to maintain its boundary based on what was right. Any encroachment should be vacated and the situation rectified. Thus the question of status quo which they agreed to in principle, could in real terms be violated should India decide to reaffirm its legitimate boundary. He, therefore, advised caution at this stage but made it clear that India would insist on the evacuation of Aksai Chin as a precondition to any talks and to avoid any border dispute. Nehru in his two letters, written a year before the public came to know of the boundary dispute, had taken a stand to which he stuck firmly in subsequent negotiations and discussions that although there was no boundary dispute with China, there could never be a question of realignment of the boundary and status quo ante was to be maintained thereby implying that the Chinese presence on the area they had occupied or claimed had to be removed. At this stage, there was no public pressure nor political compulsion. The situation was entirely that of Nehru's own making and the course was set by Nehru and his advisers. If this was not a collision course, what else was? And the architect of this course , was no one else but Nehru. The 1899 Macarthey-MacDonald Line was another curious element introduced into this murky scenario. It was the one and only boundary proposed to China by the British in Ladakh. Had China accepted it the Aksai Chin road would have been left in the Chinese possession. But the Government of India refused to accept this interpretation of the boundary and Nehru in September, 1959, less than truthfully, stated that the 1899 line 'signified beyond doubt that the whole of Aksai Chin area lay in Indian territory'. It might well have been an oversight in interpreting the British note, but it led to serious consequences.... Thus Nehru refuted the Chinese claim even on that part of Aksai Chin which the British records showed as belonging to China, and thus closed the doors for consideration of further negotiations.

There was no question of further discussions. In Nehru's own words:

"There can be no question of withdrawing any Indian personnel... No discussion can be fruitful unless the posts on the India's side of the traditional frontier held by the Chinese forces are first evacuated by them and further threat and intimidations immediately cease." Krishna Menon articulated the same position at the United Nations. The Chinese withdrawal was a precondition for any talks. By his own choice of understanding with China, unless the latter changed its position diametrically and agreed to India's demand, Nehru closed all avenues of settlement. While thus negotiating diplomatically, Nehru issued a directive to the Indian forces on the border to resist by force any 'trespass', knowing fully well that this was not a feasible military proposition.

Nehru recorded the following minutes in his directives:

(a) We must avoid actual conflict until it is actually forced down upon us. That is to say, we must avoid armed conflict not only in a big way, but even in a small way. On no account should our forces fire unless they are actually fired at.

(The 1899 proposal was for a boundary that 'follows the Lak Tsang range until that meets a spur running south from the Kuen Lun' but in the Indian version the proposal became for an alignment 'along the Kuen Lun range'.)

(b) In the event of any Chinese armed detachment coming over to our side, they should be told to go back. Only if they fire should our people fire at them.

(c) [This gave detailed instructions for the Chushul area]

(d) The Aksai Chin area has to be left more or less as it is as we have no check-posts there and practically little of access. Any questions in relation to it can only be considered, when the time arises, in the context of the larger question of the entire border. For the present, we have to put up with the Chinese occupation of this northeastern sector [of Ladakh] and their road across it.

(e) Our general instructions to our people on the border should be that they should avoid any provocative action, but should remain firmly on our side of the line and not allow themselves to be pushed away easily.

(f) I think it is unlikely that the Chinese forces will take up any aggressive line on this frontier, that is, try to enter into our territory any further. If they should do so, they will have to be stopped and the matter reported to us immediately for instructions.

At this time, an Indian patrol was sent out for Lanak Pass and on October 21, there was a clash with the Chinese at that place resulting in casualties. India bitterly complained against imperialistic designs and warned that aggression will be resisted by all possible means. This note contained a detailed delineation of the boundary as it existed according to Indian records in the western sector.

Although, Nehru had repeatedly stated during August and September in the Parliament that no clear-cut boundary existed in Ladakh, he now came out with the statement of a new boundary marked with an exact alignment, wherein the whole of Aksai Chin was shown within the Indian territory. Elaborating his stand further, he stated:

"Any person with a knowledge of history... would appreciate that this traditional and historical frontier of India has been associated with India's culture and tradition for the last two thousand years or so, and has been an intimate part of India's life and thought."

The incident at Longju, subsequent clashes and mounting casualties due to Chinese aggression into Indian territory roused public opinion at large. Speaking later at Meerut, he tried to pacify public feelings and advised caution describing that he viewed the above incidents more in anguish than anger. But he stressed the friendship with China, rather than denouncing it which he emphasised, would not be in India's long term interest. After this rather incoherent statement of Nehru the public opinion was roused all the same. Nehru's handling of the entire border dispute evoked a strong reaction from the opposition and the media for the first time, and Nehru's speeches were considered not only irrelevant and fatuous but also dishonest. The press pointed him as bending over backward to please the Chinese while ignoring the susceptibilities of the Indian masses whom he was alleged to be treating as grown-up children. There were also demands that India should drop its policy of nonalignment, join military pacts against China and make its armed forces strong to resist the Chinese in a full scale war. Nehru dismissed such talks as "utterly wrong and useless."

He assured the country that our armed forces were strong enough. He assured the Lok Sabha:

"That at no time since our independence, and of course before it, were our defence forces in better condition, in finer fettle, and with the background of our far greater industrial production.... to help them, than they are today. I am not boasting about them or comparing them with any other country's, but I am quite confident that our defence forces are well capable of looking after our security." I being in the Army at that time knew fully well how weak was our tactical position and logistic support to undertake any worthwhile operations against China. This was Nehru's bluff, pure and simple.

Nehru, the less than a sagacious statesman, then lost all control on his China policy. He made it a matter of public concern and unleashed a war psychosis. Cool reason now took a backward seat and mob hysteria steered the wheel of the nation's destiny. Nehru a man of masses now allowed the masses to decide the intricate and delicate question of diplomacy and war.

All diplomatic exchanges on the issue of border dispute were placed before the Parliament and released to the press in the form of a 'White Paper'. Nehru under his self-imposed obligations to keep Parliament informed abdicated his own power as the nation's first executive even in the matter of detailed conduct of foreign affairs. This was to keep up the facade that India was still maintaining diplomatic exchanges with China and not resorting to the use of arms in an uncivilized manner. Having once aroused the public deliberately, as mentioned earlier, Nehru now lost all control and left the national policy to follow its own destined course, with disastrous consequences. Nehru had always buckled under public pressure. Now he passed the buck to the Parliament and drifted along. To be fair, the people and the Lok Sabha were asking him to do only what to them appeared as matters of national concern. They did not restrain Nehru from doing anything which he considered in the national interest. However, political opinion in India was sufficiently aroused by the end of 1959, and it was plain that any attempt to compromise with China would be denounced as appeasement, or cowardice, or worse, thus leaving Nehru helpless in the whirlpool of the fast changing events.

The failure of Chou-En-lai-Nehru summit in April, 1959, is common knowledge and then came the so-called 'Forward Policy'. Briefly stated, it meant moving forward from our existing positions and covering the space upto the line of claim by patrolling and establishment of posts even though unsupported by reinforcements, firepower and logistics adequate to meet the Chinese reaction, should it materialise. It was more like successive batches of Satyagrahis and flag waving volunteers, laying claim to territory than a well planned and prepared military advance to capture and consolidate the claimed territory. It was a balloon that was bound to burst with the slightest Chinese prick and this is precisely what happened. By occupying untenable forward positions, juxtaposed to the well prepared Chinese dugouts was nothing short of provocation and we simply asked for trouble. It was not long in coming. Nehru's earlier ambivalent policy on war with China later changed to an unwise and hasty one. (As far as preparedness for such a contingency is concerned, the record is dismal.) During the 1950s the exclusive concern in our planning was Pakistan and our armed forces were deployed and disposed towards that objective. Further, though it had been suggested that an infantry manual may be given to our Defence Forces about Chinese tactics and to plan for a possible war situation against it, such counsels met with derision and disdain. Even the proposals that a study of Chinese battle tactics as experienced by the British and Americans in Korea be given due importance in training our Defence Forces were similarly rejected. In fact, even in 1958, to the horror and amazement of senior Army officers, a Chinese Military Mission was allowed to proceed on a visit to our key military establishments. Not only that, they were invited to witness a demonstration of firepower and infantry capability in the attack, organized by an Infantry division, then under the command of Major General B.M. Kaul. This division and this General later met their nemesis in the China war barely after a lapse of four years.

Though not clearly defined there was an unmistakable intent in Nehru's speeches that India would insist on the vacation of the territory of Aksai Chin. Even at this stage, Nehru would make the nation believe that India would resort to arms only after having been foiled in its attempt to gain by peaceful means what it considered its legitimate territory. It never crossed his mind that the Chinese might decide to strike first. This lack of farsightedness was the basic weakness in Nehru's forward policy and his foolish attempt to challenge a military power far superior to his own.

To return for a while to documentary evidence, records in the Ministry of External Affairs reveal that a note was prepared to get at least the eastern boundaries accepted and signed during Chou-En-lai's visit to India in 1956, the hey days of Hindi-Chini-Bhai-Bhai.' Nehru, the idealist, scoffed at the idea and the note was never put up. Had we got one part of the border dispute settled, time was with us and we could have taken up the case of Aksai Chin later. A large part of our defence forces would have been released from the North-East frontier and diverted to the western sector in Ladakh. There would have been no reverses, such as at Se La or Walong for our Army. Much as Chou-En-lai was prepared to sign such an agreement, Nehru's curious desire not to embarrass him foreclosed such a possibility. If we could have bought time by freezing the border on the McMahon Line in the east, we could have then tackled Aksai Chin later, through diplomacy or force, if necessary. It was an even playing field for both the forces. Our existing troops in J&K could be counted upon as a firm base for the newly inducted force to advance into Aksai Chin, and then we could match our words with the force of our action. Nehru, however, wanted a total solution to the boundary problem. It was to be all or nothing. This is not the course of a wise statesman. You go by stages to the goal, not by a leap, especially if you are not strong enough on the ground. Wisdom lies in waiting for the opportune time. Chinese speak less, their actions speak volumes. Inspite of his admiration for China, Nehru never really knew the Chinese . In my army service of ten years in Assam, I have spent four and a half years in North-East Frontier Agency (NEFA) with forces deployed on the India-China borders from East Sikkim upto Burma. Similarly, out of my three and a half years of service in J&K, I have spent two years in Ladakh. I know the Chinese well. I reached Kashmir in early 1963, almost on the heels of the China war. During these years, I have found many myths exploded. These I have discussed elsewhere in my military work. But I shall make a few statements of facts. The Chinese were not 10 feet tall. There were no human waves ever, which attacked isolated picquets. There was no Chinese perfidy in their attack on the Indian border. They left no one in doubt, least of all Nehru, about their intentions in Tibet, NEFA and Ladakh. If we wish to delude ourselves, it is entirely our fault. The case of Tibet has been discussed earlier. Also as has been pointed out earlier, the proposal to accept McMahon Line as de facto and de jure boundary between India and China in the North-East was acceptable to the Chinese. But they wanted to negotiate on Aksai Chin. There is not a shred of evidence to suggest that the Chinese attack on NEFA (now Arunachal Pradesh) and Ladakh was not anticipated by our forces and information of such developments was not sent to the Prime Minister. In the east, geography and terrain was against us. While the Chinese could easily move large scale forces on an almost even terrain right upto the border, we had long and tenuous lines of maintenance passing through jungles involving steep climbs from 2000 to 14000 feet to reach upto our forward positions. While the Chinese had prepared carefully for a contingency of conflict we had not. While the Chinese were improving roads and sending arms forward to their troops, our ordnance factories till as late as July, 1962, were manufacturing coffee percolators and Krishna Menon, our Defence Minister, was proud of the fact. So much for the industrial base for supporting any war against China that Nehru boasted. The outcome of the war was not only a foregone conclusion but inevitable. Ill prepared, ill fed, ill supplied, ill clothed, ill armed, our troops fought gallantly and suffered reverses. Nehru was never a war leader. His neglect of the sane advice given earlier by Patel and later by his military advisers, came home to roost.

Nehru had stated earlier:

"Perhaps there are not many instances in history where one country, that is India, has gone out of her way to be friendly with the Chinese Government and to plead their cause in the councils of the world, and then for the Chinese to return evil for good and even go to the extent of invading our sacred land." "However, I may sometimes lose my temper, but I never lose my nerve."

He did precisely that. He lost his nerve. In one of his broadcasts, he literally bade farewell to the people of Assam. Contrast this with Churchill's determination after Dunkirk to fight till the end.

We shall not concern ourselves with the details of military operations which have been described in great detail elsewhere and are by now common knowledge. However it will be in order to mention a few points here. Lt. Gen. B.M. Kaul, more of a politician than a military leader and Nehru's protege, was posted sometime in July 1962 as General-Officer-Commanding (GOC) IV Corps to throw out the Chinese from the Indian territory. As events progressed he realised the unenviability of the task entrusted to him and which, used as he was to bask in military glory of easy pe acetime exhibitions, he had accepted with alacrity. As reverse followed reverse, the General, who came to conquer was suddenly paranoid about Army shortcomings and ordered withdrawal. From the extremes of exultation he drooped to depths of despair and sent alarming signals to Delhi as also to the local administration.

On November 18, General Kaul having taken into consideration the prevailing military situation, painted a dismal picture to his superiors. The civil administration became non-existent and loudspeakers blared out warnings to the local population for evacuation since their safety could no longer be ensured. Some local politicians did try to restore the confidence of the civilian population by assuring them safety. However, the people at Tezpur could not be reassured and some of them ferried across

River Brahmputra southwards. There was an attempt to burn the currency notes and the people tried to throw the coins in the lake. The confusion continued. There was some talk of a "scorched earth" policy to be followed. The Director Civil Defence sent by the Government of India to enforce the so-called policy was even prepared to destroy the airport and the oil-fields at Digboi. Even the burning of tea gardens was mooted and, of course, all power house, waterworks and the like could have gone up, if personnel had been available to do the job. However, the soldiers posted in Army establishments went out without waiting for orders to protect the power house and other civil services. Later, the Central Government in an effort to whitewash its pusillanimous attitude blamed the State Government for this, knowing fully well that such instructions had been issued from the Union Home Ministry.

As the news of the fall of Walong reached Delhi on November 18, 1962, there was consternation in political circles and then the fall of Se La Pass on November 19 came as the deathknell to any lingering hopes that Nehru might have harboured. Much confusion persisted. And then on November 20, Nehru gave up.

That night he broadcast to the nation bemoaning the present situation and discouraging further the people of the country; his earlier confidence had gone up in smoke. The fall of Bomdi La did nothing to restore confidence of the country and then Nehru's famous appeal to people of Assam:

"Now what has happened is very serious and very saddening to us and I can well understand what our friends in Assam must be feeling, because all this is happening on their doorstep, as one might say. I want to tell them that we feel very much for them and we shall help them to the utmost of our ability."

The reaction was bitter to almost all. Though, Nehru still maintained:

"We shall not be content till the invader goes out of

India or is pushed out. We shall not accept any terms that he may offer because he may think that we are a little frightened by some setbacks..."

The same day, the American Ambassador in Delhi observed:

"It was the day of panic in Delhi, the first time I have ever witnessed the disintegration of public morale."

There were rumours of Chinese capture of Tezpur and a possible paradrop in Delhi itself. General Kaul was reported captured by the Chinese. On this, the then President Radhakrishnan, sadly remarked, "It is unfortunately untrue."

The same night Nehru appealed for assistance from the United States seeking bombers and fighters squadrons to strike against the Chinese. It was possible that this decision might have been taken on the advice of his service chiefs, but his Cabinet colleagues were kept in the dark.

The Chinese had cleared all Indian positions south of the McMahon Line and in Ladakh pushed the Indian forces to the outskirts of Chushul. They had made their point in diplomatic language and consummated it by military means.

Nehru showed no inclination to resign, something that could not have happened in a democratic country. The failure of Nehru's leadership and his conduct of military affairs was there for everyone to see. After this debacle, the political and moral high ground which he occupied within and outside the Parliament slipped away from his feet. There was a stormy meeting of the Congress Parliamentary party where Nehru's authority was challenged for the first time and there was a demand for Krishana Menon's resignation. Nehru tried to shield him and hinted that if Menon had to go he might himself do the same. This gambit, however, did not work and the party was insistent even to ask Nehru to go if he felt that way. Nehru had lost his preeminence for ever.

This position on the ground now was precisely as Chou-En-lai had suggested to Nehru in his letter of November 7, 1959, and reiterated after the battle of Namka Chu. China had been consistent in its stand over the border dispute to be resolved by settlement while India had rejected and brushed it aside even on October 24, after the first Chinese attack. Now China could force India to keep its forces 20 kms. away from the line of actual control. Later, the Chinese explained their plan. They had advanced into the territory south of the McMahon Line in order to thoroughly rout the Indian reactionaries and to shatter their plan of altering the border status quo by the force of arms, and thus create an atmosphere for negotiations. The unilateral cease-fire and the halting of the offensive by China came as a surprise to the country since it could not get rid of the idea dinned into its ears by Nehru and his team regarding China's reprehensible intentions. This was not the truth. All that the Chinese wanted was to settle for a trouble-free border with India. Misinformed throughout this sorry episode, Indian public did not expect the Chinese withdrawal to their original line of claim after their victory. Lord Cacia remarked: "The Chinese withdrawal to their original line after a victory in the field was the first time in recorded history that a great power has not exploited military success by demanding something more." This is what China had always sought, not territory but a settled border.

To revert back to the chronology of events, on the morning of November 21, India woke up to learn about the Chinese announcement of a unilateral cease-fire. The Government, incredulous at first, came to accept the reality that China far from waging a war on India, had successfully completed its great punitive expedition. After this catastrophe any Government in the world would have fallen and a Prime Minister would have voluntarily resigned or pressed to do so. Not so Nehru. The ship of the State had become rudderless and Nehru's

China policy already in a tail spin, now hurtled towards an abyss.

Nehru's moral authority received a severe blow from which it never recovered. This was a catastrophe that was of Nehru's own making and the buck could not be passed to anyone else. Like the unfolding of a Sophoclean tragedy, he initiated the moves over which he lost all control and then remained a helpless spectator to witness the inevitability of the disaster.

While India was fighting an unequal battle against China, what was the response of the world nations? America had promised and did send help in the form of small arms, wireless sets, high altitude clothing, logistic support and transport, to mention just a few items. All type of equipments flowed in. I myself on reaching Ladakh in November, 1964, used most of it as a souvenir.

The western nations were sympathetic to India, but the non-aligned nations so assiduously cultivated by Nehru were almost aloof. There was no word of sympathy or solidarity with the Indian cause by any of these nations even a week after the invasion. According to a reporter, 'Kenyatta and other leaders were being non-committal' and Nkrumah, President of Ghana, claiming to be Nehru's close friend said, "Whatever the rights and wrongs of the present struggle between India and China", he wrote to Macmillan, "I am sure that we can all serve the cause of peace best by refraining from any action that may aggravate the situation." And this statement came soon after Nehru's visit to Ghana.

And then the unkindest cut of all. What of the Soviet Union for whom Nehru had incurred the opprobrium of the United States Administration and the western countries on his so-called non-alignment policy which appeared to them not so equidistant after all from the two poles. To their 'warped' view it appeared, to quote a Naval terminology, 'listing more to the port (Left) side. Nehru had constantly carped against the USA and talked of keeping equal distance from the western countries and the Soviet block. *Pravada*, the official news bulletin of the Soviet Union, observed:

"The question of the China-India frontier is a heritage from those days when British colonialists—who drew and redrew the map of Asia at their own will—ruled on the territory of India. The notorious 'McMahon Line', which was never recognized by China, was foisted on the Chinese and Indian peoples. Imperialist circles have done everything in their power to provoke an armed clash by speculating on the border conflicts connected with this Line. The imperialists are dreaming day and night of setting these great powers at loggerheads, as well as undermining the Soviet Union's friendship with fraternal China and friendly India."

We should have known the difference between a fraternal country and a mere 'friend.' Our demand for MIG fighters was turned down. We had the same problem with America, nine years later during the Bangladesh war when the United States lined up with Pakistan and threatened us with their Seventh fleet. But the statesman in Nehru should have known that amongst nations, there are no permanent friends or permanent enemies but only permanent interests. His principle of Non-alignment was too straightjacketed, a policy to subserve national interests in the world of realpolitic.

The Chinese disaster left a permanent scar on Nehru, the author of Panchsheel, friendship with China and Non-alignment. It grievously hurt the Indian psyche, not to speak of the morale of the Armed Forces which were the helpless victim of a great tragedy. Nehru was the producer, storywriter, the actor, director and the distributor of this great Indian tragedy.

Epilogue

Unadorned by rhetoric, unhampered by prejudice, untainted by personal malice and unencumbered by political compulsions, a stocktaking has been made, through a scrutiny of the facts of history bearing on the man under study, Jawaharlal Nehru. Was Nehru's emergence and efflorescence as a leader during the freedom struggle and later as a Prime Minister, a blessing or a blight to the fortunes of this country? The answer lies somewhere between the two extremes. A man of high pedigree, elitist education, tremendous enthusiasm and great personal charm Nehru stands alone next only to Gandhi in his hold on the minds of our people. He could think big and within the limits of his inner lights go to any length to achieve his goals. The nation owes much to the man for steering us on a path of democracy and self-reliance, inculcating a scientific temper and taking the first steps towards building an infrastructure for economic development. But here the positive side ends. The negative side is what this book is all about. It is ironic that some of Nehru's greatest failures arose out of his virtues. His overweening confidence led to arrogance and ascerbity. The knowledge of his superior birth gradually turned into a scorn for the countrybred and the son of the soil. His limited Cambridge built knowledge of Indian history resulted in misreading the all-pervasive and immanent message of the cultural heritage of this country which centuries of oppression could not wipe out. His socialism was rather superficial.

His posturing as a radical, a convenient ploy to win the hearts of the true radicals and the youthful masses, while keeping an eye on the conservative power centre in the Congress completely and rightly under the influence of Gandhiji. As mentioned earlier he hobnobbed with Subhas Bose, a radical, holding an occasional olive branch, but always followed Gandhiji when the crunch came. There was thus an element of opportunism inbuilt in Nehru's basic nature. But mercifully, this was confined to matters of promoting himself and search for personal power. He was democratic to a degree but was a despot to his own partymen. His hectoring tone was not unoften heard in the party or parliamentary fora. His emaphasis on self-reliance, though, well meant could not be translated into a concerted national effort towards rapid economic growth. His scientific temper could promote individual scientists like Dr. Homi Bhabha and Shanti Swaroop Bhatnagar but left little impact on the scientific community at large. His efforts merely amounted to tokenism as a substitute for a sustained movement towards laying the foundations for production of a competitive scientific manpower by providing them with incentives as Lee Kuan Yew did in Singapore. Oversensitive to public opinion, he could hardly be called practical. The hesitant Hamlet had in Sardar Patel, the bold Bismarck, to help him in building up this nation. But he tried to sideline him and his ego prevented the two working as a team. The Nehru-Patel duumvirate which was a heady mix of complementality with tremendous potential could have carved greatness for this nation. Nehru, the Greek hero, counselled and sustained by the Roman patrician Patel could have worked wonders for this country if only the two as Gandhiji desired, had worked together. This was not to be. That was Nehru's greatest failure. Alexander, the youthful conqueror, had Aristotle by his side as his friend, philosopher and counsellor. If Nehru could have used Patel the same way our story would have been different. There would have been no socialistic drag on our economy, no imbroglio in Kashmir and later no Chinese Debacle. The nation's integrity would have been maintained and the grammar of political dialogue in this country very different from what it is today. Nehru's western education, largely washed away Nehru, the Indian. Gandhiji and Patel too had done their law degrees in England, but neither returned as a Westernised Oriental Gentleman (WOG). They retained their roots firmly in the Indian soil and could empathise with the thought of an average Indian with his deep religious moorings and love of his past. Nehru tried to implant Western values in this soil which did not take kindly to it. He hardly understood the Indian mind or the spirit of Hinduism, a concept that was later upheld by the Supreme Court as 'Hindutva'.

Nehru's handling of linguistic Provinces and the issue of national language brings out a man who lacks an insight into the Hindu mind. His failure to introduce a Uniform Civil Code as enshrined in the Indian Constitution shows his endemic infirmity to take the bull by the horn and stand firm on what he thought right. It also reinforces the belief that his modernistic reforming zeal against outdated religious practices was confined only to the majority community. His secularism was tilted just as his non-alignment was asymetric. Self-effacement was never Nehru's strong point. Equally, he could stand no rivals. His differences with Patel were the inevitable outcome of this overweening compulsion to wield unbridled power, as was evident from the "Guru Chandal Yog" in his horoscope. While he could be large-hearted and over-indulgent to some, he could be down-right petty to others. His silent encouragement of a whispering campaign branding Patel as fascist is too well known.

Nehru had read widely but not wisely. His knowledge did not bless him with humility. He had many beads of knowledge, but there was no running thread. His philosophy of action was fragmented to a fault.

Exactitude, mastery of detail and sense of timing were not Nehru's strong points.

His romantic love for the antiquity of this great country was like the awestruck hypnotism of a juvenile and not a deeper understanding of a mature man that could enable him to assimilate its millenia old spirit. On issues of great national concern, he could fret and fume but could not initiate cool, reasoned, timely and effective action. This was amply evident during the Kashmir crisis, Hyderabad action and the Chinese Boundary Dispute and subsequent military action. Here was a man who was so assiduosly nourished on mass adulation that sent so much political adrenalin racing in his veins that bereft of mass support he could collapse into an ineffective had been. By no stretch of imagination could Nehru be described as a good loser. Used to the cast of a prima donna, he could not take the second place or a lesser role; nor was he capable of building a team that could act on its own in his absence. There was a certain kind of emptiness in Nehru's make-up resembling the empty space which surrounds the electrical particles constituting matter. Matter as we all know consists of a solid nucleus surrounded by infinite space through which charged bodies move with tremendous velocity giving the illusion of continuity and solidity of substance. Likewise, there was a certain kind of superficiality about Nehru that could go unnoticed by a less perceptive observer. Inspite of long hours at work, he lacked a deep insight into any vital issue. It was the veneer of superficiality and concomitant emptiness as described above, that made it difficult for Nehru to sustain himself during adverse political weather or national crises.

The gravamen of history against Nehru would be a question mark, not on the earnestness of the man but on the limitations of his perception; not on his lack of patriotism but on the substance of his endeavours; not on lack of enthusiasm but that of sustained action; not on lack of emotion but that of unfailing purpose; not on want of trying but on absence of direction; not on lack of articulation but that of decisive and timely action.

A nation newly born, aspiring to greatness, needs firm hands and a strong will, clarity of perception, an unwavering aim and the right direction from its leader. Given the unquestioning love and loyalty showered on Nehru by the credulous and fawning masses, and an eternal mandate, he could have led this nation through its childhood and adolescent years in his seventeen long years of rule to great heights. But he betrayed that trust and failed his people. Nehru's life and endeavours is a sad story of a betrayal of this great country which deserved better.

The following could well be history's epitaph on Nehru:

"Here lies the man to this nation born, whom nature and man had gifted all that a mortal could wish for. But he allowed those treasures to remain his frozen assets. He could, but did not rise to the call of destiny and led this country not to glory but ignominy."

A Select Bibliography

1. Nehru—Biography by Michael Fletcher.
2. Nehru—A Political Biography by Michael Edwardes.
3. Living an Era by D.P. Mishra.
4. Freedom at Midnight by Larry Collins and Dominique Lapierre.
5. My Autobiography by Jawaharlal Nehru.
6. Discovery of India by Jawaharlal Nehru.
7. Glimpses of World History by Jawaharlal Nehru. (Foreword by V.K.Krishna Menon, May 1939). (Note to 4th edition by V.K. Krishna Menon 1948). (Being further letters to his daughter written in prison and containing a rambling account of history for young people with 60 maps by J.F.Horrabin.)
8. The Collected Works of Mahatma Gandhi by Publications Division, Ministry of Information & Broadcasting, Government of India.
9. India Wins Freedom by Maulana Abul Kalam Azad.
10. Sardar Patel's Correspondence 1945-50 Edited by Durga Das.
11. Dr. Rajendra Prasad Correspondence & Selected Documents by Valmiki Choudhary.
12. Patel: A Life by Rajmohan Gandhi.
13. The Irony of Patel by B. Krishna.
14. Mission with Mountbatten by Allan Campbell Johnson.
15. Nehru: An Anthology' Works by Dr. Sarvapalli Gopal.

16. A Secular Agenda by Arun Shouri.
17. The Hindu Phenomenon by Giri Lal Jain.
18. My Frozen Turbulence by Jag Mohan.
19. History of the Jews by Abram Lean Sachar Ph.D. (30 Centuries of Judaism)
20. Heros of Israel
(Profile of Jewish Courage) by Chaim Herzog.
21. Philosophy of Physical Science by Sir Arthur Eddington.
22. The General Theory of Relativity by Albert Einstein.
23. History of Western Philosophy by Bertrand Russelll.
24. Our Knowledge of The External World by Bertrand Russell.
25. Autobiography by Bertrand Russell.
26. Education and The Social Order by Bertrand Russell.
27. Freedom Verses Organisation by Bertrand Russell.
28. Sceptical Essays by Bertrand Russell.
29. Outline of Philosophy by Bertrand Russell.
30. Power by Bertrand Russell.
31. An Intelligent Women's Guide to Socialism, Capitalism, Sovietism and Fascism by George Bernard Shaw.
32. Arms Aims & Aspects by Gen. J.N. Choudhury.
33. Slender Was The Thread (Kashmir) by Lt. Gen. L.P.Sen.
34. Kashmir: A Pakistan Obsession by Lt. Gen. K.K.Nanda.
35. Official History of Kashmir Operation, by Historical Section, Army Headquarters.
36. Outline of History by H.G. Wells.
37. History and Culture of the Indian People (in 11 Volumes) Bhartiya Vidya Bhavan, Bombay.
38. Annals and Antiquities of Rajasthan by Col. James Todd.
39. Cambridge History of India.
40. The Story of Civilization by Will Durrant.
41. Pushing To The Front by Orisson Swett Marden.
42. Thimayya of India by Humphrey Evan.
43. Arthshastra by Kautilaya.

44. Some Problems of India's Economic Planning, edited by Charan D. Wadhwa.
45. State Finance in India by Ramesh Baghchi, J.L. Bajaj & William A. Byrd.
46. Essays on Finances by S.L.N. Sinha, M.A.
47. Socialism in India, edited by B.R. Nanda.
48. Socialism, Sarvodaya and Democracy by Jaya Prakash Narain.
49. Some Theoretical Doubts on India' Plan Frame by Shigito Tsuru, published in the *Economic Weekly* of January, 1957.
50. The Untold Story by Lt. Gen. B.M. Kaul.
51. Himalayan Blunder by Brig. J.P. Dalvi.
52. The Unfought War of 1962: The NEFA Debacle by Lt. Col. J.R. Saigal.
53. India's China War by Neville Maxwell.
54. The Holy Quran, Text Translation and Commentary by A. Yusuf Ali.
55. The Holy Bible King James (Authorised) Version.
56. The Bhagvad Gita.

Index